Accounting, Budgeting, and Finance

A Reference for Managers

Charles J. Woelfel

amacom

American Management Association

This book is available at a special discount when ordered in bulk quantities. For information, contact Special Sales Department, AMACOM, a division of American Management Association, 135 West 50th Street, New York, NY 10020.

Library of Congress Cataloging-in-Publication Data

Woelfel, Charles J.
    Accounting, budgeting, and finance : a reference for managers /
Charles J. Woelfel.
        p.   cm.
    ISBN 0-8144-5988-9
    1. Finance--Dictionaries.   2. Accounting--Dictionaries.
I. Title.
HG151.W62   1990
657'.03--dc20   89-7745C
                                                          CIP

©1990 AMACOM, a division of American Management Association, New York.

Portions of this book appeared previously in Charles Woelfel's books *The Complete Executive's Encyclopedia of Accounting, Finance, Investing, Banking & Economics; Budgeting, Pricing & Cost Controls;* and *The Desktop Encyclopedia of Banking*, published by Probus Publishing Co.

Printed in the United States of America

Printing number

10   9   8   7   6   5   4   3   2   1

To Colette

Preface

Accounting, Budgeting, and Finance: A Reference for Managers is a major reference and source book for managers. This comprehensive volume explains major concepts in the following business areas with an emphasis on their implications to managers:

Major concepts:
  Accounting
  Budgeting
  Finance
Supporting concepts:
  Management
  Economics
  Foreign Operations
  Business and professional ethics

Accounting, Budgeting, and Finance: A Reference for Managers is for *managers* who must have immediate access to authoritative accounting, budgeting, and financial information on a day-to-day basis. Business executives, bankers, accountants, investors, lawyers, and other professionals will also find this book useful. The book is designed specifically to be a convenient reference or source book. There are approximately 475 major entries and numerous entries within entries in the book. This one-volume source book is carefully referenced to enable the manager/user to explore a topic in greater depth. Many of the entries contain bibliographies which offer access to primary or secondary sources on the same general topic. The book contains many illustrations and exhibits which enhance the understandability of complex concepts and processes. The book is user friendly.

There are a number of ways to use this book. For the manager who needs to know what a particular accounting, budgeting, or finance concept means, the book will normally provide a particular entry that will satisfy this need. When this entry is located, carefully prepared cross-references are available to enable the reader to pursue the topic further. In addition, many references are cited that can be used obtain additional information. For someone interested in using a systematic approach to accounting, budgeting, finance and related topics, it is recommended that the outline presented below be used to become acquainted with major areas represented in this book.

Managers can be assured that the discussions presented herein are authoritative, current, relevant, and reliable. This reference book was prepared with the user in mind and so offers a practical and accessible guide to the current theory and practice of the business arts and sciences.

ACCOUNTING

Financial Accounting:
Accounting
Accounting assumptions
Accounting basis (cash and accrual basis)
Accounting changes
Accounting equation
Accounting functions
Accounting period
Accounting policies and procedures
Accounting principles:
Conservatism
Consistency
Cost principle
Full disclosure

Book value
Cash flow
Charting
Checks
Cost-benefit analysis
Credit market
Current yield
Discounted cash flows
Dividends
Earnings per share
Economic indicators
Euro market
Factoring
Federal Funds
Federal Reserve System
Finance
Financial forecast
Financial markets
Financial planning
Financial reporting
Financial statements
Financial theories and models:
    Beta coefficient
    Bond duration
    Capital asset pricing model
    Capital maintenance theory
    Coefficient of variation
    Efficient market theory
    Equation of exchange
    Expectancy theory of interest rates
    Expected value
    Forecasting financial requirements
    Loanable fund theory
    Random walk
Fiscal policy
Float
Foreign trade
Future value

Imputed and implicit costs
Inventory profit
Investing
Investment banking
Investment instruments:
    Bankers' acceptances
    Bonds
    Call options
    Capital stock
    Certificates of Accrual on Treasury securities (CATS)
    Certificates of deposit
    Collateralized mortgage obligations
    Commercial paper
    Convertible securities
    Eurobonds
    Eurodollars
    Forward contracts
    Futures market
    Government obligations
    Investment companies (mutual funds)
    Junk bonds
    Limited partnership
    Mortgage
    Options
    Petro dollars
    Preferred stock
    Put options
    Rate of return on securities
    Stock options
    Stock rights
    Tax shelters
    Treasury bills
Investment methods and strategies
Leases
Legal capital
Letters of credit
Leverage
Market structure

Money market
Mortgage
Negotiable instruments
Off-balance sheet item
Portfolio insurance
Present value
Price index
Product financing arrangements
Program trading
Prospectus
Proxy
Prudent man rule
Rational expectations
Ratios
Securities market
Stock dividends
Stock split
Takeover
Wraparound mortgage
Yield curve
Yield to call
Yield to maturity

MANAGEMENT

Analysis (with budgeting implications):
 Break-even analysis
 Contribution margin analysis
 Cost-benefit analysis
 Financial statement analysis
 Gross margin analysis
 Incremental cost analysis
 Inventory model
 Learning curve
 Network analysis
 Opportunity cost analysis
 Quantitative methods
 Ratios

Cost-push inflation
Demand-push inflation
Division of labor
Economic indicators
Economies of scale
Economics
Free enterprise system
Fiscal policy
Government Regulation of Business
Invisible hand
Law of demand
Law of diminishing return
Law of supply
Liquidity preference theory
Marginal analysis
Monetary policy
Money
Producer's index
Satisficing
Scarcity
Supply side economics

FOREIGN OPERATIONS

Eurobonds
Eurodollars
Euro Market
Exchange rates
Foreign Corrupt Practices Act of 1984
Foreign trade
Foreign trade strategies
Forward contracts
Foreign operations and exchanges
Import-Export Bank
Multinational corporation
Tariff

ETHICS

Fraud
Fraudulent financial reporting
Kiting
Lapping
Profession
Foreign Corrupt Practices Act
Insider Trading Sanctions Act of 1984
Related party transactions

The author appreciates the enthusiastic support of American Management Association throughout this project. Their guidance and insights contributed considerably to the overall design, coverage, and quality of the final product. The author also wants to express his appreciation to Probus Publishing Company for their editorial assistance throughout this project.

Charles J. Woelfel

Aa

ACCOUNT

A ledger account is an accounting form used to assemble information that affects one specific asset, liability, owners' equity, revenue, or expense. In its simplest form, a ledger account can be represented in the form of a T. The account contains the date of the transaction or event, the source of the item, and the dollar amount. Space is also available for an explanation or comment.

The left side of a T account is called the debit side; the right side is called the credit side. The dollar difference between the debit side and the credit side is called the account balance.

The rules for increasing and decreasing an account are summarized as follows:

Debit an account to:	Credit an account to:
1. increase an asset	1. decrease an asset
2. decrease a liability	2. increase a liability
3. decrease owners' equity	3. increase owners' equity

A control account is frequently used in the general ledger for a group of specific accounts contained in a subsidiary ledger. The balance in the control account on a balance sheet date equals the total balance of its related subsidiary ledger.

In banking and brokerage firms, the term account refers to a record of a depositor's or client's transactions and credit/debit balances with a firm. The term account is also used in a variety of other ways; such as, checking account, savings account, money market account, NOW account, and Individual Retirement Account (IRA).

See also: ACCOUNTING

ACCOUNTING

Accounting has been defined by a committee of the American Institute of Public Accountants (AICPA) as a service activity. Its function is to provide quantitative information, primarily financial in nature, about economic activities that is intended to be useful in making economic decisions—in making reasoned choices amoung alternative courses of action. This definition emphasized economic decision-making activities rather than the function of accounting as the major objectives of accounting. The functions of accounting are to accumulate, process, and communicate information about a specific economic entity.

Accounting principles are the guidelines, laws, or rules which are adopted by the accounting profession and which serve as guides to accounting practice. Generally accepted accounting principles (GAAP) reflect the consensus at a particular time as to which economic resources and obligations should be recorded as assets and liabilities, which changes in assets and liabilities should be recorded, when these changes should be recorded, how the recorded assets and liabilities and changes in them should be measured, what information should be disclosed, and which financial statements should be prepared.

Major organizations which are involved in the development of GAAP include the American Institute of Certified Public Accountants (AICPA), the financial Accounting Standards Board (FASB), the Governmental Accounting Standards Board (GASB), and the Securities and Exchange Commission (SEC). The AICPA is the national professional organization of practicing Certified Public Accountants. Its two committees, the Committee on Accounting Procedures (CAP)(1934–1959) and the Accounting Principles Board (APB)(1959–1973) determined appropriate account practice during the period of their existence. In 1973, the Financial Accounting Standards Board was established as the new standard-setting structure in the United States. The FASB is composed of seven members reflecting board representation, e.g., currently, it is not necessary to be a CPA to be a member of the FASB. The Governmental Accounting Standards Board was established in 1984, under the oversight of the Financial Accounting Foundation, to address state and local governmental repoorting issues. The organization structure for setting accounting standards in the United States is illustrated in Exhibit A-1.

An accounting system is a management information system within an organization which is responsible for the collection and processing of data to produce information which is useful to decision makers in planning and controlling the activities of the organization. The accounting system deals primarily with financial information which concerns the flow of financial resources through the organization. The data processing system can be conceptualized as the total structure of records and procedures that are associated with five activities: collection or recording, classifying, processing, including calculating and summarizing, maintenance or storage, and output or reporting. The processing of data in a typical accounting system is illustrated in Exhibit A-2.

Basic principles of accounting include (1) the historical cost principle, (2) the revenue recognition principle, (3) the matching principle, (4) the full disclosure principle, (5) the materiality principle, and (6) the principle of conservatism. The historical cost principle requires that most assets and liabilities be accounted for and reported on the basis of acquisition, or historical, cost. The revenue recognition principle requires that generally revenue be recognized when (1) the revenue is earned and (2) an exchange has taken place. The matching principle requires that generally costs are expensed and matched against the revenue in the period when the revenue is recognized. The full disclosure principle requires that information that is of sufficient importance to influence the judgment and decisions of an informed user be reported in the financial statements. The materiality principle states that an item is material if its inclusion or omission would influence or change the judgment of a reasonable person. If the item is material, it must be disclosed in the financial statements. The principle of conservatism states that when in doubt, the accountant should choose that principle or method that will be least likely to overstate assets and income.

Exhibit A-1
Organizational Structure for Establishing Accounting Standards

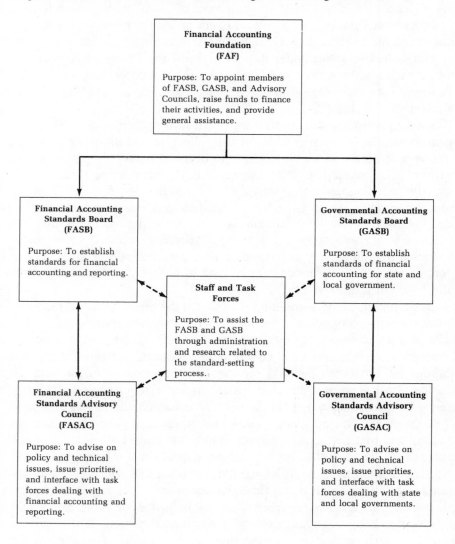

Exhibit A-2

A Conceptualized Accounting System

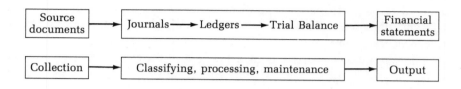

See also: ACCOUNTING ASSUMPTIONS
                  ACCOUNTING BASIS
                  ACCOUNTING PRINCIPLES

References:

Financial Accounting Standard Board, Accounting Standards (New York, NY: McGraw-Hill, latest edition).

Kieso, Donald E., et.al., Intermediate Accounting (New York, NY: John Wiley & Sons, 1986).

ACCOUNTING ASSUMPTIONS

Accounting assumptions are broad concepts that underlie generally accepted accounting principles. The major accounting assumptions include the following: the business entity assumption, the continuity assumption, the periodic and timely reporting assumption, and the monetary unit assumption.

A basic assumption in accounting is that economic activity can be identified with a particular unit (or entity) of accountability. This unit is the one to be accounted for. The business entity assumption determines the nature and scope of the reporting that is required for the unit. The entity for accounting purposes is identified as the economic unit that controls resources, incurs obligations, and otherwise is involved in directing economic activities that relate to a specific accountability unit. Accounting units (or entities) include corporations, partnerships, proprietorships, not-for-profit entities, trusts, and others.

Accounting is based on the assumption that the accounting unit is engaged in continuous and ongoing activities. The accounting unit is assumed to remain in operation into the foreseeable future in pursuit of its goals and objectives. This assumption is referred to as the continuity or going-concern assumption.

The continuous operations of a unit over an extended period of time can be meaningfully segmented into equal time periods, such as a year, quarters, or months. The periodic and timely reporting assumptions require that accounting reporting should be done periodically and on a timely basis so that it is relevant and reliable.

The monetary unit assumption requires that financial information be measured and accounted for in the basic monetary unit of the country in which the enterprise is located. The monetary value of an economic event or transaction, determined at the time it is recorded, is not adjusted for subsequent changes in the purchasing power of the monetary unit (as occurs in periods of inflation or deflation).

See also: ACCOUNTING
ACCOUNTING POLICIES AND PROCEDURES
ACCOUNTING PRINCIPLES
ASSUMPTIONS
FINANCIAL STATEMENTS
GOING CONCERN

ACCOUNTING BASIS

Major bases of accounting include the accrual, cash, and modified cash. In accrual accounting, revenue and gains are recognized in the period when they are earned. Expenses and losses are recognized in the period when they are incurred. Accrual-basis accounting is concerned with the economic consequences of events and transactions rather than only with cash receipts and cash payments. Under accrual accounting, net income does not necessarily reflect cash receipts and cash payments for a particular time period. Accrual accounting generally provides the most accurate measure of earnings, earning power, managerial performance, and stewardship.

Cash-basis accounting recognizes only transactions involving actual cash receipts and disbursements occurring in a given period. Cash-basis accounting recognizes revenues and gains when cash is received and expenses and losses when cash is paid. No attempt is made to record unpaid bills or amounts owed to or by the unit. Cash-basis accounting is generally deficient as an accounting model that attempts to produce a statement of financial position and an income statement. However, cash-basis accounting is widely used for income tax purposes.

Under a modified cash basis of accounting, certain expenditures are capitalized and amortized in the future. For example, under cash-basis accounting, the purchase of equipment for cash is expensed immediately; under a modified cash basis, the purchase is recorded as an asset. A portion of the acquisition cost is later recognized as an expense when the services of the asset are consumed.

Net income from operations computed according to generally accepted accounting principles (accrual basis) can be converted to cash flow from operations according to the following general procedures:

Net income from operations

Plus:
- Items reducing income but not using cash, such as depreciation, depletion, and amortization expenses
- Decreases in current assets other than cash
- Increases in current liabilities

Less:
- Increases in current assets other than cash
- Decreases in current liabilities

Equals:
- Cash flow from operations

ACCOUNTING CHANGES

An accounting change is any change in an accounting principle, an accounting estimate, or a reporting entity. Accounting changes can significantly affect financial statements for an accounting period, trends in comparative statements, and historical summaries, as well as the confidence that financial statement users have in the statements.

Consistency in the application of accounting principles and methods is assumed to enhance the usefulness and understandability of financial statements. Consistency does not imply uniformity or comparability among different independent entities (Company A compared to Company B) or within a company (LIFO inventory for Department A compared to FIFO for Department B). The professional judgment of the accountant or auditor must be relied upon to deal with problems related to consistency and changes in accounting.

If a firm changes the way an item is measured or reported in its financial statements, the changed situation should fit one of the three following types:

1. *Change in accounting principle.* A change from one generally accepted accounting principle to another generally accepted accounting principle: for example, a change in the method of depreciation from straight-line depreciation to double-declining method.

2. *Change in accounting estimate.* A change that results from new or additional information: for example, a change in the estimate of the useful lives of depreciable assets or a change in the estimate of uncollectible accounts receivable.

3. *Change in reporting entity.* A change from reporting as one type of entity for another type: for example, presenting consolidated or combined statements in place of statements of individual companies.

The effect of accounting changes on income should be recognized by one of the following procedures:

1. *Retroactively.* Recognize the cumulative effect of the change in prior years' earnings as a prior-period adjustment (that is, as an adjustment of the beginning balance in retained earnings for the current year and restate prior years' financial statements accordingly).

2. *Currently.* Recognize the entire cumulative effect of the change in prior years' earnings as an element in calculating net income in the year of the change. Changes in accounting principles are generally treated currently (a catch-up approach).

3. *Prospectively.* Spread the cumulative effect of the change in prior years' earnings over the year of the change and a number of future years, where appropriate. Changes in accounting estimates are treated prospectively.

The cumulative effect of an accounting change refers to the effect of the change on assets or liabilities at the beginning of the period in which the change is made. The cumulative effect is the difference between the present carrying value of the asset or liability and what the carrying value would have been if the accounting change had been in effect in all previous periods of the asset's or liability's existence.

Errors are not accounting changes. Errors in financial statements are primarily the result of a mathematical mistake, a misapplication of accounting principles, a misuse or oversight of data that were available when the financial statements were prepared, or an incorrect classification of accounting elements such as assets and liabilities. An error in a previously issued financial statement is treated as a prior-period adjustment. Retained earnings as of the beginning of the current period are charged or credited for the cumulative effect of the error on earnings or prior years. Financial statements of prior periods must be restated when presented in subsequent financial reports so as not to reproduce the errors that have been made.

See also: CONSISTENCY
ERRORS
PRIOR-PERIOD ADJUSTMENTS

ACCOUNTING CONTROLS

Accounting controls include the plan of organization and the procedures and records dealing with the broad objectives of safeguarding assets and improving the reliability of financial records required for the preparation of financial statements. Accounting controls are concerned primarily with systems of authorization and approval, controls over assets, internal auditing procedures, and other financial matters. It is management's responsibility to establish and maintain an appropriate system of internal accounting control.

According to Statements on Auditing Standards Nos. 1 and 30, the operative objectives of accounting controls are designed to provide reasonable assurance that:

1. Transactions are executed in accordance with management's general or specific authorization.

2. Transactions are recorded as necessary to permit preparation of financial statements in conformity with generally accepted accounting principles or any other criteria applicable to such statements, and to maintain accountability for assets.

3. Access to assets is permitted only in accordance with management's authorization.

4. The recorded accountability for assets is compared with the existing assets at reasonable intervals, and appropriate action is taken with respect to any differences.

Accounting control systems provide reasonable, but not absolute, assurance that the accounting control objectives are met. The concept of reasonable assurance recognizes that accounting control systems are subject to cost-benefit constraints.

See also: ADMINISTRATIVE CONTROLS
CONTROL FUNCTION
FRAUD
INTERNAL CONTROL

References:

Statement on Auditing Standard No. 1, "Codification of Auditing Standards and Procedures" (Commerce Clearing House, Chicago, Ill., 1980).

Statement on Auditing Standard No. 30, "Reporting on Internal Accounting Control" (American Institute of Certified Public Accountants, New York).

ACCOUNTING CYCLE

The accounting cycle is a sequence of activities that records, summarizes, and reports economic events and transactions. The steps in the accounting cycle include journalizing transactions, posting to a ledger, taking a trial balance, adjusting the accounts, preparing financial statements, closing the accounts, and taking a postclosing trial balance. The accounting cycle is repeated each accounting period. The operations of the cycle can be conceptualized as shown in Exhibit A-3.

Exhibit A-3
The Accounting Process (or Cycle)

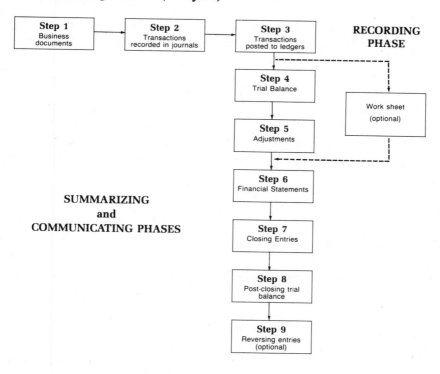

See also: ACCOUNT
                ACCOUNTING SYSTEM
                ADJUSTING ENTRIES
                CLOSING ENTRIES
                FINANCIAL STATEMENTS
                JOURNAL
                LEDGER
                OPERATING CYCLE
                REVERSING ENTRIES

ACCOUNTING EQUATION

The accounting equation expresses the relationship that exists between assets, liabilities, and owners' equity. In its simplest form, the accounting equation can be represented as follows:

$$ASSETS - LIABILITIES = OWNERS' EQUITY$$

The accounting equation states an equality and establishes a relationship among the three major accounting elements. Owners' equity is shown as the residual of assets over liabilities. The accounting equation can be restated in this form:

$$ASSETS = LIABILITIES + OWNERS' EQUITY$$

When the accounting equation is expressed in this format, owners and creditors are shown as having claims against the assets of the enterprise. The accounting equation can also be expressed in a format that combines liabilities and owners' equity into a single concept referred to as equities:

$$ASSETS = EQUITIES$$

See also: ACCOUNTING

ACCOUNTING FUNCTIONS

Accounting deals with numbers and measurable quantities. The accounting system accumulates, measures, and communicates numbers and measurable quantities of economic information about an enterprise. These three functions can be represented as a flow of information from source to destination as follows:

ACCUMULATION $\rightarrow$ MEASUREMENT $\rightarrow$ COMMUNICATION

Accumulation refers primarily to recording and classifying data in journals and ledgers. The accounting system accumulates data related primarily to completed transactions and events. Measurement refers to the quantification of business transactions or other economic events that have occurred, or that may occur. Measurement determines how to select the best amounts to recognize in the financial statements. The accounting system communicates relevant and reliable information to investors, creditors, managers, and others for internal and external decision making.

See also: ACCOUNTING
               ACCOUNTING SYSTEM
               MEASUREMENT

ACCOUNTING PERIODS

Custom as well as income tax and other legal considerations have focused on annual reporting periods and an annual accounting cycle. If the reporting period begins on January 1 and ends on December 31, it is referred to as a calendar-year accounting period. Any other beginning and ending period of one year is called a fiscal-year. The accounting period is identified on the financial statements.

When selecting an annual reporting period, some entities adopt a reporting period that ends when operations (inventories and accounts receivable) are at a low point in order to simplify year-end accounting procedures and to permit more rapid preparation of financial statements. Such an accounting period is referred to as natural business year since it conforms to the natural annual cycle of the entity.

Some firms use a 52-53-week accounting period for reporting purposes. The yearly reporting period varies from 52 to 53 weeks since it always ends on the same day of the week (for example, the last Friday of the year), either the last one of such days in a calendar month, or the closest one to the last day of a calendar month.

Financial reports for periods shorter than one year, such a quarterly reports, are referred to as interim reports or interim statements.

For income tax purposes, the accounting period is usually a year. Unless a fiscal year is chosen, taxpayers must determine their tax liability by using the calendar year as the period of measurement. A change in accounting period requires the approval of the IRS.

See also: ACCOUNTING ASSUMPTIONS
    ACCOUNTING CYCLE
    FINANCIAL STATEMENTS
    INTERIM FINANCIAL REPORTS

ACCOUNTING POLICIES AND PROCEDURES

The accounting policies of a reporting entity are the specific accounting principles and the methods of applying those principles that are judged by the management of the enterprise to be the most appropriate in the circumstances to present fairly financial position, results of operations, and cash flow in accordance with generally accepted accounting principles.

Information about the accounting policies adopted by a reporting enterprise is essential for financial statement users, and should be adequately disclosed. Accounting principles and their methods of application in the following areas are important:

1. A selection from existing alternatives.

2. Areas that are peculiar to a particular industry in which the company operates.

3. Unusual and innovative applications of generally accepted accounting principles.

Examples of commonly required disclosures by a business enterprise include those relating to depreciation methods, inventory pricing, basis of consolidations, and recognition of profit on long-term, construction-type contracts.

The preferred place to disclose accounting policies is under the caption "Summary of Significant Accounting Policies" cr as the initial note to the financial statements.

Accounting procedures can vary from company to company and from industry to industry. An accounting procedure should be selected in a given circumstance if its use reflects generally accepted accounting principles and if it is appropriate to record, process, and report the event or transaction.

See also: ACCOUNTING PRINCIPLES
          ACCOUNTING SYSTEM
          ACCOUNTING THEORY

References:

Kelly-Newton, Lauren, *Accounting Policy Formulation* (Addison-Wesley, Reading, Mass., 1980).

APB No. 22, *Disclosure of Accounting Policies* (APB, 1972).

ACCOUNTING PRINCIPLES

Accounting principles are the guidelines, laws, or rules adopted by the accounting profession to serve as guides to accounting practices. Accounting principles include the accounting and reporting assumptions, standards, and practices that a company must use when preparing external financial statements. An objective of GAAP is to reduce the differences and inconsistencies in accounting practice, thereby improving the comparability and credibility of financial reports.

The phrase "generally accepted accounting principles," or GAAP, is a technical term that identifies the conventions, rules, and procedures that represent accepted accounting practice at a particular period of time. GAAP reflect a consensus of what the professional considers good accounting practices and procedures.

GAAP are prescribed by authoritative bodies, such as the Financial Accounting Standards Board. The term "principle" does not imply a rule or law from which there can be no deviation or exception. The application of generally accepted accounting principles typically requires the professional judgment of an accountant. Accounting principles are understood to have application primarily to material and significant items. Items with little or no consequence can usually be dealt with on a basis of expediency or practicality. The Accounting Principles Board stated that:

Generally accepted accounting principles incorporate the consensus at a particular time as to which economic resources and obligations should be recorded as assets and liabilities . . . which changes in assets and liabilities should be recorded, when these changes should be recorded, how the recorded assets and liabilities and changes in them should be measured, what information should be disclosed, and which financial statements should be prepared.

Sources of generally accepted accounting principles include:

1. Pronouncements of the Financial Accounting Standards Board (FASB) and its predecessors, the Accounting Principles Board (APB) and the Committee on Accounting Procedures (CAP). These pronouncements include FASB statements of Standards and Interpretations, APB Opinions, and American Institute of Certified Public Accountants Accounting Research Bulletins (ARB).

2. FASB Technical Bulletins and AICPA's Interpretations, Audit Guides, Accounting Guides, and Statements of Position.

3. General accounting practice.

4. Securities and Exchange Commission regulations.

5. Internal Revenue Service regulations.

6. Accounting literature.

Levels of authority of sources of accounting principles are determined according to the following hierarchy:

1. Pronouncements of authoritative bodies specified by Rule 203 of the AICPA Code of Professional Ethics. These include the Financial Accounting Standards Board (FASB) Standards and Interpretations, the Governmental Accounting Standards Board (GASB) Standards and Interpretations, Accounting Principles Board (APB) Opinions, and CAP Accounting Research Bulletins.

2. Pronouncements of bodies composed of expert accountants that follow a due process procedure. These include AICPA Industry Audit Guides and Accounting Guides and Statements of Position.

3. Pronouncements, or practices, that represents prevalent practice or application to specific circumstances of generally accepted pronouncements. These include FASB Technical Bulletins, AICPA Interpretations, and industry practices.

4. Other accounting literature. These include APB Statements, AICPA Issues Papers, FASB Concept Statements, pronouncements of other professional associations or regulatory agencies, and textbooks and journal articles.

When applying the scheme, one is advised to work down from the top of the classification described in the preceding paragraph until an answer is found. Where an inconsistency between categories exists, it is recommended that the rule suggested by the higher level of authoritative literature shall prevail. In cases of a conflict between sources within a category, attempts are made to determine which treatment best presents the substance of the transaction given the specific circumstances.

Accounting principles are classified as either measurement principles or disclosure principles. Measurement principles deal with quantifying accounting events, transactions, and circumstances, and with determining the timing and accounting basis of items that impact the financial statements. Disclosure principles deal with matters which must be disclosed in the financial statements in order for the statements not to be misleading.

For recognition in financial statements, an item must comply with the following criteria, subject to constraints of materiality (the item must make a difference to a decision maker) and cost-benefit (costs must not exceed benefits):

1. *Definition*—The item must meet the definition of an element in financial statements (elements include assets, liabilities, revenue, gain, expense, loss, and others).

2. *Measurability*—The element must have an attribute (historical cost, replacement cost, market value, present value, and net realizable value).

3. *Relevance*—The capacity of information to make a difference in a decision by helping users to form predictions about the outcomes of

past, present, and future events or to confirm or correct prior expectations.

4. *Reliability*—The quality of information that assures that information is reasonably free from error and bias and faithfully represents what it purports to represent.

See also: ACCOUNTING
ACCOUNTING ASSUMPTIONS
ACCOUNTING BASIS
ACCOUNTING POLICIES **AND** PROCEDURES
FINANCIAL STATEMENTS

Reference:

Committee to Prepare a Statement of Basic Accounting Theory, A Statement of Basic Accounting Theory (AAA, Evanston, Ill., 1966).

ACCOUNTING PROFIT

In accounting, profit or income are considered net concepts and refer to amounts resulting from the deduction from revenues, or from operating revenue, of cost of goods sold or other expenses and losses. The terms are generally preceded by a qualifying adjective such as "gross," "operating," or "net."

In economics, accounting profit has a unique meaning. Accounting profit is defined, for a given time period, as total revenue minus total costs. In this calculation, total cost includes the firm's explicit costs of operation such as wage payments and interest on capital equipment.

See also: ECONOMIC PROFIT
PROFIT

ACCOUNTING SYSTEM

An accounting system is a management information system that is responsible for the collection and processing of data to produce information useful to decision makers in planning and controlling the activities of an organization. An accounting system deals primarily with one category of information, namely, financial information that concerns the flow of financial resources through the organization.

The data processing cycle of an accounting system can be conceptualized as the total structure of records and procedures that are associated with five activities: collection or recording, classifying, processing including calculating and summarizing, maintenance or storage, and output or reporting. The processing of data in a typical accounting system can be illustrated as follows:

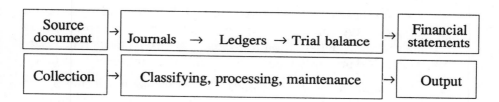

The development of an accounting information system includes the following stages: analysis, design, implementation, and operations. During the system analysis stage, the analyst determines the information needs of the system, sources of information, and the strengths and deficiencies of the current system. The design stage typically involves an evaluation of different kinds of data processing equipment, processing methods, and procedures which are suitable to the proposed project. During the design stage, the detailed system design is completed. After the system is designed, the implementation of the system commences. During the implementation stage, the system is installed and made ready to begin functioning. After the system has been implemented, it becomes operational. Modifications of the system may be required as problems arise or as new needs develop.

The essential functions of any information system include the following features:

1. *Collection of data.* Data must be collected through a selection process involving observations, measurements, and recording. In an accounting information system, this is done primarily through the use of business documents, including sales invoices, purchase orders, payroll documents, and many other forms.

2. *Information representation.* The data being collected must be described and assigned a measurement number. In accounting, this is accomplished primarily in monetary units (for example, the U.S. dollar).

3. *Storage (memory).* The acquired data must be organized, classified, and stored awaiting its use. In accounting, this function is performed primarily with journals and ledgers utilizing either manual or electronic data processing systems.

4. *Search procedures.* Data stored must be capable of being retrieved through an organized search process. The search process produces an intermediate output for the system. In accounting, this is accomplished primarily with a trial balance and worksheet procedures.

5. *Dissemination (or transmission).* The final output selected by the search process must be transmitted, distributed, or displayed in an organized physical form so that it can be made available to decision makers. Much financial reporting is disseminated through financial statements and reports.

See also: ACCOUNTING
          ACCOUNTING CYCLE
          CONTROLLER
          FINANCIAL REPORTING

Reference:

Moscove, Stephen A., and Mark G. Simkin, *Accounting Information Systems* (John Wiley & Sons, New York, 1984).

ACCOUNTING THEORY

Theory is a systematic statement of principles that serve as a foundation and explanation for underlying phenomena. In general, theory should provide an explanation, a basis for predicting outcomes or results, and guidance for practice. Accounting theory consists of a systematic statement of accounting principles and methodology.

Accounting theory has been developed using either a deductive or an inductive approach. The deductive approach involves reasoning from the general to the particular; the inductive approach involves reasoning from the particular to the general. No generally recognized, comprehensive theory of accounting exists at the present time.

The objective of accounting theory is to establish a framework or reference point to guide and evaluate accounting practice. Accounting theory also provides a basis for inherent logic, consistency, and usefulness of accounting principles and procedures. Much of accounting theory has developed over the years through the process of general acceptance by accountants, regulatory agencies, and users of financial statements. Some accounting theories have gained acceptability based on their predictive qualities. The predictive approach to the development of accounting theory relies heavily on statistical procedures and analysis. Accounting theory plays a major role in the standard-setting process which develops generally accepted accounting principles.

A committee of the American Accounting Association defined "theory" in A Statement of Basic Accounting Theory (ASOBAT) as "a cohesive set of hypothetical, conceptual and pragmatic principles forming a general frame of reference for a field of study." The committee applied this definition to accounting and assigned itself the following tasks:

1. To identify the field of accounting in order to develop a coherent theory of accounting.

2. To establish standards for accounting information.

3. To suggest ways to improve accounting practice.

4. To develop a framework for accounting research.

Accounting theory currently consists of assumptions, concepts or elements, principles, and modifying conventions used in the preparation of financial statements. A general outline of these factors is:

1. Basic assumptions:

   a. Economic (or accounting) entity

   b. Going concern

   c. Monetary measurement

   d. Periodicity

2. Basic concepts or elements:

    a. Assets, liabilities, equities

    b. Revenue, gain, expense, loss, comprehensive income

    c. Investment by owners, distribution to owners

3. Broad principles:

    a. Historical (or acquisition) cost

    b. Revenue realization

    c. Revenue recognition

    d. Matching costs and revenues

    e. Accrual accounting

    f. Consistency

    g. Adequate (or full) disclosure

    h. Objectivity

    i. Articulated (or interrelated) financial statements

4. Modifying conventions:

    a. Materiality

    b. Conservatism

    c. Industry practices.

Accounting procedures refer to specific methods for applying accounting theory in practice. Examples of accounting procedures include the following: first-in, first-out, last-in, first-out, and other cost flow assumptions for inventories; completed contract and percentage-of-completion methods of income recognition for long-term construction-type contracts; purchase and pooling-of-interest methods of accounting for business combinations.

See also: ACCOUNTING
              ACCOUNTING ASSUMPTIONS
              ACCOUNTING BASIS

ACCOUNTING PRINCIPLES
AGENCY THEORY
CONSERVATISM
CONSISTENCY
COST PRINCIPLE
ELEMENTS OF FINANCIAL STATEMENTS
FULL DISCLOSURE
GOING CONCERN
MATCHING PRINCIPLE
MATERIALITY
MEASUREMENT
OBJECTIVITY
REALIZATION
RECOGNITION

References:

American Accounting Association, *Statement on Accounting Theory and Theory Acceptance* (AAA, 1977).

American Accounting Association, *Accounting and Reporting Standards for Corporate Financial Statements and Preceding Statements and Supplements* (AAA, 1957).

American Accounting Association, *A Statement of Basic Accounting Theory* (AAA, 1966).

American Institute of Certified Public Accountants, *The Basic Postulates of Accounting*, Accounting Research Study No. 1 (AICPA, 1961).

American Institute of Certified Public Accountants, *Basic Concepts and Accounting Principles Underlying Financial Statements of Business Enterprises,* APB Statement No. 4 (AICPA, 1970).

American Institute of Certified Public Accountants, *A Tentative Set of Broad Accounting Principles for Business Enterprises,* Accounting Research Study No. 3 (AICPA, 1962).

American Institute of Certified Public Accountants, *Inventory of Generally Accepted Accounting Principles for Business Enterprises,* Accounting Research Study No. 7 (AICPA, 1965).

Belkaoui, Ahmed, *Accounting Theory* (Harcourt Brace Jovanovich, San Diego, Calif., 1985).

Paton, W.A., *Accounting Theory* (Ronald Press, New York, 1982).

Wolk, Harry I., Jere R. Francis, Michael G. Tearney, *Accounting Theory: A Conceptual and Institutional Approach* (Kent, Boston, 1984).

ADJUSTING ENTRIES

Toward the close of an accounting period, after all external transactions and events have been recorded in the accounts, additional internal changes in assets and liabilities and offsetting changes in revenue and expense items may have to be recorded so that the financial statements properly reflect the current accounting period. These adjusting entries are usually required to adjust certain accounts so that all revenues/gains and expenses/losses and balance sheet items have correct ending balances. Adjusting entries fall into one of the following categories:

1. Apportionment of prepaid and unearned items.

    a. *Prepaid expense.* A prepaid expense is an expense paid in advance. A prepaid expense (or prepaid asset) represents goods or services purchased by the company for use in operations but which are not completely consumed or used as of the end of the accounting period. Prepaid expenses consist of such items as prepaid rent, insurance, and supplies. The portion of such expenditures not consumed in the current period and hence will benefit a future period(s) is called a prepaid expense.

    b. *Unearned revenues.* Unearned revenue is revenue received from a customer prior to the delivery of a product or performance of a service. When such revenue is received in advance, the company has an obligation to deliver the product or perform the service. When the product or service has been provided, the unearned revenue is eliminated and revenue is recognized as being earned. Examples of unearned revenue include unearned rent and interest.

2. Recording accrued expense (or liability) and accrued revenue (or receivable). An accrued expense is an expense that has been incurred

during the accounting period but one which has not been paid or recognized in the accounts. Accrued expenses include such items as accrued salaries, interest, rent, and taxes. Accrued revenue is revenue for which the service has been performed but which has not been received or recorded in the accounts. Accrued revenues include such items as accrued interest, rent, royalties, and fees.

3. Items which must be estimated.

   a. *Depreciation, amortization, and depletion.* The cost of certain assets—such as machines, buildings, office fixtures, patents, goodwill, and natural resources (oil and gas reserves)—must be systematically and rationally allocated as an expense to an appropriate accounting period. This cost allocation is referred to as depreciation, depletion, or amortization.

   b. *Bad debt expense.* When sales are made on credit, some of the accounts will undoubtedly turn out to be uncollectible. An adjustment is usually required to account for the fact that the accounts receivable are probably overstated and that a bad debt expense should be reported on the income statement to match revenue and expenses.

   c. *Inventory adjustments.* When the periodic inventory method is used, the inventory account at the end of the year contains the beginning-of-the-year inventory amount. The inventory account must be adjusted to show the cost of the merchandise on hand at the end of the period and to record the cost of goods sold during the period.

To summarize, unearned (or deferred) revenue involves the receipt of cash before the revenue is recognized; prepaid (or deferred) expense involves the payment of cash before the expense is recognized. An accrued revenue is a revenue recognized before related cash is received; an accrued expense is an expense recognized before it is paid.

See also: ACCOUNTING CYCLE
　　　　　ALLOCATION
　　　　　CLOSING ENTRIES
　　　　　DEFERRED CHARGE (CREDIT)
　　　　　REVERSING ENTRIES

ADMINISTRATIVE CONTROLS

Administrative controls include the plan of organization and the procedures and records associated with the decision processes involved in management's authorization of transactions. Administrative controls are designed to facilitate management's responsibility for achieving the objectives of the organization and to improve operational efficiency and compliance with management's policies. Administrative controls are the basis for establishing the accounting control over transactions.

Administrative controls can be contrasted with accounting controls. Examples contrasting administrative and accounting controls include the following:

Accounting Controls	**Administrative Controls**
Cash	
Cash receipts are to be deposited daily; all cash disbursements are to be made by check.	Use cash forecasts to determine short-term borrowing requirements.
Inventory	
The perpetual inventory method is to be used to account for inventory.	Inventory modeling techniques are to be used to determine the quantity of inventory to order and the timing of orders.

See also: ACCOUNTING CONTROLS
               FRAUD
               INTERNAL CONTROL

Reference:

Statement on Auditing Standard No. 30, *Reporting on Internal Accounting Control* (American Institute of Certified Public Accountants, New York).

AGENCY THEORY

Agency theory involves the study of the conflict that often arises between corporate owners (principals) and managers (agents). This conflict is frequently due to a divergence in goals. While agency problems exist in the corporate world, the same concept can be applied to any situation where there is a group taking action (agents) and a group of affected parties (principals).

Within a firm there are many principals and many agents. Stockholders are the principals and the corporate executives are the agents. A corporate executive (such as the president) is affected by the actions of his or her vice president: the president is the principal and the vice president is the agent. Similarly, vice presidents are principals and their managerial staffs are agents, and so on. At every level within an organization there may be conflict between what a principal seeks to achieve and what an agent seeks to achieve.

An agency problem exists whenever the principal cannot efficiently oversee, or monitor, the activities of the agent. Monitoring involves the principal's time and energy. Both time and energy are scarce resources, and thus there are opportunity costs to their uses. Even disregarding the costs of monitoring, in most circumstances the principal will have insufficient knowledge about the specific tasks performed by the agent. Even if monitoring could be done costlessly, the principal may not be able to render a meaningful evaluation of the agent's efficiency.

The greater the cost to the principal for monitoring the actions of the agent, the less monitoring that will take place and the greater the possibility that the agent's actions will not directly coincide with the principal's goals. For example, it is extremely costly for a stockholder (who is both a corporate owner and a principal) to monitor all of the actions of a firm's vice president. Most large corporations elect a board of directors from among the major stockholders to undertake the monitoring. Boards do not monitor directly every action of the president; rather, they look to aggregate information such as current profit and projected profit to get an overall indication of the president's performance. In most instances, a board is unaware of the profit potential of the firm and looks instead for a satisficing level of profit.

In a similar fashion, the president looks for a satisficing level of performance from the vice president, and so on down the line. The lack of information and the inability of principals to monitor fully the actions of agents brings about the agency problem.

One solution practiced in corporations to overcome the agency problem is to provide the agents with an incentive to act in the best interest of the principal. For example, if stockholders want the firm to maximize profit, then there needs to be an organizational structure within the firm that provides managers with an incentive to act accordingly. That structure can take many forms. Commonly, corporations compensate their managers in one of two ways: through an annual salary and through stock options. Such a compensation package directly links the financial well-being of a manager to the long-run performance of the firm.

See also: SATISFICING

Reference:

Pratt, John W., and Zeckhauser, Richard J., eds., Principals and Agents: *The Structure of Business* (Harvard Business School Press, Boston, Mass., 1985).

AGING SCHEDULE

An aging schedule includes a breakdown of each account receivable by the length of time passed between the date of sale and the balance sheet date. The schedule is prepared primarily for the purpose of estimating the amount of uncollectible accounts receivable as of a specific date and testing the validity of the receivables. Most audit tests of accounts receivable and the allowance for uncollectible accounts are based on the aging schedule (or the aged trial balance). The auditor needs to know whether the accounts receivable in the aging schedule agree with related subsidiary ledger accounts and that the total is correctly added and agrees with the general ledger. The auditor would also want to determine whether the accounts receivable in the schedule are valid, owned by the company, properly valued, and properly classified in the financial statements. Exhibit A-4 shows a typical aging schedule for accounts receivable.

Exhibit A-4
Aging Schedule for Accounts Receivable

Customer	Balance	Amount Not Due	Number of Days Past Due			
			1–30	31–60	61–90	Over 90
X Co.	2,800	1,300			1,500	
Y Co.	1,800	1,800				
Z Co.	500	400	100			
Others	498,500	450,000	20,000	15,000	8,500	5,000
Totals Dec. 31, 1995	503,600	453,500	20,100	15,000	10,000	5,000

See also: RECEIVABLES

ALLOCATION

The term allocation has a distinct meaning in accounting and in economics. From an accounting perspective, allocation is generally considered to be the accounting process of assigning or distributing an amount according to a plan or a formula. Allocation problems arise in many situations that involve accounting, such as:

1. Reducing an amount by periodic payments or write-downs:
   a. Reducing a liability which arose as a result of a cash receipt by recognizing revenue (for example, unearned rent).

  b. Reducing an asset (for example, depreciation, depletion, amortization, including amortization of prepayments and deferrals).

  2. Assigning manufacturing costs to production departments or cost centers and subsequently to units of product to determine product cost.

  3. Apportioning the cost of a lump-sum or basket purchase to individual assets on the basis of their relative market values.

Currently, accountants recognize that within the existing framework of conventional accounting principles and methods, allocations are generally arbitrary. Current allocation theory and practice attempt to allocate portions of the costs of nonmonetary inputs in relation to benefits received from them by the enterprise. In this context, benefits involve an increase in the entity's income (or decrease in losses) or are related to cash flows. The generally recognized minimum criteria of any allocation method include the following:

  1. The method should be unambiguous.

  2. The method should be defendable (that is, theoretically justifiable).

  3. The method should divide up what is available to be allocated (that is, the allocation should be additive).

The allocation problem in accounting is related to the matching process that assigns the costs of monetary and nonmonetary inputs (such as plant assets and inventories, and revenues) to accounting periods for purposes of determining net income. The objective of this form of allocation is to systematically spread a cost or revenue over two or more time periods. For example, depreciation accounting is a system which allocates the cost of a tangible fixed asset over its estimated useful life.

The allocation of common costs to products or departments is another significant cost allocation problem. Common costs are those costs that are not directly identifiable with a product, process, or department but which result from the joint use of a facility. For example, the cafeteria of a manufacturing plant is used by employees from the manufacturing departments and office department. Some practical way must be found to allocate the cafeteria costs to the various departments (for example, the number of employees in a department). Common cost allocations are frequently arbitrary in nature.

The allocation problem also arises when dissimilar assets are acquired for a single lump-sum price. The purchase price must be allocated to the individual assets purchased. The basis for the allocation of the purchase price in lump-sum or basket purchases is usually considered to be the relative fair market values of the individual assets. To illustrate a lump-sum acquisition, assume that land and building are acquired for $1,000,000. The fair market values of the land and building are $250,000 and $1,000,000, respectively. The lump-sum purchase price would be allocated to the two assets as follows:

	Appraisal Value	Relative Fair Market Value	× Total Cost =	Allocated Cost
Land	$ 250,000	$ 250,000 / $1,250,000 ×	$1,000,000 =	$ 200,000
Building:	1,000,000	$1,000,000 / $1,250,000 ×	$1,000,000 =	800,000
	$1,250,000			$1,000,000

The common cost allocation process involves (1) accumulating costs, (2) identifying the department or process that is to be allocated the costs, and (3) selecting a basis for allocating the common costs to the recipients. Selecting a basis of allocation is often done by examining the past behavior of the cost to determine whether a relation between the costs and an allocation base (e.g., number of employees, square footage) can be identified. In some cases, it is possible to evaluate operations to find a logical relation between costs and an allocation base. If these attempts are not productive, then costs would be assigned on an arbitrary base. The table on the following page is a relatively simple illustration involving two service departments (cafeteria and personnel) and two manufacturing departments (Departments A and B).

Note that costs that can be directly associated with departments arre allocated first, e.g., the direct costs. Costs such as rent and utilities are allocated on a rational basis (for example, floor space). Next, service department costs are allocated to manufacturing departments. When serivce departments service other service departments as well as pro-

Cost	Allocation Base	Service		Manufacturing		
		Cafeteria	Personnel	Dept. A	Dept. B	Total
Direct cost	Direct	$10,000	$5,000	$50,000	$75,000	140,000
Indirect:						
Rent	Sq. foot	2,000	1,000	10,000	15,000	28,000
Utilities	Sq. foot	4,000	2,000	20,000	30,000	56,000
Totals		$16,000	$8,000	$80,000	$120,000	$224,000
Allocation of service depts.:						
Cafeteria	No. of employees	$(16,000)	$2,000	$7,000	$7,000	—
Personnel	No. of employees		(10,000)	5,000	5,000	—
Totals				$92,000	$132,000	$224,000

duction departments, their costs are usually allocated first. In the illustration, it was decided to first allocate the cafeteria costs to the personnel department and the two manufacturing departments. After a service department's costs have been distributed, no additional costs are allocated to it. The company now knows the costs allocated to the two manufacturing departments. If more than one product comes from the production process, the costs incurred prior to the split-off point of separable products are referred to as *joint costs*. Joint costs are usually allocated to the separable products based on their relative sales value or some physical measure (for example, pounds of beef, board feet of lumber).

From an economic perspective, allocation is the process of choosing. Resources that are limited are referred to in economics as scarce resources. Most resources are scarce. Because scarcity is a fact of life, choosing among alternative resources is a necessity. Economics can be defined as the study of the process of allocating scarce resources among alternative uses.

See also: COST ACCOUNTING
             JOINT PRODUCTS AND BY-PRODUCTS

Reference:

Thomas, Arthur L., *The Allocation Problem* (AAA, 1969).

AMERICAN INSTITUTE OF CERTIFIED PUBLIC ACCOUNTANTS

The American Institute of Certified Public Accountants (AICPA) is the national professional association of certified public accountants. The AICPA's involvement and focus is on the practice of public accounting and the establishing of professional standards, especially in the auditing area. Its major publications include the *Journal of Accountancy, Accounting Research Studies, Statements of Auditing Standards,* the *Accountants' Index,* and *Accounting Trends & Techniques.*

The Institute's Auditing Standards Division and its Accounting Standards Executive Committee develop issue papers that present recommendations about current financial reporting issues.

See also: PROFESSION

AMORTIZATION

Amortization is the accounting or financial process of reducing an amount by periodic payments or write-downs. Amortization refers to the liquidation, writing off, or extinguishing of a debt over a period of time and to the write-off of a portion of the book value of an asset. The periodic retirement of a debt, such as a mortgage of serial bonds, and the periodic write-down of a bond premium are examples of amortization. The write-down of the book value of intangible assets, such as copyrights and patents, also is referred to as amortization.

See also: ALLOCATION
             BOND
             DEPRECIATION
             INTANGIBLE ASSETS

ANNUITY

An annuity is a series of equal cash flows (payments or receipts) occurring at equal intervals over a period of time. The equal cash flows are called rents. Annuities can be classified as an ordinary annuity (or an annuity in arrears) or an annuity due (or an annuity in advance). If the first payment occurs at the end of the first interest period, the annuity is called an ordinary annuity. If the first payment occurs at the beginning of the first period, the annuity is called an annuity due.

The amount or future value of an ordinary annuity is the total amount on deposit immediately after the last rent in the series is made. The amount or future value of an annuity due is determined one period after the last rent in the series. The present value of an annuity is the present value of a series of equal rents made in the future. If the present value of the series of cash flows or rents is determined one period before the receipt or payment of the first rent, the series of rents is known as the present value of an ordinary annuity. The present value of an annuity due is determined on the date of payment of the first rent. A deferred annuity is an annuity that does not start to produce rents until two or more periods have passed. A perpetuity is an annuity that continues indefinitely. For-mulas for the future value and present value of an ordinary annuity are shown in Exhibit A-5.

Reference:

Woelfel, Charles J., *Financial Managers Desktop Reference to Money, Time, Interest and Yield* (Probus, Chicago, 1986).

ANTITRUST POLICY

See Government Regulation

Reference:

Sherman, Roger. *Antitrust Policies and Issues* (Addison-Wesley, Reading, Mass., 1978).

APPRECIATION

Appreciation means to increase in value. This term is used in economics to refer to an increase in the value of the dollar. The value of the dollar increases when exchange rates change so that one dollar can buy more units of a foreign currency than previously. For example, if the exchange rate 6 months ago was $1 equals 1.74 deutsche marks, and today the ex-change rate is $1 equals 1.93 deutsche marks, then the dollar is said to

Exhibit A-5
Future Value and Present Value of an Ordinary Annuity Illustrated

Formula:

$$FV = R \left[\frac{(1 + i)^n - 1}{i} \right]$$

Where FV = future value (or amount) of an ordinary annuity of a series of rents of any amount
R = value of each rent
n = number of rents
i = compound interest rate

Example 1. Compute the future amount of 4 rents of $1,000 with interest compounded annually at 14%. The first rent occurs on December 31, 1996, and the last rent occurs on December 31, 1999.

$$FV = \$1,000 \left[\frac{(1.14)^4 - 1}{0.14} \right]$$

$$= \$1,000(4.92114)$$
$$= \$4,921.14$$

Present Value of an Ordinary Annuity

Formula:

$$PV = R \left[\frac{1 - \dfrac{1}{(1 + i)^n}}{i} \right]$$

Where PV = present value of an ordinary annuity of a series of rents
R = value of each rent
n = number of rents
i = compound discount

Example 2. Use the same data in Example 1 to compute the present value of an ordinary annuity.

$$PV = \$1,000 \left[\frac{1 - \dfrac{1}{(1.14)^4}}{0.14} \right]$$

$$= \$1,000(2.91371)$$
$$= \$2,913.71$$

The Tables in Exhibit A–7 could be used to get the factors (4.92114 and 2.91371) used in Examples 1 and 2.

have increased in value against the deutsche mark, or to have appreciated. Exchange rates are reported daily in the *Wall Street Journal*.

The term is also used with reference to an asset increasing in value, such as land, a building, stock or a bond.

See also: EXCHANGE RATE

ARBITRAGE

Arbitrage is the process of simultaneously buying in one market and selling in another market in order to profit from exiting price differentials. The process of arbitrage carried out on a wide scale by speculators and others insures a rough equality of prices for the same instruments sold in different markets. Arbitrage is thus responsible for promoting efficiency in the financial marketplace.

An example of arbitrage can be seen in the actions of traders buying and selling the same commodity or financial instrument in both the cash (or spot) market and the futures market. The difference between the cash price and the futures price of a specific commodity is called the basis. Because of the arbitrage actions of traders, the basis on a commodity or financial instrument will approach the cost of carry (that is, the costs of finance and storage).

In arbitrage, a trader might buy a commodity on the cash market and store it for future delivery. At the same time, he might sell a futures contract for the same commodity. At delivery, the actual commodity which was purchased on the spot market is delivered to satisfy the trader's obligation under the futures contract. The trader's gain on this transaction is equal to the price at which he sold the futures contract minus the cash price he paid for the commodity and minus the costs of storage and finance on the cash contract. Because any profit opportunity identified by one trader will quickly be known to others, competition among arbitraging traders will usually rapidly drive the difference between the futures price and the spot price down close to the costs of storage and finance. Thus, the actions of traders in arbitraging between the cash and futures markets will tend to eliminate opportunities for further arbitrage profits.

For financial instruments, the cost of carry is determined by interest rates and dividends. Traders seeking to arbitrage between the spot market for securities and the futures market for those same securities must calculate the net interest cost of buying the securities on the spot market and holding those securities for future delivery. Arbitrage opportunities exist whenever the futures price minus the spot price is greater than the costs of carry.

ARM'S-LENGTH TRANSACTION

An arm's-length transaction is one in which buyer and seller both pursue their own best interest and both are free to act accordingly. Transactions between related parties and affiliated companies are often not arm's-length transactions. In dealings between related parties, the question that should be asked is: Would unrelated parties have handled the transaction in the same way? When assets are acquired at a cost, it is assumed that each acquisition results from an arm's-length market transaction by two independent parties who are presumed to be acting rationally in their own self-interest.

Arm's-length transactions are the basis for a fair market value determination used to record the acquisition or historical costs of assets. The arm's-length concept is also an important judicial concept relating to tax law.

See also: COST PRINCIPLE
RELATED PARTY TRANSACTIONS

ASSETS

Assets are probably future economic benefits obtained or controlled by a particular entity as a result of past transactions or events. Future economic benefits refers to the capacity of an asset to benefit the enterprise by being exchanged for something else of value to the enterprise, by being used to produce something of value to the enterprise, or by being used to settle its liabilities. The future economic benefits of assets usually result in net cash inflows to the enterprise.

To be an asset, a resource other than cash must have three essential characteristics:

1. The resource must, singly or in combination with other resources, contribute directly or indirectly to future net cash inflows.

2. The enterprise must be able to obtain the benefit and control others' access to it.

3. The transaction or other event giving rise to the enterprise's right to or control of the benefit must already have occurred.

Assets currently reported in the financial statements are measured by different attributes including historical or acquisition cost, current (replacement) cost, current market value, net realizable value (selling price of the item less direct costs necessary to convert the asset), and present value of future cash flows, depending on the nature of the item and the relevance and reliability of the attribute measured.

Assets are recognized in the financial statements when the item meets the definition of an asset, when it can be measured with sufficient reliability, when the information about it is capable of making a difference in user decisions, and when the information about the item is reliable (verifiable, neutral or unbiased, and representationally faithful). Assets need not be recognized in a set of financial statements if the item is not large enough to be material and the aggregate of individual immaterial items is not large enough to be material to those financial statements.

Assets are usually classified on a balance sheet in order of their liquidity (or nearness to cash) as follows:

1. Current assets

2. Long-term investments

3. Property, plant, and equipment

4. Intangible assets

5. Other assets (including deferred charges).

Current assets are cash and other assets which are reasonably expected to be converted into cash, sold, or consumed within the normal operating cycle of the business or one year, whichever is longer. An operating cycle is the average time required to expend cash for inventory, process and sell the inventory, collect the receivables, and convert them back into cash.

See also: ACCOUNTING EQUATION
                 CONTRA ACCOUNT
                 COST PRINCIPLE
                 CURRENT ASSETS
                 DEFERRED CHARGE (CREDIT)
                 ELEMENTS OF FINANCIAL STATEMENTS
                 INTANGIBLE ASSETS
                 OPERATING CYCLE
                 PROPERTY, PLANT, AND EQUIPMENT
                 RECOGNITION
                 WORKING CAPITAL

Reference:

SFAC No. 3, *Elements of Financial Statements of Business Enterprises,* (FASB, 1980).

AUDIT

Auditing is a systematic process of objectively obtaining and evaluating evidence by a competent independent person about a specific entity for purposes of determining and reporting on the correspondence between assertions about economic events, actions, and other information and established criteria for reporting these assertions. An audit and the auditor's report provide additional assurance to users of financial statements concerning the information presented in the statements.

Three major types of audits include the financial statements audit, the operational audit, and the compliance audit. A financial statement audit (or attest audit) is a systematic examination of financial statements, records, and related operations to ascertain adherence to generally accepted accounting principles, management policies, and other considerations. Operational auditing is a systematic review of an organization's activities for the purposes of assessing performance, identifying opportunities for improvement, and developing recommendations for improvement or further action. A compliance audit has as its objective the determination of whether the entity being audited is following procedures or rules established by a higher authority.

The audit committee is a major committee of the board of directors of a corporation. The committee usually is composed of outside directors who nominate the independent auditors and react to the auditor's report and findings. Matters which the auditor believes should be brought to the attention of the shareholders are first brought before the audit committee.

In *The Philosophy of Auditing,* R. K. Mautz and Hussein A. Sharaf identify eight tentative postulates of auditing:

1. Financial statements and financial data are verifiable.

2. There is no necessary conflict of interest between the auditor and the management of the enterprise under audit.

3. The financial statements and other information submitted for verification are free from collusive and other unusual irregularities.

4. The existence of a satisfactory system of internal control eliminates the probability of irregularities.

5. Consistent application of generally accepted principles of accounting results in the fair presentation of financial position and the results of operations.

6. In the absence of clear evidence to the contrary, what has held true in the past for the enterprise under examination will hold true in the future.

7. When examining financial data for the purpose of expressing an independent opinion thereon, the auditor acts exclusively in the capacity of an auditor.

8. The professional status of the independent auditor imposes commensurate professional obligations.

An independent auditor performs an examination with the objective of issuing a report containing an opinion on a client's financial statements. The attest function of external auditing refers to the auditor's expressing an opinion on a company's financial statements. Generally, the criteria for judging an auditee's financial statement are generally accepted accounting principles. The typical audit leads to an attestation regarding the fairness and dependability of the financial statements which is communicated to the officials of the audited entity in the form of a written report which accompanies the financial statements.

The auditing process is based on standards, concepts, procedures, and reporting practices. The auditing process relies on evidence, analysis, convention, and informed professional judgment. Auditing standards imposed by the American Institute of Certified Public Accountants are presented in Exhibit A-6 on the following page. The standards for internal auditors are established by the Institute of Internal Auditors. The General Accounting Office establishes audit standards for governmental auditors.

The auditor generally proceeds with an audit according to the following process:

1. Plans the audit.

2. Gathers evidence:

   a. Studies, tests, and evaluates the firm's internal accounting control system.

   b. Performs and evaluates substantive tests including:

      1. Independent tests of account balances and transactions. Such tests include compliance tests which answer the question: Were the accounting controls adequate and was the system operating as designed? Substantive testing answers the question: Were the dollar amounts of the transactions correctly recorded?

      2. Other general procedures, including analytical tests (ratios and trends) and background information (to understand the client's business, operations, personnel).

3. Issues a report.

Exhibit A-7 on page 43 shows a diagram of an audit.

In planning the audit, the auditor develops an audit program that identifies and schedules audit procedures that are to be performed to obtain the evidence supporting the auditor's report. Audit evidence is proof obtained to support the audit's conclusion. Audit procedures include those activities undertaken by the auditor to obtain the evidence. Evidence-gathering procedures include observation, confirmation calculation, analysis, inquiry, inspection, and comparison. An audit trail is a chronological record of

Exhibit A-6
AICPA Auditing Standards

General Standards
1. The examination is to be performed by a person or persons having adequate technical training and proficiency as an auditor.
2. In all matters relating to the assignment, an independence in mental attitude is to be maintained by the auditor or auditors.
3. Due professional care is to be exercised in the performance of the examination and the preparation of the report.

Standards of Field Work
1. The work is to be adequately planned and assistants, if any, are to be properly supervised.
2. There is to be a proper study and evaluation of the existing internal control as a basis for reliance thereon and for the determination of the resultant extent of tests to which auditing procedures are to be restricted.
3. Sufficient competent evidential matter is to be obtained through inspection, observation, inquiries, and confirmations to afford a reasonable basis for an opinion regarding the financial statements under examination.

Standards of Reporting
1. The report shall state whether the financial statements are presented in accordance with generally accepted accounting principles.
2. The report shall state whether such principles have been consistently observed in the current period in relation to the preceding period.
3. Informative disclosures in the financial statements are to be regarded as reasonably adequate unless otherwise stated in the report.
4. The report shall contain either an expression of opinion regarding the financial statements, taken as a whole, or an assertion to the effect that an opinion cannot be expressed. When an overall opinion cannot be expressed, the reasons therefor should be stated. In all cases where an auditor's name is associated with financial statements the report should contain a clear-cut indication of the character of the auditor's examination, if any, and the degree of responsibility he is taking.

Exhibit A-7

Diagram of an Audit

INTERNAL CONTROL REVIEW AND EVALUATION　　　**SUBSTANTIVE TESTS**

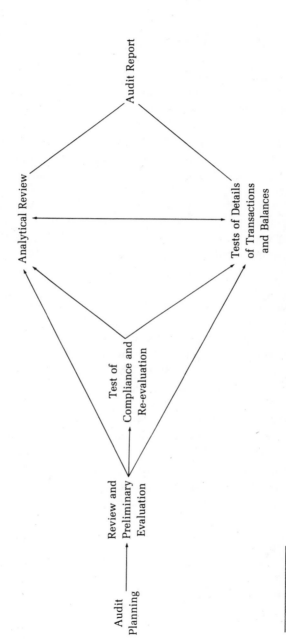

Source: Kinney, William R., Jr., "Decision Theory Aspects of Internal Control System Design/Compliance, and Substantive Tests," *Journal of Accounting Research* (Supplement, 1975), p. 16 (adpated).

Exhibit A-8
Independent Auditor's Report

We have audited the accompanying balance sheet of X Company as of December 31, 19XX, and the related statements of income, retained earnings, and cash flows for the year then ended. These financial statements are the responsibility of the Company's management. Our responsibility is to express an opinion on these financial statements based on our audit.

We conducted our audit in accordance with generally accepted auditing standards. Those standards require that we plan and perform the audit to obtain reasonable assurance about whether the financial statments are free of material misstatement. An audit includes examining, on a test basis, evidence supporting the amounts and disclosures in the fiancial statements. An audit also includes assessing the accounting principles used and significant estimates made by management, as well as evaluating the overall financial statement presentation. We believe that our audit provides a reasonable basis for our opinion.

In our opinion, the financial statements referred to above present fairly, in all material respects, the financial position of X Company as of (at) December 31, 19XX, and the results of its operations and its cash flows for the year then ended in conformity with generally accepted accounting principles.

Signature

Date

economic events or transactions that have been experienced by an organization. The audit trail enables an auditor to evaluate the strengths and weaknesses of internal control, system designs, company policies and procedures.

The independent audit report sets forth the independent auditor's opinion regarding the financial statements, that is, that they are fairly presented in conformity with generally accepted accounting principles applied on a basis consistent with that of the preceding year (or in conformity with some other comprehensive basis of accounting that is appropriate for the entity). A fair presentation of financial statements is generally understood by accountants to refer to whether:

1. The accounting principles used in the statements have general acceptability;

2. The accounting principles are appropriate in the circumstances;

3. The financial statements are prepared so as to favorably affect their use, understanding, and interpretation;

4. The information presented in the financial statements is classified and summarized in a reasonable manner; and

5. The financial statements reflect the underlying events and transactions in a way that presents the financial position, results of operations, and changes in financial position with reasonable and practical limits.

The auditor's standard report identifies the financial statements audited in an introductory paragraph, describes the nature of an audit in a scope paragraph, and expresses the auditor's opinion in a separate opinion paragraph. A typical short-form audit report on financial statements covering a single year is illustrated in Exhibit A-6.

Various audit opinions are defined by the American Institute of Certified Public Accountants' Auditing Standards Board as follows:

1. *Unqualified opinion.* An unqualified opinion states that the financial statements present fairly, in all material respects, the financial position, results of operations, and cash flows of the entity in conformity with generally accepted accounting principles.

2. *Explanatory language added to the auditor's standard report.* Circumstances may require that the auditor add an explanatory paragraph (or other explanatory language) to his report.

3. *Qualified opinion.* A qualified opinion states that, except for the effects of the matter(s) to which the qualification relates, the financial statements present fairly, in all material respects, the financial position, results of operations, and cash flows of the entity in conformity with generally accepted accounting principles.

4. *Adverse opinion.* An adverse opinion states that the financial statements do not present fairly the financial position, results of operations, or cash flows of the entity in conformity with generally accepted accounting principles.

5. *Disclaimer of opinion.* A disclaimer of opinion states that the auditor does not express an opinion on the financial statements.

The fair presentation of financial statements does not mean that the statements are fraud-proof. The independent auditor has the responsibility to search for errors or irregularities within the recognized limitations of the auditing process. An auditor understands that his or her examination based on selective testing is subject to risks that material errors or irregularities, if they exist, will not be detected. The Institute of Internal Auditors (IIA) in its Standards for the Professional Practice of Internal Auditing states:

> In exercising due professional care, internal auditors should be alert to the possibility of intentional wrong-doing, errors and omissions, inefficiency, waste, and conflicts of interest. They should also be alert to those conditions and activities where irregularities are most likely to occur. . . . Accordingly, the internal auditor cannot give absolute assurance that noncompliance or irregularities do not exist.

Auditors sometimes perform social audits and statutory audits. A social audit is an examination of an accounting entity in areas of social and environmental concerns, such as minority relations, waste managements, etc. A statutory audit is an audit performed to comply with requirements of a governing body, such as a federal, state, or city government.

Internal auditing is an independent appraisal function established by an organization to examine and evaluate its activities as a service to the organization. Internal auditors are employees of the organizations whose activities they evaluate. The primary focus of internal auditing is the determination of the extent to which the organization adheres to managerial policies, procedures, or requirements.

The legal responsibilities of the auditor are determined primarily by the following:

1. Specific contractual obligations undertaken,

2. Statutes and the common law governing the conduct and responsibilities of public accountants, and

3. Rules and regulations of voluntary professional organizations.

See also: ACCOUNTING PRINCIPLES
AMERICAN INSTITUTE OF CERTIFIED PUBLIC
  ACCOUNTANTS
CERTIFIED PUBLIC ACCOUNTANT
COMPILATION
FRAUD
PROFESSION
RELATED PARTIES TRANSACTIONS
REVIEW

References:

Taylor, Donald H., and G. William Glezen, *Auditing* (John Wiley & Sons, New York, latest edition).

Bavishi, Vinod B., and Harold E. Wyman, *Who Audits the World?* (Center for Transnational Accounting and Financial Accounting, University of Connecticut, 1983).

AICPA, *Professional Standards* (Commerce Clearing House, Inc., Chicago, latest edition).

Bb

BALANCE OF PAYMENTS

A country's balance of payments is a record of all of its international transactions for goods and services, IOUs, other financial assets, and investments. In principle, the U.S. balance of payments should be zero because every transaction is two-sided with debits balancing credits.

For example, if a U.S. computer company sells $50 million of computers to West Germany on a one-year credit, the U.S. current account shows a trade surplus of $50 million for the computer sale and the U.S. capital account shows a $50 million capital deficit from the IOU. The balance of payments nets to zero.

More generally, in balance-of-payments accounting, the total of all inflows from abroad equals the total of all outflows. This follows from the fact that the following accounting identity must always be satisfied:

$$X - M - S - T - I - R \equiv 0$$

where:

X = exports
M = imports
S = net service outflows

T = gifts, transfers, and remittances
I = net investment outflows
R = net official reserve inflows.

In practice, the balance of payments will not always equal zero. This can be due to, among other things, a country's central bank engaging in transactions that are not counted toward the country's balance of payments, or the lack of available statistical data to record all transactions.

BALANCE SHEET

See Statement of Financial Position

BANK

A bank is a company authorized by federal or state charter to perform various financial activities including:

1. *Deposit function*—Accept money as deposits

2. *Payment function*—Disburse money

3. *Credit function*—Extend credit

4. *Investment function*—Investing activities

5. *Service function*—Provide advisory, trust, safe deposit, custodianship, agency, and other financial services.

The title of bank is applied to commercial banks, investment banks, mortgage banks, industrial banks, Banks for Cooperatives, Central Bank for Cooperatives, Export-Import Bank, Federal Intermediate Credit banks, Federal Land banks, central bank, Federal Reserve banks, industrial banks, and many others. Noncommercial bank institutions include savings and loan associations, mutual savings banks, and credit unions which are sometimes referred to as thrift institutions. Thrifts have statutory authority to diversify into fields of commercial banks.

The U.S. commercial banking system includes:

1. The Federal Reserve System, the central bank, with its 12 Federal Reserve Banks

2. National banks federally charted by the Comptroller of the Currency

3. State banks chartered by the states

4. Trust companies chartered by the states

5. Miscellaneous banking institutions charted by the states (for example, private banks cooperative exchanges)

State banking laws generally allow:

1. *Unit banking*—Bank may operate in only one location.

2. *Statewide branch banking*—Bank may operate branches throughout the state.

3. *Limited branch banking*—Bank may open branches only within specifically defined geographic areas within a state.

4. *In-state multibank holding companies*—Ownership or control of a number of banks only within the state.

5. *Multistate multibank holding companies*—Out-of-state bank holding companies.

A bank holding company, as defined by the Bank Holding Company Act of 1956, is a company that has control over any bank or over any company that has control over any bank.

The federal government has developed many programs involving direct loans and insurance or guarantees of private loans dealing with housing and home ownership, agricultural and natural resources development, assistance to economic development and military assistance abroad, higher education support, and the promotion of business including exports, transportation, and small business.

High technology applications to banking, the evolution of new products, and increased competition are three major issues facing the banking industry today. Along with regulatory innovations, these issues are revolutionizing banking.

References:

Cox, Edwin B., et al., *The Bank Director's Handbook* (Dover, Mass.: Auburn House Publishing Company, 1986).

Vrabac, Daniel J., "Recent Developments at Banks and Nonbank Depositary Institutions," *Economic Review, Federal Reserve Bank of Kansas City* (July–August 1983), 33–35.

Commerce Clearing House, American Institute of Certified Public Accountants Professional Standards (4 vols).

Federal Reserve Board, *Federal Reserve Regulatory Service.*

Federal Reserve Board, *Monetary Policy and Reserve Requirements Handbook.*

Schlichting, Rice and Cooper, *Banking Law* (New York: Matthew Bender & Co., Inc., 1981) (8 vols).

BANKERS ACCEPTANCES

A bankers acceptance is a "time draft" drawn on a commercial bank ordering the bank to pay a certain sum of money at a certain date. It is called an acceptance because a bank "accepts" the responsibility of seeing that the order is carried out, thus reducing the default risk of the investor who holds the acceptance or time draft. By accepting the time draft, the bank effectively substitutes its own credit for that of the borrower and creates a negotiable instrument that may be traded in the process.

Bankers acceptances have been and continue to be widely used in international trade. Acceptances have made it possible for importers and exporters in widely separate parts of the world and unknown to each other to conduct business with each other.

Consider the example of a small retailer in Italy, Mr. Bianco, who wants to import a new video game from an American firm in California, to pay for the shipment after it arrives in Pisa, but XYZ Video is unfamiliar with Mr. Bianco and prefers immediate payment. In such a case, Mr. Bianco might suggest acceptance financing.

Mr. Bianco might offer XYZ Video $50,000 payable 60 days after shipment for a certain quantity of video games f.o.b. Pisa. XYZ Video calculates the discounted present value of $50,000 paid 60 days from now. This is the amount XYZ will actually receive when it accepts Mr. Bianco's offer. Typically in this kind of transaction, the costs of finance will be borne by the buyer, in this case Mr. Bianco.

Once XYZ accepts his offer, Bianco asks his bank in Pisa to issue a commercial letter of credit on his behalf in favor of XYZ Video. The letter of credit contains the terms of the proposed transaction and represents the Italian bank's promise to stand behind Mr. Bianco's ability to pay XYZ's invoice in 60 days when presented with the shipping documents for the video games. The American bank earns a fee or commission for accepting the time draft. The size of the fee varies with the term of the acceptance and is quoted in terms of basis points calculated on an annual basis.

When it receives the letter of credit, the American bank notifies XYZ of its arrival. With the letter of credit, XYZ feels safe to ship the games. And having done so, it presents the shipping documents and the time draft for $50,000 to its American bank. The bank takes the shipping documents representing title to the games and the time draft. The bank then pays XYZ Video the dicounted present value of the time draft. Once XYZ has shipped the games and received its money, the transaction is complete on its end.

The American bank stamps the time draft "Accepted," thereby creating a bankers acceptance and indicating its responsibility to pay whoever presents the draft for payment in 60 days. The bank sends the shipping documents to the Italian bank. The American bank can either hold the acceptance as an investment or sell it to an investor on the secondary market. If it sells the acceptance, the purchaser has the bank's promise that it will redeem the acceptance at maturity.

When the Italian bank gets the shipping documents, it informs Mr. Bianco. After he signs a note or makes other arrangements to pay $50,000 in 60 days, the shipping documents are released to him so that he may claim the games when they arrive.

At maturity of the acceptance, whoever holds it presents it for payment to the American bank which redeems it. At the same time, Mr. Bianco pays his Italian bank, which uses the funds to pay its debt to the American bank.

Although the example outlined above describes an acceptance created to finance an American export, acceptances also are used to finance imports into the United States, the shipment and storage of goods within the United States, and the shipment and storage of goods between foreign countries. Acceptances representing U.S. exports and imports used to be the largest category of traded acceptances, but today they represent less than half of the market. The largest category of acceptances arise out of the shipment of goods between foreign countries. Acceptances representing the shipment of goods within the United States are only a minor part of the total.

Virtually all acceptances traded in the United States are denominated in dollars, and most have a maturity of six months or less. The most common maturities are one, three, and six months. The market in traded acceptances is an over-the-counter market which is highly liquid and supported by around 30 dealers. Dealers and brokers quote bid and asked prices for round lots of $5 million. The typical bid-ask spread is around 5 basis points. If the transaction to be financed is larger than $5 million, it will be broken into multiples of $5 million each by drawing several drafts for the same transaction. Transactions less than $5 million are grouped together in bundles of similar maturities and sold as a package.

The major investors in bankers acceptances include money market mutual funds, insurance companies, bank trust departments, and others. For investors, buying bankers acceptances is very much like putting funds in a bank certificate of deposit. Consequently, the rates on acceptances are very close to those on CDs, usually within 10 basis points. Although acceptances are not federally insured, the default rate on them historically has been very low. And should a bank default, investors can look for payment to the firm that drew the acceptance (in the above example this would be XYZ Video).

From the standpoint of a bank, dealing in acceptances is almost like financing a loan with funds from a certificate of deposit. In both cases, the bank must pay the holder at the certificate's maturity and can expect to do so from funds generated by the repayment of the loan. In the above example, funds received from the Italian bank can be used to redeem the acceptance.

For a bank, an outstanding acceptance is like a deposit liability. But unlike deposit liabilites, acceptances are not subject to deposit insurance fees and reserve requirements. (Acceptances are exempt from reserve requirements so long as they arise out of the foreign or domestic shipment or storage of goods and have a maturity of six months or less). Accordingly, acceptance liabilities are a less costly source of funds for banks than are normal deposit liabilities.

The market for dollar-denominated acceptances grew rapidly in the 1970s but has declined somewhat since 1983. This slowdown in the growth of acceptance financing is partly attributable to the decline in commodity prices that depressed the dollar value of world trade and declines in interest rates. But it also reflects a growing use of the commercial paper and Eurodollar markets by both U.S. and foreign companies to meet their short-term credit needs.

See also   CHECKS
              MONEY MARKETS
              LETTER OF CREDIT

Reference:

Jensen, Frederick H. and Parkinson, Patrick M., "Recent Developments in the Bankers Acceptance Market," Federal Reserve Bulletin (January 1986), pp. 1–12.

BANK RECONCILIATION

A bank reconciliation is a process of bringing into agreement the balance of a depositor's account in the bank's records and the balance of the cash account in the company's books. The objective of the bank reconciliation is to disclose any errors or irregularities in either the bank's or the company's records. For purposes of internal control, the reconciliation is generally made by an individual who neither handles cash nor has access to the books of the company. The bank reconciliation illustrated in Exhibit B-1 adjusts both the book balance and the bank balance to reflect the adjusted balance (the correct balances that should exist). The bank statement balance is adjusted for items not yet recorded by the bank and for errors made by the bank. The cash account balance is adjusted for items not yet recorded in the cash account and for any errors in the company's books. The adjusted balances should be equal.

A special four-column bank reconciliation, "proof of cash," or "block reconciliation" reconciles the bank and book balances at both the beginning and end of the period as well as cash receipts and disbursements during the period. Exhibit B-2 shows this form of a reconciliation.

See also: INTERNAL CONTROL

Exhibit B-1

Bank Reconciliation in Form that Adjusts Bank and Book Balances

Bank Statement

Balance per bank statement	$15,000
Add: Deposit in transit	5,000
	20,000
Deduct: Outstanding checks	7,000
ADJUSTED BANK BALANCE	$13,000

Cash Account

Balance per cash account	$ 6,950
Add: Note collected by bank and interest	6,060
	13,010
Deduct: Bank service charge	10
ADJUSTED CASH ACCOUNT BALANCE	$13,000

Exhibit B-2

Proof of Cash

	Balance Nov. 30	December Deposits	December Withdrawals	Balance Dec. 31
Transactions per bank	$5,500	$12,300	$2,800	$15,000
Deposits in transit				
November 30	1,000	(1,000)		
December 31		5,000		5,000
Oustanding checks:				
November 30	(700)		(700)	
December 31			7,100	(7,100)
Bank service charge			10	10
Note/interest collected by bank		(6,060)		(6,060)
Customer's N.S.F. check			(50)	50
Transactions per books	$5,800	$10,240	$9,140	$ 6,900

BANK REGULATION

The structure of banking regulation that exists today in the United States has evolved slowly over a long period of time. Regulations were imposed to deal with financial crises and the changing structure of the industry (see Exhibit B-3). Much of the regulatory structure was erected to increase the safety of the banking and payments system. Generally, regulatory agencies, such as the Federal Reserve and the Federal Deposit Insurance Corporation (FDIC), were created following periods in which the banking failures injuring large numbers of people had occurred.

The structure of banking regulation in the United States is complex, and it is characterized by substantial overlap and functional duplication among the governmental bodies charged with various facets of bank regulation. Exhibit B–4 illustrates the complexity of the current regulatory environment.

Today, of the more than 14,000 commercial banks, about one-third have national charters. The remainder are chartered by the various states. If a bank has a national charter, its operations are supervised by the Comptroller of the Currency. In addition, all national banks must be members of the Federal Reserve System.

State-chartered banks are supervised by the state bank departments or equivalent agencies in the states where the banks are located. State banks may choose to be members of the Federal Reserve, in which case they become subject to its regulations the same as national banks. Or state banks may remain non-members of the Federal Reserve System, in which case they are regulated by the FDIC.

The Depository Institutions Deregulation and Monetary Control Act (DIDMCA) of 1980 made all financial institutions, including both national and state-chartered banks, subject to the same deposit reserve requirements set by the Fedearal Reserve. Moreover, if a state-chartered bank is part of a holding company, the holding company parent organization is subject to Federal Reserve regulation. Because of the tax and other financial advantages of the holding company form of organization, the Federal Reserve has some authority over the majortiy of commercial banks, especially the larger ones.

State-chartered banks are not mandated to join the DFIC, but realistically, it is a competitive necessity for a bank to have federal deposit insurance. And some state banking agencies require FDIC approval before they will grant a bank charter.

Exhibit B-3
Major Banking Legislation in the United States

LEGISLATION	MAJOR PROVISIONS
National Bank Act (1863)	Created the office of the Comptroller of the Currency. Authorized the Comptroller to charter and supervise national banks.
Federal Reserve Act (1913)	Established the Federal Reserve System and required all national banks to become members.
Banking Act of 1933 (Glass-Steagall Act)	Created the FDIC. Separated commercial from investment banking. Allowed national banks to branch where permitted by state law.
Bank Holding Co. Act (1956)	Regulated multibank holding companies (MBHCs). Prohibited MBHCs from engaging in nonfinancial business and from crossing state lines except where permitted by state law.
Bank Merger Act (1966)	Established merger guidelines.
Amendment to Bank Holding Act (1970)	Regulated one-bank holding companies.
Depository Institutions Deregulation and Monetary Decontrol (1980)	Established uniform reserve requirements for all depository institutions. Phased out depository rate ceilings. Eliminated usury ceilings. Allowed NOW accounts.
Depository Institutions Act of 1982 (Garn-St. Germain)	Gave commercial loan and demand deposit powers to thrifts. Allowed bank holding companies to acquire troubled financial institutions both in-state and out-of-state.

Exhibit B-4
Existing Regulation of Banks and Their Holding Companies
December 31, 1983

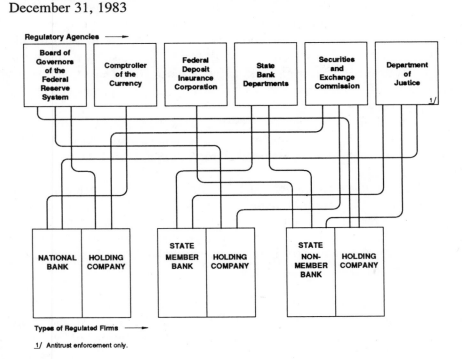

Source: *Economic Report of the President, 1984*, p.171.

The Securities and Exchange Commission (SEC) operates to guarantee that banks provide adequate disclosure of all financial information. Amendments to the Securities Act of 1934 passed in 1964, 1974, and 1975 increased the SEC's authority over banks and charged the banking agencies with following disclosure guidelines similar to those of the SEC. The SEC requires that banks provide full, fair, and timely public disclosure of corporate information. The SEC also plays a role in determining if banks may enter into various investment banking activities without violating the Glass-Steagall Act of 1933.

The U.S. Department of Justice and the Federal Trade Commission (FTC) also share in the responsibilty for bank regulation. The Bank Merger Act of 1966 gave the Department of Justice an independent role in th approval of bank mergers. It has the power to postpone a merger for 30 days with an "automatic" injunction, giving it additional time to decide whether to bring suit to prevent the merger under antitrust laws. In assessing the competitive effects of bank mergers, the Justice Department seeks to determine if the merger would significantly reduce competition in the bank's market area.

The Truth in Lending Act (1969) gave the FTC power to ensure that consumers have proper information in their dealings with banks. The FTC monitors bank behavior to assure that banks do not mislead or deceive consumers.

Over the years, controversy has continued to surround the issue of bank regulation. Government regulation of banks has focused on preventing bank failures and providing consumer protection, but many now claim that banking is overregulated. Critics charge that overregulation protects inefficient banks and hinders innovation. They contented that more competition is necessary.

The major banking acts of the 1980s, the Depository Institutions and Monetary Control Act (1980) and the Depository Institutions Act (1982), took substantial steps toward deregulating the banking industry, and many observers expect this process to continue. The challenge for public policy is to properly balance the gains from increased competition against the considerations of bank safety, stability, and consumer protection. This is no easy task, and the trade-offs are not easily resolved.

References:

Council of Economic Advisers, Economic Rep[ort of the President, 1984 (Washington, DC: U.S. Government Printing Office, 1984), Ch. 5.

Lash, Nicholas A., *Banking Laws and Regulations: An Economic Perspective* (Englewood Cliffs, NJ: Prentice-Hall, 1987).

BANKRUPTCY

Bankruptcy is a judicial procedure used to reconcile the conflicting interests that occur when a debtor has incurred too much debt. The Bankruptcy

Reform Act of 1978 is the major federal law dealing with bankruptcy. The public policy goal of bankruptcy is to allow the debtor a "fresh start" in financial dealings and to obtain a fair distribution of the debtor's assets among creditors. A discharge in bankruptcy refers to the absolution of a bankrupt's debt, by court order, upon the liquidation or rehabilitation of the bankrupt.

A bankrupt is a person recognized by law as being unable to pay debts. A business is insolvent in the legal sense when the financial condition is such that the sum of the entity's debts is greater than the entity's property at fair valuation. All federal bankruptcy cases must be filed under a specific chapter of the Reform Act. In Chapter 7 of the Reform Act, the assets of the debtor are liquidated in an effort to satisfy creditors. Chapter 11 provides for the reorganization of the debtor's finances and operations so that it can continue operating. Chapter 13 provides for the adjustment of debts of an individual with regular income to enable the person to work through financial problems while avoiding liquidation. Chapter 9 applies to municipalities and sets forth the procedures for the rehabilitation of a financially troubled municipality.

The Reform Act established a new bankruptcy court system. Special bankruptcy courts are located in each federal judicial district. These courts have judicial authority over all cases and proceedings brought under the act. The courts have exclusive authority over all property of the debtor.

Chapter 7 liquidation cases begin voluntarily when a debtor corporation files a petition with the bankruptcy court, or involuntarily when three or more entities file the petition. In Chapter 7 cases, the estate of the debtor corporation is turned over to an interim trustee until a trustee is elected by unsecured creditors. A Chapter 11 reorganization case can be initiated either voluntarily by a debtor or involuntarily by creditors. In Chapter 11 cases, a trustee may be appointed for cause; otherwise, the debtor corporation continues in possession.

A statement of affairs is a report prepared to show the immediate liquidation amounts of assets, instead of historical costs, and the estimated amounts that would be received by each class of claim or party of interest in the event of the liquidation of an enterprise. The report is essentially a balance sheet prepared on the assumption that the enterprise is to be liquidated, rather than on the going-concern assumption which normally applies to the preparation of financial statements. Emphasis is placed on the legal status of resources and claims against those resources. Creditors and owners can use the statement to estimate the amounts that could be realized on the disposition of the assets and the priority of claims as well as any estimated deficiency that would result if the enterprise were to be liquidated. A typical statement of affairs discloses the following information about assets and liabilities:

Assets
Assets pledged with fully secured creditors
Assets pledged with partially secured creditors
Free assets

Liabilities
Liabilities having priorities
Fully secured liabilities
Partially secured creditors
Unsecured creditors

A trustee or receiver is usually required to prepare a realization and liquidation account or report to summarize his/her activities during a reporting period. The report typically discloses the following information:

Realization and Liquidation Account

Assets to be realized	Assets realized
Assets acquired	Assets not realized
Liabilities liquidated	Liabilities to be liquidated
Liabilities not liquidated	Liabilities incurred
Supplementary charges (expenses)	Supplementary credits (revenues)

See also: LIQUIDATION
QUASI-REORGANIZATION
REORGANIZATION
SOLVENCY AND INSOLVENCY

Reference:

Ginsberg, Robert E., *Bankruptcy* (Prentice-Hall, Englewood Cliffs, N.J., 1985).

BENEFIT-COST ANALYSIS

See Cost-Benefit Analysis

BETA COEFFICIENT

A beta coefficient for a given stock or portfolio of stocks is a measure of the extent to which the returns on the stock or stock portfolio move with the overall market for stocks as measured by some broad stock index, such as the S&P 500 Index. Beta is a measure of the stock's volatility relative to the average stock on the market. And since market volatility is also a measure of risk, beta measures part of the overall risk of holding a security: the risk that the security will move up or down with the market. This is often called "market risk" or "systematic risk."

A hypothetical "average-risk" stock will tend to rise or fall in price in direct step with the overall stock market. Such an average-risk stock would have a beta coefficient equal to 1.0. A higher-than-average-risk stock would have a volatility greater than the average for the market as a whole, and thus its beta coefficient would be greater than 1.0. A stock with lower than average volatility would have a beta coefficient less than 1.0. If B = 0.5, the stock is only half as volatile as the market, and holding a portfolio of such stocks would be only half as risky as holding a diversified portfolio of "average-risk" stocks. Alternatively, if B = 2.0, the stock is twice as volatile as the market; that is, it tends to rise and fall twice as much. Holding a portfolio of such stocks would be twice as risky for the average investor.

Because rational investors do not take on additional risk without demanding additional returns to compensate them for the additional risk, investors who hold high-beta stocks will likely demand above-market returns. Similarly, investors who hold low-beta stocks can usually expect to be compensated with below-average returns.

The beta coefficients for most publicly traded companies are published by Merrill Lynch, Value Line and other investor advisory services.

These values are calculated using actual trading data. Usually, beta is tabulated by estimating a regression line as follows:

$$R_i = A + B \times R_m$$

where

R_i =   return on the stock
R_m =   return on the market
B   =   beta coefficient

The estimated slope of this regression line is equal to the beta coefficient for the individual stock.

See also: INVESTING

Reference

Brigham, Eugene F., *Fundamentals of Financial Management* (Chicago, Ill.: Dryden Press, 1986), Chapter 6.

BOND

A bond is a written, unconditional promise made under corporate seal in which the borrower promises to pay a specific sum at a determinable future date, together with interest at a fixed rate and at fixed dates. A bond issuer is a debtor. The bondholder is a creditor of the issuer and is not an owner as is a stockholder.

Corporate bonds are usually issued in denominations of $1,000. The amount shown on the bond is the face value, maturity value, or principal of the bond. Bond prices are usually quoted as a percentage of face value. For example, a $1,000 bond priced to sell at $980 would be quoted at 98 which means that the bond is selling at 98 percent of $1,000.

The nominal or coupon interest rate on a bond is the rate the issuer agrees to pay and is also shown on the bond or in the bond agreement. Interest payments, usually made semiannually, are based on the face value of the bond and not on the issuance price. The effective or market interest rate is the nominal rate adjusted for the premium or discount on the purchase and indicates the actual yield on the bond. Bonds that have a single fixed maturity date are term bonds. Serial bonds provide for the repayment of principal in a series of periodic installments.

If bonds are sold above face value, they are said to be sold at a premium. If bonds are sold at a premium, the effective interest rate is less than the nominal rate since the issuer received more than the face amount of the bond but is required to pay interest on only the face amount. If bonds are sold below face value, they are said to be discount. If bonds are sold at a discount, the effective interest rate paid is more than the nominal rate since the issuer received less than the face amount of the bonds but is required to pay interest on the face amount.

Callable bonds are bonds which can be redeemed by the issuer at specific prices, usually at a premium, prior to their maturity. Convertible bonds are bonds which at the option of the bondholder can be exchanged for other securities, usually equity securities, of the corporation issuing the bonds during a specific period of time at a determined or determinable conversion rate. The conversion price is the price at which convertible securities can be converted into common stock. The conversion ratio is the number of shares of common stock that may be obtained by converting one convertible bond or share of convertible preferred stock.

Secured bonds are bonds that have a specific claim against assets of the corporation. If the corporation fails to make interest payments or the maturity payment, the pledged assets can be seized by the bondholder or his representative. Real estate mortgage bonds have a specific claim against certain real property of the issuer, such as land and building. A chattel mortgage bond has a claim against personal property, such as equipment or livestock. Collateral trust bonds are secured by negotiable securities owned by the bond issuer, such as stocks or bonds. Guaranteed bonds are bonds on which the payment of interest and/or principal is guaranteed by another party. Income bonds are bonds on which interest payments are made only from operating income of the issuing entity. Unsecured bonds, or debentures, are bonds the holder of which has no claim against any specific assets of the issuer or others but relies on the general creditworthiness of the issuer for security.

Senior securities are securities that have claims that must be satisfied before payments can be made to more junior securities. Junior securities have a lower-priority claim to assets and income of the issuer than senior securities.

Zero-coupon (or compound discount) bonds are noninterest-bearing bonds issued by many companies at a substantial discount. Zero-coupon bonds sell for much less than their maturity value. The discount on the bonds represents the interest earned over the life of the bonds. For example, if an investor purchased a $1,000 ten-year maturity zero-coupon bond for $300, he would be receiving a compound interest yield of approximately 12.79 percent annually. At the end of the ten years, he would redeem the bond for $1,000 from the issuing company.

Registered bonds are issued in the name of the owner and are recorded in the owner's name on the records of the issuer. Coupon bonds are bearer bonds which can be transferred from one investor to another by delivery. Interest coupons are attached to the bonds. On interest payment dates, the coupons are detached and submitted for payment to the issuer or an agent. Sinking fund bonds are bonds for which a fund is established into which periodic cash deposits are made for the purpose of redeeming outstanding bonds.

Bonds may be sold by the issuing company directly to investors or to an investment banker who markets the bonds. The investment banker might underwrite the issue, which guarantees the issuer a specific amounts or sell the bonds on a commission (best efforts) basis for the issuer.

The price of bonds can be determined either by a mathematical computation or from a bond table. A bond table shows the current price of a bond as a function of the coupon rate, years to maturity, and the effective yield to maturity (or effective rate). An excerpt from a bond table is presented in Exhibit B-5 on the following page. When mathematics is used, the price of a bond can be computed using present value tables. The price of a bond is:

1. The present value at the effective rate of a series of interest payments (that is, an annuity) and

2. The present value of the maturity value of the bonds.

To determine the price of a $1,000 four-year bond having a 7 percent nominal interest rate with interest payable semiannually purchased to yield 6 percent, use the following procedure:

Exhibit B-5
Excerpts form Bond Table

Four Years Interest Payable Semiannually

Per Cent Per Annum	Nominal Rate						
	3%	3½%	4%	4½%	5%	6%	7%
4.00	96.31	98.17	100.00	101.83	103.66	107.33	110.99
4.10	95.98	97.81	99.63	101.46	103.29	106.94	110.60
4.125	95.89	97.72	99.54	101.37	103.20	105.85	110.50
4.20	95.62	97.45	99.27	101.09	102.92	106.56	110.21
4.25	95.45	97.27	99.00	100.91	102.73	106.38	110.02
4.30	95.27	97.09	98.91	100.73	102.55	106.19	109.83
4.375	95.00	96.82	98.64	100.45	102.27	105.90	109.54
4.40	94.92	96.73	98.55	100.36	102.18	105.81	100.44
4.50	94.56	96.38	98.19	100.00	101.81	105.44	109.06
4.60	94.21	96.02	97.83	99.64	101.45	105.06	108.68
4.625	94.13	95.93	97.74	99.55	101.36	104.97	108.58
4.70	93.87	95.67	97.47	99.28	101.08	104.69	108.30
4.75	93.69	95.49	97.30	99.10	100.90	104.51	108.11
4.80	93.52	95.32	97.12	98.92	100.72	104.32	107.92
4.875	93.26	95.06	96.85	98.65	100.45	104.04	107.64
4.90	93.17	94.97	96.77	98.56	100.36	103.95	107.54
5.00	92.83	94.62	96.41	98.21	100.00	103.59	107.17
5.10	92.49	94.28	96.06	97.85	99.64	103.22	106.80
5.125	92.40	94.19	95.98	97.77	99.55	103.13	106.70
5.20	92.15	93.93	95.72	97.50	99.29	102.86	106.43
5.25	91.98	93.76	95.54	97.33	99.11	102.67	106.24
5.30	91.81	93.59	93.37	97.15	98.93	102.49	106.06
5.375	91.55	93.33	95.11	96.89	98.67	102.22	105.78
5.40	91.47	93.25	95.02	96.80	98.58	102.13	105.69
5.50	91.13	92.91	94.68	96.45	98.23	101.77	105.32
5.625	90.71	92.48	94.25	96.02	97.79	101.33	104.86
5.75	90.30	92.06	93.83	95.59	97.35	100.38	104.41
5.875	89.88	91.64	93.40	95.16	96.92	100.44	103.96
6.00	89.47	91.23	92.98	94.74	96.49	100.00	103.51

(Effective Rate — left margin label)

Example: A $1,000 4-year, 6% bond purchased at 104.69 (= $1,046.90) yields 4.70% effective interest. Interest is payable semiannually. To purchase this bond to yield 4.70% effective interest, an investor should pay $1,046.90.

1. Present value of maturity value at effective rate (3%) for eight periods:

$1,000 × .789409 (= present value of 1 at 3% when the number of periods is 8) $ 789.41

2. Present value of an annuity of eight interest receipts of $35 each at effective interest rate of 3%:

$35 × 7.01969 (= present value of an annuity of 1 at 3% for 8 periods)   245.69

Price of the bond $1,035.10

The carrying value (or book value) of the bond issue at any time is the face value plus any amortized premium or minus any unamortized discount. The periodic write-off of a bond discount or bond premium adjusts the carrying value of the bond toward the bond's face value. Amortization of the discount increases the amount of interest expense while the amortization of a premium decreases the amount of interest expense reported. Exhibit B–6 on the following page illustrates the amortization of a bond premium using the effective interest method. The total interest expense each year is computed by multiplying the carrying value of the bond at the beginning of the period. The difference between the interest paid or payable during the period and the total interest expense represents the discount or premium amortized for the period. The carrying value of the bond increases (decreases) each year as the discount (premium) is amortized to interest expense until maturity. At maturity, the carrying value of the bonds is their face amount. The use of the effective rate method recognizes a constant rate of interest on the bonds over the life of the bonds. The straight-line method of amortization is sometimes used to amortize bond premiums and discounts. This method amortizes an equal amount of premium or discount each period. When this method is used, the interest expense for the periods remains constant over the life of the bonds.

In reporting long-term debt on the balance sheet, the nature of the liability, maturity date, interest rate, conversion privileges, borrowing restrictions, and other significant matters should be disclosed.

Exhibit B-6
Schedule of Bond Premium Amortization—Effective Interest Method

Date	Cash	Interest Expense	Amortization of Bond Discount	Carrying Value of Bonds
1/1/90				$108,530
7/1/90	$ 4,000[a]	$3,256[b]	$ 744[c]	107.786[d]
1/1/91	4,000	3,234	766	107,020
7/1/91	4,000	3,211	789	106,231
1/1/92	4,000	3,187	813	105.418
7/1/92	4,000	3,162	838	104,580
1/1/93	4,000	3,137	863	103.717
7/1/93	4,000	3,112	888	102,829
1/1/94	4,000	3,085	915	101,914
7/1/94	4,000	3,057	943	100,971
1/1/95	4,000	3,029	971	100,000
	$40,000	$31,470	$8,530	

[a]$4,000 = $100,000 \times .08 \times 6/12$

[b]$3,256 = $108,530 \times .06 \times 6/12$

[c]$744 = $4,000 - $3,256$

[d]$107,786 = $108,530 - 744

Credit rating agencies, such as Standard and Poor, Moody, and others, report on the quality of corporate and municipal bond issues. The reports of these agencies serve as a basis for evaluating the risks, profitability, and probability of default on bond issues. Bond ratings are based on various factors including the following: issuer's existing debt level; issuer's previous record of payment; the safety of the assets or revenues committed to paying off principal and interest. Symbols such as AAA or Aaa (referred to as triple A) refer to the highest-quality rating. Other symbols are used to refer to high-quality bonds, investment grade bonds, substandard bonds, and speculative bonds. Exhibit B-7 on the following page shows several ratings of bonds' default risks.

Exhibit B-7
Ratings of Bonds' Default Risks

Moody's	Standard and Poor's	Definition*
Aaa	AAA	The highest rating assigned. Capacity to pay interest and principal extremely strong.
Aa	AA	Very strong capacity to pay interest and principal. Differ from highest-rated issues only in small degree.
A	A	Strong capacity to repay interest and principal but may be susceptible to adverse changes in economic conditions.
Baa	BBB	Adequate protection to repay interest and principal but more likely to have weakened capacity in periods of adverse economic conditions.
Ba	BB	Some speculation with respect to repayment capacity. Have some quality and protection characteristics, but major uncertainties exist.
B	B	Moderate default risk.
Caa	CCC	High default risk. May be in default or in servere danger of default.
Ca	CC	Highly speculative and likely to be in default.
C		For Moody's, the lowest-rated bonds. Can be regarded as having extremely poor prospects of ever attaining any real investment standing.
	C	For S&P, income bond on which interest is not being paid.
	D	In default. Payment of interest and/or principal in arrears.

*Adapted from Standard and Poor's *Bond Guide* and Moody's *Bond Record.*

See also: ANNUITY
                 BOOK VALUE
                 CONVERTIBLE SECURITIES
                 FINANCIAL MARKETS
                 LEVERAGE
                 LIABILITIES

Reference:

Darst, David M., *The Handbook of the Bond and Money Markets* (McGraw-Hill, New York, 1981).

BOND DURATION

Bond duration is a measure of the weighted average life of a bond. The present values of the cash flows expected from the bond each period are used as weights in calculating the average.

Duration is defined as follows:

$$D = \Sigma\, t \times PVF_t\, /\, \Sigma\, PVF_t$$

where

D   = duration
t   = length of time (number of years, etc.) to the date of
          each payment
PVF_t = present value of the payment (F) made at (t), or
          $F_t\, /\, (1 + i)^t$
          where i = the market rate of interest paid on bonds
          of similar risk
S   = a summation from the first (1) to the last (n) payment

Calculation of bond duration yields a single number that measures average age of the security in units of time such as months or years. If a security yields only one payment at maturity, for example, a zero-coupon bond, duration is equal to the maturity of the security. For securities, which yield periodic payments of interest and principal up until maturity, duration is less than maturity.

Duration is useful in measuring the sensitivity of bond value to changes in the market rate of interest. The fractional change in the value of a bond resulting from a change in interest rates is given by

$$DS/S = -D \times (\Delta i / (1 + i)) \cong -D\Delta i$$

where

S = market price of the bond
i = market rate of interest
Δ = change from the previous period

The fractional change in the market price of a bond is equal to its duration (with a minus sign) times the change in the interest rate, divided by 1 plus the interest rate prior to the change. This fractional change is approximately equal to duration (with a minus sign) multiplied by the change in the rate of interest.

Knowledge of a bond's duration provides the bondholder with an easy way to measure the interest rate risk associated with the bond. For example, assume the duration of a bond is 5 and that the current rate of interest is 10 percent. If the market rate were to rise to 11 percent, the value of the bond would fall by [5 × (.01/(1 + .1)) = .0455] 4.55 percent, approximately [5 × .01 = .05] 5 percent.

Since duration is nothing more than the weighted average life of a bond, it is not a constant. As a bond ages, its duration changes and must be recalculated.

The concept of duration was first proposed by Frederick R. Macaulay in 1938. Although it usually is not included in the standard statistics presented in the normal bond reference guides, such as Moody's and Standard & Poor's, it is discussed in modern investment textbooks, and computer programs to calculate duration are commercially available.

The concept of duration can be used to help eliminate interest rate risk. If, for example, an investor knows that he will need a certain amount of money at a known future date, he should invest in bonds of matching duration. A family saving for expected college expenses in 10 years should invest in bonds having an average duration of 10 years to reduce interest rate risk exposure.

Because duration is an *additive* concept, it is possible to calculate the average duration of a bond portfolio. Such a calculation provides a measure of the interest rate risk associated with the portfolio as a whole.

The concept may also be applied to expected cash outflows. Thus, an institution such as a pension fund or institutional trust may calculate the average expected duration of its liabilities. It is then possible for a portfolio manager to offset the institution's interest rate risk by investing its funds in a portfolio of bonds with an average duration that matches the duration of the liabilities of the institution.

See also: BOND
            YIELD TO MATURITY

References:

Macaulay, Frederick R., *Some Theoretical Problems Suggested by Movements of Interest Rates, Bond Yields, and Stock Prices in the United States since 1856* (New York, NY: National Bureau of Economic Research, 1938).

Radcliffe, Robert C., *Investment Concepts, Analysis, and Strategy* (Glenview, IL: Scott, Foresman and Company, 1987), pp. 400–401.

BOND RATINGS

Corporate and municipal bonds are assigned categorical ratings which are designed to provide investors with information on the probability of default. These ratings are produced by private bond rating services. The two major bond rating services are Moody's Investors Service (Moody's) and Standard & Poor's Corporation (S&P).

	High Quality		Investment Grade		Substandard		Speculative	
Moody's	Aaa	Aa	A	Baa	Ba	B	Caa	C
S&P	AAA	AA	A	BBB	BB	B	CCC	D

Although each service uses its own rating system, their ratings can be grouped into comparable categories. Within each category below triple A, both services employ modifiers to further refine their ratings. Moody's uses the modifiers of 1, 2, and 3, with 1 signifying the strongest bonds within the category and 3 the weakest.

For example, within the single A category, A1 is the best, A2 is average, and A3 the weakest. Standard and Poor's uses a plus and minus system, so that within the single A category, for example, A+ is the most secure and A- the weakest.

In both rating systems, triple A and double A bonds are extremely safe and free from the risk of default. Single A and triple B bonds are termed "investment grade" securities. They are the lowest that many banks and investment companies are permitted to hold. Double B and lower-rated bonds are assumed to have a substantial probability of default, either because the organizations which have issued them are in financial difficulty or because they are so new that they have little financial history. These lower-rated bonds are often termed "junk bonds."

Because bondholders normally demand higher returns for accepting increased risk, low-rated bonds usually pay higher returns than higher-rated securities. The spread between the average rate on triple A and triple B corporate bonds varies with economic conditions, but the average rate on triple B bonds is always higher, reflecting their generally higher risk of default.

The rating of bonds as to their default risk is largely a subjective process. The rating firms insist that they do not employ precise quantitative formulas, but they do consider a wide variety of factors including the current level of debt, the stability of earnings, the mortgage provisions in the bond indenture, the existence of a sinking fund, etc.

Once established, the rating on a particular issue of corporate or municipal debt is reviewed periodically by the rating agencies. Occasionally, existing issues will be upgraded or downgraded to reflect changes in the financial condition of the issuing firm or municipality. When rating changes occur, they almost always have a substantial effect on the market price of the securities.

Usually, when a company announces a large new public debt issue, the rating agencies will review the ratings on all of the company's outstanding securities. If the company's financial condition has declined, it may find that the ratings on all of its outstanding bonds have been downgraded. In order to avoid triggering such an overall rating review, companies have been known to turn to bank financing in the hope of postponing a rating review until their financial condition improves.

See also: BOND

Reference:

Belkaoui, Ahmed, *Industrial Bonds and the Rating Process* (London: Quorum Books, 1983).

BOOK VALUE

Book value is a term that refers to the carrying value of an item in the financial statements, accounts, or books. The book value of plant assets is the difference between cost and accumulated depreciation. The book value of an enterprise is the excess of total assets over total liabilities (or net assets).

The book value per share of stock is the total stockholders' equity divided by the total number of shares outstanding. In other words, the book value per share is the dollar amount per share a shareholder would receive if assets were liquidated and liabilities settled at the amounts reported on the financial statements. If the preferred stock is outstanding, the book value per share of common stock is computed after deducting from total stockholders' equity the equity assigned to the preferred stock. To determine the book value of preferred stock, it is customary to begin with the liquidating value to which any dividends in arrears are added. This total is divided by the number of preferred shares outstanding.

The book value of bonds payable is affected by any premium or discount related to the bond issue. The book or carrying value of the bonds changes each period by the amount of amortized discount or premium. It equals the face amount minus any unamortized discount or plus any unamortized premium.

Caution should be exercised in interpreting the meaning of book value. It should be understood that market value per share is usually different from book value per share. Market value is influenced by a variety of factors that may not be reflected in book value. Book value reflects the accounting principles and methods used in preparing the financial statements.

See also: AMORTIZATION
BOND
CONTRA ACCOUNT
DEPRECIATION

BOOKKEEPING

A distinction is made between accounting and bookkeeping. Bookkeeping is usually associated with the mechanical, routine, and repetitive aspects of the accounting process, such as journalizing, posting, and taking a trial balance. Accounting relates to the theoretical, conceptual, and logical relationships of the entire information system as well as to the practical operations of the system. Accounting is concerned with such matters as the preparation of financial statements, compliance with generally accepted accounting principles, the fairness of the financial statements, system design, transaction analysis, budgeting, income taxes, and cost reports. Accounting includes bookkeeping.

See also: ACCOUNTING
CERTIFIED PUBLIC ACCOUNTANT

BREAK-EVEN ANALYSIS

Break-even analysis is conducted by managers in an attempt to identify a level of output at which to produce in the short run so as to cover all of their fixed and variable costs of production. This output level corresponds to where total revenue becomes greater than total costs. In most situations managers have information about what their total revenue and total costs will be at various output levels; therefore, they can predict a minimum level of sales that is needed in order to make a profit.

In Figure 1 on the following page, the firm will break even when 10,000 units of its product are sold. At the output level 10,000, total costs are $20,000 and total revenue is $20,000. Profit at the break-even level of output is zero.

Refer to Contribution Margin Analysis for additional discussion of break-even analysis.

Figure 1
Break-Even Analysis

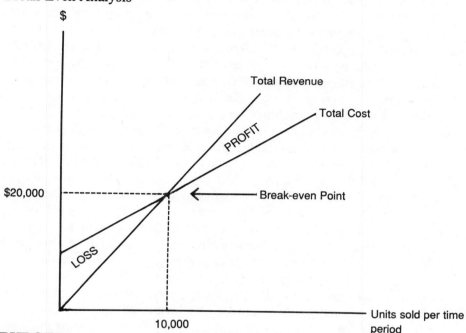

BUDGET

A budget is an orderly and coordinated plan of financial planning and management. It is a major tool for planning, motivating, and controlling business operations. The budgeting process forces management to determine its goals and objectives and to develop a coordinated plan for achieving these ends.

The master or comprehensive budget is a relatively complete "blueprint" of the future operations of the firm. The budget period is usually short enough to permit reasonably accurate predictions and long enough to allow time for implementation. The budget period usually coincides with the fiscal period of the business so that actual results of operations can be compared with budgetary estimates. An operating budget is usually prepared for a year, with supporting schedules in monthly or quarterly terms. A capital expenditure or project budget is usually developed for a longer time period.

The budgeting process usually involves the determination by a budget committee of basic assumptions under which the details of the budget are to be prepared. The board of directors (or other high-level, decision-making group) approves the assumptions set forth by the budget committee. Detailed budgeting usually begins with a forecast of revenue from sales of products or services. Estimates are made of expenses, costs, collections, and payments. Budgeted financial statements are then compiled and examined to determine how the budgeted activities will affect the company, stockholders, creditors, and other external parties. After this phase of the budgeting process is completed, the budget is implemented.

The second phase of the budgetary control process involves monitoring operations so that operating plans and targets can be attained. Budgetary control relies primarily on analyses of differences between actual costs/revenues and budgeted costs/revenues and between actual costs and standard costs. Aspects of the control process involve establishing lines of responsibility for performance, communicating plans to those assigned performance responsibilities, evaluating variances between actual results and budgeted estimates, and taking appropriate action thereon.

This master budget is primarily a planning tool. It is often a static or inflexible budget and is usually prepared for one level of activity—the anticipated or normal level of output. A flexible or variable budget is usually used as the tool for controlling costs and evaluating performance. A flexible budget is prepared for a range of activity because costs are affected by changes in the level of activity. Flexible budgets are often expressed in terms of units of output or in standard direct-labor hours allowed for that output. A simplified flexible budget prepared in terms of product output for three activity levels is:

	Levels of Output Activity		
	10,000	**15,000**	**20,000**
Direct materials	$100,000	$150,000	$200,000
Direct labor	50,000	75,000	100,000
Variable factor overhead	20,000	30,000	40,000
Fixed factory overhead	30,000	30,000	30,000
Total costs	$200,000	$285,000	$370,000

If the actual level of output for the period is 15,000 units, actual costs would be compared with the flexible budget prepared at the 15,000 unit level. Any cost variances between actual and budgeted should be explained and corrected, if necessary. Performance reports for cost control purposes could be prepared using the following format:

Item	Actual Cost	Budgeted Cost	Variance	Explanation

A capital budget is a plan for acquiring and maintaining long-term assets and providing the means of financing these activities. Financial theory strongly supports the separation of the investment decision from the financing decision. A capital budget typically includes one or more of the following items:

1. New facilities and major additions.

2. Major renovations and repairs to existing facilities.

Several methods are used for making capital budgeting investment decisions. The net present value method or some modification thereof, is preferred. The application of the net present value method of capital budgeting involves the following processes:

1. Estimate the future cash inflows and outflows for each alternative project under consideration.

2. Discount the future cash flows to the present using the firm's cost of capital.

3. Accept or reject the proposed project according to a decision rule that will maximize the firm's wealth.

Budgeting is considered especially important in governmental accounting. Governmental accounting requires that an annual budget(s) be adopted by every governmental unit. The accounting system should provide the basis for appropriate budgetary control. Budgetary comparisons should be included in the appropriate financial statements and schedules for governmental funds for which an annual budget has been adopted.

See also: BUDGET MANUAL
          FORECASTING
          BUDGETS, TYPES OF

BUDGET MANUAL

The preparation of a budget can be simplified to some extent if a firm has a budget manual which documents the budgeting procedures and provides guidelines to be followed throughout the budgeting process.

The budget manual should be designed with the end users in mind. Participation in the preparation of the budget manual should include major participants in the budgeting process at various management levels. The person or group having authority over the budget should ordinarily draft the budget manual, e.g., the budget director, controller, or budget committee. The budget manual should define budget activities relating to the following:

1. What budget activities should be performed?
   Budget preparation; monitoring operations; operational feedback; performance evaluation.

2. How should budget activities be performed?
   Detailed instructions for completing the budget activities; forms lists, schedules, etc., to be used.

3. When should budgeting activities occur?
   A timetable for the performance of activities involved in the budgeting process.

4. Who should perform specific budgeting activities?
   The managers and subordinates who are to be assigned specific responsibilities for the performance of budgeting activities.

A survey of the contents of typical budget manuals indicates that the following information is specified in the manuals:

1. Statement of budgeting purpose (goals and objectives)

2. Statement of expected results (links budget to goals and objectives)

3. Budgetary duties of managers and employees (by position); names of persons associated with the position can be listed separately

4. Preparation of the budget (details and processes)

5. Approval of budget estimates and budget revision (positions/persons responsible for approving estimates and revisions, e.g., budget director, controller, or budget committee)

6. Budget calendar for preparing the budget (realistic and attainable)

7. Sample forms and reports (usually presented in an appendix)

8. Supplemental data (e.g., price lists, cost schedules, personnel charts, and other data requiring frequent revisions; usually reported in an appendix)

The budget manual should be updated periodically to accommodate changes in management goals and objectives, business strategies, forecasts, policies, economic conditions, and other factors.

See also: BUDGET
         BUDGETS, TYPES OF
         CAPITAL BUDGET

BUDGETS, TYPES OF

There are five major types of budgets used in business and by not-for-profit institutions:

1. Incremental budget (used with object-of-expenditure, or line-item, budgets).

2. Formula budget.

3. Planning, programming, and budgeting systems (PPBS).

4. Zero-base budgeting.

5. Performance budgeting.

Incremental budgeting incorporates an object-of-expenditure approach to budgeting. Incremental budgets show line-item categories of expenditures to be made during the year. Line item refers to objects of expenditures, such as salaries and supplies. In incremental budgeting, either each line item is considered for an increment or it remains unadjusted in the base. Frequently, increments are calculated as uniform percentage adjustments for every line item or group of line items. The basic philosophy is that the current budget is distributed properly among both the functions and objects of expenditures and that little programmatic change needs to occur. Changes in institutional priorities often result through ad hoc determination concerning what increase is needed to effect a programmatic change. When resources become scarce, incremental budgeting tends to perpetuate the existing programs regardless of how ineffective or inefficient they may be. High-cost programs continue to receive high levels of support. The status quo is reinforced and extended. Incremental budgeting emphasizes the short-run and continuity at the possible expense of the long-run goals of the organization. It also encourages spending at the risk of jeopardizing cost control efforts.

Formula budgeting is a technique by which the financial needs or operating requirements of an institution may be determined through the application of a formula. Formula budgeting is an objective procedure for estimating the future budgetary requirements of an institution by manipulating data about future programs and by utilizing relationships between program and cost. Formula budgeting is frequently used in not-for-profit institutions, such as colleges and universities.

Planning, programming, and budgeting systems (PPBS) is a managerial technique designed to merge the planning process with the allocation of funds by making it difficult to allocate funds without planning. PPBS emphasize performance (that is, output and efficiency). The focus of PPBS is essentially a planning device that ultimately leads to a conventional department budget for operation and control. PPBS is also described as a macroeconomic, centralized, top-down policy and long-range planning tool. In PPBS, planning involves the selection and identification of long-range objectives of the organization and benefit-cost analysis of various courses of action. Zero-base budgeting demands a total rejustification of every activity from base zero, instead of incrementing the new on the old. The objective of zero-base budgeting is to examine each activity in a manner similar to a proposed new activity to determine whether the activity is necessary. The major focus of zero-base budgeting is on ensuring that managers evaluate their areas of responsibility more completely and more objectively than under other budgeting procedures.

Performance budgeting is a budgeting structure that either focuses on activities or functions that produce results and from which resources are used, or promotes a budgetary process that attempts to link organizational objectives to resource utilization. Its primary focus is to improve efficiency by means of activity classifications and cost measurements. The common components of most performance budgeting systems are activity classifications, performance measurements, and performance reports. A major problem in implementing performance budgeting has been the difficulty in determining appropriate performance criteria.

Budgets can also be classified under the headings operating budgets and capital budgets. Operating budgets are general-purpose budgets used to formalize activities in relation to financial considerations for a stated period, usually a fiscal year. They represent short-term planning and control techniques. Capital budgets are budgets representing the expenditures, and the means of financing these expenditures, to be expended for long-lived, or capital, assets, including land, buildings, and equipment.

See also: BUDGET
CAPITAL BUDGET
COMPREHENSIVE BUDGET
COST-BENEFIT ANALYSIS

BUSINESS COMBINATIONS

A business combination occurs when a corporation and one or more incorporated or unincorporated businesses are brought together into a single accounting entity. This entity carries on the activities of the previously separate, independent enterprises.

Business combinations can be classified structurally into three types: horizontal, vertical, and conglomerate. A horizontal combination is one that involves previously competing companies within the same industry; a vertical combination involves a company and its suppliers or customers; a combination resulting in a conglomerate is one involving companies in unrelated industries having few, if any, production or market similarities.

Business combinations can be classified by method of combination as statutory mergers, statutory consolidations, and stock acquisitions. A statutory merger occurs when one company acquires all of the net assets of one or more other companies. The acquiring company survives; the acquired company or companies cease to exist as a separate legal entity. For example, a merger occurs between constituent corporations A and B if A remains the same legal entity (essentially with the combined assets and liabilities of A and B) and B goes out of existence.

A statutory consolidation requires the formation of a new corporation which acquires two or more other corporations; the acquired corporations then cease to exist as separate legal entities. For example, Corporations A and B agree to transfer their assets and liabilities to a new corporation C, and then go out of existence. Corporation C remains to carry on the activities of Corporations A and B.

A stock acquisition occurs when one corporation pays cash or issues stock or debt for more than 50 percent of the voting stock of another company and the acquired company remains intact as a separate legal entity. The relationship of the acquiring company to the acquired company in a stock acquisition is described as a parent-subsidiary relationship. The acquiring company is referred to as the parent (investor) and the acquired company as a subsidiary. The related companies are called affiliated companies. Each of the affiliated companies continues as a separate legal entity. The parent company carries its interest in a subsidiary as an investment in its accounts. Consolidated financial statements are prepared only when the business combination was carried out as a stock acquisition.

The parent-subsidiary relationship can be visualized as follows:

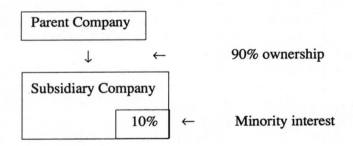

In the illustration of a parent-subsidiary relationship, the Parent Company owns 90 percent of the Subsidiary. A 10 percent interest in the subsidiary is owned by someone other than the parent. This interest is referred to as a minority interest.

The relationship between mergers, consolidations, and stock acquisitions can be summarized as shown on the following page.

Two methods of accounting are available for recording a business combination—purchase and pooling of interest. These methods are discussed separately under Purchase Accounting and Pooling of Interests.

	Prior to Combination	Survivors
Merger	A and B	A or B
Statutory consolidation	A and B	C
Acquisition	A and B	A and B

See also: CONSOLIDATED FINANCIAL STATEMENTS
GOODWILL
MERGER
POOLING OF INTERESTS
PURCHASE ACCOUNTING
SUBSTANCE OVER FORM

References:

APB No. 16, *Business Combinations* (APB, 1970).

Hartz, Peter F., *Merger* (William Morrow, New York, 1985).

BUSINESS CYCLES

Economic growth is usually defined in terms of the annual percentage change in real (inflation adjusted) GNP. The U.S. economy has experienced many business cycles—periods of fluctuation in economic activity—but real output growth has averaged 3 percent per year during this century.

Business cycles are defined by peaks and troughs. During an expansion, economic activity is increasing. The peak in a business cycle occurs when economic expansion has reached a maximum. Following a peak, economic activity decreases and a recession results. The decline in economic activity continues until real GNP reaches a minimum. Such a point is called a trough. Figure 2 on the following page shows the annual percentage change in real GNP in the United States since the late 1800s.

Figure 2

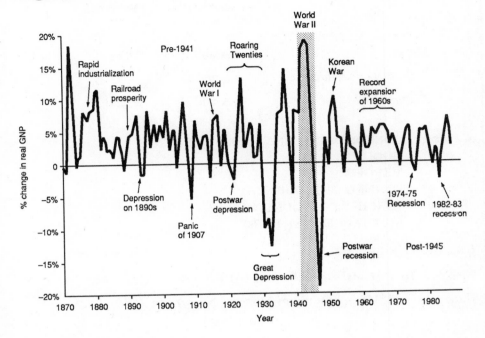

Source: Baumol, William J., and Blinder, Alan, S. *Economics: Principles and Policy*
(San Diego: Harcourt, Brace, Jovanovich, 1988, p. 82).

Cc

CALL OPTION

Options are contracts between buyers and sellers. Anyone can be either a buyer (holder) or a seller (writer) of an option. Two types of options are traded: call options and put options. A call option gives the holder the right to purchase the underlying commodity or financial instrument at a specific price during a specific period of time. The writer of the call option is obligated to make delivery of the commodity or financial instrument to the call holder if the holder wishes to exercise the option. The holder of a call option must pay the writer a sum of money, known as the permium, for the option right. The premium is kept by the writer whether or not the option is exercised.

Options have been traded on real estate and financial instruments such as common stocks for many years. There was over-the-counter trading in calls and puts on shares of common stock long before the creation of centralized exchange trading in stock options in the mid-1070s.

Buyers and sellers in the market for common stock options hope to profit from anticipated movements in the prices of the underlying securities on a leveraged basis. For example, the buyer of a call option on common stock hopes to gain from the rise in the price of the associated stock. But since his call option right costs him only a fraction of the value

88   CALL OPTION

of the underlying securities, any rise in the value of the stock will provide him with a leveraged gain. On the other hand, if the stock drops in value, so will the value of the call option.

The exercise price (strike price) is the fixed price at which an option may be exercised by its holder. The expiration date is the last day on which the option may be exercised by its holder. If it is not exercised on the expiration date, the option ceases to exist, and its value becomes zero.

At any given time there are several factors that influence the price (premium value) of a call option. Because an option is a wasting asset, the nearer the exercise date the less will be the value of the option. Other things being equal, options that have longer to run are more valuable than shorter term options.

Price expectations also influence an option's value. When expectations increase that the value of the underlying stock or asset will rise, demand for call options on the stock or asset will grow, causing the value of a call option to rise accordingly.

A call option is said to be "in the money" if its exercise price is less than the market price of the stock. the greater the positive difference between the market price of the underlying security and the exercise price of the call option, the greater will be the value of the option. For example, if the exercise price on a call option is $50 when the stock is trading for $55, the value of the options will be at least equal to $5. If the market value of the stock rises to $60, the value of the option will increase to at least $10.

A call option is "out-of-the-money" if its exercise price is greater than the market price of the stock. Nevertheless, an out-of-the-money option usually still has some value. Its price will not be zero. This is because there is always a chance, however remote, that the market price of the stock may rise, putting the call option "in-the-money" before it expires. The greater the volatility in the price of the stock the more likely this is to happen and, therefore, the greater will be the value of the call option. Accordingly, call options on more volatile securities tend to be more valuable than options on less volatile securities, everything else being equal.

The trading of options on organized exchanges began in 1973 with the formation of the Chicago Board Options Exchange (CBOE). Among the exchanges where options can now be traded are the CBOE, the American Stock Exchange, the Pacific Stock Exchange, the Philadelphia Exchange and the New York Stock Exchange. Exchange traded options offer investors a number of advantages including 1) *contract stand-*

ardization, 2) *liquidity*, 3) *disclosure and surveillance* 4) *guaranteed clearing*, and 5) *lower transaction costs*. The *options clearing corporation* of each exchange guarantees the delivery of the underlying securities and cash on all exchange-traded options. Each exchange sets the margin requirements for writers (sellers) of options.

Options are now traded not only on individual stocks but also on a whole array of contracts for various stock indexes, foreign currencies, debt securities, future contracts, and commodities. Investors may buy or sell call options—for example, on S&P 100 and S&P 500 indexes; British pounds; U.S. treasury notes and bonds; and gold, silver, and oil futures.

Anyone buying or holding a call option on a futures contract acquires the right, but not the obligation, to assume a long position in a futures contract for the strike price at any time up until the expiration of the option contract. For options on futures which are traded on specific exchanges, the exchange sets the stike price of the option when it is listed.

A trader writing (selling) a call option on a futures contract sold on an exchange undertakes a firm commitment to assume a short position in the futures market at the stike price if the option is exercised. To protect option holders and the exchange, sellers of futures options are required to deposit margin money when assuming a position. Margin accounts are marked to market daily to reflect change in the option's value, and sellers may be subject to margin calls.

Buyers (holders) of call options on futures contracts are never subject to margin calls. This is because the most the call option buyer can lose is the price of the option. Thus the holder of a call option can maintain his position up until expiration even if market movements result in a decline in the value of the option. This is said to give the option holder "staying power."

The availability of options and options on futures contracts has led to great variety of hedging strategies using options to protect investors from risks stemming from price fluctuations in the underlying financial instruments. For example, an investor with a short position in the futures market might buy a call option on the futures contract to hedge his position against a rise in the market. Or a corporate treasurer needing German marks in the future might buy a call option on a mark futures contract to protect his company against an appreciation in the value of the mark. Alternatively, a savings and loan institution fearing a rise in its cost of funds might buy a GNMA put option to hedge its position. In each of these transactions, the cost of the option can be viewed as an insurance premium against possible loss arising from a change in the price of the underlying asset.

See also: FUTURES MARKET
INVESTMENT METHODS AND STRATEGIES
INVESTING

Reference:

Sharpe, William F., *Investments* (Englewood Cliffs, NJ: Prentice-Hall, 1981).

CAPITAL

Capital has many different meanings in accounting, economics, and finance. In accounting, capital is the residual interest in the assets of an entity that remains after deducting its liabilities. Hence, capital is the ownership interest, or equity. Capital is the cumulative result of investments by owners, earnings, and distribution to owners. Typically, liabilities have priority over ownership interest as claims against enterprise assets. In a corporation, capital is referred to as stockholders' equity, or shareholders' equity. In accounting for stockholders' equity, the basic purposes are the following:

1. To identify the source of corporate capital.

2. To identify legal capital.

3. To indicate the dividends that could be distributed to the stockholders.

A distinction is often made between capital originating from stockholders' investments, referred to as contributed capital or paid-in capital, and the equity originating from earnings, referred to as retained earnings. Contributed or paid-in capital is usually reported as (1) capital stock representing that portion of capital contributed by stockholders and assignable to the shares of stock issued and (2) additional paid-in capital representing investments by stockholders in excess of the amounts assignable to capital stock as well as invested capital from other sources. The capital stock balance is generally considered legal capital or permanent capital of the corporation. Retained earnings is the amount of undistributed earnings of past periods. An excess of dividends and losses over earnings results in a deficit. Portions of retained earnings are sometimes restricted and unavailable as a basis for dividends.

The stockholders' equity section of a balance sheet is illustrated in Exhibit C–1.

Exhibit C–1
Stockholders' Equity Section of a Balance Sheet

Capital stock:		
Preferred stock, $100 par value, 8% cumulative, 200,000 shares authorized, 30,000 shares issued and outstanding		$3,000,000
Common stock, $10 par value, 500,000 shares authorized, 400,000 shares issued		4,000,000
		7,000,000
Additional paid-in capital		
Excess over par—preferred stock	$ 150,000	
Excess over par value common stock	50,000	150,000
Total paid-in capital		7,150,000
Donated capital		50,000
Retained earnings:		
Appropriated for plant expansion	500,000	
Unappropriated	1,500,000	2,000,000
Total paid-in capital and retained earnings		9,200,000
Less cost of treasury stock (2,000 shares, common)		(100,000)
Total stockholders' equity		$9,100,000

The term *capital* is used in many different ways including the following: in economics, a factor of production; capital goods, legal capital, stated capital; circulating capital; working capital; capital assets; assets invested in the business, liabilities and stockholders' equity; capital surplus; financial capital; physical capital; capital budgeting; capital leases, capital maintenance; capital markets; capital projects; capital stock; contributed capital; simple capital structure; complex capital structure; capital expenditure; return on capital. The term *capitalization of a corporation* is frequently used by investment analysts to refer to shareholders' equity plus bonds outstanding.

In economics, the production process is characterized as a relationship between inputs and outputs. Inputs are broadly classified under the rubrics of labor and capital. Capital refers to physical inputs such as plant and equipment. Capital includes those goods used to produce other goods and services. In a narrower sense, capital is often used to refer to money.

	Capacity Utilization Rates	
Year	**All Industries**	**Manufacturing Industries**
1980	80.9	79.3
1981	79.9	78.2
1982	72.1	70.3
1983	74.6	73.9
1984	81.0	80.5
1985	80.4	80.1
1986	79.4	79.7
1987	80.7	81.0

Source: *Economic Report of the President*, 1988.

See also: CAPITAL STOCK
             CORPORATION
             PREFERRED STOCK.

Reference:

Kieso, Donald E., and Weygandt, Jerry J., *Intermediate Accounting* (New York, NY: John Wiley, 1986).

CAPITAL AND REVENUE EXPENDITURES

A capital expenditure is an expenditure that is expected to benefit future periods. Capital expenditures are recorded as assets and are normally depreciated. Revenue expenditures are normal, recurring expenditures that benefit only the current accounting period and are expensed as they occur.

Capital expenditures either increase the quantity of services received from an asset (longer useful life or more output) or increase the quality of the service of the asset. Some firms establish a minimum amount for capital expenditures, which represents a materiality or expediency threshold.

Revenue expenditures are expenses that relate to the acquisition of property or other benefits that do not extend beyond the current accounting period. Such expenditures are matched against the revenue of the period in which they are incurred.

Expenditures related to plant and equipment include: additions, replacements and betterments (improvements); rearrangements and relocations; and repair and maintenance. An addition is a major expenditure that increases the service potential of the related asset. Additions are usually capitalized. Replacements and betterments are essentially substitutions of a new part of an asset for an existing part. Replacements involve substituting a similar asset for the existing asset. A betterment involves substituting an asset that reflects an improvement in quality for the existing asset. Replacements and substitutions are usually considered capital expenditures. Rearrangements and relocations of existing assets are capitalized if they are expected to benefit future periods. Repairs and maintenance are those expenditures that are required to maintain the current operating capabilities of the existing asset. Repair and maintenance expenditures are usually expensed unless they are considered major when they could be capitalized.

In tax law, a capital expenditure is an expenditure that must be added to the basis of the property improved. Generally, any cost recovery in the form of a tax deduction has to come in the form of depreciation.

See also: DEPRECIATION
           PROPERTY, PLANT, AND EQUIPMENT

CAPITAL ASSET PRICING MODEL

The capital asset pricing model (CAPM—pronounced "cap-m") is one method for estimating the cost of equity capital for an issuing firm. The model treats a stock as one potential element in an investor's portfolio; as such, the stock is evaluated in terms of its influence on the entire portfolio—in terms of its return and its risk.

It is assumed that the cost of equity (the return on equity required by an investor), r, equals the sum of the return on a risk-free investment, r_f, and a premium that reflects the risk of the equity, R, as:

$$r = r_f + R.$$

In the CAPM, R is assumed to be estimated as a coefficient, times the difference between the overall market return, r_m, and r_f as:

$$r = r_f + \beta \ (r_m - r_f)$$

where β is referred to as the beta coefficient.

See also: BETA COEFFICIENT

CAPITAL BUDGET

Capital budgeting is a formal process of long-term planning for relatively large, permanent acquisitions and commitments of a firm's economic resources. Long-term investment decisions relate to the following basic areas that have as their objective profit maximization:

1. equipment acquisition and replacement required (for example, to deal with obsolescence, competition, or legal requirements);

2. cost-saving investments to promote efficiency; and

3. expansion opportunities (for example, diversification, product lines, and research and development investments).

In evaluating capital budgeting projects, management must consider two major factors:

1. the cost of the investment, and

2. the potential net increase in cash inflows (or reduction in cash outflows) resulting from the proposed investment.

Four methods of capital budgeting are widely used in business:

1. the accounting method

2. the payback method

3. the net present value method, and

4. the discounted cash flow method.

Accounting method—The accounting method is based on the application of the following equation to evaluate capital projects:

$$\text{Accounting rate of return} = \frac{\text{Expected increase in income}}{\text{Expected increase in investment}}$$

To illustrate the accounting method, assume that management is considering the purchase of a new machine for $11,000. The machine has an expected useful life of five years and a scrap value of $1,000 at the end of this useful life. For the next five years, the machine will create cost savings of $4,000 per year. The accounting rate of return can be calculated this way:

$$\text{Acounting rate of return} = \frac{\$4,000}{(\$11,000 - \$1,000)}$$

$$= 40\%$$

The firm must now decide whether a rate of return of 40 percent is adequate for this project. The accounting rate of return's most serious shortcoming is that it ignores the time value of money. Expected future dollars are regarded as equal to present dollars.

Payback method—The payback period is the time required for the cash inflow from an investment to accumulate to a total equal to the original cash outlay required for the investment. Using the above data, the payback period for the new machine can be calculated as:

Payback period   = Initial investment/Annual cash savings
                            = $11,000/$4,000
                            = 2.75 years

When using this method, management chooses the investment that provides the quickest payoff regardless of which investment gives the highest rate of return over the long run. Also, management often sets a maximum payback period for acceptable investments. Investments that exceed the maximum period are rejected. A reasonable payback period is usually considered to be between two and five years.

If the inflow of cash savings is not the same from year to year, the payback period may be calculated by adding the cash proceeds in successive years until the total equals the original outlay.

Net present value method—The net present value method uses present values of streams of earnings or costs for evaluating investment decisions. When this method is employed, expected future cash inflows and outflows associated with the investment are discounted to the present using a minimum discounting rate acceptable to management. The net present value is the difference between the present cost of the investment and the present value of the cash inflow expected from the investment. If the net present value is positive, the investment is acceptable. If the net present value is negative, the investment does not promise to provide a return at a minimum level and should be rejected. Net present value can be conceptualized as:

Net present value = present value of net cash inflows − cost of the investment.

To illustrate the net present value method, consider an $11,000 machine with a scrap value of $1,000 and a useful life of five years. If the company expects a 16 percent minimum rate of return for this type of investment, the machine should not be purchased. The rationale for this decision is given in the illustration shown in Exhibit C-2.

1. Dollar amounts of cash inflows and outflows are recorded in the columns for the appropriate periods.

    a. Direction of each cash inflow is indicated. Cash outflows are negative amounts, and cash inflows or savings are shown as positive amounts.

    b. The timing of each flow is indicated by recording it in the appropriate period.

2. Present value discounting factors are determined from present value tables and entered in the appropriate column (note that the cash operating savings can be treated as an annuity since they are equal each period).

3. Present values of each item are computed and entered in the last column whose figures are then totaled to determine the net present value of the investment.

Exhibit C-2
Discounted Cash Flows

	0	1	2	3	4	5	Discount factor	Total present value
		Cash flows at end of period						
Initial cost	$(11,000)						1.0000	$(11,000)
Cash operating savings		$4,000	$4,000	$4,000	$4,000	$4,000	3.2741	13,096
Disposal value						1,000	.4761	476
Net present value								$ 2,572

Because the net present value of the investment in the machine is positive, the investment in the new machine is considered desirable. The underlying concept for this method is the idea that the company can earn more by buying the machine than it could by putting the same amount of cash into some other investment that earns a 16 percent rate of return. The effect of this decision rule is to accept any proposed investment that offers more than a 16 percent rate of return.

If income taxes are considered, the payment of income taxes represents a cash outflow; a tax savings represents a cash inflow. For a 48 percent income tax rate, each dollar of cash revenue equals only $0.52 after-tax cash inflow while each dollar of cash expense equals only $0.52 after-tax cash outflow. Cash savings on depreciation equals depreciation expense multiplied by the income tax rate. If the problem involving the machine is reworked to take a 48 percent income tax into consideration, the problem would be solved as shown in Exhibit C-3. In this case, the net present value of the investment is negative, so the investment in the machine is rejected.

Exhibit C-3
Net Present Value Method Including Income Tax Implications

| | Cash flows at end of period | | | | | Discount factor | Total present value |
	0	1	2	3	4	5		
Initial cost	$(11,000)						1.000	$(11,000)
Cash operating savings		$2,080	$2,080	$2,080	$2,080	$2,080	3.2741	6,810
Disposal value						1,000	.4761	476
Depreciation impact on income taxes		960	960	960	960	960	3.2741	3,143
Net present value								$ (571)

Discounted cash flow method. The discounted cash flow method of capital budgeting finds the discounting rate that results in a net present value of zero for the cash flows. This rate is the expected rate of return on the investment project. The discounting rate can be determined through the use of tables or with a trial-and-error approach. With the discounted cash flow approach, the decision rule takes the following form: if the computed rate of return on the investment exceeds a minimum acceptable rate imposed by management, the investment is considered acceptable. Otherwise, it is rejected.

Using data for the machine purchase above, and taking income taxes into consideration, the following computations are made:

1. Determine the expected after-tax savings from the investment ($2,080 + $960 = $3,040) per year for five years.

2. Determine the cash outflow for the initial cost of the investment, $11,000.

3. Determine the present value of other cash inflows such as salvage value, $1,000 at the end of five years or $476 now ($1,000 × .476 = $476).

4. Find the discount factor that will equate the expected cash inflows to the present value of the cash outflows.

5. Find the discounting rate that gives a discount factor of 3.4618 for a five-year annuity at an unknown discount rate. This is the discounting rate for which an annuity of $3,040 for five years has a present value of $10,524. Refer to the present value of annuity table to find the discount rate that, for five periods, equals or approximates the com-

puted "factor value." The factor is about 14 percent which is less than the 16 percent minimum rate acceptable to management. The project is rejected. Capital budgeting projects are frequently complicated when

a. the amounts to be invested occur over a period of time,

b. the amounts differ, and

c. the timing is irregular.

These problems can usually be dealt with by converting all investments and returns to their discounted total values, at a particular point.

See also: BUDGET
COMPREHENSIVE BUDGET
INTERNAL RATE OF RETURN

Reference:

Bierman, Harold, Jr., and Seymour Smidt, *The Capital Budgeting Decision: Economic Analysis of Investment Projects* (Macmillan, New York, 1980).

CAPITAL MAINTENANCE THEORIES   24/933

Accountants generally recognize that earnings result only after capital has been maintained or costs have been recovered. In this context, capital ordinarily refers to owners' equity or net assets of a business enterprise. Capital at the beginning of a period is maintained during the period if earnings for the period equal or exceed dividends (withdrawals) for the period. Earnings in excess of dividends for a period become part of investment capital or net assets to be maintained in the following period. There are two major views concerning the type of capital to be maintained:

1. Financial capital maintenance (for example, dollars invested directly by owners or through nondistribution of earnings in the past). Financial capital maintenance can compute income measurement in terms of historical cost or current cost. Under financial capital maintenance, earnings occurs if a company recovers more from revenues than the nominal dollars invested in the asset sold. This concept is associated with the conventional accounting and reporting system.

2. Physical capital maintenance (for example, physical properties of assets required to produce goods or services or productive capacity). Income arises only if an enterprise recovers in revenues more than the replacement cost of items sold.

The primary difference between these two concepts involves certain changes in prices of assets during accounting periods that result in "holding gains and losses." Holding gains and losses are amounts that arise solely because of price or value changes in assets. For example, assume that an item of inventory is purchased on January 1 for $10,000 and its price at December 31 is $12,000. The asset is unsold at the end of the year. A holding gain of $2,000 resulted from holding the asset. The decision paths that result from the different views of capital are diagrammed as shown on the following page.

The two capital maintenance concepts can be illustrated by a simple example. Assume that initial capital of $15,000 cash is invested in inventory and a machine priced at $8,000 and $7,000, respectively. The machine has a 10-year life that will be depreciated using straight-line depreciation. Inventory transactions during the year are shown below the diagram.

Valuation View

Assets are resources/Liabilities are obligations

Net asset changes are earnings

Capital measured in dollars	Capital is physical capacity
Holding gains in income	Holding gains in capital

Inventory purchased as described above	$8,000
Inventory sold for $9,000; replacement cost	
at time of sale (inventory not replaced at this time)	8,300
Actual cost to replenish stock	8,500
Year-end inventory replacement cost	8,700

Exhibit C-4 on the following page shows an income statement and a balance sheet assuming financial capital maintenance (at historical cost and current value) and physical capital maintenance.

Under the financial capital maintenance approach (historical cost), the company maintained its beginning of the year $15,000 capital and earned $300 in income during the year. Accountants have generally used the concept of maintenance of financial capital based on historical cost because investors are assumed to be interested primarily in the monetary (dollar) return on their investment. Holding gains are not recognized until assets are sold. When holding gains are realized, they are not identified separately on the income statement. Under the current value concept of financial capital maintenance, inventory and depreciable assets are revalued every year at current cost, usually replacement cost. Holding gains are considered to be income but are separately identified in the income statement. Under the financial capital maintenance approach, holding gains and losses are included in income (or loss).

Under the physical capital maintenance concept, the cost of capital consumed (inventories sold and depreciation of asset) exceeded revenues by $90. Physical capital was not maintained. Notice that an additional charge must be made against income for the additional cost of sales and depreciation necessary to reflect those higher replacement costs. In the illustration, physical capital was eroded. Holding gains or losses are not reported on the income statement but are shown as a separate component of capital on the balance sheet.

It is also possible to adjust capital to reflect changes in the purchasing power of the dollar resulting from inflation or deflation. Income is then shown after maintenance of the purchasing power of the investor's capital. Income results only if the company can recover from revenues more than the general purchasing power equivalent of its investment. The basic concept of capital maintenance is not changed as a result of this additional consideration.

See also: CAPITAL
           CURRENT VALUE ACCOUNTING

Reference:

FASB, SFAC No. 5, *Recognition and Measurement in Financial Statements of Business Enterprises* (FASB, 1984).

Exhibit C-4
Theories of Capital Maintenance—Financial Capital and Physical Capital

| | Financial Capital | | Current Value/ |
	Historical Cost	Current Value	Physical Capital
INCOME STATEMENT			
Sales	$ 9,000	$ 9,000	$ 9,000
Cost of Sales	8,000	8,300	8,300
Depreciation	700	790	790
	8,700	9,090	9,090
	300	(90)	(90)
Holding gains (inv. sold $300; inv. held $200; lathe $900)	—	1,400	—
Income (loss)	$ 300	$ 1,310	$ (90)
BALANCE SHEET			
Cash	$ 500	$ 500	$ 500
Inventory	8,500	8,700	8,700
Lathe-net	6,300	7,110	7,110
Total	$ 15,300	$ 16,310	$ 16,310
Capital	$ 15,000	$ 15,000	$ 15,000
Undistributed income (loss)	300	1,310	(90)
Capital Maintenance	—	—	1,400
Total	$ 15,300	$ 16,310	$ 16,310

CAPITAL STOCK

Ownership in a corporation is divided into shares of capital stock with the physical evidence of ownership being a stock certificate. The following terms are associated with capital stock:

1. *Authorized capital stock*—Shares that can be legally issued as specified by the corporate charter.

2. *Issued capital stock*—Authorized shares that have been issued by the corporation.

3. *Unissued capital stock*—Shares of authorized capital stock that have never been issued.

4. *Outstanding capital stock*—Shares of authorized stock held by shareholders at a specific time.

5. *Subscribed capital stock*—Stock for which a purchase agreement has been entered into but the agreed amount has not yet been paid. Subscribed stock is normally issued when the subscriber pays the full agreed price of the stock.

Par value stocks are shares of corporate stock having a specified dollar amount per share assigned to each share by the articles of incorporation and designated on the face of the stock certificate. Stock issued at a price above par is issued at a premium, while stock issued below par value is issued at a discount. The original purchases of stock at a price below par are usually liable to creditors for the discount. Par value should not be taken as an indicator of the market value or book value of the stock. No-par value stock is stock that has not been assigned a par value in the articles of incorporation. The board of directors is generally given the power to determine whether no-par value stock is to have a stated value. True no-par value stock has neither a par nor a stated value assigned to it.

Common stock is the basic capital stock of a corporation and carries with it major rights, including:

1. A share in the management of the corporation by voting, especially as reflected in the election of the board of directors and by participation at stockholders' meetings.

2. Participation in the earnings of the corporation through dividends when declared by the board of directors.

3. A share in the assets of the corporation if the corporation is dissolved.

4. A pro rata participation in the acquisition of additional shares of capital stock issued by the corporation. This right is referred to as the preemptive right; its purpose is to protect the proportionate interests of shareholders. Currently, many shares are issued without this right.

Common stock may be classified into Class A and Class B stock. One class usually has the basic features of common stock while the other has restrictions, such as the denial or deferment of voting rights.

Common stockholders are referred to as the residual owners of the business because their interest in liquidation is subordinate to the claims of all other stockholders, such as preferred stockholders, and creditors.

Preferred stock is a form of capital stock that possesses certain preferences or priorities over common stock. The preferences are usually associated with a prior claim to dividends and the distribution of assets upon the liquidation of the corporation.

See also: CAPITAL
             CORPORATION
             PREFERRED STOCK

CAPITALISM

Capitalism is an economic structure wherein economic activity occurs through the operation of a free market. In a capitalistic society, property and factors of production are privately owned. Alternatively stated, a capitalistic economy is one that is market-based.

See Also: COMMUNISM
             ECONOMIC ENVIRONMENT
             FREE ENTERPRISE SYSTEM
             SOCIALISM

Reference:

Friedman, Milton, *Capitalism & Freedom,* (University of Chicago Press, Chicago, 1962).

CAPITALIZATION OF INTEREST

Companies frequently borrow money in order to finance the construction of an asset. The question arises as to whether interest charged on such borrowings should be considered a cost of the asset constructed. Interest has usually been considered a financing charge and not a part of the cost of an asset. Currently, generally accepted accounted principles require the capitalization of interest cost incurred in financing certain assets that take a period of time to prepare for their intended use, if its effect is material. In effect, interest should be capitalized as a part of the historical cost of acquiring certain assets. The historical cost of acquiring an asset includes the costs necessarily incurred to bring it to the condition and location required for its intended use. Qualifying assets include assets that an enterprise constructs for its own use, such as new facilities, and assets intended for sale or lease that are constructed as separate projects, such as ships or real estate developments.

The objectives of capitalizing interest are to obtain a measure of acquisition cost that more clearly reflects the enterprise's total investment in the asset, and to charge a cost that relates to the acquisition of a resource that will benefit future periods against the revenues of the periods benefited.

The amount of interest cost to be capitalized for qualifying assets is that portion of the interest cost incurred during the asset's acquisition period that theoretically could have been avoided if expenditures for the assets had not been made. The amount capitalized in an accounting period is computed by applying an interest rate to the average amount of accumulated expenditures for the asset during the period. The interest rate used is usually the rate charged on funds actually borrowed to finance the construction of the asset, the rate on other recent borrowings, or a weighted-average interest rate on old borrowings. The amount of interest capitalized cannot exceed the total interest costs incurred during the period.

See also: CAPITAL AND REVENUE EXPENDITURES

Reference:

SFAS No. 34, *Capitalization of Interest Cost* (FASB, 1979).

CARTEL

The joining together of a group of suppliers of a good or a service in order to control output or price is known as a cartel. The purpose of a cartel is to confer a monopoly advantage on its members. Perhaps the most noteworthy cartel in recent years was the Organization of Petroleum Exporting Countries (OPEC), formed in 1973 to control petroleum prices.

All members of the cartel are better off with the cartel's structure in place than without it because competition would reduce their profits. However, any one member of the cartel has an incentive to "cheat" and lower prices in order to capture the lion's share of the customers. If this one firm's actions were to go unnoticed, this firm would benefit financially. For this reason, cartel arrangements, in addition to being illegal in the U.S., are inherently unstable.

See also: COLLUSION

CASH

For accounting purposes, cash consists of any item that would be accepted for deposit in a checking account in a commercial bank. Cash includes coins, paper currency, checks, money orders, bank drafts, certified checks, cashiers' checks, and demand deposits in banks. Savings accounts are often classified as cash even though the bank retains the legal right to require notice before a withdrawal can be made. Items such as postage stamps, postdated checks, IOUs, dishonored checks, and deposits in closed banks are excluded from cash. When the use of cash is restricted for a particular purpose, such as for the retirement of bonds, it would be excluded from cash and classified under either investments or other asset categories on a balance sheet.

To provide for cash disbursements involving small amounts, many firms establish a petty cash fund to handle such payments. Under an imprest petty cash fund, a fund is established for a specific amount. When the fund is to be replenished, a check equal to the payments made from the fund is cashed and deposited in the fund to bring the fund balance up to the original amount established in the fund.

Two major issues are paramount when managing cash: how much cash should be maintained to carry out the operations of the business, and how cash can be safeguarded against theft, misappropriation, and similar irregularities. Safeguarding cash is usually accomplished by establishing control procedures for cash receipts and disbursements, using an imprest petty cash system, reconciling bank accounts periodically, utilizing cash forecasts, and using a voucher system for cash payments.

See also: BANK RECONCILIATION
CHECKS
INTERNAL CONTROL

Reference:

Garbutt, Douglas, *How to Budget and Control Cash* (Gower, Brookfield, Vermont, 1985).

CASH BUDGET

The management of cash is of major importance to most organizations. Cash management involves two problems: (1) the determination of the most desirable balance for the cash account, and (2) the safeguarding of cash. Cash budgeting can deal effectively with both of these problems.

Cash budgeting is one of the most essential parts of a company's planning and control process. The objective of cash budgeting is to project all cash receipts and disbursements with the maximum accuracy and detail, including any arrangements to ensure an adequate supply of cash to meet the needs of the firm.

A cash forecast requires the projection of the plans and estimates of activities that cause cash flows—for example, sales, inventory acquisitions, and operation expenses. The forecast of cash must be corrdinated with available information about accounts receivable, investment, accounts payable, etc. These are the steps involved in preparing a cash forecast:

1. Estimate cash receipts for the period. This requires estimates of such items as cash sales of merchandise, collections of receivables, sales of assets, etc.

2. Estimate cash disbursements for the period. This requires estimating cash purchases of merchandise, payments of expenses, repayments of loans, etc.

3. Estimate cash balance at the end of the period. This is done by taking the beginning cash balance, adding estimated cash receipts, and subtracting estimated cash disbursements.

4. Forecast the financing that will be required to maintain a desired minimum cash balance, or forecast the amount of excess cash that will be available for investment or other uses.

5. Prepare the cash budget.

6. Revise and update the cash budget as necessary throughout the year.

Exhibit C–5 illustrates a format that can be used to develop a cash budget.

Exhibit C–5
Cash Budget

Super-Glo, Inc.
Cash budget
For the year ended December 31, 1985

	Total	1st Quarter	2nd Quarter	3rd Quarter	4th Quarter
Beginning cash balance	$ 3,000	$ 3,000	$ 1,480	$ 2,430	$ 6,415
Cash collections (ex. C-12)	182,650	35,500	43,650	53,550	49,950
Total	185,650	38,500	45,130	55,980	56,365
Cash payments:					
Purchases (ex. C-15)	$92,000	$ 9,500	$21,000	$30,000	$31,500
Selling expense (ex. C-8)	40,500	11,200	8,400	9,400	11,500
Administratative expense (ex. C-10)	18,750	4,900	4,200	4,250	5,400
Federal income taxes (ex. C-11)	5,580		680	3,735	1,165
Dividends	5,000				5,000
Land purchase	25,000	25,000			
Total	186,830	50,600	34,280	47,385	54,565
Cash excess (deficiency)	(1,180)	(12,100)	10,850	8,595	1,800
Financing:					
Borrowing	14,000	14,000			
Repayment	(10,000)		(8,000)	(2,000)	
Interest	(1,140)	(420)	(420)	(180)	(120)
Net	2,800	13,580	(8,420)	(2,180)	(120)
Ending balance	$ 1,680	$ 1,480	$ 2,430	$ 6,415	$ 1,680

CASH FLOW

Cash flow refers to the total cash receipts from sales less actual cash expenditures required to obtain those sales. The term *cash flow* can also be used in a broader sense to indicate a company's sources and uses of cash during an accounting period.

The statement of cash flows is required to be presented for each period. This statement provides information about cash receipts and cash payments and sets forth information about investing and financing activities. This statement helps users of financial statements to assess the firm's ability to generate future net cash flows, to meet obligations and pay dividends, to account for differences between income and related cash receipts and payments, and to analyze the entity's investing and financing activities. This statement reports the cash effects during a period from (1) operating activities, (2) investing activities, and (3) financing activities. The statement explains changes during the period in cash and cash equivalents, i.e., short-term, highly liquid investments.

A condensed cash flow statement is presented below:

XYZ CORPORATION
Statement of Cash Flow
(For the Year ended December 31, 19XX)

Cash flows from operating activities	
Net income	$500,000
Add (deduct) items not affecting cash	
Depreciation	$20,000
Decrease in accounts receivable	10,000
Increase in prepaid expenses	(5,000)
Increases in accounts payable	15,000
Net cash flows from operating activities	40,000
Cash flows from investing activities 460,000	
Purchase of land	(70,000)
Purchase of equipment	(30,000)

(continued)

Cash flows from investing activities	(100,000)	
Cash flows from financing activities		
Issuance of bonds		100,000
Payment of cash dividends		60,000
Cash provided by financing activities	40,000	
Net increase in cash	$ 400,000	

CASH MANAGEMENT

Cash is an important working capital asset. As a major resource, it should be managed. The objectives of cash management are to keep the amount of cash available to an organization within prescribed limits, to borrow cash at minimum cost, and to invest cash at the maximum return acceptable to the company. Cash management is usually defined as having four major elements: forecasting cash, managing cash flows, investing surplus cash, and maintaining banking relations.

Cash is an unproductive asset; excessive cash retained on hand is undesirable. Insufficient cash creates liquidity and credit problems for the firm.

The preparation of a cash budget is a basic tool of forecasting cash. The cash budget establishes the sources, timing, and amounts of cash receipts and disbursements. Cash budgets can identify the high and low points in a company's cash cycle. Low points alert management not to schedule large discretionary payments during these periods. High points enable management to plan a short-term investment strategy to utilize profitability and excess funds.

Cash management requires that good internal control procedures be established for cash receipts and cash payments. These cash receipt controls are recommended:

1. All cash receipts should be recorded immediately upon receipt.

2. Total cash receipts should be deposited daily in a bank account.

3. The custody of cash should be entrusted to a person who is not entitled to authorize or record cash transactions.

4. The bank statement should be periodically reconciled to the company's records by a person not involved either in the receipt or disbursement of cash or in authorizing and recording cash transactions.

5. An internal audit or count of cash on a surprise basis should be conducted at irregular intervals.

6. A fidelity bond should be required for persons who have custody of cash.

7. A cash budget should be used to plan and control the use of cash. The two objectives of managing cash flows are efficiency and profit.

Managing cash flows is performed primarily by:

    a. forecasting cash receipts and disbursements (cash flow statement; sales forecasts; surplus/deficiency noted),

    b. accelerating cash receipts (bill faster, bill accurately, offer discounts, place invoices with shipped goods, instruct customers to send payments to regional offices),

    c. planning and slowing cash disbursements (slow the payment of bills, take advantage of float), and

    d. investing excess cash balances (safety/liquidity; return on investment).

See also: BUDGET
                COMPREHENSIVE BUDGET
                FORECASTING
                FORECASTING FINANCIAL REQUIREMENTS
                WORKING CAPITAL

CASH SURRENDER VALUE

The cash surrender value of a life insurance policy is that portion of the annual life insurance premium that will be returned to the policyholder in the event the policy is canceled. The cash surrender value of the policy increases each year as long as the policy is in force. Part of each annual premium represents an investment and part represents insurance expense. The portion of the yearly premium that does not increase the cash surrender value of the policy represents insurance expense. The amount of the cash surrender value of the policy is reported on the balance sheet as an asset under the investment classification. At death, the difference between the proceeds from the policy and the cash surrender value is reported on the income statement as an extraordinary gain or as income before extraordinary items.

CENTERS

Organizations typically are organized in terms of responsibility centers, depending upon the type and extent of authority and responsibility assigned to the center. Four major types of centers are used by businesses: profit centers, cost centers, investment centers, and revenue centers.

A profit center is a subunit or segment of an organization that is accountable for planning and controlling both revenues and expenses. A profit center is analogous to an independent business, although certain investment and financing activities are sometimes not delegated. A department in a department store could be organized as a profit center. In such cases, the department store itself would serve as the investment center.

Subunits of an organization are frequently organized as cost centers where managers have no control over sales revenue or investment decisions. Cost centers exercise control over costs through the use of standard costs systems and operating budgets. Manufacturing companies frequently use cost centers to establish areas of responsibility.

An investment center can be conceptualized as a profit center that also has planning and controlling responsibilities for investment decisions associated with capital assets. These combined responsibilities make managers of investment centers similar to managers of independent businesses. Long-term financing decisions are frequently reserved to the home office or parent corporation. Managers of such centers are responsible both for the profitability and the return on investment of their centers. Individual stores in a food chain could be organized as investment centers.

In relatively rare situations, an organization may establish revenue centers which are responsible solely for the production of revenue. In such cases, special provision must be made at the entity level to control costs and secure an acceptable return on assets invested in the center.

Companies ordinarily use multiple factors to evaluate the performance of centers. Depending upon the type of center, such factors could include:

profitability; productivity (ratio of output to input); market position; product leadership; personnel development (ratio of persons promoted to the number considered promotable); employee attitudes (surveys on job satisfaction, pay policies, and promotion opportunities); public responsibility (surveys of suppliers, customers, local community, etc.); and balance between short- and long-range goals and objectives.

See also: CENTRALIZATION versus DECENTRALIZATION
CONTROL FUNCTION

CENTRALIZATION VERSUS DECENTRALIZATION

Organizations can be organized in two ways: centralized or decentralized. From an organizational perspective, centralization and decentralization are issues of how authority is delegated to the different organizational levels. Centralization refers to the organizational level that has authority to make a decision. When decisions are delegated to lower organizational levels, the organization is decentralized.

Decentralization gives greater autonomy to subunits of the organization. In a decentralized firm, decision-making authority is pushed downward through the organizational levels to enable effective planning and activities at the most appropriate level. Decentralized operations enable the firm to fulfill its objectives while providing sufficient autonomy to managers to enable them to test their ideas, skills, and to develop their potential. Communication and coordination are more effective and decisions can be made more quickly in a decentralized organization. In a decentralized organization, the risk exists that managers will promote their decentralized unit at the expense of the company as a whole. The extent to which a firm centralizes its operations depends upon the firm's environment (for example, competitive situation, market characteristics), the size and growth rate of the firm, and the firm's characteristics (for example, costs and risks involved; top management's preference; available managerial skills; the history of the entity; and cost-benefit considerations). Delegation of authority requires that authority, responsibility, and accountability be coextensive.

In a centralized organization structure, decision making and coordinating functions are concentrated at the higher levels of the organization structure. Operational activities and responsibilities remain at the lower levels. Centralized operations are usually used by a firm that wants to provide greater uniformity of actions or integration of organizational effort.

See also: CONTROL FUNCTION
                MOTIVATION
                PERFORMANCE EVALUATION

Reference:

Fallon, William K., ed., AMA Management Handbook (AMACOM, New
     York, 1983).

CERTIFICATES OF ACCRUAL ON TREASURY SECURITIES

Certificates of accrual on treasury securities (CATS) is one of several securities created by investment bankers in recent years in response to the increased fluctuation in interest rates. Other securities of this type include treasury investment growth receipts (TIGERS) and separate trading of registered interest and principal securities (STRIPS).

Securities such as CATS and TIGERS are created by investment baning firms. They do this by first buying a large pool of U.S. Treasury securities and placing them with a custodian such as a commercial bank. The investment bankers then sell new securities to the public that represent the legal rights to specific cash flows generated by the treasury portfolio. The new securities promise investors a single future lump-sum cash payment for a set price. In effect, the new securities are zero-coupon bonds created by the investment banking companies by "stripping" the cash flows of interest and principal from the treasury securities which are held by the custodian. For those investors who may want to sell their CATS and TIGERS before they mature, the investment banks maintain a secondary market.

For many investors, the purchase of CATS and TIGERS enable them to avoid the reinvestment risks inherent in treasury bonds, because they can lock in a certain interest rate for a set period of time and not have to worry about how to invest coupon payments received prior to maturity. Because they represent a claim to treasury securities, they are considered free from default risk and are largely noncallable.

The STRIPS program was introduced by the Treasury in 1985. Under this program, selected treasury securities are maintained in the book-entry system operated by the Federal Reserve in a manner that allows separate ownership and trading of the interest and principal payments. Once the securities have been sold at normal auction by the Treasury, the Federal Reserve facilitates trading in the secondary market by maintaining separate ownership records for specific interest and principal payments. Trading takes place in $1,000 units.

See also: BOND
          GOVERNMENT OBLIGATIONS

CERTIFICATES OF DEPOSIT

A certificate of deposit (CD) is issued by a depository institution as evidence that the holder has deposited at the institution a certain amount of money for a certain period of time. By issuing a certificate of deposit, a bank, or thrift institution, gives its pledge to redeem the certificate at maturity and to pay a certain rate of interest for the use of the deposited funds.

Certificates of deposit are issued in several different forms. They may be negotiable or nonnegotiable. If a CD is negotiable it may be sold on the secondary market prior to maturity. Usually only large CDs are issued in negotiable form. CDs may also be issued either in bearer or registered form. Negotiable CDs are usually always issued in bearer form because of the ease with which ownership may be transferred.

The interest rate on CDs often is quoted on the basis of a 360-day year. And the rates may be either fixed or variable. Variable-rate CDs are also called floating-rate or variable-coupon CDs; they accounted for about 15 percent of domestic CDs in 1988. The interest rate on large variable-rate CDs in often tied to either the composite CD rate published by the Federal Reserve or the London interbank offered rate.

The rate of interest paid on large CDs over $100,000 is higher than the rate on treasury bills (T-bills) of equivalent maturity. The spread between the CD rate and that on T-bills varies over time and with economic conditions. The spread tends to widen in poor economic times as investors seek the additional security of T-bills.

CDs never have maturities less than 7 days because of Federal Reserve regulations that limit the minimum maturity on time deposits.

The maturities on most CDs range from 14 days to 12 months, with the average maturity being about 5 months.

As a money market instrument, large negotiable CDs are relatively new. They were first issued by Citibank of New York in 1961 as a way to compete for funds that were being shifted into investments in T-bills and commercial paper. The volume of large CDs issued by banks in the domestic market has grown steadily since the 1960s, and negotiable CDs presently rival commercial paper as the second most popular money market instrument being T-bills.

Large negotiable CDs are now issued by savings banks and savings and loans as well as commercial banks. Ratings of the credit quality of negotiable CDs issued by depository institutions are available from the major rating services, such as Moody's and Standard & Poors.

The secondary market in negotiable CDs is large and efficient. It is an over-the-counter market made up of a network of dealers, brokers, and investors connected by telephone. The bid-ask spread on CDs sold in the secondary market is typically around 5 basis points. The typical size of a CD transaction in the market is between $5 and $10 million. Currently, the CDs of 25 U.S. banks, 15 resident-foreign banks, 20 London banks, and 10 thrifts are actively traded in the market. The principal investors in the market include money market mutual funds, insurance companies, and banks.

See also: MONEY MARKET

Reference:

Willemse, Rob, "Large Certificates of Deposit," in Timothy Q. Cook and Timothy D. Rowe, eds., *Instruments of the Money Market* (Richmond, Va.: Federal Reserve Bank of Richmond, 1986), pp. 3652.

CERTIFIED PUBLIC ACCOUNTANT

A certified public accountant is an accountant who has fulfilled certain requirements established by a state law for the practice of public accounting in that state. The intent of legislation governing public accounting is to regulate the practice of the profession so as to ensure that certain basic standards of practice and professional conduct are maintained because of the public interest that is directly involved.

To become a CPA, an accountant must pass a comprehensive examination that includes: accounting practice, accounting theory, auditing, and business law. Some states also require that an examination on professional ethics be passed before the CPA certificate is issued. The CPA examination is designed to measure the competence of candidates, including technical knowledge of accounting, the ability to apply this knowledge to practical problems, and the candidate's understanding of professional responsibilities. Membership in the major professional association (AICPA) is over 200,000.

See also: ACCOUNTING
            PROFESSION

CHART OF ACCOUNTS

A chart of accounts is a list of a firm's general and subsidiary ledger accounts and numbers systematically organized. An account-numbering system is usually designed as a code that indicates classifications and relationships of accounts. For example, each asset account might be assigned a number between 101 and 199. General ledger accounts are usually arranged in the order in which they appear on the financial statements. First, assets, liabilities, and permanent owners' equity accounts appear in the order of their listing on the statement of financial position. Then revenue and expense accounts appear in the order of their listing on the income statement. This arrangement facilitates the preparation of financial statements.

See also: ACCOUNT
            LEDGER

CHECKS

A check is a written instrument which by its terms directs a bank at which the drawer of the check (the person making out the check) has a deposit to pay on demand a certain sum of money to a payee (the party to whom the check is to be paid). The balance in the cash account is reduced when a check is issued, not when it clears the bank.

A certified check is a check drawn by a depositor and taken by the depositor to his/her bank for certification. When a check is certified by the bank at the request of the holder, the bank becomes primarily responsible. It is almost the same as the holder's obtaining the cash and redepositing it. If a bank certifies a check at the request of the drawer, the drawer's liability continues. A cashier's check is a check drawn by an officer of a bank on that bank and payable to some other persons. A traveler's check is a credit instrument or draft drawn upon a company (such as American Express) or a bank by one of its officers. Traveler's checks are frequently used as substitutes for cash when traveling or making payment where the risks of losing cash are to be avoided.

A letter of credit is a written promise by a bank to accept and pay orders for money drawn upon it up to the amount stated and for the party named in the letter of credit. A certificate of deposit is a written instrument in the form of a receipt given by a bank or other type of financial institution for a sum of money it has received on deposit. A trade acceptance is a draft drawn by a seller of goods and services on the buyer of those goods or services that is payable either to the seller or to the seller's bank. Trade acceptances are usually drawn to require payment at a future date which allows the buyer to receive the goods or services and possibly sell them before payment is required.

See also: CASH
              NEGOTIABLE INVESTMENTS

CHARTING

Technicians rely on charts of prices and trading volume to serve as a basis for analysis of the market and individual stocks. Technical analysts hold that stock price fluctuations tend to form patterns which have predictive value. The value of chart reading has been expressed as follows:

> The purpose of "chart reading" or "chart analysis" is to determine the probable strength of demand versus pressure of supply at various price levels and thus to predict the probable direction in which a stock will move, and where it will probably stop.

Clues are provided by the history of a stock's price movements, as recorded on a chart. In the market, history does repeat itself—often. On the charts, price fluctuations tend, with remarkable consistency, to fall into a number of patterns, each of which signifies a relationship between buying and selling pressures. Some patterns, or "formation," indicate that demand is greater than supply, others suggest that supply is greater than demand, and still others imply that they are likely to remain in balance for some time.

Types of charts used by technicians include the line, bar, vertical bar, and point-and-figure charts.

Market trends that chartists follow include basic trend of the market, leadership reflected in quality of stocks leading advances or declines, advance-decline ratio, short position, low-priced stock activity, odd-lot ratio, support and resistance levels of the market and individual stocks, a confidence index, and other internal market factors.

Chartists provide a technical analysis approach to stock evaluation and selection. They attempt to predict future price levels of stocks by analyzing previous data from the market. Technical analysts assume that the price patterns and trading volumes of the stock market and individual stocks predict a future condition, that every major downturn in a stock is preceded by a period of distribution; every major advance is preceded by a period of accumulation, and that movements in the market have a relationship to one another. Technical analysts based their judgments on such factors as activity, market strength, direction, contrary opinion, and confidence. Technical analysis of individual stocks examines pattern signals which may forecast major or minor upward or downward movement in the stock (for example, head and shoulders, triangles, wedges, flags, saucers, etc.)

Many investors are skeptical of charting techniques and practices. Such investors hold that technical analysis techniques have not been confirmed by empirical testing.

See also: INVESTING
           INVESTING METHODS AND STRATEGIES

CLASSIFIED FINANCIAL STATEMENTS

A classified balance sheet arranges the major categories of assets, liabilities, and owners' equity into significant groups and subgroups. Classifying items on the balance sheet provides information concerning the liquidity of the assets and the maturity dates of liabilities. For example, assets, liabilities, and shareholders' equity are usually classified on a classified balance sheet as:

Assets
Current assets
Long-term investments (or Investments)
Property, plant, and equipment
Intangible assets
Deferred charges

Liabilities
Current liabilities
Long-term liabilities

Shareholders' equity
Capital stock
Additional paid-in capital
Retained earnings

See also: STATEMENT OF FINANCIAL POSITION

CLASSICAL ECONOMICS

With the publication of *An Inquiry into the Nature and Causes of the Wealth of Nations,* by Adam Smith in 1776, began the classical school of thought regarding macroeconomics. Classical macroeconomic economics believed that the economy has the capabilities to sustain itself at a full employment level without government intervention. They admitted that there would be business cycles, but in the long run full employment would be obtained as long as prices (including wages and interest rates) were flexible. Influential writers in this period of economics included, among others, Thomas Robert Malthus, Jean-Baptiste Say, David Ricardo, and John Stuart Mill.

See also: ECONOMICS
            FREE ENTERPRISE SYSTEM

Reference:

Needy, Charles W., ed., *Classics of Economics* (Moore Publishing, Oak Park, Ill., 1980).

CLOSING ENTRIES

Closing entries are general journal entries made at the end of an accounting period to reduce the balance in revenue and expense accounts to zero and to transfer the balances to related balance sheet accounts. Revenue and expense accounts are temporary accounts and are used during an accounting period to accumulate and summarize information relating to net income for the period. The balances in these accounts are no longer required once the accounting period is over. By reducing these account balances to zero, the accounts are ready to begin accumulating and summarizing data for the following period. The dividends account is also closed out for the same reason.

See also: ACCOUNTING CYCLE
             ADJUSTING ENTRIES
             REVERSING ENTRIES

COEFFICIENT OF VARIATION CRITERION

One criterion for deciding between two investment alternatives, where the risk and the expected return from one is greater than the risk and the expected return from the other, is to select that investment opportunity with the lower coefficient of variation. A coefficient of variation measures the relative risk of an investment, that is the risk per dollar of expected return. It quantifies risk by the standard deviation of the expected returns of an investment, σ, per dollar of expected returns, $E[\Pi]$, as:

$$C.V. = \sigma / E[\Pi].$$

C.V. is a useful decision-making index for at least two reasons: (1) it is relatively easy to calculate and (2) it is a unitless measure, that is it allows for comparisons between investments whose returns are measured in different units (dollars, thousands of dollars, etc.)

The coefficient of variation is a standard output from most statistical software packages.

COINCIDENT ECONOMIC INDICATORS

Coincident indicators are those indicators that move with (as opposed to before or after) the business cycle. These include an index of industrial production, levels of nonagricultural employees, real personal income (less transfer payments) and sales in the manufacturing sector.

See also: ECONOMIC INDICATORS

COLLATERALIZED MORTGAGE OBLIGATIONS

In 1983, the Federal Home Loan Mortgage Corporation (FHLMC) developed a new security tailored to the needs of investors with different maturity preferences by effectively dividing the cash flows on mortgage-backed securities into groups and issuing new securities, termed collateralized mortgage obligations (CMOs), against each group.

Mortgage-backed securities usually pass on to investors the principal and interest received each month from mortgagors on a pro rata basis. However, because mortgagors may prepay their mortgages when they move or refinance, holders of mortgage-backed securities may get their principal back sooner than expected and, thus, be subject to reinvestment risk.

To reduce this problem, CMOs are divided into several different maturity classes, for example, short-, medium-, and long-term. In each class, CMO holders receive interest at the certificate rate. As mortgagor principal is repaid, it is passed through first to holders of short-term CMOs. After all principal has been fully repaid to investors in the short-term class, it is paid to holders in the medium-term class, and then finally to those in the long-term class. This repayment schedule reduces the un-certainty of CMO investors as to the term of their investment. And both short- and long-term investors are able to satisfy their preferences for mortgage-backed securities.

Although all CMOs share the same basic structure, numerous differences exist. The most important difference is the nature of the underlying mortgage collateral. Most CMOs are collateralized by a single type of mortgage-backed security: Freddie Mac PCs, Fannie Mae MBSs, or Ginnie Maes. However, some CMOs are backed by some combination of these securities, and some are backed by conventional mortgage loans.

The individual mortgages in the package may all have the same coupon rate, or there may be a range of coupons. There also is no set number of maturity classes. Having a large number of maturity classes (or tranches) may make it easier to match the securities with investor preferences, but it may also reduce the liquidity of the CMOs in the secondary market. Most existing CMOs have four maturity classes, but some have as few as two and others as many as ten.

Another difference is the frequency with which investors receive payments of interest and principal. Most CMOs pay quarterly or semiannually, but some pay monthly. When payments are not received monthly, the issuer has the responsibility of reinvesting the cash in-flows received from mortgagors until the next payment date.

Despite the lack of a standard formula for all CMOs, they have proved to be very popular and are widely available. Innovations to the basic CMO structure continue as underwriters learn the features most valued by investors. So far, banks and thrift institutions have been the largest buyers of shorter-term CMOs, while pension funds have been the dominant investors in longer-term issues.

See also: MORTGAGE

COLLUSION

Collusive activity involves any agreement, explicit or implicit, between firms that affects the competitive process. Firms have an incentive to set prices or limit output, thereby creating an arrangement through which collective profits are greater than they would be under a competitive situation. Collusion is illegal, as outlined in the Sherman Antitrust Act. However, William Baldwin notes that "price-fixing and other collusive activities are pervasive features of economic life even when subject to legal prohibitions, but their effectiveness is determined in large part by features of market structure, and their success is often problematic." As with cartels, collusive arrangements are unstable owing to the financial incentive to cheat (if that conduct can go undetected).

See also: CARTEL
                FRAUD

Reference:

Baldwin, William L., *Market Power, Competition, and Antitrust Policy* (Richard D. Irwin, Homewood, Ill., 1987).

COMMERCIAL BANKS

Commercial banks acquire funds by selling liabilities, such as checking accounts, certificates of deposit, etc. They use the funds they acquire to purchase income-earning assets. Banks make money on the spread between the rate that they must pay for funds and the rate they can earn on their loans and investments. They also make money on the fees they charge for the various services they offer their customers.

Traditionally, a sharp distinction is drawn between commercial banks and other financial institutions because the liabilities of commercial banks serve as the principal medium of exchange in modern economies. Today, that distinction has been blurred by financial deregulation, which has allowed other institutions like savings and loans, savings banks, and money market mutual funds to issue liabilities that also serve as money. Commercial banks as well as these other institutions create money when they increase their liabilities, and they destroy money when they reduce them. If a commercial bank fails, the value of its outstanding liabilities is reduced, and money is destroyed.

Because of the major role played by the industry in the economy and the financial system, commercial banking is one of the most heavily regulated industries in the nation. In 1983, there were some 14,789 commercial banks in the United States. Of these, 4,752 (32%) were federally chartered institutions, and 10,037 (68%) were state chartered.

Federally chartered banks are chartered by the Comptroller of the Currency. They must include "national" (or "national association"—"N.A.") in their name and must be members of both the Federal Reserve System (Fed) and the Federal Deposit Insurance Corporation (FDIC).

State-chartered banks are chartered by the state banking commission or equivalent organization within the state where they are located. They cannot use the word "national" in their title. And they are not required to be members of the Federal Reserve System or the FDIC, although they may choose to do so. Competitive pressures have made membership in the FDIC a virtual necessity for most banks.

The Depository Institutions Deregulation and Monetary Control Act (DIDMCA) of 1980 made all depository institutions, including state-chartered banks, subject to the same Federal Reserve requirements as national banks. National banks must conform to the same state banking laws established by the states in which they operate as do state banks, including any limitations on branching.

National banks are examined by the Office of the Comptroller of the Currency. State banks that are members of the Federal Reserve System are examined by the Fed. And state banks that are not members of the Fed but which are insured by the FDIC are examined by the FDIC. In addition, state banks are subject to examination by state bank examiners in coordination with the Fed and the FDIC.

Compared to other financial intermediaries, commercial banks are larger and more diversified. In 1987, commercial banks in the United States had total assets in excess of $2.7 trillion, and in terms of asset size, they were more than twice as large as savings and loan associations, the next biggest financial intermediary.

To understand how commercial banks operate, it is helpful to examine a consolidated balance sheet for the banking industry like that compiled each month by the Federal Reserve System (see Exhibit C-6). Listed first on the liability side are checkable deposits. These are liabilities of the banking system that entitle the owners of these accounts to write checks payable to third parties. They include all types of accounts where checks may be drawn, including non-interest-bearing demand deposit accounts, interest-bearing NOW (Negotiable Order of Withdrawal) accounts, Super NOW accounts, and money market deposit accounts (MMDAs). Until the early 1970s, checkable deposits were the largest source of bank funds. Today, however, they represent only 22 percent of total bank liabilities and equity.

Nontransaction deposits have become the largest source of banking funds, comprising 49 percent of bank liabilities and equity. These deposits include savings accounts and certificates of deposit. Owners of these accounts are not allowed checking privileges. Small passbook savings accounts were once the major part of nontransaction deposits, but certificates of deposit now represent the biggest component. Many large certificates of

Exhibit C-6

Assets and Liablilities of Commercial Banking Institutions,
April 1987 (billions of dollars)

Assets		Liabilities & Equity	
Reserves	$ 54	Checkable Deposits	$ 591
Cash Items in Process of Collection	$ 75	Nontransaction Deposits	$1,329
		Borrowings	$ 618
Deposits at Other Banks	$ 34	Equity	$ 183
Other Cash Assets	$ 48		
Securities:			
U. S. Govt.	$ 305		
Other	$ 211		
Loans:			
Commercial	$ 556		
Real Estate	$ 519		
Consumer	$ 315		
Other	$ 401		
Other Assets	$ 204		
Total	$2,720	*Total*	$2,720

Source: *Federal Reserve Bulletin* (July 1987), p. A18.

deposit (those over $100,000) are negotiable and are traded on the secondary market prior to maturity.

Borrowings by banks from other banks, nonfinancial corporations, and the Federal Reserve System make up 23 percent of bank liabilities and equity. This is a major change from the early 1960s, when borrowings represented only 2 percent of the total funds of the banking system. Bank borrowings from the Federal Reserve are called *discount loans and advances*, but this source accounts for only a small fraction of the total funds borrowed by the banking system. Borrowings from other banks or financial institutions are said to take place in the *federal funds market*. Such borrowings are often only for overnight, but may be arranged for longer terms. Other sources of bank borrowings include loans from bank holding companies to their bank subsidiaries, loans from nonfinancial corporations arranged through *repurchase agreements*, and loans from the *Eurodollar market*.

The smallest source of banking system funds is equity capital, that is those funds supplied by the owners of commercial banks. Equity capital represents somewhat less than 7 percent of total liabilities plus equity. The equity account (also called the *capital account*) at commercial banks is composed of common stock, surplus, and retained earnings. Bank capital provides a cushion to protect depositors and other creditors against losses from bad loans and other hazards. But the small size of the capital account means that banks have only a limited ability to take on additional risk.

On the asset side of the balance sheet, commercial banks and other depository institutions are required by the Federal Reserve System to maintain reserves against their deposit accounts. Reserves must be maintained in the form of non-interest-bearing deposits at the Federal Reserve banks or in vault cash. The level of reserves required by law are called *required reserves*. Reserves in excess of those required by law are termed *excess reserves*. Reserves limit the ability of banks to expand their deposit liabilities and reduce their profitability.

Cash items in the process of collection (CIPC), or what is often termed *bank float*, represents checks which have been deposited in one bank but which are drawn on another bank and which have not yet resulted in an actual transfer of funds. This category of assets represents funds owed but not yet paid.

Deposits at other banks arise because many smaller banks hold deposits at larger banks in return for a variety of other services including check collection, help with security purchases, and foreign exchange transactions. This system of bank relationships is called *correspondent banking*.

Other cash assets include bank holdings of Treasury bills, bankers acceptances, commercial paper, and other money market assets.

Among the *securities* included on the asset side of balance sheets of commercial banks are bank holdings of U.S. government securities, federal agency securities, the obligations of state and local governments, and other securities. U.S. government and agency securities are the most easily convertible into cash and are sometimes called *secondary reserves*. Bank holdings of securities are an important source of commercial bank income.

Loans are the largest single category of commercial bank assets and the largest source of income. Traditionally, larger commercial banks have specialized in *commercial and industrial loans*. These are loans to businesses for business purposes. They usually are short term, with maturities from a few months to five years. Smaller banks traditionally have invested a larger fraction of their loan portfolios in *consumer loans.* These are usually installment loans to individuals to finance purchases other than housing (including mobile homes). In recent years, most large financial institutions have entered the consumer loan business, increasing the level of competition.

Real estate loans (or mortgage loans) are another area of lending which has become increasingly competitive in recent years, as more commercial banks and other financial institutions have entered the field. Real estate loans are secured by real property and consist primarily of commercial and residential mortgages. Among the other types of loans made by commercial banks are loans of non-federal funds to other financial institutions; loans to finance the purchase of securities by brokers, dealers, and individuals; loans to not-for-profit organizations; and loans to governments.

The final category of bank assests is a catchall termed *other assets.* It includes bank buildings, computers, and other equipment.

Three financial ratios are often used to measure the profitability of bank performance. The first is *net interest margin.* This ratio is similar to the gross margin on sales of a nonfinancial corporation. It measures the difference between a bank's interest income and its interest expense. Net interest margin is calculated by taking revenue from interest, net of loan losses, minus interest expense. The result is divided by the total of the bank's assets. Interest from tax-exempt securities is often adjusted upward to reflect an equivalent return on taxable investments.

A second commonly used ratio is *return on assets* (ROA). It is tabulated by dividing net after-tax income by total assets. ROA measures the success of bank management in employing the assets of the bank. *Return on equity* (ROE) measures the return to the shareholders of the bank. It is calculated by dividing net after-tax income by total equity.

Since banks are heavily leveraged organizations, ROE will be substantially higher than ROA in good years. By definition, ROE is equal to ROA times assets over equity, as follows:

$$\text{Income/Equity} = \text{Income/Assets} \times \text{Assets/Equity} \quad (1)$$
$$(\text{ROE}) = (\text{ROA}) \times (\text{Leverage Multiplier})$$

Assets divided by equity is referred to as the *leverage multiplier.* It measures the degree of financial leverage (debt) in the bank's capital structure, and since financial leverage increases risk, it also measures the degree of risk assumed by the bank. Equation (1) states a fundamental identity: ROE can be increased either by raising ROA or by increasing the leverage multiplier, that is, taking on additional risk.

Exhibit C–7 shows the average net interest margin, return on assets, and return on equity for all insured commercial banks during 198186. While net interest margin has remained relatively constant, both ROA and ROE have declined.

Exhibit C–7
Insured Commercial Banks, 1981–86

	81	82	83	84	85	86
Net Interest Margin	3.17%	3.28%	3.25%	3.26%	3.38%	3.28%
Return on Assets	0.76%	0.71%	0.67%	0.64%	0.70%	0.64%
Return on Equity	13.09%	12.10%	11.24%	10.60%	11.32%	10.23%

Source: *Federal Reserve Bulletin.*

See also: BANK
            BANK REGULATIONSS

References:

Compton, Eric N., *Inside Commercial Banking* (New York, NY: John Wiley and Sons, Inc., 1983).

Wall, Larry D., "Profits in '85: Large Banks Gain While Others Continue to Lag," Federal Reserve Bank of Atlanta, *Economic Review* (August/September 1986), pp. 1831.

COMMERCIAL PAPER

Commercial paper is a term used to represent the unsecured notes of private companies. In general, commercial paper is issued by large companies with very good credit ratings. Maturities on commercial paper are always 270 days or less and generally vary from two to six months. Most issues carry a minimum denomination of $25,000. And they are usually sold at discount without an explicit coupon rate. Interest is calculated on a bank discount basis, using a 360-day year.

Commercial paper is one of the largest of all money market instruments and the volume outstanding has grown very rapidly during the past two decades. This type of short-term financing has become cheaper for many larger private corporations than borrowing from banks. At the same time, the yields on commercial paper are usually competitive with those on bank certificates of deposit and have proved attractive to large institutional investors. Rates on commercial paper recently have averaged one to two percentage points below the bank prime rate and one-quarter of a percentage point above the Treasury bill rate, although this spread varies with economic conditions.

Firms issuing commercial paper avoid the cost of compensating-deposit-balance requirements that many banks tie to their loan agreements. However, issuers must usually be prepared to back an issue with a line of credit at one or more commercial banks, and to sustain the cost of obtaining a credit rating. By keeping maturities 270 days or less, firms avoid the cost of registration with the Securities and Exchange Commission.

See also: NEGOTIABLE INSTRUMENTS

COMMON STOCK

See Capital Stock

COMMUNICATION FUNCTION

Communication is defined as the reporting of pertinent information to management and others for internal and external uses. Communication can also be considered as the process of transmitting and receiving information that is relevant to the management of an enterprise. Communication is a function of the organizational structure and relationships. Major managerial functions of planning, organizing, directing, and controlling are carried out through communication. Exhibit C-8, on the following page shows the major elements of a communication model.

Issues associated with communication, as noted on Exhibit C-8, include:

1. What should be communicated?
2. Who should communicate?
3. When should information be communicated?
4. Where should information be communicated?
5. How should information be communicated?

The human element in communication is affected by cognitive and affective factors. Cognitive factors relate to content and rational thought contained in the message; affective factors relate to values, emotions, and feelings. For communication to be effective, both the cognitive and affective factors must be in harmony. To reduce or eliminate error in communicating, communication models provide for repetition and verification. For example, repetition may involve the use of both written and oral forms of the same message. Verification involves procedures for independent feedback.

Communication models include one-way and two-way communication. The difference between these two models can be summarized as follows.

	One-way (without feedback)	Two-way (with feedback)
Speed	Faster	Slower
Accuracy	Less	More
Noise	Relatively quiet	Relatively noisy
Order	Relatively orderly	Relatively disorderly
Feelings of receiver	Anxiety, insecurity	More confident, less anxious

Exhibit C-8
Communication Flows

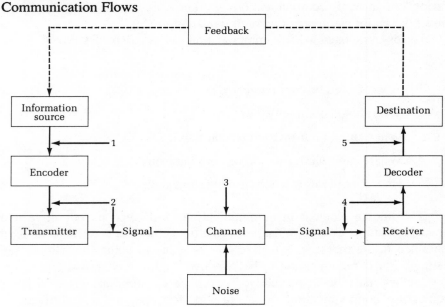

Source: Robert N. Blakeney and Eugene C. Bell, *Advanced Leadership* (Houston, Human Resources Center, College of Business Administration, University of Houston).

In interpersonal communication, communicating per se is generally improved if both parties understand that communication has both cognitive and affective components and verify to each other (provide feedback of) their understanding of what the other party means.

In formal communication, the organizational structure of the entity establishes the channels of communication. In informal communications, networking and the grapevine supplement the formal structure provided by the enterprise. In the formal structure, communication occurs in four directions: downward, upward, horizontally (across boundaries on the same organizational level), and diagonally (across both a horizontal and a vertical boundary). Horizontal and diagonal directions are commonly referred to as cross communication. Some organizational behaviorists maintain that where cross communication is allowed, all parties should obtain advance permission from their superiors and should inform their superiors of any significant developments resulting form the communication. Formal communication systems involve policies (principles or rules of action), standards (for conformity and evaluation), and procedures (detailed instructions, usually provided for in procedural manuals).

Research in organizational communication suggests that:

1. As information flows through an organization, it is frequently translated, altered, filtered, sharpened (highlighted) or leveled (selectivity), and evaluated. These transformations can either facilitate or distort communication.

2. Downward communication is more easily accomplished than is upward communication. Downward communication tends to be unfavorable and important while upward communication tends to be favorable and unimportant.

3. Trust and accuracy are essential in interpersonal and organizational communication. Trust is reflected in the openness and honesty of the communication; accuracy is reflected in the content of the communication. Trust is established by a communicator who is trustworthy (believable, ethical) and informed (experienced, competent).

4. Performance is improved when subordinates are provided with information required to improve performance along with accurate information about their performance.

See also: CONTROL FUNCTION
LEADERSHIP FUNCTION
MANAGEMENT
MOTIVATION
ORGANIZATIONAL BEHAVIOR
PERFORMANCE EVALUATION
PLANNING FUNCTION

Reference:

Dessler, Gary, *Organizational Theory* (Prentice-Hall, Englewood Cliffs, N.J., 1985).

COMPARATIVE ADVANTAGE

See Foreign Trade.

COMPILATION

A compilation is presenting in the form of financial statements information that is the representation of management (owners) without undertaking to express any assurance on the statements. A compilation requires that the accountant understand the industry and nature of the business in which the client is engaged, including the accounting records, qualifications of personnel, and the accounting basis on which the financial statements are presented. The accountant is not required to make inquiries or perform other procedures to verify, corroborate, or review information supplied by his client. A compilation report states that a compilation has been performed, describes a compilation, and states that no opinion or other form of assurance is expressed on the statements.

See also: AUDIT
         REVIEW

Reference:

Burton, John C., et al., *Handbook of Accounting and Auditing* (Warren, Gorham & Lamont, Boston, 1981).

COMPREHENSIVE BUDGET

The comprehensive budget, sometimes referred to as the master budget, is a complete expression of the planned operations of the firm for a period. The master budget typically has two elements: an operating budget and a financial budget.

The operating budget describes the relationship of the input (efforts) of the firm to final output and sales (accomplishments). The financial budget describes the impact of budgeting on the balance sheet, especially as it relates to economic resources and obligations.

The preparation of a comprehensive budget usually begins with the anticipated volume of sales or services, which is a crucial factor that determines the level of activity for a period. In other cases, factory capacity, the supply of labor, or the availability of raw materials could be the starting point.

A top-down or a bottom-up approach can be used to forecast sales. The top-down approach would first forecast sales based on an examination of the economy, then the company's share of the market and the company's sales, and would proceed to a forecast of sales by products or other category. The bottom-up approach would forecast sales by product or other category, then company sales, and then market share. Both methods should result in sales forecasts of materially the same amount. Quantitative methods of forecasting include historical projections; time series analysis relating to secular trend, cycles, seasonal fluctuations, and random fluctuations using methods such as moving average, exponential smoothing, time series analysis, and regression analysis.

See also: BUDGET
            BUDGET MANUAL

CONSERVATISM

Conservatism is a basic accounting convention that requires the reasonable anticipation of potential losses in recorded assets or in the settlement of liabilities at the time when financial statements are prepared. The principle of conservatism is sometimes expressed as follows: "Recognize all losses and anticipate no profit," or "Recognize the lowest of possible values for assets and the highest of possible values for liabilities." The application of the principle does not require the deliberate understatement of assets or overstatement of liabilities. The application of the principle requires astute professional judgment by the accountant or auditor. Application of conservatism typically requires that sales and other revenues are not to be anticipated, and that all liabilities or losses should be properly recorded and recognized in the reporting process.

Conservatism is sometimes justified on the grounds that it compensates for the over-optimism of managers and owners. Another view is that it is preferable to understate net income and net assets rather than overstate them since the consequences of loss or bankruptcy are more serious than those associated with profitable operations. It should be remembered, however, that accounting reports should provide users with sufficient information to allow them to make their own evaluation of risks and opportunities.

See also: ACCOUNTING ASSUMPTIONS
            ACCOUNTING PRINCIPLES

QUALITATIVE CHARACTERISTICS OF ACCOUNTING
INFORMATION

References:

Grady, Paul, "Inventory of Generally Accepted Accounting Principles for Business Enterprises" (AICPA, 1965).

SFAC No. 2, "Qualitative Characteristics of Accounting Information" (FASB, 1980).

CONSIGNMENT

A consignment is an arrangement whereby one party transfers to another for purposes of sale without the ownership of the goods changing hands. The company delivering the goods (the consignor) retains ownership while the company (the consignee) attempts to sell them. If the merchandise is sold, the consignee returns the sales price to the consignor minus a commission and related expenses. Since the consignor has title to the goods, the goods are included in the consignor's inventory until they are sold.

See also: INVENTORY

CONSISTENCY

In accounting, consistency means conformity from period to period by a firm, with accounting policies and procedure remaining unchanged. Consistency is essential to improving comparability across accounting periods. Should change be required because of a more relevant or objective accounting policy or procedures, full disclosure must be made so that users of financial statements are aware of the change. Auditors are required to qualify their opinions for changes in accounting methods so that users of the financial statements are informed that a firm has not used the same methods of accounting consistently over time.

See also: ACCOUNTING CHANGES
           ACCOUNTING PRINCIPLES
           AUDIT

CONSOLIDATED FINANCIAL STATEMENTS

A stock acquisition is one form of business combination. In a stock acquisition, one corporation acquires all or part of the voting stock of another company, and the acquired company remains intact as a separate legal entity. The relationship of the acquiring company to the acquired firm is described as a parent-subsidiary relationship. The acquiring company is referred to as the parent (investor) and the acquired company as a subsidiary. The related companies are called affiliated companies. Consolidated financial statements are generally prepared for affiliated companies.

There are certain advantages to acquiring the majority of the voting stock of another company rather than purchasing its resources. For example:

1. Stock acquisition is relatively simple by open market purchases or by cash tender offers to the subsidiary's stockholders.

2. A smaller investment is typically required to obtain control of the subsidiary since only a majority of the stock must be purchased.

3. The separate legal existence of the affiliated companies provides a degree of protection of the parent's assets from creditors of the subsidiaries.

Consolidated financial statements include a complete set of statements prepared for the consolidated entity and include the sum of the assets, liabilities, revenue, and expenses of the affiliated companies after eliminating the effect of any transactions among the affiliated companies. The consolidated statements present the financial position and results of operations of the economic unit controlled by the parent company as a single accounting entity. Emphasis is placed on the economic unit under control of one management rather than upon the legal form of the separate entities. The consolidated financial statements are prepared primarily for the benefit of the shareholders and creditors of the parent company. There is a presumption that consolidated statements are more meaningful than the separate statements of members of the affiliation. However, subsidiary creditors, minority shareholders, and regulatory agencies must rely on the statements of the subsidiary to assess their claims.

The usual condition for controlling financial interest is ownership of a majority voting interest in common stock. As a general rule, ownership by one company, directly or indirectly, of over 50 percent of the outstanding voting shares of another company is required for consolidation.

A subsidiary would ordinarily not be consolidated:

1. where control is likely to be temporary;

2. where the subsidiary is in legal reorganization or in bankruptcy;

3. where the subsidiary is a foreign company in a country that has expropriated the company or has imposed currency restrictions that prohibit cash remittances to the parent company.

When a parent company owns at least an 80 percent interest in a domestic subsidiary, the companies may elect to file a consolidated income tax return. When consolidated income tax returns are filed, intercompany transactions are eliminated. Consolidated net income usually approximates taxable income. If separate income tax returns are filed, consolidated net income will usually differ from taxable income because intercompany transactions would not be eliminated. These timing differences usually require special accounting recognition.

Push-down accounting is an approach to accounting for an acquisition which involves establishing a new basis of accounting and reporting for a subsidiary in its separate financial statements. According to this method, the parent company's cost of acquiring a subsidiary is "pushed down" and used to establish a new accounting basis for the assets and liabilities of the subsidiary. The assets and liabilities of the subsidiary would be updated to report the amounts at which they are shown on the parent's consolidated statements. The SEC has required push-down accounting under special circumstances since 1983.

When an enterprise owns a substantial but not controlling interest in another company, some accountants prefer to use "proportionate consolidation" for the arrangement. For example, if a company has a one-third interest in a noncorporate joint venture, the investor company would include in the consolidated financial statements one-third of each of the assets, liabilities, revenues, and expenses of the venture. Proportionate consolidation of joint ventures is used primarily in the real estate and construction, oil and gas, and utilities industries.

In some situations, enterprises are affiliated as a result of common management or common control instead of as a result of a majority voting interest held by a parent in its subsidiaries. Combined statements are sometimes prepared for some arrangements. The procedures used to prepare combined statements are similar to those used when preparing consolidated statements. Any intercompany investment is eliminated against the related equity of the other enterprise. Where there is no intercompany investment but merely common management, the individual company equities are combined.

One-line consolidation occurs when an investment in another company is accounted for by the equity method of accounting. The effect of using the equity method on reported income and the total balance sheet assets of the investee are identical to those that would be reported if the investee were consolidated. The difference would be that income and total assets of the investee would be reported on a single line in the income statement and balance sheet of the investor.

See also: BUSINESS COMBINATIONS
              GOODWILL
              POOLING OF INTERESTS
              PURCHASE ACCOUNTING
              SUBSTANCE OVER FORM

References:

Burton, John C., Russell E. Palmer, Robert S. Kay, eds., *Handbook of Accounting and Auditing* (Warren, Gorham & Lamont, Inc., Boston, 1981).

Haried, Andrew A., et al., *Advanced Accounting* (John Wiley & Sons, New York, 1985).

ARB 51, "Consolidated Financial Statements" (AICPA, Committee on Accounting Procedures, 1959).

CONSTRUCTION-TYPE CONTRACTS

A construction-type contract is one which involves a construction project and extends over more than one accounting period. Two methods are currently used to account for such contracts:

1. *Completed contract method*—When this method is used, all of the profit from the contract is recognized in the accounting period the contract is completed. An expected loss on such a contract is recognized in the period when the loss is first forecast.

2. *Percentage-of-completion-method*—When this method is used, profit is allocated to each of the construction periods ordinarily based on estimates of cost incurred during the period to total costs of the project or on an efforts-expended method.

The completed contract method would be used only when the seller is unable to determine reliably either the amount of progress made in each year or the amount of costs needed to complete the entire project.

The major advantage of the completed contract method is that gross profit is objectively determined when the project is completed rather than on estimates. The disadvantages of this method is that income does not reflect current performance and that any income recognition is deferred until complete performance under the contract. The percentage-of-completion method recognizes income currently and does not wait until final performance under the contract. The percentage-of-completion method reflects the application of accrual accounting, and usually produces a better measure of periodic income. This method also emphasizes the economic substance of the contract rather than the legal form of the contract. The major disadvantage of this method is that it relies on estimates for measuring income and inventory.

See also: REALIZATION
            RECOGNITION
            REVENUE
            SUBSTANCE OVER FORM

Reference:

AICPA, "Statement of Position 81-1, Accounting for Performance of Construction-Type Contracts" (AICPA, 1981).

CONSULTING PROCESS

The consultant's role is varied, but generally should consist of helping an organization by providing advice and solving problems. Consultations should result in the company's becoming more competent in solving similar problems in the future without outside assistance.

The consultant can be a listener or a sounding board to assist the client in solving his/her own problems. The consultant can also be viewed as a coach (jointly solving problems) or an intervener who solves problems and takes action directly. Consultant and client should have a clear understanding of what role the consultant is to provide.

While the consulting process used on particular assignments varies, the process typically follows a basic pattern:

1. Summary of the organization's environment, history, goals, and objectives
2. Objective of the consultation:
   a. Problem(s) identified by client
   b. Problem(s) identified by consultant
3. Method and procedures to be used
4. Consultant's expectation from the client (meetings, records, staff)
5. Scheduling/timetable
6. Nature and scope of the report
7. Follow-up
8. Remuneration for engagement

The consultant usually presents the report in both written and oral forms. The final report should typically adhere to the agreed upon plan, indicating which problems have been investigated, which recommendations have been made, and what future commitments have been made. Recommendations should be made in specific terms along with detailed descriptions of how they can be carried out. In the concluding interview, the consultant and the client have the opportunity to discuss the engagement, the findings, and the recommendations.

See also: PLANNING FUNCTION

CONTINGENCIES

A contingency is an existing condition, situation, or set of circumstances involving uncertainty as to the possible gain or loss to an enterprise that will ultimately be resolved when one or more future events occurs or fails to occur. The resulting gain or loss is referred to as a "gain contingency" or a "loss contingency." Gain contingencies do not receive accounting recognition. Loss contingencies are related to the possible incurrence of liabilities or the impairment of assets. Examples of certain loss contingencies include the following: collectibility of receivables, obligations related to product warranties and product defects and customers premiums, threat of expropriation, litigation, claims and assessments, and guarantees of indebtedness of others. Three terms are used to describe the range of possibilities of an event occurring: probable, reasonably possible, and remote. Different accounting is prescribed for contingencies which fall within these ranges. These situations are outlined in Exhibit C–9.

Loss contingencies related to general or unspecified business risks, such as losses related to a strike or recession, are not disclosed in financial statements.

Exhibit C–9
Ranges for Contingencies

Term	Definition	Accounting Action
Probable	The future event(s) is likely to occur.	Record the probable event in the accounts if the amount can be reasonably estimated. If not estimable, disclose facts in note.
Reasonably possible	The chance of the future event(s) occurring is more than remote but less than likely.	Report the contingency in a note.
Remote	The chance of the future event(s) occurring is slight.	No recording or reporting unless contingency represents a guarantee. Then note disclosure is required.

See also: LIABILITIES

Reference:
SFAS No. 5, "Accounting for Contingencies" (FASB, 1975).

CONTRA ACCOUNT

Special accounts are frequently used to recognize the fact that the balance in a related account is not a complete description of the account. If the account is a deduction from the regular account, the account is referred to as a contra account. Control accounts are also referred to as offset, valuation, and negative-asset accounts. The accumulated depreciation account is as a contra account to the plant or equipment account. The allowance for uncollectible receivables account is a contra account to the accounts receivable account. On the income statement, the sales returns and allowance account is a contra account to the sales account. A contra account would be reported as follows on the balance sheet:

Accounts receivable	$100,000	
Less: Allowance for uncollectible receivables	5,000	$95,000

The difference between the asset account and its related contra account ($95,000) is referred to as the book value or carrying value of the asset.

If the special account is an addition to the regular account, it is referred to as an adjunct account. A premium on bonds payable account is an adjunct account to the bonds payable account. The liability is the sum of the two account balances at a specific date.

Contra and adjunct accounts are neither assets nor liabilities in their own right.

See also: ASSETS

CONTRIBUTION MARGIN ANALYSIS

Contribution margin is defined as sales less variable expenses and can be illustrated as shown on the following page.

Sales (50,000 units)	$100,000
Less: Variable expense	60,000
Contribution Margin	40,000
Less: Fixed expenses	10,000
Net income	$ 30,000
Contribution margin per unit (50,000 units)	$0.80
Contribution margin rate (on sales)	40%

Variable expenses are those expenses that change in direct proportion to the change in volume of sales over the relevant range of business activity. The total variable expense fluctuates as sales volume fluctuates. The variable expense per unit remains constant. Fixed expenses are those expenses that remain constant at any relevant range of volume within the operating capacity of the firm. The total fixed expenses remain constant; the per unit fixed expense varies with changes in volume. Contribution is that portion of revenue that is available to cover fixed expenses and produce a profit.

The contribution margin can be used in a variety of ways. For example, the break-even point of a business can be computed using the contribution-margin approach. The break-even point in units can be computed using the following formula:

$$\text{Sales at break-even point} = \frac{\text{Fixed expense}}{\text{Contribution margin per unit}}$$

$$= \frac{\$10,000}{\$0.80 \ (= \$40,000/50,000 \text{ units})}$$

$$= 12,500 \text{ units}$$

The contribution margin rate is computed as follows: contribution margin divided by sales. Sales at the break-even point in dollars can be computed using the contribution-margin rate as follows:

$$\begin{array}{rl}\text{Sales at break-even point} & = \dfrac{\text{Fixed expense}}{\text{Contribution rate}} \\ \text{in dollars} & \end{array}$$

$$= \frac{\$10,000}{.40 \ (= \$40,000/\$100,000)}$$

$$= \$25,000$$

Using data on contribution margin per unit, management can make quick estimates of the impact on net income resulting from changes in sales:

Change in net income = Change in volume × Contribution margin per unit
Change in net income = Change in sales revenue × Contribution margin rate

Change in selling price or unit cost = Desired change in total
required to achieve a desired   contribution margin
contribution margin   Number of units to be sold

Sales required = Fixed expenses + Desired net income income
for desired   Contribution margin rate
net income

A cost-volume-profit chart (Exhibit C-10 on the following page) shows the profit or loss potential for an extensive range of volume. At any level of output, the profit or loss is the vertical difference between the sales line and the total cost line. The break-even point is the intersection of sales and total costs. The contribution margin at any level of output is the vertical difference between the sales line and the variable expenses line. The total expenses and variable expenses lines are parallel; the difference between them equals fixed expenses.

The margin of safety is the dollar difference between break-even sales revenue and sales revenue at a certain volume level. Margin of safety can be expressed as a rate:

M/S = Sales at given level – Break-even sales
              Sales at given level

If break-even sales were $1,000,000 and current period sales were $1,200,000, the margin of safety would be $200,000 sales. Expressed as a rate, the margin of safety would be 16.7%:

M/S = ($1,200,000 – $1,000,000)/$1,200,000 = 1/6 = 16.7%.

Exhibit C–10

Contribution Margin Analysis— Cost-Volume-Profit Chart

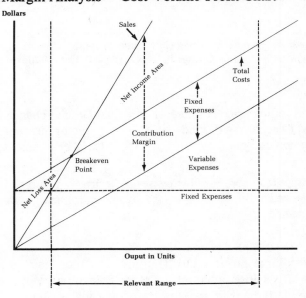

If a firm has relatively large fixed expense, relatively small variable expense rate, and a low margin of safety, it would usually try to improve its profit position by increasing volume or by reducing fixed expense. If the margin of safety for a firm is relatively small and the unit contribution margin is also small, the firm might consider the advisability of increasing selling price or reducing variable expense. Managers should appreciate the fact that, if they operate with a small margin of safety, a small decline in sales is likely to bring net losses.

The principal uses of break-even analysis are summarized here:

1. To understand the relationships between costs, volume, and price.

2. To test the profit impact of a sales forecast.

3. To find the break-even volume of sales in dollars and/or in units of sales.

4. To determine the volume of sales required to attain certain profit goals.

5. To estimate the effect on the break-even point and on profits of changes in the firm's cost and revenue structures.

Major assumptions underlying break-even analysis include the following:

1. All costs can be reliably separated into their variable and fixed components within a relevant range of activity.
2. Fixed costs remain constant in total amount throughout a relevant volume range.
3. Variable costs do not change per unit and fluctuate in total in direct proportion to volume.
4. Selling prices remain constant at any relevant volume.
5. Production and sales volume will be equal.

Contribution margin analysis facilitates other decisions such as the utilization of scarce resources, make-or-buy equipment, sell now or process further, and plant acquisition decisions. To illustrate several applications, assume the following data about a company that can produce and sell three products or any combination thereof. However, the company's production capacity is limited by the number of machine hours available to produce the products.

	Product A	Product B	Product C
Sales price per unit	$12	$15	$18
Variable expense per unit	7	9	10
Contribution margin per unit	5	6	8
Machine hours to produce one unit	5	3	16
Contribution margin per machine hour	$1	$2	0.80

Although Product C has the largest contribution margin per unit, Product B should be produced since it has the largest contribution per the constraining factor (machine hours).

The illustration below shows the income statement for a company that has revenue but is operating at a $20,000 loss. This is considered to be a temporary situation. Should the company continue operations or shut down? If the company closes down, the fixed expenses will continue.

	Continue operations	**Shut down**
Sales	$1,000,000	– –
Less: Variable expense	900,000	– –
Contribution margin	100,000	– –
Less: Fixed expense	120,000	$120,000
Net loss	$20,000	$120,000

The firm should continue to operate because the contribution margin is larger than zero. The contribution margin from continued operations helps pay some of the fixed expenses.

See also: BREAK-EVEN ANALYSIS
CONTROL FUNCTION
GROSS MARGIN ANALYSIS
PLANNING AND FUNCTION

Reference:

Liao, Woody M., and James L. Boockholdt, *Cost Accounting for Managerial Planning, Decision Making and Control* (Dame, Houston, Texas, 1985).

CONTROL FUNCTION

Control is a managerial function that provides a degree of assurance that the organization's activities are being performed effectively and efficiently. One of the better-known definitions of control is provided by Henry Fayol:

Control consists of verifying whether everything occurs in conformity with the plan adopted, the instructions issued, and principles established. It has for an object to point out weaknesses and errors in order to rectify and prevent recurrence.

The control function consists of setting standards, measuring performance, evaluating results, and taking appropriate action. There is a direct linkage between controlling and planning. Planning provides the institution's goals and objectives; control provides one of the means for achieving those goals and objectives. The planning and control cycle is illustrated in Exhibit C-11 on the following page.

Control consists primarily of the acts of:

1. determining that actions undertaken are in accordance with plans, and

2. using feedback to assure that goals and objectives are being attained.

Control techniques include both financial and nonfinancial controls. Financial controls focus on monitoring costs, assessing profits or benefits attained, and evaluating asset utilization. Nonfinancial controls monitor important activities and programs as they relate to nonfinancial aspects of efficiency, economy, and effectiveness.

Organizational controls are used to evaluate overall performance, often in terms of profitability, goal attainment, changes in organizational structure, plans, and objectives. Operational controls are used to measure the period-to-period performance by establishing standards which can be used to monitor the performance. Operational controls include such tools and techniques as productivity ratios, unit costs, and workload measures.

Supervisory control relates primarily to control at the operational level. Two generally recognized supervisory controls include output controls and behavior controls. Output controls are usually based on formal measurement records of outputs and productivity. Behavior controls are based upon personal observations of employees and their performance.

The information managers ordinarily need to control effectively can be classified as (1) score-card information, (2) attention-directing information, and (3) problem-solving information. Score-card information responds to the question: How well or poorly are we doing? Attention-directing information answers such questions as: Is the company performing according to plans? What problems or opportunities exist? What areas of the enterprise need to be changed, if any? Problem-solving information helps management resolve a particular problem: What is the problem or concern? What are the alternatives? Which alternative is preferable? Reporting and analysis of data developed through a control system is communicated to concerned parties through formal and informal reports.

Exhibit C-11
Steps in Planning and Control Cycle

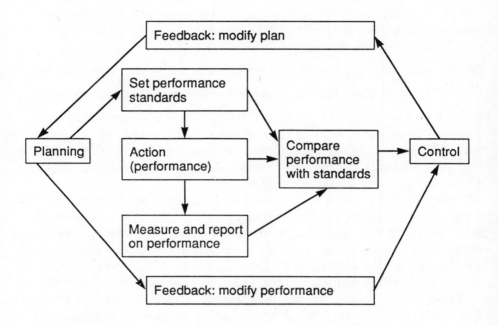

See also: ACCOUNTING CONTROLS
ADMINISTRATION CONTROLS
BUDGET
CENTER
COMMUNICATION FUNCTION
DECISION MAKING
DISTRIBUTION COST CONTROL
GOALS AND OBJECTIVES
INTERNAL CONTROL
LEADERSHIP FUNCTION

MANAGEMENT
MANAGEMENT THEORIES
MOTIVATION
NETWORK ANALYSIS
ORGANIZATIONAL BEHAVIOR
ORGANIZING FUNCTION
PERFORMANCE EVALUATION
PLANNING FUNCTION
QUALITY CONTROL
RESPONSIBILITY ACCOUNTING

Reference:

Woelfel, Charles J., and Charles D. Mecimore, *The Operating Executive's Handbook of Profit Planning Tools and Techniques* (Probus Publishing Co., Chicago, 1986).

CONTROLLER

The controller (or comptroller) is the chief accounting executive in most business organizations. Major functions performed by the controller include internal auditing, general accounting, tax planning, cost accounting, and budgeting. The treasurer is responsible for assuring that the firm has the financial resources required to conduct its activities. In addition, the treasurer usually has responsibilities relating to the custody of cash, banking, investments, and insurance. The treasurer's function is basically custodial; the controller's function is basically an information and reporting function. The following functions are usually assigned to controllers and treasurers:

Controller:

1. Planning for control

2. Reporting and interpreting reports and statements

3. Evaluating and consulting on financial matters

4. Evaluating and consulting on financial matters

5. Tax administration

6. Protection of assets

7. Economic appraisal

Treasurer:

1. Provision of capital

2. Investor relations

3. Short-term financing

4. Banking and custody

5. Credit and collections

6. Investments

7. Insurance

See also: ACCOUNTING
ACCOUNTING SYSTEM
CERTIFIED PUBLIC ACCOUNTANT
PROFESSION

CONVERTIBLE SECURITIES

Convertible securities are bonds or preferred stocks that can be exchanged for common stock at the option of the holder. Deferred securities are often used as a form of deferred common stock financing, as a device to assist debt or preferred financing, and for raising relatively less expensive financing.

Convertible securities are usually convertible only within or after a certain time period. Time limits are imposed primarily to meet the issuer's long-term financial needs. The conversion ratio is the ratio in which the convertible security can be exchanged for common stock or preferred stock. If the conversion ratio is known, the conversion price can be computed by dividing the face value (not the market value) of the convertible security by the conversion ratio. For example, a $1,000 face value bond convertible into 25 shares of common stock has a conversion ratio of 25 and a conversion price of $40 ($1,000 divided by 25). The issuer of convertible securities usually establishes a conversion price or ratio so as to make the conversion price at the time of issuance of the security somewhere between 10 and 20 percent above the current market price of the firm's stock. A predictable opportunity to convert must be available in order to improve the marketability of a convertible security. The conversion value of a convertible security is the value of the security measured in relation to the market value of the security into which it can be converted. The conversion value can usually be determined by multiplying the conversion ratio by the current market price of the firm's common stock (if convertible into common stock). If the conversion ratio of a bond is 20 and the market price of the common stock is $60, the conversion value is $1,200. A conversion premium is the percentage difference between the conversion price and the issuance price of a security.

See also: BOND
LIABILITIES
PREFERRED STOCK

CORPORATION

A corporation is an entity created by law, capable of owning assets, incurring liabilities, and engaging in specified activities. The corporation is a legal entity separate from its owners (shareholders). Ownership in a corporation is evidenced by a stock certificate, a serially numbered document that shows the number of shares owned and the par value, if any. Ownership in a corporation is readily transferable and shareholders have no personal liability for the corporate debts and frequently have little active role in its management.

To form a corporation, three or more individuals, called incorporators, must file an application (articles of incorporation) with the proper state official. Articles of incorporation are the legal documents that specify a corporation's name, period of existence, purpose and powers, authorized number of shares, classes of stock, and other information related to the corporation's existence and operations. When approved, this becomes the corporate charter which authorizes the company to do business. Incorporators next hold a stockholders' meeting to elect a board of directors and to pass bylaws to guide the operations of the corporation. The directors then hold a meeting to elect officers of the corporation, who manage the enterprise. The "cumulative method" of voting is sometimes used when electing a board of directors. When the cumulative method of voting is used, the owner of any one share is allowed as many votes for one or more candidates as there are directors to be elected. The activities of the board are recorded in a minutes book that becomes the official record of policy decisions. A typical corporate structure is shown here:

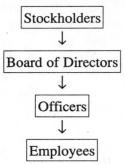

When a corporation issues stock, it gives the stockholders a stock certificate for the number of shares acquired, as evidence of ownership. The corporation maintains a shareowners' ledger that contains an account for each stockholder, showing the number of shares held by each owner of shares. When stock that has been issued is transferred from one owner to another, the transfer is recorded in a stock transfer book. Larger corporations often arrange for a transfer agent to maintain their stock transfer books and shareowners' ledgers. To ensure independent control over the process of issuing stock, many corporations engage a stock registrar to countersign stock certificates and to insure that each certificate is properly issued. Banks and trust companies in financial centers often serve as stock registrars and transfer agents.

A de jure corporation is a corporation formed in compliance with the provisions of an incorporation statute. A de facto corporation is a corporation formed without full compliance with all material, mandatory provisions of an incorporation statute. Acts beyond the scope of corporate powers are referred to as ultra vires acts. Directors are personally liable for such acts which they approve.

Corporations are classified as public or private corporations. Private corporations may be stock or nonstock corporations. Stock companies normally operate for profit, while nonstock corporations such as certain hospitals and churches usually are not-for-profit organizations. Corporations can also be classified as:

1. Public corporations are government-owned entities, such as the Federal Deposit Insurance Corporation.

2. Open corporations are private stock corporations whose stock is available to the public and is usually traded on a stock exchange (a listed corporation) or in the over-the-counter market (unlisted).

3. Closed corporations are private corporations whose stock is not offered for sale to the general public but rather is usually held by a few individuals.

4. Domestic corporations are corporations incorporated in a particular state.

5. Foreign corporations are companies that operate in a state other than the one in which they are incorporated.

The major advantages associated with the corporate form of business organization include limited liability to stockholders, ease of capital formation, ease of transfer of ownership, lack of mutual agency relationships, continuous existence, and centralized authority and responsibility. The major disadvantages of the corporate form include government regulation and taxation. A corporation, unlike a partnership or single proprietorship, is subject to taxation on income. Individual stockholders are subject to taxation on the dividend distributions of net income which results in a form of double taxation.

The comparative advantages and disadvantages of the corporate, partnership, and sole proprietorship types of business are presented in Exhibit C-12 on the following page.

Professional corporations are closely held corporations established by members of legally recognized professions, such as accountancy, law, and medicine. Membership in professional corporations is limited to members of the profession to ensure the integrity of the profession and to minimize professional compromises. Subchapter S corporations are also closely held corporations and are created through income tax legislation. Such corporations have the usual advantages of the corporate form of business organization but do not have the disadvantage of double taxation.

See also: PARTNERSHIP
                PROPRIETORSHIP

Exhibit C-12
Comparison of Legal Forms of Business Organization

FEATURE	PROPRIETORSHIP	PARTNERSHIP	CORPORATION
Number of owners	One.	Two or more.	Usually three or more.
Assets owned by	Proprietor.	Partners as co-owners.	Corporation.
Liability	Sole proprietor is personally liable for all business debts. *Unlimited liability.*	Each partner is personally liable for all business debts. *Unlimited liability.*	Stockholder's liability is usually limited to his own investment. *Limited liability.*
Legal existence	Extension of proprietor.	Extension of partners.	Separate entity, distinct from stockholders.
Life	Ends with change in ownership—for example, death or insolvency of proprietor.	Ends with change in ownership—for example, death or insolvency of a partner, withdrawal of a partner.	Perpetual unless limited by charter.
Organization agreement	Unnecessary.	Should have formal Articles of Copartnership setting forth agreement among partners.	Must be chartered by state.
Ownership powers	Complete.	Complete; any partner binds all other partners unless a partner is restricted.	Certain rights given by stock agreement to stockholders—for example, the right to vote, to receive declared dividends, to buy additional issues of stock.
Federal income tax	Proprietor reports income statement data on his personal tax return and is taxed on profit of the business; the business pays no income tax.	Partners report income statement data of partnership and show income distribution among partners on their personal tax returns; each partner is taxed on his share of the business' net income; the partnership pays no income tax.	Corporation pays income tax; shareholders report dividends as income on their personal tax returns (double taxation of corporate income).
Owners' salary	Personal withdrawal from owner's equity.	Division of net income among partners.	Salaries paid as operating expense; net income may be paid out as dividends.
Advantages	a. Relatively easy to start. b. Relatively free from government regulation. c. Profits taxed once to owner.	Approximately the same as those for proprietorship.	a. Ability to raise large sums of money. b. Ownership shares are relatively easy to transfer. c. Limited liability of shareholders. d. Life of corporations can be perpetual.
Disadvantages	a. Unlimited liability of owner. b. Difficulties of raising large amounts of money. c. Lack of permanency as a form of organization.	Approximately the same as those for proprietorship.	a. Double taxation of income distributed to shareholders. b. Subject to government regulation not required of other forms of business organization.

Reference:

Muller, Dennis, C., *The Corporation: Growth, Diversification, and Mergers* (Harwood Academic Publishers, London, 1987).

COST

A cost is an expenditure (a decrease in assets or an increase in liabilities) made to obtain an economic benefit, such as resources that can produce revenue. A cost can also be defined as the sacrifice to acquire a good or service. Used in this sense, a cost represents an asset. An expense is a cost that has been utilized by the company in the process of obtaining revenues (that is, the benefits associated with the good or service have expired). Costs can be classified in many ways including:

1. Direct and indirect costs:

   a. Direct costs are outlays that can be identified with a specific product, department, or activity. For example, the costs of material and labor that are identifiable with a particular physical product are direct costs for the product.

   b. Indirect costs are those outlays that cannot be identified with a specified product, department, or activity. Taxes, insurance, and telephone expense are common examples of indirect costs.

2. Product and period costs:

   a. Product costs are outlays that can be associated with production. For example, the direct costs of materials and labor used in the production of an item are product costs.

   b. Period costs are expenditures that are not directly associated with production, but are associated with the passage of a time period. The president's salary, advertising expense, interest, and rent expenses are examples of period costs.

3. Fixed, variable, and mixed costs:

   a. Fixed costs are costs that remain constant in total (not per unit) regardless of the volume of production or sales, over a relevant range of production or sales. Rent and depreciation are typically fixed costs. Total depreciation remains constant; depreciation per unit of output changes with changes in volume or activity.

b. Variable costs are costs that fluctuate in total (not per unit) as the volume of production or sales fluctuates. Direct labor and direct material costs used in production and sales commissions are examples of variable costs. Total commission expense varies with changes in sales volume; commission expense per unit of sales remains constant as sales volume changes.

c. Mixed costs are costs that fluctuate with production or sales, but not in direct proportion to production or sales. Mixed costs contain elements of fixed and variable costs. Costs of supervision and inspections are often mixed costs.

4. Controllable and uncontrollable costs:

a. Controllable costs are costs that are identified as a responsibility of an individual or department, and that can be regulated within a given period of time. Office supplies would ordinarily be considered a controllable cost for an office manager.

b. Uncontrollables cost are those costs that cannot be regulated by an individual or department within a given period of time. For example, rent expense is uncontrollable by the factory foreman.

5. Out-of-pocket costs and sunk costs:

a. Out-of-pocket costs are costs that require the use of current economic resources. Taxes and insurance are generally out-of-pocket costs.

b. Sunk costs are outlays or commitments that have already been incurred. The cost of equipment already purchased is a sunk cost.

6. Incremental, opportunity, and imputed costs:

a. Incremental (or differential) cost is the difference in total costs between alternatives. Incremental costs can also be considered as the total cost added or subtracted by switching from one level or plan of activity to another.

b. Opportunity cost is the maximum alternative benefit that could be obtained if economic resources were applied to an alternative use.

c. Imputed costs are costs that can be associated with an economic event when no exchange transaction has occurred. For example, if a company "rents to itself" a building that it might otherwise have rented to an outside party, the rent for the building is an imputed cost.

7. Relevant cost.

A relevant cost is an expected future cost and a cost that represents difference in costs among alternatives. Assume you purchased an airline ticket from New York to London at a cost of $300 and that you have made a nonrefundable $75 downpayment on the ticket. The remaining $225 still must be paid when you pick up the ticket. The ticket is nontransferable. You later discover that you can purchase a ticket to London on another airline for $200. Everything related to the two tickets is equal. The $75 downpayment is not relevant to this decision because it is not a future cost that differs among alternatives. You should buy the new ticket for $200.

See also: FIXED COST
IMPLIED AND IMPLICIT COSTS
OPPORTUNITY COST ANALYSIS
VARIABLE COST

COST ACCOUNTING

Cost accounting is a subset of accounting that develops detailed information about costs as they relate to units of output and to departments, primarily for purposes of providing inventory valuations (product costing) for financial statements, control, and decision making.

Manufacturing costs flow through three basic responsibility centers: raw materials storeroom, the factory, and the finished goods storeroom. Three inventory accounts are usually provided to accumulate costs as they relate to the three responsibility centers: raw material inventory, work-in-process inventory, and finished goods inventory. When goods are sold, costs are transferred from the finished goods inventory account to the cost of goods sold account. The flow of costs through the manufacturing process can be illustrated as follows:

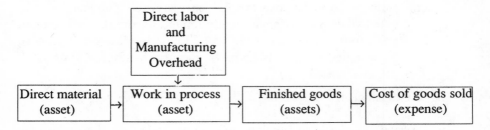

A job-order cost system or a process cost system are used to assign costs to manufactured products for purposes of controlling costs and costing products:

1. A job-order (or production order) cost system accumulates costs of material, labor, and manufacturing overhead by specific orders, jobs, batches, or lots. Job-order cost systems are widely used in the construction, furniture, aircraft, printing, and similar industries where the costs of a specific job depend on the particular order specifications.

2. A process cost system accumulates costs by processes or departments over a period of time. Product cost systems are used by firms that manufacture products through continuous-flow systems or on a mass-production basis. Industries that use process cost systems include chemical, petroleum products, textiles, cement, glass, mining, and others. In a process cost system, costs for a department or process are accumulated. Per-unit costs are obtained by dividing the total departmental costs by the quantity produced during a given period in the department or process.

Direct material and direct labor costs can usually be traced directly to particular units manufactured. Manufacturing overhead costs incurred during a period are usually allocated to units manufactured based on a predetermined overhead rate. This overhead rate is based on the budgeted overhead costs for the period and the estimated level of activity (for example, units produced, direct labor hours, direct labor costs).

Standard cost systems are widely used for budgeting and performance evaluation purposes. Standard costs can be used in both job-order and process cost systems. In a standard cost system, product costing is achieved by using predetermined standard costs for material, direct labor, and overhead. Standard costs are developed on the basis of historical cost data adjusted for expected changes in the product, production technology, engineering estimates, and other procedures. Standards may be established at any one of the following levels:

1. Ideal standards are set for the level of maximum efficiency.

2. Normal standards are set to reflect the conditions that are expected to exist over a period of time sufficient to take into consideration seasonal cyclical fluctuations.

3. Currently attainable standards are set at a level which represents anticipated conditions assuming efficient operations.

Because predetermined standards usually differ from actual costs incurred, a variance typically exists. An unfavorable variance results when actual cost exceeds standard cost; a favorable variance results when standard cost exceeds actual cost. The usual approach followed in standard cost analysis is to separate price factors from efficiency factors. When the actual amount paid differs from the standard amount, the variance is referred to as a price, rate, or spending variance. When the actual input quantity (ton, labor hours) differs from the standard input quantity, the variance is referred to as a quantity, volume or yield variance. The relationships between actual and standard price/quantity is illustrated in the diagram on the following page. The diagram shows two types of prices and quantities: actual and standard. A price variance is conceptualized as the difference between quadrants 1 and 2. A quantity variance is reflected in the difference between quadrants 2 and 4.

	Actual Price	**Standard Price**
Actual Quantity	1 Actual quantity at actual price	2 Actual quantity at standard price
Standard Quantity	3 Standard quantity at actual price	4 Standard quantity at standard price

The formulae for typical direct material and direct labor variances include the following:

1. Direct material price variance =
    Actual quantities purchased × (Actual price − Standard price).

2. Material quantity (usage, efficiency) variance =
    (Actual quantity used − Standard quantity allowed)× Standard price.

3. Direct labor rate variance =
    Actual hours used × (Actual labor rate − Standard labor rate).

4. Direct labor efficiency variance =
    (Actual hours used − Standard hours allowed)× Standard labor rate.

COST BEHAVIOR

How costs react to changes in activity (volume) is referred to as cost behavior. Different types of costs behave differently in response to different activity levels and within a relevant range. In the short run, costs are of three types: fixed costs, variable costs, and mixed, or semivariable, costs.

Fixed costs are those costs that remain constant at any relevant range of volume within the existing operating capacity of the firm. The term fixed cost relates to total dollar cost. For example, the rent expense of a firm is assumed to be $100,000 for the year. If 1,000 or 10,000 items are manufactured, rent expense remains fixed at $100,000. Note that per unit fixed cost for rent varies inversely with volume because the cost is spread over more units. Rent expense per unit is $100; if 10,000 units are produced, rent expense per unit is $10 per unit.

Variable costs are those costs that change in direct proportion to the change in volume of sales over the relevant range of business activity. The total variable expense fluctuates as the volume fluctuates. The term variable cost refers to the variability of the total dollar cost. Assume that a company sells a magazine for $2 per issue. Commission expense is $1 per issue. If 1,000 units are sold, the total sales commission is $1,000; if 10,000 units are sold, the total sales commission is $20,000.

Mixed costs are those costs that contain both a fixed and a variable element. Mixed costs change with increases or decreases in volume but do not change in direct proportion to the volume changes. Telephone expense, maintenance and repair expense, and utilities are usually mixed expenses. If volume should drop to zero, these costs would probably decrease somewhat, but they would not decrease proportionately with the decrease in volume.

Fixed and variable costs are illustrated in Exhibit C–13.

See also: COSTS
        BUDGET
        FIXED AND FLEXIBLE BUDGET

Exhibit C–13
Variable and Fixed Costs Behavior

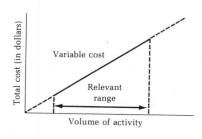

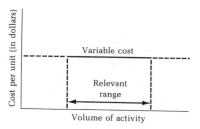

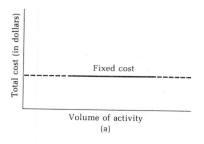

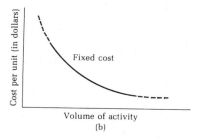

(a)

(b)

COST-BENEFIT ANALYSIS

Cost-benefit analysis is one of several methods for evaluating a project. Unlike other methods of analysis, cost-benefit analysis attempts to include in the calculations estimates of both primary and secondary costs and benefits. Usually, this decision-making approach is used to evaluate public programs where there are a large number of secondary recipients.

Cost-benefit analysis attempts to maximize benefits for a prescribed level of costs, determine the minimum level of expenditures to achieve a pre-specified level of benefits, or maximize net benefits. The methodology involves a comparison, in present value, of benefits and costs. Often, if the ratio of benefits to costs is greater than unity, the project will be selected (unless competing projects have a lower cost-to-benefit ratio).

Cost-benefit analysis has a subjective element, namely the identification of the secondary recipients of the benefits and the secondary parties incurring costs. For example, if a project were being contemplated to improve the water quality of a recreational lake, the number of individuals currently using the lake could be identified, but projections of those who would use the lake only if it were cleaner is more difficult. Other areas of application relate to pollution in general, employee morale, and safety.

Cost-benefit analysis has occasionally been applied to the auditing and accounting standard setting process. As applied to auditing, costs often include audit fees and other costs incurred by the entirety being audited. Benefits often relate to the reliability of the financial statements being audited and to the discovery or prevention of fraud. It is important to note that many of the benefits associated with an audit are usually paid for by a particular entirety.

See also: CONTROL FUNCTION
          INCREMENTAL COST ANALYSIS
          PLANNING FUNCTION

Reference:

Prest, A.R., and Turvey, R. "Cost-Benefit Analysis: A Survey," *Economic Journal* (December 1965).

COST METHOD

The cost method of accounting for investments in common stock records the investment at cost. Dividends received from the investment are recognized as income. However, dividends received in excess of the investor's share of earnings after the investment is acquired are considered a return of capital and are recorded as a reduction in the investment account. If the securities are considered marketable equity securities, the lower-of-cost-or-market procedure is usually applied. The cost method contrasts with the equity method of accounting for stock investments. When the equity method is used, the investment is recorded at cost and is adjusted for earnings, losses, and dividends.

See also: COST PRINCIPLE
EQUITY METHOD OF ACCOUNTING

Reference:

Beams, Floyd A., *Advanced Accounting* (Prentice-Hall, Inc., Englewood Cliffs, N.J., 1985).

COST OF CAPITAL

The cost of capital usually refers to the cost of funds invested in an enterprise. In this sense, the cost of capital is the weighted average of the cost of each type of debt and equity capital. The weight for each type of capital is the ratio of the market value of the securities representing that particular source of capital to the market value of all securities issued by the company. To illustrate, assume that the market value of a company's common stock is $600,000 and the dividend yield is 10 percent. The market value of the company's interest-bearing debt is $400,000 with an average after-tax yield of 8 percent. The average cost of capital for the company can be estimated as follows:

Source	Proportion of Total Capital	Cost	
Common stock	0.60	0.10	0.06
Debt	0.40	0.08	0.032
Average cost of capital			0.092

Cost of capital also refers to the discount rate that equates the expected present value of future cash flows to common shareholders with the market value of the common stock at a specific time.

See also: DISCOUNTED CASH FLOW

Reference:

Bierman, Harold, Jr., and Seymour Smidt, *The Capital Budgeting Decision* (Macmillan, New York, 1966).

COST OF GOODS SOLD

Cost of goods sold is the expense that was incurred for the merchandise (or goods) that was sold during the period. Cost of goods sold can be computed as follows:

Beginning inventory, January 1, 1985	$100,000
Add: Purchases (net) during the year	700,000
Goods available for sale during the year	800,000
Less: Ending inventory, December 31, 1985	60,000
Cost of goods sold	$740,000

Gross margin is the excess of sales over cost of goods sold:

Sales (net)	$950,000
Less: Cost of goods sold	740,000
Gross margin	$210,000

Gross margin is available for other expenses and net income.

See also: GROSS MARGIN ANALYSIS
INCOME STATEMENT

COST PRINCIPLE

The cost (or initial recording) principle requires that assets, liabilities, owners' equity, revenue, expenses, and other elements of accounting be initially recorded in the accounting system at the time of exchange and at the prices agreed upon by the parties to the exchange. The cost principle is also referred to as the historical (or acquisition) cost principle. Acquisition cost is equal to the amount of cash given or the cash equivalent value of other consideration exchanged. When an asset is acquired from a donation, its "cost" is assumed to be its fair market value. When an asset is acquired in an exchange, the accounting required to record the acquisition depends on whether the two assets exchanged are similar or dissimilar, and whether a cash difference (boot) is paid or received. The general rule for recording an exchange of assets is as follows: If the assets exchanged are similar, the exchange should be recorded on a "book value" basis because the earning process on the old asset is not completed. The book value of the old asset is assigned to the asset acquired in the exchange. If the assets exchanged are dissimilar (equipment for land), the exchange should be recorded on a "fair market value" basis because the earning process on the old asset has been completed.

The cost principle is based on the assumption that cost represents the fair market value at the date of acquisition. Those who advocate historical cost measurement emphasize that such costs are objective and reliable. Opponents of the historical cost principle argue that historical costs lack relevance because they do not reflect current market values or the effects of inflation when included in financial statements subsequent to the time the assets are acquired. Nevertheless, the cost principle is one of the most basic concepts in accounting theory.

See also: ARM'S-LENGTH TRANSACTION
MEASUREMENT
PROPERTY, PLANT, AND EQUIPMENT

Reference:

Grady, Paul, "Inventory of Generally Accepted Accounting Principles for Business Enterprises" (AICPA, 1965).

COST-PUSH INFLATION

Inflation is a continuous increase in the average price level. One explanation for inflation is that increases in the cost of production "push" the prices of final goods and services up. A key cost element is wages, and it is believed that excessive union demands for higher wages fuel inflation. Similarly, monopoly control over key resource inputs will have the same effect.

See also: INFLATION

CREDIT MARKET

The credit market is composed of borrowers who obtain money from lenders at a predetermined price. The price that borrowers pay to lenders is an interest rate. This flow of money between borrowers and lenders is called credit. Households, firms, and the government supply and demand credit. The exchange of credit between these groups occurs in the aggregate in the credit market. Facilitating the working of this market are financial institutions which act as intermediaries in the exchange process.

Figure 3 shows the exchanges that occur in the aggregate credit market.

Figure 3

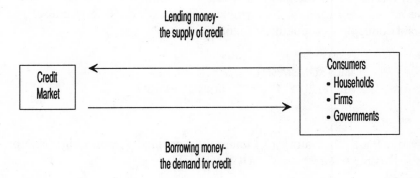

See also: CREDIT

CURRENT ASSET

Current assets include those economic resources of the entity that are in the form of cash and those that are reasonably expected to be sold, consumed, or converted into cash during the normal operating cycle of the business or within one year if the operating cycle is shorter than one year. The normal operating cycle of a business is the average time it takes to convert cash into inventory, sell the inventory, and collect the amount due that results from the sale. Typical items included among current assets include cash, temporary investments, accounts receivable, notes receivable, inventory, and prepaid expenses. In the balance sheet, current assets are usually listed in the order of their liquidity—that is, the ease and speed with which they could be converted into cash.

See also: ASSET
        CURRENT LIABILITY
        OPERATING CYCLE
        WORKING CAPITAL

CURRENT LIABILITY

A current liability is an obligation that must be discharged within the normal operating cycle of the business or within one year, whichever is longer. Current liabilities are normally expected to be paid using existing resources properly classified as current assets or by creating other current liabilities. Items commonly included in current liabilities include accounts payable, collections received in advance of delivery of goods or services, and other debts resulting from the normal operations of the enterprise. Current liabilities are usually listed on the balance sheet in the order of their liquidation date and are usually reported at the amount to be paid. Current liabilities are important in computing working capital which is the excess of current assets over current liabilities.

Current liabilities are commonly classified as either definitely determinable liabilities or estimated liabilities. Current liabilities that can be measured precisely are referred to as definitely determinable liabilities and include obligations that are established by contract or by statute. Estimated liabilities are definite obligations of the enterprise, the exact amount of which cannot be determined until a later date. Examples of estimated liabilities include product warranties, vacation pay, income taxes, and property taxes.

See also: CURRENT ASSET
                LIABILITIES
                OPERATING CYCLE
                WORKING CAPITAL

CURRENT VALUE ACCOUNTING

Current value (or cost) accounting is a procedure that attempts to measure the current values of assets, liabilities, and equities. The objective of current value accounting is to report the effects of specific price changes on the operating performance and financial position of the firm. It provides a measurement of current value as distinguished from historical acquisition cost. Current values can be measured in nominal dollars or in constant dollars (dollars adjusted for changes in the general purchasing power of the dollar).

Current costs can be expressed as:

1. *Current cost*—The current cost of an item is the amount of cash or equivalent that would be required on the date of the balance sheet to obtain the same items (an identical asset or one with equivalent productive capacity).

2. *Current exit value*—The current exit value of an item is the amount of cash which could be obtained on the date of the balance sheet by selling the asset, in its present condition, in an orderly liquidation.

3. *Expected exit value*—The expected exit value of an asset is the amount of cash or equivalent into which the asset is expected to be converted in the ordinary operations of the entity, less any expected costs related to completion and disposal. Expected exit value is also referred to as net realizable value.

4. *Present value*—The present value of an asset is the amount of discounted expected cash inflows less the discounted expected cash outflows relating to the item.

See also: COST ACCOUNTING

CURRENT YIELD

The current yield on a bond is its coupon interest payment divided by its closing market price. The current yield on bonds traded each day on the New York Stock Exchange is shown in the *Wall Street Journal*'s daily report of trading activity. The prices reported in the *Journal* reflect the price per $100 valuation. Thus in Exhibit C-11, the closing price of ARX Corporation bonds is reported as 112 and 1/2. If this bond has a par value of $1,000, it would sell for $1,125.

In the *Wall Street Journal* listing shown in Exhibit C-6, the current yield can be easily calculated by taking the listed closing price and dividing it by the coupon rate. For ARX bonds, the coupon rate is 9 and 3/8, so the current yield on this bond is calculated by taking (9 3/8)/(112 1/2), or 9.375/112.5. The current yield is 0.0833, or 8.3 percent. The *Journal* does not report the current yield on convertible bonds, so "cv" appears under the current yield column for ARX Corporation in Exhibit C–14.

Exhibit C–14

Corporation Bonds—Volume, $33,110,000

Bonds		Current Yield	Volume	High	Low	Close	Net Change
ARX	9⅜ O5	cv	8	112½	112½	112½ +	⅞
AlrbF	7½ 11	cv	1	121	121	121	- - -
AlaBn	6.7 s99 +	6.7	5	100⅛	100⅛	100⅛	- - -
AlaP	9¾s 04	9.8	6	100	100	100	- - -
AlaP	10⅞ 05	10.4	25	105	104¾	105 +	1½
AlaP	10½ 05	10.1	8	103½	103½	103½ +	½
AlaP	8¾07	9.5	10	91⅞	91⅞	91⅞ -	⅛
AlaP	8⅜07	8.7	7	100	100	100 -	3/18
AlaP	9¼07	9.8	10	94¾	94¾	94¾ -	⅜
AlaP	9⅜08	9.8	8	99¾	98⅛	98⅛ +	⅛
AlaP	12⅜10	11.9	58	106⅛	106	106⅛ +	⅛
AlskH	16¼99	14.6	50	111	111	111 +	⅞
AlskH	15¼92	14.1	1	108½	108½	108½	- - -
AlskH	11½93	11.1	25	104	104	104 -	¾
AlskH	12⅞93	12.3	10	105	105	105	- - -

For the Alabama Power Company bonds with a coupon rate of 9 and 3/4, the current yield is 9.55/100, or 9.75 percent. Note that the *Journal* reports the yield as 9.8 percent, which is the current yield rounded to the nearest one-tenth of a percent.

The current yield provides an investor with one measure of the return he/she can expect from his/her investment. But as a measure of return, it is generally considered to be inferior to "yield to maturity." If a bond is purchased by an investor at its par value, the current yield will equal its yield to maturity. This is because the yield on a bond purchased at par consists entirely of its current yield. If the bond is purchased at a price in the market that is different from its par value, its return to the investor will consist of its current yield plus a positive or negative capital gain on the redemption of principal at maturity. If the bond is purchased at a price below its par value, the current yield will be less than its yield to maturity. And if it is purchased at a premium, current yield will be above the yield to maturity.

See also: BOND

Dd

DATA

Data refers to factual information. Generally, data are in a numerical form, such as a series representing the annual rate of inflation since, say, 1950 or the rate of unemployment in selected U.S. cities. Data are usually categorized as time series data or cross-sectional data.

Time series data refer to information on a specific variable (for example, the annual rate of inflation) over a specified period of time. These time periods can be years, quarters, months, or the like. In financial research, it is common to study time series of daily stock and bond prices.

Cross-sectional data refer to information about an economic variable measured at one point in time, across observations. For example, managers may have information about a group of their customers in 1988. This sample of data refers to behavior across customers in one particular year. Information on voters' preferences at a selected point in the election is a cross-sectional set of data.

One useful source of economic and financial data is the *Statistical Abstract of the United States,* published annually by the U.S. Government Printing Office. This reference is available in most public libraries.

173

DEBENTURE

A debenture is an unsecured bond. Unlike a mortgage bond or other secured obligation, a debenture provides holders with no lien against specific property as security for the obligation in case of default. Holders of corporate debentures are general creditors of the corporation. Their claims are protected by income and assets not otherwise pledged as security against other debt obligations.

The decision of a firm to issue debentures depends upon both the general financial strength of the corporation and the nature of the business in which it is engaged. IBM Corporation, for example, has been so financially sound that it usually has issued debentures because investors simply did not require the additional security of specifically pledged assets. Debentures also are issued by companies in industries where physical capital is a small part of the overall production process. For example, large mail-order houses and commercial banks fall into this category.

Sometimes corporations will issue subordinated debentures. In such a case, the claims of the holders of the subordinated debentures are "inferior" to the claims of some other creditors of the firm. In the event of bankruptcy, the holders of the subordinated debentures will be paid off only after the claims of the senior debt-holders have been satisfied. Oftentimes debentures are subordinated to outstanding bank loans or other outstanding bonds.

See also: BOND

DECISION MAKING

One of the most important characteristics of a business executive is his or her ability to make appropriate decisions. A decision is an action. The result of a decision is that one course of action is taken instead of an alternative course. Decision making is essentially problem solving:

1. What is the problem or concern?

2. What are the alternatives?

3. Which alternative is preferable?

Major factors associated with decision making include:

1. Quantitative data

2. Analysis of quantitative data: systematic method(s) of organizing, summarizing, and analyzing facts.

Decision models are frequently used in making business decisions. Decision models provide some assurance that alternatives are evaluated logically as related to specific criteria and assumptions. Modeling is generally economical in terms of time and effort: it is readily understood by the decision maker and decision user, and it can be modified as circumstances dictate.

Probability can be used to measure the degree of the likelihood of a particular event occurring. Estimates of probability may be subjective, based on personal estimates of the decision maker, or objective, based on historical experience or logical processes. The decisions typically faced in the business world can be classified as:

1. Decisions under certainty (all facts are known); decisions under uncertainty (where the event that will occur—the state of nature) is now known with certainty but probabilities can be assigned to the possible occurrences (the process is stochastic). Decision making under uncertainty typically requires that judgments be made about future events to which outcomes are more likely than others (probability distribution about possible outcomes) and correlates this knowledge with the consequences associated with specific decisions.

2. Decisions where the opponent is nature, or a rational opponent.

3. Decisions by an individual or by a group.

When mathematical models are used to solve the decisions described in the preceding paragraph, the following general process can be used:

1. Establish the criterion to be used—the decision rule.

2. Select the model to use and the values of the parameters of the process.

3. Determine the decision which optimizes the criterion.

Decision rules under uncertainty where the decision maker must choose a course of action without knowing the probabilities for the occurrences of the various states of nature include:

1. *Maximin rule*—Maximize the minimum profit of the various alternatives or, if costs (losses) are involved, minimize the maximum cost.

2. *Maximax rule*—Maximize the maximum (where a large gain is considered attractive).

3. *Minimax regret rule*—Minimize the maximum regret.

Decision trees are useful for analyzing a series of decisions and for clarifying complex situations. Various stages of the decision-making process are shown graphically as separate branches of a decision tree. The decision maker would evaluate the expected payoffs at the far right side of the tree and work back (left) to a decision. This process provides the expected value of making a specific decision; this expected value can be used to work backward to evaluate the payoff from the initial decision. A partial decision tree is shown in Exhibit D-1.

Exhibit D-1
Decision Tree for a Project

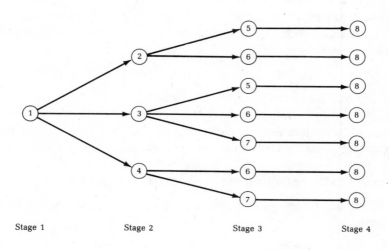

Stage 1   Stage 2   Stage 3   Stage 4

Errors in decision making typically are those which represent a mistake in logic in reasoning from premises to conclusions, or which involve the selection of the wrong variables or not enough variables.

General rules for noninvestment decisions where the flow of benefits and costs is even include:

Decision factors	Decision rule
Revenues only	Maximize revenue
Variable costs only	Minimize costs
Costs and benefits within relevant range and below capacity	Maximize contribution margin
Costs and benefits within relevant range and at capacity	Maximize unit contribution per unit of constraining factor

General rules for noninvestment decisions where the flow of benefits and costs is uneven:

1. Maximize the net present value of net after-tax benefits.

2. If there are no net benefits, minimize the net present value of after-tax costs.

Special approaches to business decision making discussed in this book include:

Situation	Reference entry
1. Cost-volume-profit relationships	Break-even analysis
2. Alternative course of action	Incremental cost analysis
	Opportunity cost analysis
3. Profitability	Contribution margin analysis
	Gross margin analysis
4. Investment analysis	Return on investment
5. Short-term planning and control	Budgeting
6. Long-term capital projects	Capital budgeting
7. Inventory order point	Inventory model

See also: BUDGETING
              CONTROL FUNCTION
              FORECASTING
              GOALS AND OBJECTIVES
              MANAGEMENT THEORIES
              ORGANIZATIONAL BEHAVIOR
              PERFORMANCE EVALUATION
              PLANNING FUNCTION
              PRICING POLICY

References:

Baker, Kenneth R., and Dean H. Kropp, *Management Science* (John Wiley & Sons, New York, 1985).

Buffa, Elwood S., *Modern Production/Operations Management* (John Wiley & Sons, New York, 1983).

DEFEASANCE

In addition to retirement at maturity or prior to maturity, debt can be extinguished by defeasance or by in-substance defeasance. Defeasance of debt refers to a release from the legal liability related to the debt. The debtor is legally released from being the primary obligor for the debt either by law or by the creditor. The debtor eliminates the liability from its statements and can recognize an extraordinary gain. For example, a parent company in an affiliation might agree to become the primary obligor for a debt of a subsidiary company.

In-substance defeasance is an arrangement whereby a company provides for the future repayment of one or more issues of its long-term debt by irrevocably placing with an independent trustee essentially risk-free securities to be used solely for satisfying the debt service requirements. The assets held in the trust must provide cash flows from interest and principal that are similar as to timing and amount to the scheduled interest and principal payments on the debt being extinguished. In most cases, the debtor is not legally released from being the primary obligor under the debt obligation. In periods when interest rates are relatively high, a company can service its debt profitably by purchasing and placing in an irrevocable trust U.S. Government securities at a cost less than the carrying amount of the debt. This procedure can result in an immediate gain for accounting purposes. For financial reporting purposes, the debt is removed from the balance sheet and an extraordinary gain is usually recognized in the income statement. For tax purposes, no gain or loss is currently recognized because no cancellation of debt occurs.

See also: LIABILITIES
   OFF-BALANCE SHEET ITEMS

Reference:

FASB, SFAS No. 76, "Early Extinguishment of Debt" (FASB, 1983).

DEFERRED CHARGE (CREDIT)

Deferred charges are long-term prepayment of expenses and include prepaid income taxes, bond issues costs, and organization costs. They represent prepaid costs which have a future benefit in the form of reduced future cash outflows for services. Deferred charges (delayed debits) are amortized over their expected economic lives but not to exceed forty years, usually by the straight-line method. Certain deferred charges represent a cost which is deferred from expense recognition because of income measurement rules, such as situations where the income tax liability exceeds accounting-based tax expense. Deferred credits refer to certain long-term liabilities (delayed credits) which will increase income in future accounting periods. Deferred credits include deferred income taxes resulting from the application of income measurement rules and collections received in advance of performing services on a long-term basis (prepaid revenue).

See also: ADJUSTING ENTRIES
   ASSETS
   LIABILITIES

DEFICIT

Retained earnings is the amount of undistributed earnings of a past period. An excess of dividends and losses over earnings results in a negative retained earned balance which is referred to as a deficit. The retained earnings account has a debit balance when a deficit exists.

See also: BUDGET DEFICIT
QUASI-REORGANIZATION
RETAINED EARNINGS

DEFINED BENEFIT PENSION PLANS

A defined benefit pension plan is one in which the benefits payable to the employee are determinable at any time. The plan specifies the benefits employees will receive upon retirement. The amounts usually depend on a formula that includes employee's earnings, years of employment, age, and other variables. The determination of periodic contributions to the plan is made by actuaries based on estimates of the variables.

A defined contribution plan is essentially a money purchase (pension) plan or arrangement, usually based on a formula, where the employer makes a cash contribution to eligible individual employee accounts according to the terms of the plan. Benefits received by an employee are dependent on the rate of return on the assets invested in the plan. The amount to be contributed annually by the employer is specified rather than the benefits to be paid.

The primary purpose of a pension plan's financial statements is to provide financial information that is useful in assessing the plan's present and future ability to pay benefits when due. The primary users of these statements are the plan's participants. The reporting focuses on the needs of plan participants, especially their need to evaluate the fund's ability to provide current and future benefits to employees. Information relating to the following matters is ordinarily considered necessary: fair value of plan investments, present value of estimated future pension benefits, and changes in asset values and the present value of future benefits during the year.

See also: PENSIONS

DEFLATE

A nominal value is deflated to a real value by dividing the nominal value by the relevant price index. To illustrate, economic activity, as measured by GNP, can increase for two reasons: more goods and services are being produced and sold each year, and the average price of these goods and services is increasing. The importance of deflating the nominal GNP series (converting it to a real series) is to remove the price change influence so as to isolate the changes in GNP due only to increased production and sales. Below are listed nominal values of GNP, the GNP deflator (1982=100), and values of real GNP for selected years. The nominal values are deflated by dividing by the GNP deflator (divided by 100).

Year	GNP ($ billions)	Deflator ÷100	Real GNP ($ billions)
1940	$ 100.4	0.130	$ 772.31
1950	288.3	0.239	1206.28
1960	513.3	0.309	1661.17
1970	1015.5	0.420	2417.86
1980	2732.0	0.857	3187.86
1985	4010.3	1.112	3606.38
1986	4235.0	1.141	3711.66
1987	4486.2	1.175	3818.04

Source: *Economic Report of the President*, 1988.

DELEGATION

The delegation of authority and responsibilities is an essential part of the organizing process. Delegation is the primary mechanism for establishing organizational relationships. Delegation assigns managerial and operational functions to specific individuals.

Organization authorities have identified various aspects of delegation:

1. assigning responsibilities;

2. granting authority commensurate with the assigned responsibilities, including making commitments, using resources, and performing similar managerial duties;

3. establishing an obligation for effective and efficient performance; and

4. providing for feedback and evaluation of performance.

See also: CENTRALIZATION VERSUS DECENTRALIZATION
MANAGEMENT THEORIES
ORGANIZATIONAL BEHAVIOR

Reference:

Daft, Richard L., *Organization Theory and Design* (West, St. Paul, Minn., 1983).

DEMAND FOR MONEY

Individuals hold money (currency or non-interest checking accounts) in response to the opportunity cost of investing it elsewhere. The interest rate on alternative forms of savings deposits and IOUs represents the opportunity cost of holding money. As the interest rate increases, the quantity of money demanded to be held will decrease. The interest rate represents a price of holding money because it represents the amount that an individual "pays" or foregoes to hold money as opposed to invest it.

The two reasons that individuals demand to hold money is for transaction purposes (although the wide acceptance of credit cards is reducing this need) and for precautionary purposes (although the availability of automatic teller machines is reducing this need, too).

Graphically, an individual's demand for money is illustrated by the downward sloping demand for money curve, shown in Figure 4 on the following page. The quantity of money demanded is inversely related to the price of holding money; the interest rate.

See also: MONEY MARKET

DEMAND MANAGEMENT POLICY

Macroeconomic policies that affect economic activity by changing the aggregate demand for goods and services are called demand management policies. In other words, the government attempts to "manage" aggregate demand. With reference to the aggregate supply and demand model shown in Figure 5 on the following page, demand management policies are intended to shift aggregate demand, AgD, to the right or to the left. A rightward shift will expand the economy: the expansion is accompanied by

Figure 4

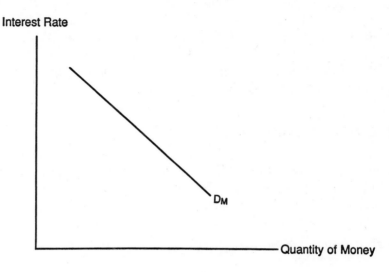

Figure 5

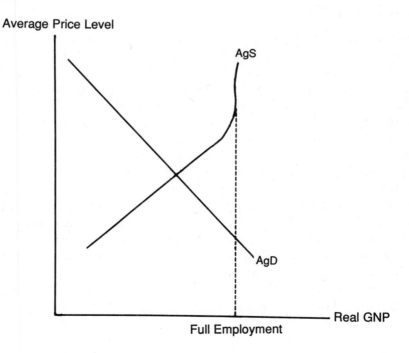

a rising price level. A leftward shift will contract the economy: the contraction is accompanied by a falling price level.

Aggregate demand (Y) is composed of four expenditure categories: consumption (C), investment (I), government purchases (G), and net exports (NX): (Y = C + I + G + NX). A policy designed to change at least one of these expenditure categories will impact on aggregate demand and is a demand management policy.

DEMAND-PULL INFLATION

Inflation is a continuous increase in the average price level. One explanation for inflation is that increases in demand pull prices upward, thus creating inflationary pressures in the economy. When an economy is near full employment, increases in demand cannot be met and hence prices must increase as consumers bid for the limited products.

See also: COST-PUSH INFLATION
INFLATION

DEPRECIATION

Depreciation is the accounting process of allocating in a systematic and rational manner the cost or other basic value of a tangible, long-lived asset or group of assets, less salvage value, if any, over the estimated useful life of the asset(s). Systematic means methodical or with design and regularity. Rational means that the depreciation method used should relate to the expected benefits to be obtained from the asset being depreciated. Depreciation can also be conceptualized as the expiration of service potential of an asset. Depreciation is a process of allocation, not of valuation. Recording depreciation is not an attempt to determine the market value of an asset at a balance sheet date.

Depreciation expense for an accounting period is the portion of the total cost of an asset that is allocated to that period. Depreciation charges are noncash expenses that reduce net income. The depreciation allowance is not a cash fund accumulated to cover the replacement cost of an asset. The accounting entry that records depreciation does not of itself accumulate any cash. A typical accounting entry made at the end of an accounting period to record depreciation expense for the period is shown here:

| Depreciation Expense | 50,000 | |
| Accumulated Depreciation—Equipment | | 50,000 |

Depreciation expense is reported on the income statement. The accumulated depreciation account is a contra asset account and is deducted from the related asset—equipment in the illustration.

In making a determination of the amount of depreciation to be taken in an accounting period, three factors are considered: acquisition cost, salvage value, and useful life. The estimated useful life of an asset is related to both physical and functional factors:

1. *Physical factors*—Decay and deterioration from wear and tear of use, passage of time, and other factors which affect the physical life of the asset.

2. *Functional (or economic) factors*—Obsolescence arising from technological improvements, inadequacy of the asset for its intended purpose(s) or ecological and energy-saving considerations.

The useful life of an asset may be expressed in terms of

1. time (for example, a certain number of years);
2. operating periods (for example, a certain number of working hours); or
3. units of output (for example, a certain number of items).

Various methods of computing depreciation are available. Major methods of depreciation currently in use include the following:

1. *Straight-line depreciation*—Under straight-line depreciation, the cost, less salvage value, of the asset is spread in equal periodic amounts over its estimated useful life.

2. *Accelerated depreciation*—Accelerated depreciation methods recognize relatively larger amounts of depreciation in the earlier years of the asset's useful life and smaller amounts in later years. Two such methods are the declining-balance method and the sum-of-the-years'-digits method. Declining-balance depreciation is computed by

applying a constant rate (generally a rate double the straight-line rate) to the remaining undepreciated balance. When the sum-of-the-years' depreciation method is used, the sum of the total years of life of the asset is used as a denominator of a fraction of the depreciable base (cost of the asset less estimated salvage value). The numerator is always the remaining years of life. For example, assume that an asset acquired for $900 has a three-year life and no salvage value. Depreciation would be computed as follows for the three years:

Year 1:	3/6 × $900	=	$450
Year 2:	2/6 × $900	=	300
Year 3:	1/6 × $ 90	=	150
Total			$900

3. *Unit-of-production method*—The useful life of certain assets, such as machinery, can be estimated in terms of units produced or hours of operations rather than years. Depreciation would be computed as the ratio of the actual number of units produced or hours operated during the period to the total number of units or hours in the estimated useful life of the asset.

The various depreciation methods are illustrated in Exhibit D-2 using the following information concerning a machine acquired at the beginning of the company's fiscal year:

Cost of equipment	$1,100
Salvage value	100
Estimated useful life	
Years	5
Working hours	500
Units of production	1,000
Hours worked this period	75
Units of production this period	300

Exhibit D-2
Depreciation Methods Illustrated

1. *Straight-line depreciation:*

$$\text{Depreciation} = \frac{\text{Cost} - \text{Salvage value}}{\text{Estimated number of years of service life}}$$

$$= \frac{\$1,100 - 100}{5}$$

$$= \$200$$

2. *Rate per working hour:*

$$\text{Depreciation rate} = \frac{\text{Cost} - \text{Salvage value}}{\text{Estimated life of asset in working hours}}$$

$$= \frac{\$1,100 - \$100}{500 \text{ working hours}}$$

$$= \$2 \text{ per hour}$$

$$\text{Depreciation expense} = 75 \text{ hours} \times \$2$$

$$= \$150$$

3. *Unit-of-production method (activity-based method)*

$$\text{Depreciation rate} = \frac{\text{Cost} - \text{Salvage value}}{\text{Estimated units of production during life}}$$

$$= \frac{\$1,100 - \$100}{1,000 \text{ widgets produced}}$$

$$= \$1 \text{ per widget produced.}$$

$$\text{Depreciation expense} = 300 \text{ widgets produced} \times \$1$$

$$= \$300$$

4. *Double-declining-balance method (An accelerated method):*

$$\text{Depreciation rate} = (\text{Straight-line rate}) \times 2$$

$$= (100\%/\text{life in year}) \times 2$$

$$= (1/5 = 20\%) \times 2$$

$$= 40\% \text{ per year of carrying value}$$

Year	Computation	Annual Depreciation	Accumulated Depreciation	Carrying Value
1	40% × $1,000	$400	$400	$600
2	40% × 600	240	640	360
3	40% × 360	144	784	216
4	40% × 216	86*	870	130
5	40% × 130 = $52	80†	950	50

*Rounded to nearest dollar.
†In the last year of the estimated life of the asset, the annual depreciation charge is adjusted to the amount needed to bring the carrying value of the asset to its salvage value.

The inventory (or appraisal) method of depreciation is sometimes used. Under this method, the company takes a physical inventory of its tangible, long-lived assets at the end of the period and assigns a value to them. The difference between the book value of the assets at the beginning of the year and the assigned value at the end of the year represents depreciation expense for the period, after allowing for acquisitions and disposals during the period.

Retirement and replacement depreciation methods are also sometimes used to record depreciation. Under the retirement method, the company records depreciation expense only when the asset is retired from use; the cost of the retired asset is recognized as depreciation expense for the year that the asset is retired. Under the replacement method, the acquisition cost of the replacement asset, net of any salvage proceeds from the asset being replaced, represents depreciation expense in the year of replacement.

Companies frequently account for depreciation on a composite or group basis. The composite method of depreciation applies depreciation to a collection if dissimilar assets; the group method applies depreciation to a collection of similar assets. These two methods are illustrated in Exhibit D-3 on the following page. Procedures for applying the two methods are identical, with depreciation expense being computed by applying the average depreciation rate times the balance in the group asset account at the beginning of the year.

The Economy Recovery Tax Act (ERTA) of 1981 provided for the use of a new method of computing depreciation for tax purposes called the accelerated cost recovery system (ACRS). The new depreciation rules were developed to simplify the computation of depreciation and to provide for a more rapid recovery of asset costs to offset depreciation and stimulate investment in the economy. ACRS requires that certain property provided after December 31, 1980, be depreciated over three, five, ten, or fifteen years, depending on the type of property. Cost recovery tables for each class of property specify the percentage of cost recovery for each year.

See also: AMORTIZATION
            PROPERTY, PLANT, AND EQUIPMENT

Reference:

Lamden, Charles W., et al., "Accounting for Depreciable Assets" (AICPA, 1975).

Exhibit D-3
Group Depreciation Illustrated

Asset	Cost	Estimated Salvage Value	Depreciable Cost	Estimated Useful Life (in years)	Annual Straight-Line Depreciation
1	$10,000	$ 0	$10,000	10	$1,000
2	5,500	500	5,000	2½	2,000
3	2,200	200	2,000	5	400
	$17,700	$700	$17,000		$3,400

$$\text{Average life} = \frac{\text{Depreciable cost}}{\text{Annual depreciation}} = \frac{\$17,000}{\$3,400/\text{year}} = 5 \text{ years.}$$

The annual rate of depreciation (rounded value) is computed as follows:

$$\text{Annual rate} = \frac{\text{Annual depreciation}}{\text{Total cost}} = \frac{\$3,400/\text{year}}{\$17,700/\text{year}} = 19.21\% \text{ per year.}$$

Depreciation per year at the average rate of 19.21% (rounded) applied to total cost of $17,700 is $3,400 (rounded).

DEVALUATION

Devaluation is an official reduction in the value of a nation's currency. Under the Bretton Woods system of fixed exchange rates, a currency could be devalued if there was a long-term persistent excess supply of the currency in the foreign exchange market. Temporary situations of excess supply might be handled by a county's central bank if it had sufficient foreign exchange reserves or borrowing capacity at the International Monetary Fund. But long-term excess supply could usually only be managed by devaluation or the imposition of foreign exchange controls.

Because devaluation is a decline in the official value of a currency, it is usually applied only under a system of fixed exchange rates where currency values are officially set by central banks. In contrast, the term depreciation is used to denote a market-driven reduction in the price of a nation's currency that takes place under a system of flexible exchange rates in response to the forces of demand and supply.

Whether the decline in value is termed a devaluation or a depreciation, its effects are the same. For residents of the country sustaining a
currency devaluation, the prices of foreign goods and foreign travel rise
relative to domestically produced goods and domestic travel. Foreigners
are able to purchase the country's exported goods at lower relative prices,
while domestic residents must pay higher relative prices for imports.

The changes in relative prices brought on by devaluation usually will
affect a country's balance of trade, resulting in higher exports and lower
imports. But there may be substantial lags in the process. A devaluation
results in immediate changes in relative prices, but the quantity of exports
and imports responds more slowly, because it takes time for purchasing
and production patterns to change. During the adjustment process,
countries often find that their balance of payments situation actually
deteriorates immediately following devaluation. Improvement may take
months or years, and in the interim currency reserves may continue to fall
and borrowings from the IMF may have to rise.

The length of the adjustment period depends on how domestic and
foreign producers choose to respond. If domestic producers use the rise in
the cost of imported products as an excuse to raise prices, domestic inflation may be stimulated and the nation's trade balance may show little or
no improvement. Likewise, if foreign producers absorb much of the price
increase in lowered profit margins, the devaluation may not create much of
a price advantage for domestic producers and their market shares will
show little improvement.

Often, a substantial devaluation will create social and political distur-
bances because of the differential impacts of the currency realignment
across producers, consumers, and other wealth holders in the economy.
Large capital movements may take place in expectation of devaluation or
in its wake, and these movements may force further change. Labor may
suffer because devaluation raises the cost of imported products while gains
in domestic production and employment appear only with substantial lags.

If devaluation is brought on by domestic inflation, it may do little to
restore balance of payments equilibrium and may actually stimulate the
pace of inflation unless it is part of a general anti-inflation policy. To be
effective, a devaluation must be accompanied by domestic monetary and
fiscal policies designed to slow the inflationary process.

DEVELOPMENT STAGE COMPANIES

An enterprise is a development stage company if substantially all of its efforts are devoted to establishing a new business and either of the following is present:

1. principal operations have not begun, or
2. principal operations have begun but revenue produced is insignificant.

Activities of a development stage enterprise frequently include financial planning, raising capital, research and development, personnel recruiting and training, and market development.

A development stage enterprise must follow generally accepted accounting principles applicable to operating enterprises in the preparation of its financial statements. In its balance sheet, the company must report cumulative net losses separately in the equity section. In its income statement it must report cumulative revenues and expenses from the inception of the enterprise. In its statement of cashflows, it must report cumulative sources and uses of cash from the inception of the enterprise. Its statement of stockholders' equity should include the number of shares issued and the date of their issuance as well as the dollar amounts received for its shares from the date of inception. Notes to the financial statements should identify the entity as a development stage enterprise and describe the nature of development stage activities. During the first period of normal operations, the enterprise must disclose in notes to the financial statements that the enterprise was, but is no longer, in the development stage.

See also: ACCOUNTING PRINCIPLES

Reference:

SFAS No. 7, "Accounting and Reporting by Development Stage Companies" (FASB, 1975).

DIRECT COSTING AND ABSORPTION COSTING

Direct (or variable) costing and absorption costing are two approaches to product costing. With direct costing, ending inventory includes only variable production costs, such as direct materials, direct labor, and variable manufacturing overhead. Fixed overhead costs, that do not change with changes in production levels (such as rent, insurance), are expensed when incurred. With absorption costing, the cost of inventory includes both variable and fixed factory overhead costs. Variable costing is frequently used for decision-making purposes but is not generally accepted for external financial reporting. The differences between the two methods are due entirely to the treatment of fixed factory overhead. To illustrate the difference between direct and absorption costing, assume the following data. A company that manufactures radios incurred the following costs for the year: raw material costs, $100,000; direct labor costs, $200,000; variable factory overhead, $50,000; fixed factory overhead, $25,000. There was no beginning or ending work in process inventories.

	Direct Costing	Absorption Costing
Direct materials	$100,000	$100,000
Direct labor	200,000	200,000
Variable factory overhead	50,000	50,000
Fixed factory overhead	————	25,000
Ending finished goods inventory	$350,000	$375,000

When production exceeds sales, absorption costing will cause net income to exceed net income under direct costing because some fixed overhead costs are deferred in inventory rather than being written off as a period cost. When sales exceed production, the opposite effects on net income occur because some previously deferred fixed factory costs are included with current fixed overhead costs in cost of goods sold.

Direct costing is useful for controlling current costs, and profit planning (sales promotions; special pricing; make or buy decisions). When direct costing is used, periodic net income varies directly with sales volume since variable costs are proportional to sales. When absorption costing is used, the volume/profit relationship becomes more difficult to estimate since fixed costs are a component of inventory.

See also: COST
             INVENTORY

Reference:

Morse, Wayne J., *Cost Accounting* (Addison-Wesley, Reading, Mass., 1978).

DIRECTING

Directing is a management function that involves guiding and supervising subordinates in order to achieve goals and objectives of the enterprise. Directing can be justified in relation to what an organization does (its purpose), what it accomplishes (results), how it accomplishes what it does, and why it does what it does (motivation).

The basic ingredients of directing are motivation and leadership. Content and process theories of motivating people have been suggested. Content theories describe the needs that motivate people: incentive payments, human relations (group approval and personal satisfaction), the hierarchy of needs (physiological, security, social, ego needs, and self-actualization, and Theory X and Theory Y. Process theories of motivation describe how needs motivate people. Process theories generally fall into one of three groups:

1. *Expectancy theory*—The expectation that effort will be rewarded;

2. *Equity theory*—How outcomes measure up against inputs; or

3. *Positive reinforcement*—Behavior is the result of conditioning.

See also: CONTROL FUNCTION
             LEADERSHIP FUNCTION
             MOTIVATION
             PERFORMANCE EVALUATION
             PLANNING FUNCTION

Reference:

Fallon, William K., ed., *AMA Management Handbook* (AMACOM, New York, 1983).

DISCONTINUED OPERATIONS

Discontinued operations are those operations of an enterprise that have been sold, abandoned, or otherwise disposed of. The results of continued operations must be reported separately in the income statement from discontinued operations and any gain or loss from disposal of a segment must be reported along with the operating results of the discontinued segment. A segment of a business is a component of an entity whose activities represent a separate major line of business or class of customer. A segment may be a subsidiary, a division, or a department if its assets, results of operations, and activities can be distinguished physically and operationally, and for financial reporting purposes, from those of the entity.

The presentation of discontinued operations should be reported as follows:

Income from continuing operations before taxes		$500,000
Provision for income taxes		150,000
Income from continuing operations		350,000
Discontinued operations:		
Income from operations of		
discontinued division		
(less applicable income taxes of $50,000)	$200,000	
Loss on disposal of Division	(350,000)	150,000
Net income		$200,000

See also: INCOME STATEMENT

Reference:

APB No. 30, Reporting the Results of Operations (APB, 1973).

DISCOUNT

Discounts from the list price of goods can be classified as trade discounts and cash discounts. A cash discount is the amount allowed as a deduction from the selling price if payment is made within a specific time period. Cash discounts are used as incentives for prompt payment. Credit terms of 2/10, n/30, means that a 2 percent discount is allowed on the invoice price if the account is paid within 10 days. In any event, the account is due within 30 days. Failure to take advantage of the discount means that the customer is paying approximately 36 percent interest for the extra 20 days available under the credit terms.

A trade discount is a reduction from list price that is offered to purchasers who fit into certain categories—for example, wholesalers and retailers. The gross purchase price is the price after any applicable trade discount but before any cash discount. For example, suppose that merchandise with a list price of $1,000 is purchased at $1,000 less trade discounts of 30% and 10% and a cash discount of 2%. In this case, the gross and net purchase prices are computed as follows:

$1,000 less 30% = $700
700 less 10% = $630, the gross purchase price
630 less 2% = $617.40, the net purchase price

See also: PRICING POLICY: DISCOUNTS

DISCOUNTED CASH FLOW

The discounted cash flow technique is a tool used in evaluating investment decisions. When this method is used, expected future cash inflows and outflows associated with the investment are discounted to the present time, using a minimum discounting rate acceptable to management. The net present value is the difference between the present value of the cost of the investment and the present value of the cash inflow expected from the investment. If the net present value of the cash flows is positive (cash inflows exceed cash outflows), the investment is acceptable.

To illustrate the discounted cash flow method, assume that management is considering the purchase of a new machine for $11,000. The machine has an expected life of five years and a scrap value of $1,000 at the end of its life. Management assumes a minimum desired rate of return of 10 percent on the investment. The new machine will create cost savings of $4,000 per year for the next five years; the cost savings are realized at the end of each year. Exhibit D-4 shows a worksheet used to solve this problem. Dollar amounts of cash inflows and outflows are recorded in the columns for the appropriate period. Cash outflows are recorded as negative amounts. Cash savings are considered cash inflows. Present-value discounting factors are determined from present-value tables and entered in the appropriate column. Note that the cash operating savings can be treated as an annuity. Present values of each item are computed and entered in the last column. These values are totaled to determine the net present value of the investment.

Exhibit D-4
Discounted Cash Flow Procedures

	Cash flows at end of period						Discount factor	Total present value
	0	**1**	**2**	**3**	**4**	**5**		
Initial cost	$(11,000)						1.0000	$(11,000)
Cash operating savings		$4,000	$4,000	$4,000	$4,000	$4,000	3.2741	13,096
Disposal value						1,000	.4761	476
Net present value								$ 2,572

The initial cash outflow for purchase of the machine is not discounted because it is made at the beginning of the first period. The cash inflows due to operating savings are discounted as a $4,000 annuity for five years at a 10 percent discount rate. The disposal value is discounted as a sum of $1,000 to be received five years in the future at 10 percent discount rate. Because the net present value of the investment is positive (cash inflows exceed cash outflows), the investment is considered desirable.

See also: ANNUITY
              COST OF CAPITAL
              PRESENT VALUE

DISCOUNT RATE

The discount rate is the rate of interest charged by the Federal Reserve on discount loans and advances made through the discount window to depository institutions. The discount rate is established by the Boards of Directors of the 12 regional Federal Reserve Banks (Fed), subject to review and final determination by the Board of Governors.

The spread between the discount rate and the federal funds rate affects the incentive of depository institutions to borrow from the Fed through the discount window. When the Fed sets the discount rate above the federal funds rate, there is little incentive for institutions to borrow from the discount window except in emergencies. But when the discount rate is set below the funds rate, the incentive of institutions to borrow is substantially increased. Since the 1960s, the discount rate has more often than not been set below the funds rate.

The discount rate is a major tool of monetary policy. By changing the discount rate the Fed can affect the volume of loans made to banking institutions through the discount window, and thus the monetary base and the supply of money. A rise in the discount rate tends to discourage discount loans and thereby reduces the monetary base and decreases the money supply, while a reduction in the discount rate encourages discount loans, increasing the monetary base and expanding the supply of money.

Since the discount rate is set by the Fed, changes in the discount rate serve as an important signal of the Fed's intentions about future monetary policy. For example, if the Fed decided to slow the economy by raising interest rates, it can signal its intentions by raising the discount rate. The announcement effect of Fed intentions signaled by a rise in the discount rate may itself be an important force in slowing the economy, causing businesses and consumers to rein in their spending plans in anticipation of an economic slowdown brought about by the change in Fed policy.

Federal Reserve policy in setting the discount rate relative to the rate on federal funds also has been debated. Several arguments have been advanced in favor of setting the rate at or above the federal funds rate. Some economists have suggested that such a policy would allow the Fed to ensure that discount loans are extended only to those institutions placing a high value on such credit and that the facilities of the discount window would be used in emergencies. Such a policy also would remove the current need for the Fed to police the use of discount credit through administrative rules about what is and what is not appropriate use of such credit. Finally, it has been suggested that such a change would simplify the mechanics of monetary policy by reducing the volume of borrowed reserves to an insignificant level. Thus open market operations could concentrate on setting the level of total reserves and need not be concerned about separate policy instruments to affect the magnitude of borrowed and nonborrowed reserves.

See also: FEDERAL RESERVE SYSTEM

Reference:

Mengle, David L., "The Discount Window," *Economic Review,* Federal Reserve Bank of Richmond (May/June 1986), pp. 2-10.

DISCRIMINATION

In economics, discrimination refers to equivalent inputs (for example, labor) receiving different compensation (for example, salary, benefits, working conditions, etc.) when the contribution of the inputs is equal. Examples of such discrimination may be unequal pay between whites and nonwhites or between males and females when the inputs are equivalent and the output is equivalent. It is not discriminatory for there to be differences in pay, say, when there are differences in experience, schooling, or other training.

References:

Becker, Gary, *The Economics of Discrimination* (University of Chicago Press, Chicago, 1971).

DISTRIBUTION COST CONTROL

The marketing function includes all activities involved in the flow of goods from the point of production to consumption. Distribution or marketing costs include such costs as promotion, advertising, transportation, insurance of goods transported, selling expenses, and others. A company attempts to control marketing costs to increase profits, to better control marketing costs, and to justify a company's actions before regulatory bodies which are concerned with marketing policies.

Cost control tools available for controlling marketing operations are usually budgets and standards. Cost controls measure the actual performance of a function against a predetermined standard and investigate any differences between actual performance and standard performance. Cost analysis refers to searching for better ways of performing marketing tasks.

Marketing costs are usually classified as order-getting and order-filling costs. Order-getting costs are costs incurred by direct selling, advertising, and sales promotion functions for the purpose of persuading customers to purchase a product or service. Order-filling costs are marketing costs incurred to perform the sale and include such costs as handling, transportation, and credit and collection functions. Order-filling costs are usually repetitive in contrast with order-getting costs. Order-filling costs tend to vary with sales volume (for example, warehousing costs normally increase as the number of shipments increase).

Most enterprises keep accounting records which express costs by nature or object of expenditure (for example, wages, rent, insurance) for product line, territory, customers, distribution channel. This classification is sometimes referred to as the natural expense classification which describes the kind of service the company obtained for the expenditures. For analysis purposes, the natural expense item must be distributed to functions, such as credit and collections, transportation, or sales promotion. Certain of these costs are directly related to the function and require no allocation. Other costs are indirect costs which must be distributed to the functions on some rational basis. This requires the allocation of costs to functional areas.

To allocate marketing costs to functions, the factor which causes the marketing costs to vary must be identified. Whatever unit of variability is adopted, the results should be reasonably accurate and economical in application. For example, unit costs for advertising and sales promotion can be determined by using the following units of variability:

Function	Unit of Variability
Direct media costs:	
Newspaper	Newspaper inches or gross sales
Radio and television	Minute of radio/television time
Direct mail	Number of items mailed
Sales distributed	Number of samples distributed

Total sales promotion	Sales transactions or units sold
Personnel expense	Number of employees
Filing	Number of units filed
Credit investigation	Credit sales transactions
Mail handling	Number of pieces

If variance analysis is to be used, the variance between actual and standard costs should be explained in terms of price and efficiency variances. These variances are computed as:

Price variance = (Standard price – Actual price) × Actual work units
Efficiency, or quantity, variance = (Budgeted work units – Actual work units) × Standard price

Marketing costs are usually budgeted on the basis of:

1. A given amount which is thought adequate to meet expected demand for service;

2. Percentage of expected unit sales;

3. A variable (flexible) budget is used based on a fixed amount per period plus a variable amount per unit sold; or

4. Standard costs multiplied by estimated number of measures.

Short-term profit measures of marketing performance include:

1. budgeted sales and gross margin versus actual,

2. marginal contribution analytical techniques,

3. sales (dollars or physical units),

4. return on assets, and

5. net income.

General administrative costs are incurred to facilitate both the production and marketing functions. Such costs include management salaries, financial accounting, clerical costs, rent, legal fees, telephone, and other costs. General and administrative costs can usually be controlled through budgeting and standards in a manner similar to that demonstrated for marketing costs.

See also: ALLOCATION
BUDGET
CONTROL FUNCTION
COST
EFFECTIVENESS
EFFICIENCY
PLANNING FUNCTION
VARIANCE

DIVIDENDS

A dividend is a distribution of cash, other assets, liabilities, or a company's own stock to stockholders in proportion to the number of shares owned. The distribution is usually generated from earnings of the corporation. The board of directors of a corporation is responsible for determining dividend policy including the amount, timing, and type of dividends to be declared. The dividend policy usually takes into consideration applicable state legislation concerning dividends, the impact on legal capital, contractual restrictions, the financial feasibility of the dividends, and the needs of shareholders.

The types of dividends can be classified as:

1. Dividends that decrease total stockholders' equity:

   a. Cash dividends

   b. Property dividends

   c. Script dividends

2. Dividends not affecting total stockholders' equity:

   a. Dividends decreasing retained earnings and increasing contributed capital (stock dividends)

   b. "Dividends" not affecting any stockholders' equity account (stock splits in the form of a dividend)

A cash dividend is one in which cash is used as the method of paying the dividend. A property dividend is a dividend that is paid in noncash assets of the corporation. Such dividends could include distributions of stocks, bonds, inventory, or other assets. A liability dividend is a dividend in which the corporation distributes promissory notes to its stockholders. The notes are to be redeemed at a future date and generally pay interest. A stock dividend is the issuance by a corporation of its own shares of common stock to its common stockholders without consideration.

Corporations sometimes issue stock dividends when they want to make a distribution to their stockholders but either do not want to distribute assets or do not have enough assets to distribute. Stock dividends have also been used to reduce the market value of a corporation's stock, thereby making it available to a larger number of potential investors and hopefully increasing the demand for the stock. In other cases, tax considerations have prompted the issuance of stock dividends. When a corporation distributes a stock dividend, each stockholder receives additional whole shares, fractional shares, or fractional share warrants of a corporation's stock in proportion to the stockholder's holding of that stock. The net assets of the corporation are not affected by a stock dividend, and each stockholder's total interest in the corporation is unchanged. Each stockholder owns a larger number of shares, but the total book value of the shares remains the same after the dividend as before the dividend.

Occasionally, corporate dividends reflect a distribution from capital rather than retained earnings. Such dividends are commonly referred to as liquidating dividends if they represent a return of contributed capital to investors. In the extractive industries, some firms distribute regular dividends equal to accumulated income and liquidating dividends equal to the depletion allowance. This practice is used when there are no plans to replace the natural resource and operations will cease upon their exhaustion.

Constructive dividends are a taxable benefit derived by a shareholder from a corporation although such benefit was not designated as a dividend. Constructive dividends could include unreasonable compensation, excessive rent payments, shareholder use of corporate property, and bargain purchases of corporate property.

Except for stock dividends, dividends become a liability of the corporation when they are declared by the board of directors. Most state laws specify that dividends can be distributed only to the extent of a credit balance in the retained earnings account. A few states permit dividends up to the amount of net income for previous years even though the retained earnings account may have a deficit. Some states permit dividends from retained earnings and contributed capital to the extent that it does not impair legal capital (which is often the par or stated value of the issued stock). Undeclared dividends on cumulative preferred stock are not recognized as liabilities since there is no legal obligation on the part of the corporation to pay such dividends. Undeclared dividends are referred to as dividends in arrears.

The date of declaration is the date the directors declare a dividend. The date of record is a date the board establishes to whom the dividend will be paid on the payment date. Stockholders who purchased shares in the market before the ex-dividend date (usually four trading days before the date of record) receive the dividend regardless of whether they own the shares at the declaration or payment dates. Generally, the market price of the shares traded between the declaration date and the ex-dividend date will increase by the amount of the dividend. From the declaration date to the ex-dividend date, the shares trade "dividends on." After the ex-dividend date, the shares sell "ex-dividends" and the person who purchases the shares after this date will not receive the dividend.

The dividend yield is a ratio of dividends declared for the year divided by market price of the stock as of a specific time.

See also: CAPITAL STOCK
CORPORATION
PREFERRED STOCK
STOCK DIVIDENDS
STOCK SPLIT

DIVISION OF LABOR

The origin of the belief that there are efficiency gains in production from specialization of labor stems from the writings of Adam Smith. He arrived at this conclusion based on his observations of the production activities of a pin factory. As he wrote in *The Wealth of Nations*, "The division of labor, however, so far as it can be introduced, occasions, in every art, a proportionable increase of the productive powers of labor." According to Smith, there are three advantages associated with the division of labor: an "increase of dexterity in every particular workman," a "savings of the time which is commonly lost in passing from one species of work to another," and to the invention of machines which "enables one man to do the work of many."

DOUBLE-ENTRY SYSTEM

The double-entry system of accounting requires that for each transaction or event recorded, the total dollar amount of the debits entered in all the related accounts must be equal to the total dollar amount of the credits. For example, a journal entry recorded in a double-entry system would take the following form:

Equipment (debit)	10,000	
Cash (credit)		8,000
Notes Payable (credit)		2,000

    To record the acquisition of equipment
equipment with cash and a note payable.

Note the dollar equality of debits and credits. Double-entry accounting also maintains the following equality:

Total dollar amount assigned	=	Total dollar amount assigned
to assets		to liabilities and equities

A single-entry accounting system makes only a record or memorandum entry of a transaction and does not record the double entry or dual effect of each transaction. Single-entry accounting does not involve equal debits and credits. On the balance sheet, owners' equity is calculated as the excess of total assets over total liabilities. The single-entry system does not provide for the simultaneous determination of net income and the ending balances of assets and liabilities. In order to get the customary financial statements, single-entry transactions have to be analyzed as to their dual effects on other accounts. A single-entry accounting entry to record the purchase of the equipment illustrated above could assume this form:

Equipment was purchased for $8,000 cash and a $2,000 note payable.

See also: ACCOUNT
                JOURNAL

Reference:

Sterling, Robert R., *An Explication and Analysis of the Structure of Accounting—Part One* (School of Business, University of Kansas, Lawrence, Kansas, 1971).

DOUBLE TAXATION

Corporations are owned by investors. The return that investors receive is related to the profitability of the corporation. In general, the more profitable the corporation, the higher the dividend payments and the greater the worth of the company. However, the profits of corporations are taxed. Now, the highest tax rate on corporate net earnings is 34 percent. Add to that state taxes, and less than 60 percent of corporate earnings are available for distribution to owners. The dividends that are paid by the corporation to owners are also taxed at the individual investor's marginal tax rate. Therefore, there is a double taxation of owner's earnings: one tax at the corporate level and one tax at the individual level.

The implication of double taxation is that corporations will not become involved in certain types of activities that may be profitable owing to the fact that the required return will be higher for them than for a proprietorship. However, because of this, investors are protected on the down side from marginal investments that a firm may otherwise make.

DUOPOLY

A duopoly is a market structure in which there are only two firms. Although not observed with any degree of regularity in the real world, this construct is useful in economic theory for illustrating the principles of gaming and competitive behavior.

DUMPING

Dumping refers to a country selling a product in a foreign market at a price below that which it charges in its home market. Often, the price in the foreign market is near or below the cost of production. The Japanese have been accused of this behavior with respect to semiconductors.

Opponents of dumping in the country receiving the lower priced goods are generally associated with the competing domestic industry. The strategy of dumping is to flood a market with low cost products to prevent the domestic industries from gaining a competitive position. If the domestic industry can not successfully compete in its own home market, it is believed that it will not be able to grow and compete internationally.

Ee

EARNINGS PER SHARE

Earnings per share of stock is one of the most significant ratios in financial management and investment analysis. If the capital structure of a corporation contains only common stock, earnings per share is computed as follows:

$$\text{Earnings per common share} = \frac{\text{Net income}}{\substack{\text{Weighted number of} \\ \text{common shares outstanding}}}$$

If the capital structure contains common stock and nonconvertible, cumulative preferred stock or noncumulative preferred stock on which the dividends have been paid, the earnings per share is computed as follows:

$$\text{Earnings per common share} = \frac{\text{Net income} - \text{Preferred stock dividends}}{\substack{\text{Weighted number of} \\ \text{common shares outstanding}}}$$

The weighted average number of shares outstanding in the denominator is equal to the number of common shares outstanding at the end of the accounting period if no shares have been issued or reacquired during the year. If shares have been issued or reacquired, a weighted average of these shares must be calculated. For example, if 10,000 shares were issued on July 1, these shares would be included in the denominator as 5,000 shares.

Corporations issue a variety of securities that can be converted into common stock—for example, convertible bonds and convertible preferred stock. Stock options and warrants are other securities that can be converted into common stock under specified conditions. If these common stock equivalents were converted, they would increase the number of shares of common stock outstanding and could decrease (dilute) earnings per share. If such securities exist, generally accepted accounting principles require a disclosure of the dilution that would develop if all possible contingencies occurred. In such cases, a dual presentation of earnings per share would usually be required:

1. Primary earnings per share. This presentation is based on the outstanding common shares and those securities that are in substance equivalent to common shares and have a dilutive effect.

2. Fully diluted earnings per share. This is a pro forma presentation which affects the dilution of earnings per share that would have occurred if all contingent issuances of common stock that would individually reduce earnings per share had taken place at the beginning of the period.

The details of earnings-per-share computations are highly technical and are not the proper subject of this book. The basic factors entering into the computations of primary and fully diluted earnings per share are summarized here:

$$\text{Primary earnings per share} = \frac{\begin{array}{l}\text{Net income after taxes} - \text{preferred} \\ \text{dividends on noncommon stock} \\ \text{equivalents} + \text{interest and} \\ \text{dividends (net of tax effect) on} \\ \text{securities considered to be} \\ \text{common stock equivalents}\end{array}}{\begin{array}{l}\text{Weighted average of common shares} \\ \text{outstanding} + \text{shares issuable from} \\ \text{common stock equivalents}\end{array}}$$

$$\text{Fully diluted earnings} = \frac{\text{The numerator for primary EPS + interest and dividends (net of tax effect) on securities assumed converted for fully diluted purposes}}{\text{The denominator for primary EPS + all other contingently issuable shares}}$$

In the formulae, common stock equivalents are securities that, in substance, can be considered common stock. These include convertible debt and preferred stock, stock options and warrants, and contingent shares. Securities which have an antidilutive (increase earnings or reduce loss) effect on primary earnings per share are excluded from the computations. In the numerator of the formula, the addition to net income for adjustments for common stock equivalents could include such items as the after-tax effect of interest on convertible bonds and dividends on preferred stock that were subtracted in determining net income available to common stock which must be added back. The special treatment given to stock options could also result in increasing the numerator of the formula.

Earnings per share data are widely used in judging the operating performance of a business. This ratio frequently appears in financial statements and business publications. It is, perhaps, the one most significant figure appearing on the income statement because it condenses into a single figure the data reflecting the current net income of the period in relation to the number of shares of stock outstanding. Separate earnings per share data must be shown for income from continuing operations and net income. Earnings per share may be reported for the results from discontinued operations, extraordinary items, or cumulative effects of changes in accounting principles if they are reported on the income statement. Current accounting practice requires that earnings per share be disclosed prominently on the face of the income statement.

See also: INCOME STATEMENT
          RETAINED EARNINGS

Reference:

APB No. 15, *Earnings per share* (APB, 1969).

ECONOMETRICS

There are a number of useful statistical techniques for testing empirically fundamental economics-, finance-, and management-related topics. The collection and application of these techniques is known as econometrics. The primary techniques used by analysts and researchers is regression analysis.

See also: REGRESSION ANALYSIS

ECONOMIC INDICATORS

Economic activity varies over time. Such fluctuations are called business cycles. It is useful, for both policy makers and managers, to be able to predict cyclical activity on demand. To do this at the macroeconomic level the U.S. Department of Commerce publishes a monthly listing of data series that describe past, present, and expected future economic activity. These indicators are published in *Business Conditions Digest.*

Leading indicators are those that foretell cyclical changes. These indicators increase ahead of the business cycle and decrease prior to the beginning of an economic slowdown. One such indicator is the number of contracts and orders for new plants and equipment. Another leading indicator is the average weekly hours worked by production workers in manufacturing.

Coincident indicators are those that move with the business cycle. For example, the number of employees on nonagricultural payrolls varies directly with the business cycle.

Lagging indicators generally turn after the business cycle. For example, the reciprocal of the average duration of unemployment will begin to increase after the business cycle indicates that the economy is growing.

Because no single indicator is representative of the economy as a whole, the Department of Commerce publishes composite indices. These composite indices are weighted averages of all of the indicators in a particular group. The most widely cited composite index is the composite index of leading economic indicators. Managers use such indices as a barometer for forecasting the demand for their own products.

The following table shows recent data for leading, coincident, and lagging indices:

Index (1982=100)

| | 1988 | | 1989 | |
	II	III	IV	I
Leading index	142.3	143.5	144.3	145.4
Coincident index	127.8	129.2	130.9	132.5
Lagging index	115.6	116.2	117.5	120.5

ECONOMIC PROFIT

In economics, the term profit refers to economic profit. Profit is defined, for a given period of time, as the difference between total revenue and total cost. In the calculation of economic profit, all costs are subtracted, including opportunity costs. Thus, because resources have productive alternative uses, economic profit is less than accounting profit for any particular evaluation.

One of the theoretical conclusions from an economic analysis of a perfectly competitive market is that the firm will earn zero economic profit. When a firm earns zero economic profit, it earns a positive level of accounting profit. Zero economic profit is not bad. When economic profits are zero, all resources are being used efficiently and are being paid at a rate equal to their highest valued use.

See also: ACCOUNTING PROFIT
PROFIT

ECONOMIC RENT

All resources have alternative uses. Accordingly, resources will be reallocated if they are paid less than their highest valued alternative use. For example, a firm will not be able to retain an employee if that employee is paid below a fair market salary (where the salary includes an evaluation of the intangible characteristics of the job). Economic rent refers to the amount that a resource earns above the minimum amount to keep that resource employed in its present use.

ECONOMICS

Economics is concerned with choices—how choices are made, why they are made, and what consequences these choices have. Economists study the choices made by individuals, families, businesses, and nations, as well as the outcomes of these choices.

Resources are defined to be anything available for use. Resources include time, property, equipment, natural materials, intellectual skills, creative abilities, talents and money, to name only a few. Resources that are limited in quantity and quality are called scarce resources. Most resources are scarce. There are very few resources that everyone in the world has in abundance. Air is abundant, but clean air is scarce.

Because scarcity is a fact of life, choosing among alternative uses of limited resources is a necessity. Allocation is the process of choosing. Economics can be defined as the study of the allocation of scarce resources among alternative uses. If scarcity did not exist, there would not be an economic problem. The scarcity of resources necessitates that choices be made. Choosing is the basic issue in economics.

One defining characteristic of a social science is its perspective on human behavior. Economics focuses on both the choices that are made and the consequences of these choices in a world of scarce resources. Therefore, economics is a social science that analyzes the decision-making aspect of human behavior.

Objective inquiry is called scientific or positive analysis. In the case of economics, it is called positive economics and it requires economists to sort out fact from opinion. Positive economics is practiced when one predicts that if event A occurs, event B will follow. The distinguishing characteristic of positive economics is that the predictions are testable, if given sufficient information. Thus, positive economic analysis may be either true or false. In contrast, when an economist provides a personal preference for one outcome over another, normative economics is being practiced. Normative economics is not testable, it contains personal value judgments for what ought to be or what is believed to be desirable.

See also: ALLOCATION

ECONOMIES OF SCALE

In the long run, there are no fixed factors of production; all factors are variable. This means that a firm can expand its output by hiring more of all resources, such as labor and capital. However, there is a limit to the size to which a firm can expand and still continue to improve its efficiency, that is, to lower its average cost of production.

Larger-sized firms can often operate at a lower average cost of production than smaller-sized firms. One advantage of size is that it allows for specialization of the factors of production. Larger firms can hire specialists to direct various production operations and can use more efficient technical machinery, for example. Average cost will decrease as output expands as a result of the efficiency gains associated with size.

Economies of scale (efficiencies of size) refers to such efficiencies associated with size. As noted in Figure 11 below, because of economies of scale a firm's long-run average total cost of production will decrease as output is increased. There is, however, a limit to which such scale efficiencies can be realized. When a firm becomes too large, inefficiencies result and the average cost of production begins to increase. Diseconomies of scale, meaning inefficiencies associated with size, come about when a firm becomes so large that the production process can no longer be supervised properly and the management of the firm can no longer be coordinated effectively. In the figure below, long-run average total cost increases owing to diseconomies of scale.

Figure 6

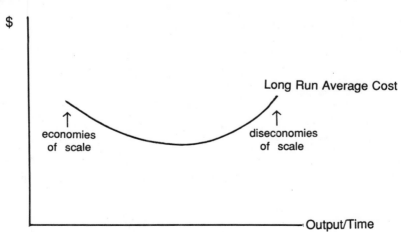

ECONOMIES OF SCOPE

A cost advantage can be gained by a firm when it produces several different products using similar production processes. One of the cost-related advantages associated with flexible manufacturing is that the same capital equipment can be used to produce a number of different products. This avoids duplication in labor and capital as well as in the administrative infrastructure of the firm.

EFFICIENCY AND EFFECTIVENESS

Effectiveness refers to how a job is performed, i.e., doing things right: does it produce the intended results? Effectiveness of an organization is evaluated in terms of how what is done relates to goals and objectives, i.e., doing the right thing. Efficiency is the relationship of outputs per unit of input. Efficiency relates to an activity performed with the lowest consumption of resources.

Efficiency is related to productivity. Workload, or output, measures refer to the volume of goods or services produced or delivered; unit cost, or input, measures show the resources are used to operate a program or activity. When output measures are related to input measures, the result is a performance measure.

Increased productivity is the result primarily of the division of labor and the intensive use of capital. Productivity measures are a subset of performance measures that deal directly with the production process. Productivity can be measured in terms of the relationship between the (1) total units of output and the total units of input of all factors of production used or (2) only one factor of production, e.g., labor cost, capital, or materials:

$$(1) \quad \text{productivity} \quad = \quad \frac{\text{Units of output}}{\text{Factors of production}}$$

$$(2) \quad \text{productivity} \quad = \quad \frac{\text{Units of output}}{\text{Labor costs}}$$

Productivity models are available to make the computations. Work measurement and time and motion studies are sometimes used to measure productivity.

A firm can change its cost per unit of output by improving production techniques, by spreading fixed cost over a greater range of output, and by other methods. Production costs are influenced by relationships between factor-of-production inputs and product outputs. This relationship reflects the production function of the firm. The production function describes the way in which costs vary with output.

The optimum proportion of the factors of production is determined by the law of diminishing returns, or diminishing productivity. This economic law states that:

> ...as additional units of factor of production are combined with fixed quantities of other factors, a point will be reached where the increase in output resulting from the use of an additional unit of that factor will not be as large as was the increase in output due to the addition of the preceding unit. Exhibit E-1 illustrates the law of diminishing returns as reflected in productivity curves.

A relationship also exists between the size of the production unit (the plant) and the cost of production. If the average cost of production per unit decreases as the size of the plant increases, economies of scale result, i.e., increasing returns to scale. Economists refer to constant, increasing, or decreasing returns to scale if, when all inputs are increased in a given proportion, the output of the commodity increases in the same, in a greater, or in a smaller proportion, respectively.

See also: BREAK-EVEN ANALYSIS
COST-BENEFIT ANALYSIS
GOALS AND OBJECTIVES
PERFORMANCE EVALUATION

Reference:

Rayburn, L. Gayle, *Principles of Cost Accounting With Managerial Applications* (Irwin, Homewood, IL, 1979).

Exhibit E-1
Productivity Curves

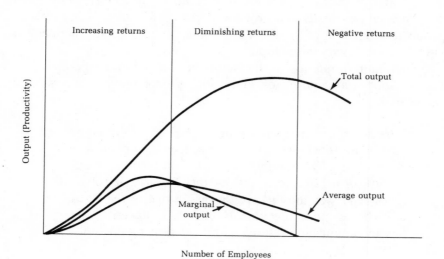

Number of Employees

EFFICIENT MARKETS THEORY

The efficient markets theory, or what is also called "the new investment technology," is the idea that security markets are efficient and that investment rewards are related to risk.

According to this theory, a market is said to be efficient if it functions in such a way that transaction costs to buyers and sellers in the market are relatively low and information on new developments is quickly disseminated to all parties. Market prices will reflect such new information.

Advocates of the efficient markets theory stress that risk has its rewards, and, on average, investors obtain greater returns for incurring greater risks. They emphasize that if investments are always efficiently priced in the market, the only way for the average investor to obtain returns above the average for the market is to take on more risk.

Efficient market theorists have defined three levels, or forms, of market efficiency:

1. Weak-form efficiency means that all information about market trends contained in past price movements is always fully reflected in current

market prices. If a market is weak-form efficient, then past trends in prices or price changes cannot be used to consistently obtain above normal returns, that is, returns above what is justified by the level of risk assumed. Thus, technical stock market analysis which seeks to discern the future prices of securities based on past trends is of little value if the stock market is weak-form efficient.

2. Semi-strong-form efficiency suggests that current market prices accurately reflect all publicly available information. Semi-strong efficiency implies that market prices adjust so quickly that it is impossible for investors to get above normal returns by buying and selling securities on the release of new public information on such things as earnings or industry conditions. Thus, fundamental stock market analysis that seeks to uncover underpriced securities by scrutinizing earnings and balance-sheet information is not useful if the stock market is semi-strong-form efficient.

3. Strong-form efficiency means that current market prices accurately incorporate all information about the product or security traded in the market, not just all publicly available information. Thus, if a market is strong-form efficient, it is impossible to make above normal returns even on inside information.

Over the past several decades, numerous academic studies have examined the question of the relative efficiency of security markets. Most of these studies have found that the money and capital markets are weak-form efficient, and some have reported semi-strong-form efficiency. Markets do not appear to be strong-form efficient, so that the possessors of inside information have a definite advantage over the average investor.

The efficient markets theory suggests that even professional money managers, unless they have access to inside information, cannot consistently obtain returns above the average for the market as a whole unless they are willing to take on an above average level of risk. Some of the most convincing evidence in support of the theory has been amassed by studies that show that the great majority of professional investment managers do not consistently outperform the market averages. Indeed, Burton Malkiel, one of the foremost proponents of the efficient markets theory, claims that "no scientific evidence has yet been assembled to indicate that the investment performance of professionally managed portfolios as a group has been any better than that of randomly selected portfolios."

See also: BETA COEFFICIENT
INVESTMENT METHODS AND STRATEGIES

References:

Malkiel, Burton G., *Winning Investment Strategies* (New York, N.Y.: W. W. Norton & Co., 1982), Ch. 2.

Radcliffe, Robert C., *Investment Concepts, Analysis, and Strategy* (Glenview, Ill.: Scott, Foresman & Co., 1987), Ch. 10.

ELEMENTS OF FINANCIAL STATEMENTS

Elements of financial statements are described as the building blocks with which financial statements are constructed, that is, the classes of items that financial statements comprise. There are currently ten interrelated elements that are directly related to measuring performance and status of an enterprise, as defined in the FASB's Statement of Financial Accounting Concepts No. 3, Elements of Financial Statements of Business Enterprises:

Assets—are probable future economic benefits obtained or controlled by a particular entity as a result of past transactions or events.

Liabilities—are probable future sacrifices of economic benefits arising from present obligations of a particular entity to transfer assets or provide services to other entities in the future as a result of past transactions or events.

Equity—is the residual interest in the assets of an entity that remains after deducting its liabilities. In a business entity, the equity is the ownership interest.

Investments by Owners—are increases in net assets of a particular enterprise resulting from transfers to it from other entities of something of value to obtain or increase ownership interests (or equity) in it.

Distributions to Owners—are decreases in net assets of a particular enterprise resulting from transferring assets, rendering services, or incurring liabilities by the enterprise to owners. Distributions to owners decrease ownership interest (or equity) in an enterprise.

Comprehensive Income—is the change in equity (net assets) of an entity during a period from transactions and other events and circumstances from nonowner sources. It includes all changes in equity during a period except those resulting from investments by owners and distributions to owners.

Revenues—are inflows or other enhancements of assets of an entity or settlement of its liabilities (or a combination of both) during a period from delivering or producing goods, rendering services, or other activities that constitute the entity's ongoing major or central operations.

Expenses—are outflows or other using up of assets or incurrence of liabilities during a period from delivering or producing goods or rendering services, or carrying out other activities that constitute the entity's ongoing major or central operations.

Gains—are increases in equity (net assets) from peripheral or incidental transactions of an entity and from all other transactions and other events and circumstances affecting the entity during a period except those that result from revenues or investments by owners.

Losses—are decreases in equity (net assets) from peripheral or incidental transactions of an entity and from all other transactions and other events and circumstances affecting the entity during a period except those that result from expenses or distributions to owners.

See also: ASSETS
            EXPENSES
            GAINS
            LIABILITIES
            LOSSES
            REVENUE

Reference:

SFAC No. 3, "Elements of Financial Statements of Business Enterprises" (FASB, 1978).

ENTREPRENEUR

The history of economics holds diverse opinions on the nature and role of the entrepreneur. Contemporary economic theory recognizes entrepreneurship as an independent factor of production on a more-or-less equal footing with land, labor, and capital. The distinction between manager and entrepreneur is now firmly drawn. However, the ultimate place of risk and uncertainty in the theory of entrepreneurship remains ambiguous. The exact relationship between entrepreneurship and economic development is also a matter of ongoing debate.

Throughout intellectual history as we know it, the entrepreneur has worn many faces and played many roles. At least twelve distinct themes have been identified in the economics literature:

1. The entrepreneur is the person who assumes the risk associated with uncertainty.

2. The entrepreneur is the person who supplies financial capital.

3. The entrepreneur is an innovator.

4. The entrepreneur is a decision maker.

5. The entrepreneur is an industrial leader.

6. The entrepreneur is a manager or superintendent.

7. The entrepreneur is an organizer and coordinator of economic resources.

8. The entrepreneur is the owner of an enterprise.

9. The entrepreneur is an employer of factors of production.

10. The entrepreneur is a contractor.

11. The entrepreneur is an arbitrageur.

12. The entrepreneur is an allocator of resources among alternative uses.

The entrepreneur is a person, not a team, committee or organization. This person has a comparative advantage in decision making, and makes decisions that run counter to the conventional wisdom either because he has better information or a different perception of events or opportunities. An entrepreneur must have the courage of his convictions and face the consequences of his actions, whether they produce profits or losses.

Entrepreneurial actions are performed in all societies by individuals whose judgment differs from the norm. Military and political life provide as much scope for entrepreneurship as economic life, but capitalism is a peculiar set of institutions and property relations that provides the widest berth for entrepreneurship.

Reference:

Hébert, Robert F., and Albert N. Link, *The Entrepreneur: Mainstream View and Radical Critiques* (Praeger, New York, 1988).

EQUATION OF EXCHANGE

Changes in the money market affect the level of economic activity in the output market. The relationship between money and aggregate output, or GNP, is related to the concept of velocity. The velocity of money is the number of times money is exchanged for final goods and services within a given year. In other words, velocity refers to the average number of times any given dollar changes hands in transactions for final goods and services in a year.

The equation of exchange relates money (M), velocity (V), and the total output of final goods and services in the economy (Y = GNP) as:

$$M \times V = Y$$

where M refers to M1 money. The equation states that the money supply times the number of times money is used to buy final goods and services is equal to nominal GNP.

See also: MONETARISM

EQUILIBRIUM

A market is said to be in equilibrium when there is no tendency for price or quantity to change. In the supply and demand diagram below, P* is the equilibrium price and Q* is the equilibrium quantity. Diagrammatically, as shown in Figure 7 on the following page, an equilibrium occurs where supply equals demand.

Figure 7

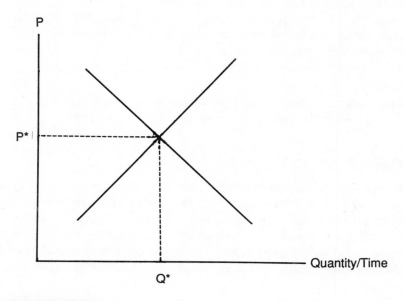

EQUITY METHOD

When an investor corporation can exercise significant influence over the operations and financial policies of an investee corporation, generally accepted accounting principles require that the investment in the investee be reported using the equity method. Significant influence can be determined by such factors as representation on the board of directors, participation in policy-making processes, material intercompany transactions, interchange of managerial personnel, and technological dependency. It is presumed that an investor can exercise significant influence if he or she owns 20–25 percent of the outstanding common stock of the investee, unless evidence to the contrary is available.

The equity method of accounting for common stock investments reflects the economic substance rather than the legal form that underlies the investment in common stock of another company. When the equity method of accounting is used, the investor initially records the investment in the stock of an investee at cost. The investment account is then adjusted to recognize the investor's share of the income or losses of the investee after the date of acquisition when it is earned by the investee. Such amounts are included when determining the net income of the investor in the period they are reported by the investee. This procedure reflects accrual-basis accounting in that revenue is recognized when earned and losses when incurred. Dividends received from an investee reduce the carrying amount of the investment and are not reported as dividend income. As a result of applying the equity method, the investment account reflects the investor's equity in the underlying net assets of the investee. As an exception to the general rule of revenue recognition, revenue is recognized without a change in working capital.

In the investor's income statement, the proportionate share of the investee's net income is reported as a single-line item, except where the investee has extraordinary items that would be material in the investor's income statement. In such a case, the extraordinary item would be reported in the investor's income statement as extraordinary. Intercompany profits and losses are eliminated. Any excess of price paid for the shares over the underlying book value of the net assets of the subsidary purchased must be identified (for example, purchased goodwill) and, where appropriate, amortized or depreciated.

When an investor owns over 50 percent of the outstanding common stock of an investee and so can exercise control over the investee's operations, consolidated financial statements for the affiliated group are normally presented.

Investments in unconsolidated subsidiaries are reported in consolidated financial statements by the equity method. In unconsolidated financial statements of parent company, investments in subsidiaries are reported by the equity method.

The relationship of ownership and the proper accounting method to use for investments in common stock can be illustrated as follows:

Percentage of Ownership

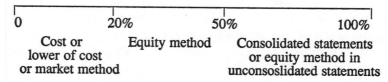

0	20%	50%	100%
Cost or lower of cost or market method	Equity method	Consolidated statements or equity method in unconsoslidated statements	

See also: CONSOLIDATED FINANCIAL STATEMENTS
COST METHOD
COST PRINCIPLE
LOWER OF COST OR MARKET

Reference:

APB No. 18, "The Equity Method of Accounting for Investments in Common Stock" (APB, 1971).

ERISA

The Employee Retirement Income Security Act of 1974 (ERISA) established procedures for protecting employee pension rights. The act established strict minimum funding, vesting, benefit requirements, and employees' participation. In addition, certain types and amounts of transactions are prohibited, such as one that states that not more than 10 percent of a plan's assets can be represented by securities of the sponsoring enterprise. The law requires that the financial statements of all employee benefit plans with more than 100 participants that are not fully insured must be examined and reported on by an independent, qualified public accountant.

ERISA created the Pension Benefit Guaranty Corporation (PBGC) to insure pension plans and administer terminated plans. In situations where a plan is unfunded or terminates, the PBGC can establish a lien on the employer's assets that takes precedence over almost all other creditor claims.

See also: PENSIONS

ERRORS

Accounting errors result from mistakes or omissions in the financial accounting process. Typical errors include mathematical mistakes, mistakes in the application of accounting principles, or oversight or misuse of facts. A change from an accounting principle that is unacceptable to a generally acceptable accounting principle is considered a correction of an error (and not a change in accounting principle). The information required for the correction of an error was available during a prior period. The use of newly acquired information or new facts resulting in a change of estimate is not an error. For example, a building was originally estimated to have a 20-year life and was being depreciated over that period. Several years later an engineering review of the building lowered the estimate to 15 years. Subsequent charges for annual depreciation would take this new information into consideration. Depreciation already recorded in prior years would not be adjusted. This situation is considered a change in estimate and is not an accounting error. The information required to revise the accounting estimate was not available in a prior period when the financial statements were issued.

Correction of an error should be reported as a prior-period adjustment which requires an adjustment to the beginning retained earnings on the Statement of Retained Earnings (and is not reported on the income statement). Disclosure would include the nature of the error, the effect of correcting it on the income before extraordinary items, net income, and related per share amounts.

See also: ACCOUNTING CHANGES
CONSISTENCY
PRIOR-PERIOD ADJUSTMENTS

Reference:
APB No. 20, "Accounting Change" (APB, 1971).

EUROBOND MARKET

Eurobonds (or international bonds) are corporate bonds denominated in a currency other than the one in which they are sold. Often these securities are dollar-denominated debt instruments sold in Europe, but they may be denominated in any currency and may be sold in markets worldwide.

The currencies in which the bonds are denominated generally are those for which there is a market in more than one country, so that the bonds can be sold in more than one national market either initially or later on the secondary market. Eurobonds also may be denominated in more than one currency or in a bundle of currencies such as special drawing rights (SDRs).

In the late 1960s, American companies began to sell bonds in Europe denominated in dollars because dollars obtained in Europe could be used more easily than funds raised in the United States and transferred abroad during periods of exchange restriction. But because of less regulation abroad, it became apparent to many borrowers in the United States and elsewhere that funds raised overseas often could be obtained at lower rates than funds raised at home. By the 1980s, even some U.S. savings and loans were selling Eurobonds to obtain funds.

See also: BOND
EURODOLLARS

EURODOLLARS

Eurodollars are dollar-denominated deposits held in banks outside the United States. These deposits generally are time deposits with maturities ranging from a few days up to one year. The rate on such deposits is closely tied to the London Interbank Offered Rate, which is the prevailing interbank deposit rate.

The Eurodollar Market has been created by banks accepting and lending Eurodollar deposits. This market is very large, amounting to an estimated $2.0 trillion in 1984. While the market is worldwide, its major center is London. Other centers are in Luxembourg, Paris, Zurich, Amsterdam, Rome, Hong Kong, and Singapore.

Eurodollar certificates of deposit trade in secondary markets. Default risk and marketability depend on the issuing bank so that the market is usually limited to the largest banks with strong international reputations.

Markets also have developed for loans and deposits denominated in other currencies, such as the West German mark, Swiss franc, and Japanese yen, but maintained outside these countries. These markets are referred to collectively as the Eurocurrency Market.

Interest rates on Eurodollar deposits are higher than the rates paid on deposits in the United States, while Eurodollar market lending rates tend to be somewhat lower. Because Eurobanks operate with lower spreads than banks in the United States, they are able to compete effectively with domestic U.S. banks for loans and deposits. Their lower spread is possible because they do not have the additional costs associated with statutory reserve requirements, deposit insurance fees, and other regulatory constraints imposed on banks in the United States.

The Eurodollar market has grown rapidly since the 1950s. Growth was spurred by the U.S. banking regulations (particularly Regulation Q) that have prevented U.S. banks from paying competitive interest rates on savings accounts and have raised the costs of lending. Persistent deficits in the U.S. balance of payments increased the dollar holdings of foreigners as did the steep rise in petroleum prices which created enormous wealth in the petroleum-exporting countries. These factors, combined with the relative freedom allowed foreign-currency banking in many countries, were the main reasons for the rapid growth of the market.

Eurodollars come into existence whenever individuals, corporations or governments choose to hold bank balances outside the United States which are denominated in dollars. Individuals may be seeking the somewhat higher returns available on short-term overseas deposits or the privacy of a numbered foreign bank account. Corporations may be looking for a temporary place to hold the earnings from their foreign investments prior to reinvestment. And governments may be seeking a safe place to hold foreign exchange reserves or a haven for funds free from domestic scrutiny. (Eurodollars held by petroleum-exporting countries are sometimes referred to as petrodollars.)

Eurodollars are in essence international money, and as such they increase the efficiency of international trade and finance. As money, they provide an internationally accepted store of value, standard of value, and medium of exchange. Because the costs and risks associated with converting from one currency to another are eliminated with Eurodollars, they allow savers to more easily scan the world for the highest returns and borrowers to search out the lowest cost of funds. They are a worldwide link among various regional capital markets helping to create a global market for capital.

See also: MONEY

Reference:

Dufey, Gunter and Ian H. Giddy, *The International Money Market* (Englewood Cliffs, N.J.: Prentice-Hall, 1978).

EUROMONEY MARKET

The Euromoney market refers to the markets for issuing or trading bank deposits and debt instruments denominated in currencies other than those of the country in which they are issued. The Euromoney market includes the market for Eurodollars as well as markets dealing in instruments denominated in West German marks, Swiss francs, and Japanese yen.

The Edge Act of 1919 (passed as an amendment to the Federal Reserve Act) authorized the Board of Governors of the Federal Reserve System to allow U.S. commercial banks to establish corporations to engage in international banking. Under this act, U.S. banks may engage in foreign banking activities and acquire foreign banks by creating subsidiary Edge Act Corporations (EACs).

Acting through an EAC, a U.S. bank may acquire foreign banking subsidiaries and may locate offices of the EAC throughout the United States to service its multinational customers. EACs may accept deposits related to foreign transactions and may refer potential new customers to the parent bank. EACs have allowed large U.S. banks to develop networks of interstate branches. In 1979, the Federal Reserve, acting under a mandate from the International Banking Act of 1978, excluded EACs from the interstate branching rule.

EACs are subject to regulation by the Federal Reserve. The Federal Reserve controls the scope of operation of EACs both domestic and foreign and must approve all equity participators in foreign institutions. EACs generally have been permitted to engage in activities common to the foreign banking practices in the host country, even though such activities may be prohibited to banks in the United States. A number of large U.S. banks, for example, operate overseas investment banking subsidiaries.

See also: EURODOLLARS

EUROPEAN COMMUNITY (EC)

The European Community (EC) has 12 member nations: Belgium, Denmark, France, Greece, Italy, Ireland, Luxembourg, the Netherlands, Portugal, Spain, United Kingdom, and West Germany. The EC was formed in 1967 with the merger of the European Coal and Steel Community, the European Economic Community, and the European Atomic Energy Community. Plans are now in place to abolish the EC by December 31, 1992, in favor of free trade across nations and industrial cooperation.

EVENTS, TRANSACTIONS, EXCHANGES, AND CIRCUMSTANCES

Events, transactions, exchanges, and circumstances affecting an entity describe the sources or causes of revenue, expense, gains, and losses as well as changes in assets, liabilities, and equity. An understanding of events, exchanges, transactions, and circumstances is important because they change or affect in some manner the underlying assets, liabilities, and equity of an enterprise. They consequently determine the contents of an enterprise's financial statements and have economic consequences.

Events, transactions, and exchanges can be outlined as follows:

1. *Event*—An event is a happening or occurrence that has economic consequences to an entity. Economic events may be external or internal to the entity.

   a. *Internal event*—An internal event occurs within an entity, such as the use of raw material in the production process.

   b. *External event*—An external event is an event that requires an interaction between an entity and its environment, such as the sale or purchase of a product.

2. *Transaction*—A transaction is a particular kind of external event that requires accounting recognition. A transaction involves the transfer of something of value between two or more entities. An investment purchased from a stockbroker is a transaction. Transactions are classified as either an exchange or a nonreciprocal transfer.

   a. *Exchange*—In an exchange, each participant receives and sacrifices something of value, such as the acquisition of inventory for cash.

   b. *Nonreciprocal transfer*—A nonreciprocal transfer involves the transfer of assets in one direction. Transfers can occur between the enterprise and its owners and between the enterprise and other entities than its owners. The acquisition and disposition of assets by donation or gifts and property dividends are examples of nonreciprocal transfers.

See also: ACCOUNTING
DOUBLE-ENTRY SYSTEM

EXCHANGE RATE

The price at which one country's currency can be exchanged for another is called the exchange rate. The value of the exchange rate, like any other price, is determined by the interaction of supply and demand in the foreign exchange market. Changes in the economic activity of any one country will affect that country's exchange rate with all other currencies.

Exchange rates can be expressed in terms of foreign currency per $U.S., or in terms of $U.S. per unit of foreign exchange. One expression is simply the reciprocal of the other. Listed in the table below are selected foreign exchange rates. Current rates are published daily in the *Wall Street Journal*, among other places, and are often posted in major financial institutions.

Country	Currency	Currency per $1
Argentina	Austral	11.96
Australia	Dollar	1.2243
Austria	Schilling	13.23
Britain	Pound	0.593
Canada	Dollar	1.2333
China	Yuan	3.722
France	Franc	6.3825
India	Rupee	14.35
Israel	Shekel	1.646
Japan	Yen	133.7
Mexico	Peso	2270.0
Sweden	Krona	6.4725
Switzerland	Fran	1.584
West Germany	Deutsche mark	1.879

Source: *Wall Street Journal*, August 24, 1988.

EXCISE TAX

Excise taxes are levied on specific products such as gasoline, alcohol, and tobacco products. These taxes are either a fixed dollar amount per unit consumed or a fixed percentage of the sale price. The excise tax on gasoline may reflect the benefit principle of taxation because such taxes are earmarked for highway expenditures. In general, excise taxes raise tax revenues while making the price of consuming the taxed goods more expensive in order to limit their consumption.

EXPECTATIONS THEORY OF INTEREST RATES

The expectations theory of interest rates purports to explain the shape of the yield curve, or the term structure of interest rates. The forces that determine the shape of the yield curve have been widely debated among academic economists for a number of years. The American economist Irving Fisher advanced the expectations theory of interest rates to explain the shape of the curve. According to this theory, longer-term rates are determined by investor expectations of future short-term rates.

In mathematical terms, the theory suggests that:

$$(1 + R^2)^2 = (1 + R^1) \times (1 + E(R^1))$$

where
R^2 = the rate on two-year securities,
R^1 = the rate on one-year securities,
$E(R^1)$ = the rate expected on one-year securities one year from now

The lefthand side of this equation is the amount per dollar invested that the investor would have after two years if he invested in two-year securities. The righthand side shows the amount he can expect to have after two years if he invests in one-year obligations. Competition is assumed to make the lefthand side equal to the righthand side.

The theory is easily generalized to cover any number of maturity classes. And however many maturity classes there may be, the theory always explains the existence of longer-term rates in terms of expected future shorter-term rates.

The expectations theory of interest rates provides the theoretical basis for the use of the yield curve as an analytical tool by economic and financial analysts. For example, upward-sloping yield curve is explained as an indication that the market expects rising short-term rates in the future. Because rising rates normally occur during economic expansions, an upward-sloping yield curve is a sign that the market expects continued expansion in the level of economic activity.

Financial analysts sometimes use this equation to obtain a market-related forecast of future interest rates. It can be rewritten as follows:

$$E(R_1) = [(1 + R_2)^2/(1 + R_1)] - 1$$

suggesting that the short-term rate expected by the market next period can be obtained from knowledge of rates today.

See also: YIELD CURVE

Reference:

Malkiel, Burton G., "The Term Structure of Interest Rates: Theory, Empirical Evidence and Applications," in Thomas M. Haurilesky and John T. Boorman, eds., *Current Issues in Monetary Theory and Policy* (Arlington Heights, Ill.: Harlan Davidson, 1980), pp. 395–418.

EXPECTED VALUE

The probability weighted value of a variable is the expected value of that variable. If a firm's decision makers think, for example, that there is a 10 percent probability that next year's profit will be $100,000; a 55 percent probability that it will be $200,000; and a 35 percent probability that it will be $300,000, then the expected value of profit is:

$$
\begin{aligned}
\text{E[profit]} &= 0.10 \times (\$100,000) + 0.55 \times (\$200,000) + 0.35 \times (\$300,000) \\
&= \$10,000 + \$110,000 + \$105,000 \\
&= \$225,000.
\end{aligned}
$$

EXPENSES

Expenses are outflows or other using up of assets or incurrence of liabilities (or a combination of both) during a period from delivering or producing goods, rendering services, or carrying out other activities that constitute the entity's ongoing major or central operations.

Expenses represent actual or expected cash outflows that have occurred or will eventually occur as a result of the enterprise's ongoing major or central operations during a period. The matching principle of accounting requires that expenses be matched with revenues whenever it is reasonable and practicable. Three major expense recognition principles have been established for determining the accounting period in which expenses are recognized and reported:

1. *Associating cause and effect*—Some costs are recognized as expenses on the basis of a presumed direct association with specific revenues. For example, a sale of a product involves both sales revenue and cost of goods sold. The cost of the goods sold would be recognized in the accounting period that the sales revenue was recognized.

2. *Systematic and rational allocation*—Where there is no cause and effect relationship, an attempt is made to associate costs in a systematic and rational manner with the products of the periods affected. Costs that are associated with periods in a systematic way include depreciation and amortization expenses.

3. *Immediate recognition*—Costs that cannot be related to revenues either by associating cause and effect or by systematic and rational allocation are recognized as expenses of the current period. Such costs could include auditor's fee, research and development costs, and officers' salaries.

Expenses never include such items as dividend payments, repayment of loan principal, and expenditures to acquire items having future value (assets) to an enterprise.

The term cost should not be used to refer to expense. An expense is an expired cost. A cost can refer to an item that has service potential (an asset). An expense would arise when the cost no longer has service potential.

See also: COST
           INCOME
           INCOME STATEMENT
           MATCHING PRINCIPLE
           MATERIALITY

Reference:

SFAC No. 3, "Elements of Financial Statements of Business Enterprises" (FASB, 1981).

EXPORT-IMPORT BANK

The Export-Import Bank (Eximbank) was established in 1934 to help promote U.S. exports. The Eximbank guarantees export-related loans to foreign purchasers of U.S. goods and services, and it may participate in such loans. It also insures U.S. exporters against losses arising from the sale of their products and services overseas. The Eximbank gets most of its funds from loans provided by the Federal Financing Bank (FFB). At the end of 1986, the Eximbank's outstanding debt totaled some $14.2 billion.

EXPORTS

The goods and services sold by the United States to foreign households, businesses, and governments are called exports. The net export component of GNP is the value of U.S. exports less the value of U.S. imports over a specified time period. Net exports are negative when the United States buys more goods and services from foreign countries than it sells to these nations. Net exports are positive when the United States is selling more goods and services to foreign countries than it is purchasing.

Listed on the following page are data on U.S. exports and U.S. net exports.

EXTRAORDINARY ITEM

Extraordinary items are material events and transactions that are both unusual in nature and infrequent of occurrence. To be unusual in nature, the underlying event or transaction must have a high degree of abnormality and be of a type clearly unrelated to, or only incidentally related to, the ordinary and typical activities of the entity, taking into account the environment in which the entity operates. Infrequency of occurrence related to the requirement that the underlying event or transaction should be of a type that would not reasonably be expected to recur in the foreseeable future, taking into account the environment in which the entity operates. The

Year	Exports ($billions)	Net Exports ($billions)
1950	14.5	2.2
1960	29.9	5.9
1970	68.9	8.5
1980	351.0	32.1
1981	382.8	33.9
1982	361.9	26.3
1983	352.5	−6.1
1984	383.5	−58.9
1985	369.9	−79.2
1986	376.2	−105.5
1987	426.7	−119.9

Economic Report of the President, 1988

materiality effect of individual events or transactions is considered separately and not aggregated unless the effects result from a single identifiable transaction or event that meets the definition of an extraordinary item.

Extraordinary items could result if gains or losses were the direct result of any of the following events or circumstances:

1. a major casualty, such as an earthquake,

2. an expropriation of property by a foreign government, and

3. a prohibition under a newly enacted law or regulation.

The income statement should disclose captions and amounts for individual extraordinary events or transactions on the face of the statement. Income taxes applicable to the extraordinary item should be disclosed. Extraordinary items can be reported as follows:

Income before extraordinary items	$XXX
Extraordinary items (less applicable income taxes of $XXX)	XXX
Net income	$XXX

A material event or transaction that is unusual in nature or occurs infrequently is reported as a separate element of income from continuing operations and is not classified as an extraordinary item.

See also: INCOME STATEMENT

Reference:

APB No. 30, "Reporting the Results of Operations" (APB, 1973).

Ff

FACTORING

Factoring is a method of financing where a firm sells its accounts receivable to another party, called a factor, for cash. Receivables can be assigned to a factor in a variety of ways:

1. Selling with recourse (seller collects).
2. Selling with recourse (factor collects).
3. Selling without recourse.

Exhibit F-1 describes a typical factoring relationship.

When receivables are sold with recourse, the seller guarantees the receivables; the seller has an obligation to the buying firm if the collections of receivables are less than anticipated. In factoring arrangements, the accounts receivable are physically transferred to the factor and the selling firm gives up all rights to future collections. The factor does not pay face value for the receivables purchased.

Accounts receivable are sometimes pledged as collateral for a loan. The borrower agrees to collect the receivables and to use the proceeds to repay the loan. In an assignment of accounts receivable, a borrower (the assignor) transfers its rights in certain receivables to a lender (the assignee) in exchange for a loan. When the receivables are collected, the proceeds are used to repay the loan. The assignment is on either a notification or a nonnotification basis. When the assignment is on a notification basis, customers are informed that their accounts have been assigned and that they are to make payments directly to the assignee.

Exhibit F-1
Typical Factoring Arrangement

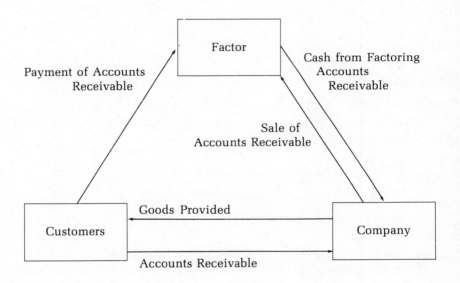

See also: RECEIVABLES

Reference:

Smith, Jay M. and K. Fred Skousen, *Intermediate Accounting* (South-Western, Cincinnati, Ohio, 1985).

FACTORS OF PRODUCTION

A firm uses many factors to assist in the production process. If the output of a firm is viewed in terms of the number of units produced, then there are four important factors. These factors include capital, labor, land and raw materials. In economics, the output from production is often measured as value added, the value that is added to the final product in the last stage of production. Therefore, the relevant inputs are reduced to only capital and labor. Thus, it is common to see in introductory economics texts a production function written as $Q = f(K,L)$, meaning that value added is derived in the final stage of production from only the contribution of capital and labor.

More and more economists are incorporating technology as an input into their theoretical models. The empirical application of these models is limited by the availability of useful measurements of technology inputs.

See also: CAPITAL
LABOR
PRODUCTION FUNCTION

FEDERAL DEPOSIT INSURANCE CORPORATION (FDIC)

During the Great Depression, large numbers of banks went bankrupt and depositors lost all of their savings. The Federal Deposit Insurance Corporation (FDIC) was established in 1934 to protect deposits. All nationally chartered banks and all state chartered banks that are members of the Federal Reserve system are required to have FDIC insurance. Nonmember state chartered banks may also apply. Today, checking, savings and money market deposits accounts are insured up to $100,000. Most money market mutual funds are not insured.

Rather than have a bank fail, the FDIC will often arrange a merger between a weaker bank and a stronger bank. One special case when the FDIC actually took control over a failing bank and reorganized it with assistance from the Fed was the National Bank & Trust Company in 1984.

FEDERAL FUNDS

The term federal funds refers to immediately available money (funds) that can be transferred between depository institutions in a single business day. Federal funds are liabilities of depository institutions. As outlined in the Monetary Control Act of 1980, these institutions are required to hold reserves in their regional Federal Reserve Banks.

About 80 percent of federal funds are overnight borrowing. Longer loans are known as term federal funds, and are usually unsecured.

Since 1982, the Fed has followed a policy known as borrowed reserve targeting. Under this policy, the Fed attempts to set the level of reserves borrowed by a depository institution through the discount window. It adjusts the level of nonborrowed reserves using open market operations so that the level of borrowed reserves falls within a target band. With a fixed discount rate, the effect of setting the level of borrowed reserves is to fix the federal funds rate, except for unpredictable instability in the demand for borrowed reserves.

FIDUCIARY

A fiduciary is a person who holds something in trust for another. Executors and administrators of estates and trusts are often referred to as fiduciaries. The term can also be applied to agencies, guardianships, directors of corporations, trustees of not-for-profit organizations, and others.

Financial reporting places considerable emphasis on the stewardship function of the management of an enterprise. Managers are accountable not only for the custody and safekeeping of an enterprise's resources but also for the efficient and effective use of those resources, including protecting the enterprise from the unfavorable impact of inflation, deflation, technological and social change, and similar environmental factors. In a larger sense, society may impose stewardship functions on enterprises and their managements. Statements of financial position and income statements are basic references for evaluating how managers have performed their stewardship function, especially to owners.

See also: PRUDENT MAN RULE

FINANCE

Finance is the science of managing money. Finance is closely related to both economics and accounting. Economics provides an understanding of the institutional structures in which money and credit flow (macro-economics) and the profit maximization guidelines associated with the theory of the firm (microeconomics). Accounting provides the source of financial and other data for financial management.

Financial theory deals primarily with the accumulation and allocation of economic resources in relation to time and under varied states of the world. Finance also attempts to explain how money and capital markets facilitate the allocation of resources. Finance is concerned with the valuation of the firm as a going concern, and with investment opportunities and factors that can change these values. It deals with the acquisition and use of funds, including their impact on the profitability and growth of the firm. Financial theory is applicable to nonprofit entities as well as for-profit enterprises.

The functions of a financial manager are financial analysis and planning, the management of the firm's asset structure, and the management of its financial structure. A firm's asset structure refers to both the mix and type of assets reported on the firm's balance sheet. Financial structure refers to the appropriate mix of short-term and long-term financing, including both debt and equity financing. The goal of financial management is to achieve the objectives of the firm's owners, which is sometimes considered to be the maximization of profit or wealth. The maximization of profit and wealth requires financial managers to consider the owner's realizable return on the investment (a short-run and a long-run viewpoint) the timing of benefits, risks, and the distribution of returns.

See also: ACCOUNTING
            ECONOMICS

Reference:

Pringle, John and Robert J. Harris, *Essentials of Managerial Finance* (Scott, Foresman & Co., Glenview, Ill., 1984).

FINANCIAL ACCOUNTING

Financial accounting is a subset of financial reporting that is concerned primarily with measuring and reporting financial information in a set of basic general purpose financial statements. Financial accounting is designed to meet the needs of external users of the financial statements of an enterprise. General purpose financial statements are statements designed to meet the needs of most users, primarily investors and creditors. Managerial accounting is concerned primarily with internal reporting. It relates essentially to planning, controlling, evaluating performance, and product costing for income valuation and income determination. There is some overlap between financial accounting and managerial accounting.

See also: FINANCIAL REPORTING
STATEMENTS OF FINANCIAL ACCOUNTING STANDARDS

FINANCIAL FORECAST

A financial forecast for an enterprise is an estimate of the most probable financial position, results of operations and changes in financial position for one or more future periods. "Most probable" means that the forecast is based on management's judgment of the most likely set of conditions and its most likely course of action. A financial projection is an estimate of financial results based on assumptions which are not necessarily the most likely (SOP 75-4). A financial projection is sometimes used to present hypothetical courses of action for evaluation. A feasibility study is an analysis of a proposed investment or course of action (SOP 75-4).

A financial forecast presents a prediction of an entity's expected financial position, results of operations, and changes in financial position. A forecast is based on assumptions about expected conditions and expected courses of action, prepared to the best of the preparer's knowledge and belief. A financial projection differs from a financial forecast in that a projection depends upon one or more hypothetical assumptions. A projection responds to the question: "What might happen if...?" Multiple projections consist of two or more projections based on a range of hypothetical assumptions.

Public accountants are primarily associated with forecasts and projects to lend their credibility to them. A client typically initiates the request that the accountant compile or review prospective financial information. In a review engagement, the accountant performs some procedures to achieve a level of assurance on which he/she bases an opinion. The accountant must perform inquiry and analytical procedures to achieve a reasonable basis for expressing limited assurance that there are no material modifications that should be made to the statements in order for them to be in conformity with generally accepted accounting principles; or, if applicable, with another comprehensive basis of accounting. In a compilation service, the accountant performs few, if any, procedures; the accountant merely assists the client to "write-up" the financial information. Accountants are expected to render a report on compiled or reviewed prospective financial statements. The compilation report contains a disclaimer and offers no conclusions or any form of assurance. The review report gives the accountant's conclusions about proper presentation and about the reasonableness of the assumptions. The reports are either unqualified, adverse, or disclaimers resulting from scope limitations.

AICPA Rule of Conduct 201(e) prohibits an accountant from being associated with a forecast or projection which may lead readers to believe that the accountant vouches for the authenticity of the forecast or projection.

See also: BUDGET
CONTROL FUNCTION
FINANCIAL PLANNING
FORECASTING
PLANNING FUNCTION

References:

Burton, John C., et al., eds. *Handbook of Accounting and Auditing* (Warren, Gorham & Lamont, Boston, 1981).

Auditing Standards Board, *Statement on Standards for Accountants' Services on Prospective Financial Information—Financial Forecasts and Projections* (AICPA, N.Y., 1986).

FINANCIAL MARKETS

A financial market brings together borrowers and lenders or investors and establishes and communicates the prices at which they are willing to make transactions. Financial markets assume many shapes and forms.

Credit markets, or "money markets," include financial markets in which instruments of short-term maturity (up to one year or slightly longer) as well as bank loans, trade credit, and other forms of indebtedness of short duration are involved. Capital markets, or "bond markets," usually include notes, bonds, and most other forms of intermediate and longer-term indebtedness. Capital markets exist for new issues of stocks and bonds and secondary capital markets include the stock exchanges and brokers and dealers in securities. Money markets and bond markets identify separate maturity subdivisions of the fixed-income securities markets. Other markets include (1) the foreign exchange market, which involves international financial transactions between the United States and other countries and agencies, (2) the commodity markets, such as the cotton, grain, and sugar exchanges, (3) futures and options markets, and (4) the insurance, shipping, and other markets requiring short-term credit accommodations in their operations.

The open market for credit instruments is subdivided as follows: (1) short-term government securities including Treasury bills and certificates, (2) the commercial paper market, (3) the bankers acceptance market, (4) negotiable certificates of time deposits issued by commercial banks, and (5) federal funds market.

Exhibit F-2 on the following page describes in general terms the American financial system as it relates to the credit and capital markets.

Commercial paper is unsecured, short-term notes issued by large firms to meet seasonal financing requirements, and it serves as a tool for raising short-term corporate funds. Bankers acceptances are bills for goods shipped for which a commercial bank accepts the obligation to pay the amount stated on the face of the bill on the date specified. Certificates of deposit (CDs) are evidence of short-term debt issued by a commercial bank, with a specified rate of interest and maturity date, to a depositor of funds. Banks are required to maintain a certain amount of reserves against deposits at Federal Reserve Banks. At times, banks may be deficient in reserves or have a surplus. Commercial banks can adjust their reserve positions by borrowing from other banks in a well-organized market known as

Exhibit F-2

Diagram of Flows in U.S. Financial System

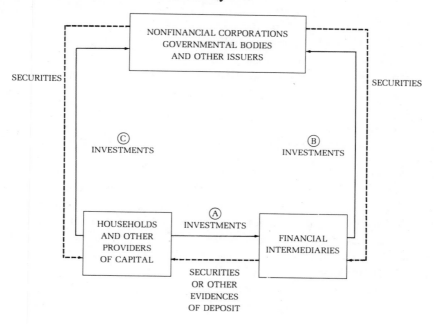

Source: The Handbook of the Bond and Money Markets. David M. Darst. McGraw-Hill Book Co., New York, N.Y. 1981.

the federal funds market. Banks, U.S. Government security dealers, and others borrow and lend federal funds in this market from time to time.

Credit and capital market instruments are sometimes classified as follows: U.S. government securities, state and local government obligations, corporate and foreign bonds, mortgages, consumer credit, bank loans, and other loans (open-market paper, commercial paper, bankers acceptances, Federal funds and security repurchase agreements, finance company loans to business, U.S. government loans, sponsored credit agency loans, and loans on insurance policies).

A stock exchange is an auction market in which securities are sold to the highest bidder and bought from the lowest seller. In the United States, the New York Stock Exchange (the Big Board) and the American Stock Exchange are the two national marketplaces for transactions in stocks. In addition to these national exchanges, there are regional exchanges located in principal cities throughout the country.

A listed security is one that has been accepted by an exchange as being qualified for trading on the exchange. Basic standards for listing on the New York Stock Exchange include the following: a going concern, national investors' interest in the firm, good standing in the industry, net assets and earnings above a specified amount, and a minimum number of shares outstanding. Trading on the exchange is done in standard numbers of shares, called round lots, usually 100 shares or a multiple thereof.

For bonds, the standard unit is one $1,000 bond. Lots smaller than round lots are called odd lots. In an odd-lot transaction, one-eighth of a point is added to (or deducted from) the price of each share purchased (or sold). Market prices are listed in points; a point is equal to a market price of $1 per share. Listings normally are given to the nearest one-eighth of a point. The execution price for an odd lot includes the price differential charged for handling the odd lot. The delivery and settlement of securities traded on the exchanges are closely regulated. In most cases, a transaction is settled "regular way"—that is, payment for and delivery of the securities on the fifth full business day following the transaction. A commission is imposed on both buyers and sellers of securities on an exchange.

The over-the-counter or unlisted market consists of a network of dealers in cities throughout the country, linked together by telephone and teletype. In this market, securities not listed on the exchanges are bought and sold. Transactions are arranged by "negotiation" rather than by auction.

Exhibit F-3 on the following page summarizes typical investment characteristics of bonds, preferred stock, and common stock.

The securities markets involve many complex trading practices and procedures. A list of such arrangements includes the following: market orders, limited orders, stop-loss orders, buy-stop orders, quotations, time limits, bonds sold flat, call and put options, long holdings, selling against the box, short sales, trading on margin, and others.

When an investor sells short, the investor sells a security that he/she does not own, intending to purchase the security before the time when the security must be delivered. A short sale is practically the reverse of a normal securities transaction. The major reason for an investor to sell short is that he/she expects the price of the security to decline.

Exhibit F-3
Investment Characteristics of Stocks and Bonds

Type of Security	Safety of Principal	Income	Growth
Bonds	Best	Very stable	Very limited
Preferred stock	Good	Stable	Variable
Common stock	Least	Variable	Considerable

In a margin transaction, the investor purchases securities and pays only a percentage of their cost; the balance is paid by the broker and is treated as a loan to the investor. The Federal Reserve System sets margin requirements. The investor who buys on margin expects the price of the stock to rise. If the price of the stock declines, the investor could sell the stock at a loss. If the investor does not sell the stock and the price declines significantly, the buyer will receive a margin call from his broker, asking that the investor put up additional cash or collateral to keep the investor's equity up to a required level. If the additional resources are not forthcoming, the broker sells the stock to recover the amount of the loan and any interest due.

A mutual fund combines the investment resources of many investors who purchase shares in a large investment pool. This pool is managed by the directors or trustees of the funds, who use the available resources to acquire stocks or bonds of other companies or of governments. Mutual funds provide investors an opportunity to diversify their investments and to obtain some benefit from professional management and supervision of their investments. The price of mutual fund shares is usually calculated daily by taking the net value of securities and cash owned by the fund and dividing by the number of fund shares outstanding. This calculation yields a "net asset value," which is the "bid" price used in the negotiation process to arrive at an "asked" price. A money market fund is a mutual fund whose investments are in short-term, money market instruments such as commercial paper, certificates of deposit, or government securities. A unit investment trust is a fixed portfolio of securities designed to achieve specific investment objectives, usually monthly income and preservation of capital through diversification. Such trusts are held in trust on behalf of investors by a bank trustee. They are called "unit" investment trusts because ownership interests in them can be purchased in one or more units valued in most circumstances at about $1,000 each.

Mortgage-backed government securities, for example Ginnie Maes (GNMA), are made up of pools of FHA and VA residential mortgages. A mortgage banker assembles a pool of mortgages guaranteed by either the Federal Housing Administration or Veterans' Administration. The Government National Mortgage Association issues securities against these mortgages, which can be sold to investors. As homeowners pay down their mortgages each month, principal and interest are passed through the pool to holders of Ginnie Mae securities.

A stock option is a right to buy or sell a given number of shares of specific stock, usually 100 shares, within a certain time. A call option ("call") gives a person the right to buy, and a put option ("put"), the right to sell. The advantages of option buying are usually related to leverage, reduced cost, and limited risk. The risk in buying an option is that the option may expire prior to its exercise or sale and so become worthless. Covered writing refers to selling call options on stocks owned.

A futures position is a commitment to buy or sell a specified quantity and quality of a product at a designated time in the future at a price which is agreed upon when the commitment is made. The person taking a futures position, as with commodity futures, will either fulfill the agreement to buy or sell when it matures, or liquidate it prior to the position's maturity date.

Underwriters play a major role in advising companies on opportunities for financing and in structuring security issuances as well as assisting companies in selling the securities to the public. In underwriting an offering, the underwriter usually operates under one of the following arrangements:

1 *Best efforts.* The underwriter agrees to his or her best efforts to sell the issue but assumes no obligation to purchase unsold securities.

2. *Best efforts, all or none.* Under this arrangement, the offering is cancelled if the underwriter is unable to sell the entire issue.

3. *Firm commitment.* Under this arrangement, the underwriter agrees to purchase all of the offering and assumes the risk for any unsold securities.

Comfort letters usually are supplied by accountants and others prior to the offering of the securities to the public. These letters usually provide the following assurances: (1) that the accountant is independent and that the financial statements covered in the auditor's report comply with the requirements of securities legislation; and (2) that nothing came to the attention of the party supplying the comfort letter indicating that discrepancies were found (negative assurance).

Federal and state governments and the securities industry attempt to protect investors through detailed regulations and supervision. Every state has "blue sky" laws that set forth requirements relating to licensing of securities representatives as well as registration and disclosure procedures for products offered for sale.

See also: BONDS
ECONOMICS
FEDERAL RESERVE SYSTEM
FINANCE
INVESTING
SECURITIES AND EXCHANGE COMMISSION

Reference:

Darst, David M., *The Handbook of the Bond and Money Markets* (New York, NY: McGraw-Hill, 1981).

FINANCIAL PLANNING

Financial planning is the art and science of putting money to work for an individual or enterprise. Personal financial planning involves the evaluation of a person's current financial position and financial goals leading to a presentation of a plan to achieve those goals. A personal financial planner is a person who assists individuals to arrange and coordinate their personal and financial affairs to enable them to achieve their goals and objectives.

A typical financial plan includes the following:

1. A balance sheet analysis.

2. Projection of cash flow.

3. Long-term accumulation plans for retirement, education, etc.

4. Statement of individual's goals.

5. Insurance analysis.

6. Estate and tax planning.

7. Projection of income taxes.

8. Overview of weaknesses and strengths in the individual's financial outlook.

9. Recommendations for implementing the plan.

Although there are many approaches to financial planning, most personal financial plans take into consideration such factors as available cash reserves, adequate protection (primarily insurance), fixed assets (funds set aside or invested at fixed rates of return to provide income and growth), and equity assets (funds invested in enterprises whose value and rate of return can vary).

Financial planners charge clients in one of three major ways: on a fee-only basis, on a fee-and-commission basis, or on a commission basis.

Currently two professional organizations accredit planners after they have completed certain educational and professional requirements: the College for Financial Planning confers the Certified Financial Planner (CFP) and the American College confers the Chartered Financial Consultant (ChFC) designation. Two major professional organizations are associated with financial planning: the International Association for Financial Planning and the Institute of Certified Financial Planners.

Reference:

Bailard, Thomas E., et al., *Personal Money Management* (Chicago, IL: Science Research Associates, 1986).

FINANCIAL REPORTING

Financial reporting includes not only financial statements but also other means of communicating information that relates, directly or indirectly, to the information provided by the accounting system. Financial reporting is intended primarily to provide information that is useful in making business and economic decisions.

Financial reporting is a broad concept encompassing financial statements, notes to financial statements (and parenthetical disclosures), supplementary information (such as changing prices disclosures and oil and gas reserves information), and other means of financial reporting (such as management discussion and analysis, and letters to stockholders). Financial reporting is but one source of information needed by those who make economic decisions about business enterprises. Exhibit F-4 on the following page, illustrates the relationship of financial reporting to other information useful for investment, credit, and similar decisions.

The primary focus of financial reporting is information about earnings and its components. Information about earnings based on accrual accounting usually provides a better indication of an enterprise's present and continuing ability to generate positive cash flows than that provided by cash receipts and payments.

See also: ACCOUNTING
ACCOUNTING BASIS
FINANCIAL ACCOUNTING
FINANCIAL STATEMENTS
OBJECTIVES OF FINANCIAL REPORTING BY
BUSINESS ENTERPRISES

Reference:

FAC No. 1, "Objectives of Financial Reporting by Business Enterprises" (FASB, 1978).

FINANCIAL STATEMENT ANALYSIS

The purpose of financial statement analysis is to examine past and current financial data so that a company's performance and financial position can be evaluated and future risks and potential can be estimated. Financial statement analysis can yield valuable information about trends and relationships, the quality of a company's earnings, and the strengths and weaknesses of its financial position. Financial statement analysis begins with establishing the objective(s) of the analysis. For example, is the analysis undertaken to provide a basis for granting credit or making an investment? After the objective of the analysis is established, the data are

Exhibit F-4
Relationship of Financial Reporting to Other Information Sources

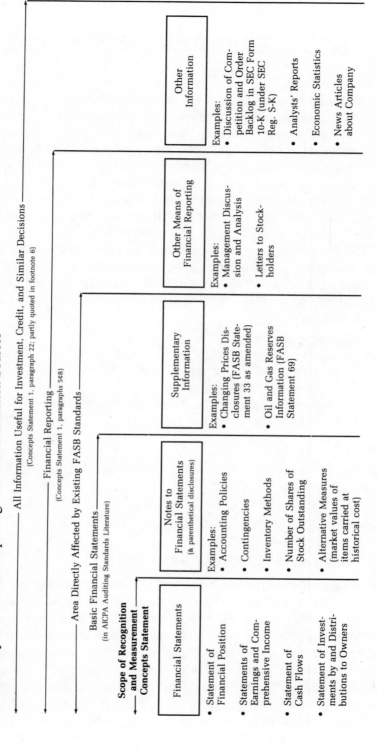

All Information Useful for Investment, Credit, and Similar Decisions
(Concepts Statement 1, paragraph 22; partly quoted in footnote 6)

Financial Reporting
(Concepts Statement 1, paragraphs 5¢8)

Area Directly Affected by Existing FASB Standards

Basic Financial Statements
(in AICPA Auditing Standards Literature)

Scope of Recognition and Measurement Concepts Statement

Financial Statements	Notes to Financial Statements (& parenthetical disclosures)	Supplementary Information	Other Means of Financial Reporting	Other Information
• Statement of Financial Position • Statements of Earnings and Comprehensive Income • Statement of Cash Flows • Statement of Investments by and Distributions to Owners	Examples: • Accounting Policies • Contingencies • Inventory Methods • Number of Shares of Stock Outstanding • Alternative Measures (market values of items carried at historical cost)	Examples: • Changing Prices Disclosures (FASB Statement 33 as amended) • Oil and Gas Reserves Information (FASB Statement 69)	Examples: • Management Discussion and Analysis • Letters to Stockholders	Examples: • Discussion of Competition and Order Backlog in SEC Form 10-K (under SEC Reg. S-K) • Analysts' Reports • Economic Statistics • News Articles about Company

accumulated from the financial statements and from other sources. The results of the analysis are summarized and interpreted. Conclusions are reached and a report is made to the person(s) for whom the analysis was undertaken.

To evaluate financial statements, a person must:

1. be acquainted with business practices,
2. understand the purpose, nature, and limitations of accounting,
3. be familiar with the terminology of business and accounting, and
4. be acquainted with the tools of financial statement analysis.

Financial analysis of a company should include an examination of the financial statements of the company, including notes to the financial statements, and the auditor's report. The auditor's report will state whether the financial statements have been audited in accordance with generally accepted auditing standards. The report also indicates whether the statements fairly present the company's financial position, results of operations, and changes in financial position in accordance with generally accepted accounting principles. Notes to the financial statement are often more meaningful than the data found within the body of the statements. The notes explain the accounting policies of the company and usually provide detailed explanations of how those policies were applied along with supporting details. Analysts often compare the financial statements of one company with other companies in the same industry and with the industry in which the company operates as well as with prior year statements of the company being analyzed.

Comparative financial statements provide analysts with significant information about trends and relationships over two or more years. Comparative statements are more significant for evaluating a company than are single-year statements. Financial statement ratios are additional tools for analyzing financial statements. Financial ratios establish relationships between various items appearing on financial statements. Ratios can be classified as follows:

1. *Liquidity ratios*—Measure the ability of the enterprise to pay its debts as they mature.

2. *Activity (or turnover) ratios*—Measure how effectively the enterprise is using its assets.

3. *Profitability ratios*—Measure management's success in generating returns for those who provide capital to the enterprise.

4. *Coverage ratios*—Measure the protection for long-term creditors and investors.

Horizontal analysis and vertical analysis of financial statements are additional techniques that can be used effectively when evaluating a company. Horizontal analysis spotlights trends and establishes relationships between items that appear on the same row of a comparative statement, thereby disclosing changes on items in financial statements over time. Vertical analysis involves the conversion of items appearing in statement columns into terms of percentages of a base figure to show the relative significance of the items and to facilitate comparisons. For example, individual items appearing on the income statement can be expressed as percentages of sales. On the balance sheet, individual assets can be expressed as a percentage of total assets. Liabilities and owners' equity accounts can be expressed in terms of their relationship to total liabilities and owners' equity.

Financial statement analysis has its limitations. Statements represent the past and do not necessarily predict the future. However, financial statement analysis can provide clues or suggest a need for further investigation. What is found on financial statements is the product of accounting conventions and procedures (LIFO or FIFO inventory; straight-line or accelerated depreciation) that sometimes distort the economic reality or substance of the underlying situation. Financial statements say little directly about changes in markets, the business cycle, technological developments, laws and regulations, management personnel, price-level changes, and other critical analytical concerns.

See also: FINANCIAL STATEMENTS
LEVERAGE
NOTES TO FINANCIAL STATEMENTS
RATIOS
RETURN ON INVESTMENT

Reference:

Woelfel, Charles J., *Financial Statement Analysis*, (Probus Publishing Company, Chicago, Ill., 1988).

FINANCIAL STATEMENTS

Financial statements are the most widely used and the most comprehensive way of communicating financial information to users of the information provided on the reports. Different users of financial statements have different informational needs. General purpose financial statements have been developed to meet the needs of the users of financial statements, primarily the needs of investors and creditors.

The basic output of the financial accounting process is presented in the following interrelated general purpose financial statements:

1. A balance sheet (or statement of financial position) summarizes the financial position of an accounting entity at a particular point in time.

2. An income statement summarizes the results of operations for a given period of time.

3. A statement of cash flows summarizes an enterprise's financing, investing, and operating activities as affecting cash flows over a given period of time.

4. A statement of retained earnings shows the increases and decreases in earnings retained by the company over a given period of time. This statement is sometimes combined with the income statement. The statement of retained earnings is sometimes expanded into a statement of stockholders' equity that discloses changes in other stockholders' equity accounts in addition to retained earnings.

Notes to financial statements are considered an integral part of a complete set of financial statements.

The major financial statements are interrelated (or articulate) with each other. The income statement and the statement of cash flows can be viewed as connecting links between the beginning and ending statements of financial position. The income statement basically describes the changes in the statement of financial position accounts that result from operations. The statement of cash flows explains changes in the balance sheet of cash or working capital between two points in time. Exhibit F-5 shows graphically the interrelationship of the financial statements.

Exhibit F-5
Articulation of Financial Statements

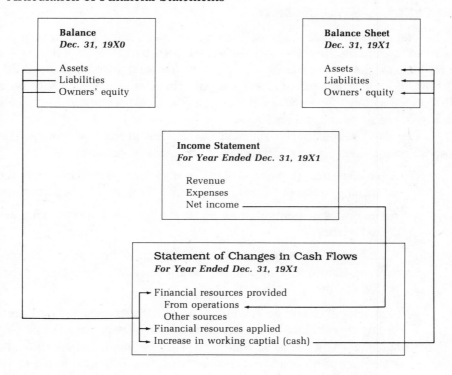

See also: AUDIT
         CURRENT VALUE ACCOUNTING
         FINANCIAL ACCOUNTING
         FINANCIAL REPORTING
         FOREIGN OPERATIONS AND EXCHANGES
         INCOME STATEMENT
         OBJECTIVES OF FINANCIAL REPORTING BY
            BUSINESS ENTERPRISES
         NOTES TO FINANCIAL STATEMENTS
         PERSONAL FINANCIAL STATEMENTS

QUALITATIVE CHARACTERISTICS OF ACCOUNTING
INFORMATION
SUBSEQUENT EVENTS

Reference:

SFAC No. 1, "Objectives of Financial Reporting by Business Enterprises"
(FASB, 1978).

FISCAL POLICY

There are two major types of demand management policies: fiscal policy
and monetary policy. Fiscal policy is formulated and implemented by Congress and the President by changing deficit expenditures and the tax system. Monetary policy is formulated and implemented by the Federal
Reserve Board by changing the money supply.

Fiscal policy is implemented either through a change in government
spending or through a change in federal tax rates. Expansionary fiscal
policy takes one of two forms: a decrease in tax rates that increase expenditures in the private sector or an increase in government expenditures. In
either case, the result is an increase in deficit spending by the government.
Contractionary fiscal policy is implemented by a decrease in deficit spending resulting from either an increase in taxes that decreases private sector
expenditures or by a decrease in government expenditures.

Household consumption is positively related to disposable income
(after-tax income). Thus, a reduction in personal taxes increases disposable
income and consumption, which in turn increases aggregate demand. The
Economic Recovery and Tax Act of 1981 lowered individual income marginal tax rates by 23 percent over a three-year period in a effort to stimulate the economy. These tax cuts increased the size of the federal deficit
and contributed to fiscal policy being expansionary between 1982 and
1985.

Aggregate demand also increases whenever government expenditures
increase. Whether the government increases the purchase of goods and services or increases transfer payments to private individuals allowing them
to increase their consumption expenditures, aggregate demand increases.
For example, the expansion of the military budget and the overall level of
government expenditures under President Ronald Reagan's administration

represented expansionary fiscal policies. Thus, the simultaneous tax decrease and expenditure increase during Reagan's terms resulted in an expansionary fiscal policy and economic growth.

FIXED AND FLEXIBLE BUDGETS

A fixed, or static budget is a planning document that assumes or estimates a volume prior to the beginning of the budget period. The budget is dependent upon the selection of the estimated volume and is not adjusted when actual volume differs from the estimated volume.

A flexible, or variable budget is defined as one that can be adjusted to show what revenue and expenses should have been at the actual volume achieved. Flexible budgets are ordinarily more valid for comparing budgets with actual results than are fixed budgets. Flexible budgets are used primarily for control purposes, including variance analysis and performance evaluation. A flexible budget is illustrated on the following page. The basic budget formula for overhead is $3.50 per unit and $800 per month. Three possible volumes within the relevant range of this cost center are shown. Budgets at other volume levels would be computed in a similar manner.

FIXED COST

Fixed costs are incurred in the short run (the long run being defined as a period of time long enough for all costs to be variable). Fixed costs are those costs that are invariant to changes in the level of output. For a firm, such costs include rent and payments on capital equipment. Capital, as opposed to labor, is generally considered that fixed factor of production in the short run.

Total fixed cost (TFC) represents all payments to factors of production that are invariant to changes in output. Average fixed cost (AFC) equals total fixed cost divided by output. As output increases, average fixed cost will continually decrease. Figure 8 illustrates these concepts.

See also: COST
            VARIABLE COST

Cost Center ABC
Variable Budget/Factory Overhead   (January 2, 19**)

Production units	1,500	2,000	2,500	
Variable costs				
Indirect materials	$1,500	$2,000	$2,500	$1.00 per unit
Indirect labor	3,000	4,000	5,000	2.00 per unit
Supplies	750	1,000	1,250	.50 per unit
Total variable costs	$5,250	$7,000	$8,750	3.50 per unit
Fixed costs:				
Depreciation	$500	$500	$500	$500 per month
Insurance	300	300	300	300 per month
Total fixed costs	$ 800	$ 800	$ 800	$800 per month
Total overhead	$6,050	$7,800	$9,550	

Figure 8

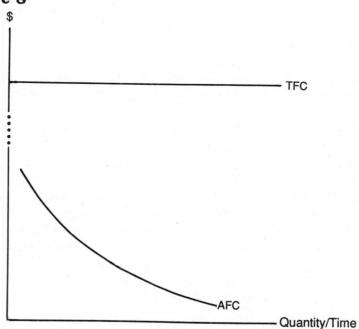

FLOAT

Float is the value of checks that have been written but not yet collected. The volume of float on checks processed by the Federal Reserve System (Fed) is often more than $2 billion daily. Federal Reserve float occurs when funds are transferred by check from one bank to another. The Fed frequently credits the amount of a check to a bank that has deposited it before it debits the bank on whom the check is drawn. When this occurs, there is a temporary net increase in the reserves of the banking system, which is called Federal Reserve float. At any point in time, the volume of float on the Fed's books is equal to the difference between cash items in the process of collection, that is, checks for which it has not yet collected, and deferred availability cash items, that is, checks that have not yet been debited from the account of the banks on which they are drawn.

Float occurs because of a number of highly variable and unpredictable factors, including unrealistic collection schedules, clerical errors, equipment failures, bad weather, poor transportation, strikes, and other disruptions. Changes in Federal Reserve float cause unexpected changes in the level of bank reserves and weaken the Fed's control over the nation's money supply. It also causes a loss in interest revenue to the Fed because to compensate for unexpected increases in bank reserves caused by changes in float, the Fed must often sell government securities from its portfolio, reducing its interest revenues.

Private corporations and individuals have long taken advantage of private float, that is, the difference between the balance shown on the firm's (or individual's) checkbook and the balance on its account at the bank. For example, it is common for firms and individuals to write checks on Friday knowing that the checks won't clear until Tuesday, giving them time to go to the bank and deposit funds.

For larger firms which receive and pay checks daily, there is a financial incentive to use float to their advantage. If their check collections are more efficient than those of the recipients of their checks, they can take advantage of net float, giving them the use of sometimes substantial sums of money for short periods of time essentially interest free. Many firms go to great lengths to speed up the processing of incoming checks, thus putting the funds to work faster, while at the same time, they try to stretch out the time it takes for their checks to clear the banking system. It is common for large firms to use bank lock-box deposit services to speed up the processing of incoming checks, and at the same time, write checks from accounts located in distant areas of the country, thus maximizing the time it takes for their checks to clear.

Reference:

Young, John E., "The Rise and Fall of Federal Reserve Float," *Federal Reserve Bank of Kansas City, Economic Review* (February 1986), pp. 20–35.

FORECAST

A forecast is a technique which purports to estimate some aspect of the future. Forecasting business activity consists of:

1. understanding the reason(s) for past changes.
2. determining which phase or activity of business should be measured.
3. selecting and compiling data which is to be used for measuring, and
4. analyzing and interpreting the data.

Forecasting future activity is related to measuring changes in business activity. Forecasters frequently classify data on the basis of intervals of time, since this is usually an effective method of identifying changes that have occurred. Data classified according to periods of time can be classified according to type of economic change:

1. Secular trend
2. Seasonal variation
3. Cyclical fluctuations
4. Random or erratic fluctuation

Secular trends refer to the effect of forces influencing growth or decline over relatively long periods of time. Seasonal variations represent regularly recurring or periodic movements with the seasons of the year. Cyclical movements refer to recurring changes that do not necessarily occur in a fixed period of time, e.g., as in a business cycle with periods of depression, recovery, prosperity, and recession. Random movements refer to small variations that are typically random or erratic in nature, resulting from many factors which are usually not considered important.

There are three basic methods of forecasting:

1. *Qualitative methods.* Qualitative methods of forecasting rely primarily on human judgment, including logical, unbiased, and systematic techniques. The Delphi method of forecasting is an example. Under this method, a forecasting group performs a succession of repeated brainstorming rounds which produce, develop, and comment on the ideas of others until a consensus is reached. The name refers to the oracle of Apollo, near Delphi in Greece.

2. *Casual methods.* Casual methods forecast about one or more known factor (a dependent variable). For example, the demand for a product might be casually related to the gross national product. Forecasting sales in budgeting often is based on historical projections which assumes there is a casual relationship between past sales trends and future sales. Correlation models are sometimes used to develop the relationship.

3. *Time series methods.* A time series is a set of data arranged chronologically. Underlying time patterns include trends, seasonal variations, cycle, and randomness. Indexes and regression models are sometimes used to develop the relationship.

Significant methods of analysis used to summarize the characteristics of one time series include:

1. *Secular trend:* linear or nonlinear least squares method or moving average method. For example, linear, least squares method, odd number of time periods.

$$Y = a + bX \quad a = \frac{EY}{n} \quad b = \frac{EXY}{EX^2}$$

where

Y' =		trend value
a	=	average (arithemetic mean) trend value
b	=	rate of change in trend
X	=	any time value

EY =   sum of values of variable

N =   Number of time periods for which there are observations

EXY =   Sum of products formed by multiplying the value of each Y by each corresponding X

EX^2 =   Sum of all X's after they have been squared

2. *Seasonal variations:* indexes, e.g., ratio moving average method.

Formula:
$$S = \frac{T \times C \times S}{T \times C}$$

where

S   =   seasonal value

T   =   secular trend value

C   =   cycle value

$T \times C \times S$ =   original data

$T \times C$ =   trend cycle measurement

3. *Cyclical movement:*

Formula
$$C \times R = \frac{T \times C \times S \times R}{T \times S}$$

where

T   =   secular trend value

C   =   cycle value

S   =   seasonal index

R   =   value of random element

Significant methods of analysis used to study the variations in one series as related to variations in another series include:

1. *Regression analysis:* a procedure which used a known variable and an unknown variable to estimate the unknown variable, i.e., how the variables are related, e.g., linear and nonlinear regression.

$$X_1 = b_{11} + b_{12} X^2 + b_{13}X^3$$

where

X_1 =   any value of dependent variable on the net regression line (same as Y used on page 262

b_{11} =   point of intersection of the regression lines of the planes

$$b_{12} \quad = \quad \text{rate of change in } X_1 \text{ as } X^2 \text{ changes}$$
$$X^2 \quad = \quad \text{any value of first independent variable}$$
$$b_{13} \quad = \quad \text{rate of change in } X_1 \text{ and } X^3 \text{ changes}$$
$$X^3 \quad = \quad \text{any value of second independent variable}$$

Formula: linear relationships, more than one independent variable

2. *Correlation analysis:* a procedure for measuring the degree of relationship between two or more variables. The closer the relationship, the greater the confidence that can be placed in the estimate. Correlation analysis can be linear, nonlinear, multiple, partial, or rank correlation.

Formula: $$r = \frac{NEXY - (EX)\,(EY)}{[NEX^2 - EX^{2]}\ [NEY^2 - (EY)^2]}$$

where

r	=	coefficient of correlation
$NEXY$	=	Multiply each X by each corresponding Y. Add these products. Then multiply this sum by N, the total number of paired observations.
$(EX)\,(EY)$	=	Add all X values. Add all Y values. Multiply sum of X values by sum of Y values.
NEX^2	=	square each X value. Add squared X values. Multiply this sum by N, the total number of paired observations.
$(EX)^2$	=	Add all X values. Square this sum.
NEY^2	=	Square each Y value. Add squares. Multiply sum by N.
$(EY)^2$	=	Add all Y values. Square sum.

The quality of a forecast is evaluated in terms of bias and precision. Bias indicates whether forecasts are consistently higher or lower than observations. Precision is a measure of variability in the forecast error.

Forecasts can be monitored by using a data filter test and a tracking signal test. The data signal test is used to detect unusual occurrences such as clerical errors or unexpected large changes in the data pattern. The tracking signal test is used to identify a basic change in the data pattern and other changes.

See also: BUDGET
              COMPREHENSIVE BUDGET
              FINANCIAL FORECAST
              FORECASTING FINANCIAL REQUIREMENTS

Reference:

Fallon, William K., ed., *AMA Management Handbook* (AMACOM, New York, 1983).

Makridakis, S., and Wheelwright, S.C., *Forecasting, TIMS Studies in Management Studies,* vol 12, 1980.

FORECASTING FINANCIAL REQUIREMENTS

Working capital is the basis for forecasting financial requirements. A percentage of sales approach, using financial ratios, can be used to forecast financial requirements.

To illustrate forecasting financial requirements, assume that the data in Exhibit F-6 are available. The company wants to know what amount of additional financing is required if sales are expected to reach the $600,000 level (a 20 percent increase). The percentage of sales approach will be used to provide the answer.

Exhibit F-6
Hypothetical Data for Financial Forecasting

Assets		**Liabilities and owners' equity**	
Cash	$ 10,000	Accounts payable	$ 50,000
Receivables	30,000	Notes payable	150,000
Inventory	60,000	Common stock	100,000
Plant and		Retained earnings	200,000
equipment (net)	400,000		
Total assets	$500,000		$500,000

Additional data:

Sales	$500,000
Net income	50,000
Profit margin on sales	10%
Plant capacity utilized	100%
Dividend payout rate	25% of net income

(earnings retention rate is 75%)

Step 1: What balance sheet items vary directly with sales?
Assume that the assets and accounts payable vary directly with sales.

Step 2: Express the balance sheet items that vary directly with sales as a percentage of sales ($500,000).

Cash	2.0	Accounts payable	10.0
Receivables	6.0		
Inventory	12.0		
Plant and equipment	80.0		——
Total	100.0		10.0
Assets as a percent of sales			100.0
Less: available credit from suppliers			10.0
Percentage of each additional sales dollar to be financed			90.0

For each $1.00 of sales, assets will increase $1.00. This increase must be financed. Accounts payable are assumed to be financed by suppliers who make credit available and so provide 10 percent of new funds. The firm must find additional financing from internal or external sources for 90 percent of each sales dollar.

If sales are to increase from $500,000 to $600,000, then $90,000 (=$100,000 increase in sales × 90%) in new funds are required.

Step 3: How much of the financing required ($90,000) can be financed internally from operations?

Because the sales revenue will be $600,000 and the profit margin is 10 percent, profit will be $60,000. Of this amount, $15,000 is required for dividends ($60,000 × 25% dividend payout). This leaves $45,000 of net income available to finance some of the additional sales.

Step 4: How much of the financing requirement must be financed externally?

If $45,000 of the $90,000 total requirement is provided internally, then $45,000 must be obtained from external sources. The relationships reflected in this illustration can be summarized in the following formula:

$$\text{External funds needed} = (A/TR)(S) - (B/TR)(S) - bm(Q)$$

where

A/TR = assets that increase spontaneously with total revenues or sales as a percentage of total revenues or sales

B/TR = those liabilities that increase spontaneously with total revenues or sales as a percent of total revenue or sales

S = change in total revenue or sales

m = profit margin on sales

b = earnings retention ratio

Q = total revenues projected for the year

$$
\begin{aligned}
\text{External funds required} = \ & \frac{(\$500,000)}{(\$500,000)}(-\$100,000) \\
& - \left(\frac{\$50,000}{\$500,000}\right)(-\$100,000) \\
& - (75\%)(10\%)(\$600,000) \\
= \ & \$45,000 \\
& \text{(same as computed in the discussion)}
\end{aligned}
$$

To summarize, the relationship between sales and assets is the key question in forecasting financing requirements. The formula used in this illustration can be used in different ways by changing the assumptions.

See also: BUDGET
CASH MANAGEMENT
FINANCIAL FORECAST
RATIOS
WORKING CAPITAL

FOREIGN CORRUPT PRACTICES ACT (FCPA)

Congress passed the Foreign Corrupt Practices Act (FCPA) in 1977. The FCPA established a legal requirement that publicly held companies must maintain internal accounting controls sufficient to provide reasonable assurances as to the achievement of the accuracy of accounting records. Two major provisions of the act are:

1. It is a criminal offense to offer a bribe to a foreign official, foreign political party, party official, or candidate for foreign political office for the purpose of obtaining, retaining, or directing business to any person.

2. Every public company must devise, document, and maintain a system of internal accounting records to ascertain that the objectives of internal control are attained.

See also: FRAUD
           INTERNAL CONTROL

Reference:

Burton, John C., et al., eds., *Handbook of Accounting and Auditing* (Warren, Gorham & Lamont, Boston, 1981).

FOREIGN EXCHANGE STRATEGIES

The dramatic expansion of foreign trade and transactions along with the growth of multinational companies have required to adjust their financial goals, policies, and techniques. A manager should realize that from the point of view of a home country, a foreign currency is a commodity that fluctuates in price as does the price of potatoes, rice, and hamburger. Like any other commodity, a country's currency is ordinarily fixed because of economic factors affecting the supply of and the demand for a nation's currency. For example, if a country is in an inflationary period, the purchasing power of its currency will decrease. This reduction in the value of a currency is reflected by a decrease in the positioning of the country's currency relative to other nations' currencies.

Additional factors affecting exchange rate fluctuations are a nation's balance of payments, changes in the country's interest rate and investment levels, and the stability of governance. For example, if interest rates in the United States are higher than in France, international investors would seek to invest in the U.S., thereby increasing the demand for U.S. dollars relative to the franc. Exchange rates are established daily and are published in financial journals, including the *Wall Street Journal.*

To begin to understand the complexities of foreign exchange rate transactions, it is necessary to become acquainted with several basic terms:

Exchange rate—the ratio between a unit of one currency and the amount of another currency into which that unit can be converted at a given time.

Free rate of exchange—an exchange rate established by supply and demand in the marketplace.

Governmental rate of exchange—an exchange rate set by a government. A government may establish a preferential rate of exchange to stimulate imports; a penalty rate of exchange to discourage certain transactions (e.g., the import of luxury merchandise); a dividend rate of exchange for the payment of dividends to nonresident shareholders.

Black-market rates of exchange—an exchange rate set by unauthorized foreign exchange dealers in violation of government regulations.

Blocked accounts—bank accounts in a foreign country which the foreign government imposes laws that restrict the bank accounts of nonresidents to use only within the country.

Direct exchange quotation—an exchange rate quotation in which one unit of foreign currency is stated in terms of its domestic equivalent. For example, if $0.40 can be exchanged for one West German mark, the quotation is direct.

$$\frac{.40 \text{ domestic currency}}{1 \text{ foreign currency}} = \$0.40$$

Indirect exchange quotation—an exchange rate quotation in which one unit of domestic currency is stated in terms of its foreign equivalent. The indirect exchange rate is the reciprocal of the direct exchange rate and represents the number of foreign currency units that can be obtained for 1 local currency unit. Using the example given in the direct exchange quotation, the indirect exchange rate is 2.50 marks for 1 U.S. dollar:

$$\frac{1 \text{ mark}}{\$0.40} = 2.50 \text{ marks}$$

Spot rate—a rate quoted for immediate delivery.

Forward rate of exchange—a rate quoted for the delivery of the exchanges (in 30, 60, or 180 days).

Forward exchange contract—an agreement to exchange currencies of different countries at a specified future date and at an exchange rate agreed upon in advance.

Premium on the forward exchange contract—a difference that arises when the forward rate is greater than the spot rate; that is, the foreign currency is selling at a premium in the forward market.

Discount on the forward exchange contract—a difference that arises when the spot rate is greater than the forward rate; that is, the foreign currency is selling at a discount in the forward market.

Denominated—Assets and liabilities are denominated in one currency if their amount is fixed in terms of that currency. When a transaction is to be settled by the receipt of payment of a fixed amount of a specified currency, the receivable or payable is denominated in that currency.

Translation—the conversion of the assets, liabilities, and operating accounts of a foreign branch or subsidiary from stated amounts of foreign currency into U.S. dollars. The purpose of translation is to enable such accounts into the financial statements of the U.S. home office or consolidated financial statements.

Financial managers have many occasions to develop strategies relating to transactions involving foreign exchange in which foreign exchange rates change. Basically, the strategies involve (1) holding monetary assets in strong currencies and (2) incurring debt in weak currencies. If inflation appears likely, it may be preferable to hold more nonmonetary assets and to use debt financing.

The typical relationship among currencies, imports, and exports can be summarized as follows:

U.S. Dollar Relative to Foreign Currency	Direct Exchange Rates	Imports into U.S.	Exports from U.S.
Dollar strengthens	Decreases	Less expensive	More expensive
Dollar increases	Increases	More expensive	Less expensive

Note that if the direct exchange rate increases, it takes more U.S. dollars to acquire one unit of foreign currency. If the direct exchange rate decreases, it takes fewer U.S. dollars to acquire one unit of foreign currency.

Financial managerial policy will be illustrated for hedging operations, debt policy and investment policy where foreign transactions are involved.

Case 1. *Hedging.* Managers can use hedging operations when sales are made to foreign customers on the basis of their currency (transaction denominated in the foreign currency) with the intention of collecting the claim at a later date and converting to domestic currency. For example, if a U.S. company makes sales to a customer in a foreign country and bills the customer 1,000,000 units of the foreign currency (Y). At the time of the sale, 50 units of currency Y were equal to $1 U.S. currency. The U.S. company will eventually collect 1,000,000 units of Y convert to $20,000 units of U.S. currency:

$$1,000,000/50 = \$20,000$$

When the receivable is collected, the exchange rate is 60 units of X for $1. The company will collect $16,667, losing $3,333 because the foreign currency weakened relative to the U.S. dollar:

$$1,000,000/60 = 16,667$$

The U.S. company could protect itself from changes in the rate of exchange by purchasing a futures contract at the time of the sale at approximately 50 foreign currency units to $1 (allowing the U.S. company to sell 1,000,000 units of the foreign currency at 50 foreign currency units at $1).

1. Collection from customer at a later date: 1,000,000 units

2. Pay 1,000,000 units of foreign currency in exchange for $20,000.

If the U.S. company could have arranged with the foreign company to have the transaction settled by sending $20,000 U.S. dollars, the U.S. company would have avoided the risk associated with changes in the exchange rate.

Case 2. *Debt policy.* Debt A company could also develop a debt strategy to deal with the possibility of changes in foreign exchange rates. If it is known that the foreign currency is a weak currency, the U.S. company could borrow in that currency, when the exchange rate is 50 to 1 ($20,000 purchasing power). If the exchange rate is 60 to 1 when the loan is repaid, the loan can be repaid with $16,667:

$$1,000,000/60 = \$16,667.$$

Case 3. *Investment policy.* As a general rule, bank balances and investments in bonds should be held in strong currencies. For example, assume that $100,000 is deposited in a country having a strong currency. At the time of the transaction, the foreign currency is quoted at 50 U.S. cents. The deposit in terms of the foreign currency is

$$\$100,000/.50 = 200,000 \text{ units of foreign currency}$$

Should the foreign currency later trade at $0.60 U.S. dollars, the 200,000 units of foreign currency is worth $120,000:

$$200,000 \times \$0.60 = \$120,000$$

See also: EXCHANGE RATES
FOREIGN TRADE
FORWARD CONTRACT
FORWARD OPERATIONS AND EXCHANGES
EURO MARKET
EXPORT-IMPORT BANK

FOREIGN OPERATIONS AND EXCHANGES

Many U.S. companies do business with foreign firms and engage in operations outside the United States. When business transactions are undertaken abroad, accounting for these transactions by a U.S. company is done in U.S. dollars—the unit of measurement in the United States. The accountant normally becomes involved in foreign operations in one of two ways:

1. *Foreign currency transactions*—A foreign currency transaction is one that requires settlement in a foreign currency. Foreign currency transactions include buying and selling, borrowing or lending, or investing in a foreign enterprise in which foreign currencies are received or paid. Transactions are normally measured and recorded in the currency of the reporting entity. A transaction is denominated in a currency if the amount is fixed in terms of that currency. For example, if a transaction is to be settled by the payment of foreign currency, the U.S. firm measures and records the transaction in dollars, but the transaction is said to be denominated in the foreign currency.

2. *Translation of financial statements denominated in foreign currency*—Translation is the process of expressing functional currency measurements in the reporting currency. The reporting currency is the currency in which an enterprise prepares its financial statements. Functional currency is the currency of the primary economic environment in which an entity operates. Normally, the functional currency is the currency of the environment in which an entity generates and expends cash. Translation usually becomes necessary when a U.S. company owns a branch, division, or subsidiary in a foreign country. The unit keeps its accounting records and financial statements in the foreign country's currency. The statements must be translated before the U.S. company can include the foreign operations in combined or consolidated statements.

Foreign currency transactions are accounted for as follows:

1. Receivables, payables, revenues, and expenses are translated and recorded in dollars at the spot rate existing on the transaction date. An exchange rate that indicates the price of foreign currencies on a particular date for immediate delivery is called a spot rate.

2. At the balance-sheet date, receivables and payables are adjusted to the spot rate.

3. Exchange gains and losses resulting from changes in the spot rate from one point in time to another are usually recognized in the current income statement.

The accounting required for forward exchange contracts depends upon management's intent when entering into the transaction. A forward exchange contract is an agreement to exchange different currencies at a specified future date and at a specified forward rate. A forward margin is the difference between today's price of a currency (the spot rate) and the price at some date in the future (the forward rate). The margin may be either a premium or a discount. A premium or discount on an identifiable hedge or on the hedge of a net investment in a foreign country is either amortized to net income over the life of the contract or recognized as part of the total gain or loss on the identifiable transaction. All other hedges are amortized to net income over the life of the forward exchange contract. A hedge is an arrangement entered into to try to avoid or lessen a loss by making a counterbalancing investment or commitment. The recognition of exchange gains and losses on forward contracts depends upon the classification of the forward contract: speculation, hedge of a net asset or liability position, hedge of an identifiable commitment (for example, the purchase or sale of equipment), and hedge of a net investment in a foreign entity. In hedging contracts, gain or loss is the difference between the balance sheet date spot exchange rate the spot exchange rate at the inception of the contract, multiplied by the amount of foreign currency involved in the transaction. In speculative contracts, gain or loss is the difference between the agreed upon forward exchange rate and the forward exchange rate relating to the remaining maturity of the contract, multiplied by amount of foreign currency involved in the transaction. FASB Statement No. 52 requires that gains and losses on foreign currency transactions generally be included in determining net income for the period in which exchange rates change unless the transaction hedges a foreign currency commitment or a net investment in a foreign entity.

Accounting principles for purposes of consolidation, combination, or reporting on the equity method for foreign operations can be summarized in broad terms as follows:

1. Foreign currency financial statements must be in conformity with generally accepted accounting principles before they are translated.

2. The functional currency of an entity is the currency of the primary economic environment in which the foreign entity operates. The functional currency may be the currency of the country in which the foreign entity is located (the local currency), the U.S. dollar, or the currency of another foreign country. If the foreign entity's operations are self-contained and integrated in a particular country and are not dependent on the economic environment of the parent company, the functional currency is the foreign currency. This type of foreign operation typically generates and spends foreign currency: the net cash flow can be reinvested, converted, or distributed to the parent company. For example, if a London subsidiary of a U.S. company purchases merchandise from a London supplier on credit, the payable will be settled with pounds sterling generated by the self-contained London subsidiary. Changes in the foreign exchange rate between dollars and pounds will have little economic significance since dollars were not used to retire the debt. On the other hand, the functional currency of a foreign company would be the U.S. dollar if the foreign operation is an integral component or extension of the parent company's operation. The daily operations and cash flows of the foreign operation of the foreign entity are dependent on the economic environment of the parent company.

3. The functional currency statements of the foreign entity are translated into the function currency of the reporting entity (the U.S. company) using the current rate of exchange method. No actual conversion of assets or liabilities from one currency to another occurs. The current rate method requires that the current rate of exchange be used to translate the assets and liabilities of a foreign entity from its functional currency into the reporting currency. The weighted-average exchange rate for the period is used to translate revenue and expenses. Gain or loss resulting from the translation of foreign currency financial statements is not recognized in current net income. Such gains or losses are reported as a separate component of stockholders' equity.

4. If a foreign entity's records are not kept in the functional currency, they must be remeasured into the functional currency prior to translation, using what is referred to as the temporal method of translation. Remeasurement is the process of measuring in the functional currency those financial statements amounts that are denominated in another currency. The temporal method requires that account balances be translated in a manner that retains their measurement basis. Under the temporal method, monetary assets and liabilities (such as cash, receivables, and most liabilities) expressed in the balance sheet of the foreign entity at current values are translated using the current exchange rate. Accounts that are carried at past exchange prices (historical cost) are translated at historical rates (rates that existed when the transaction occurred). This results in translating these amounts into dollars as of the date the transaction took place. Gains and losses resulting from the remeasurement are included in current income. The temporal method is also used when the entity operates in a highly inflationary economy.

Exhibit F-7 illustrates the temporal method, which assumes that the functional currency of a Canadian subsidiary is the U.S. dollar. The subsidiary was established at the beginning of the year. The current rate of exchange is $.80; the historical rate used for the building and common stock is $.90; the average rate for the year is $.85. The computation of the exchange loss for the year, the first year of operations, is also shown and results from the impact of rate changes on the net monetary position (monetary assets minus monetary liabilities) during the year. The $10,406 exchange loss occurred because the subsidiary held net monetary assets denominated in Canadian dollars when the Canadian dollar decreased in value relative to the U.S. dollar.

Exhibit F-8 reworks the problem and assumes that the foreign currency is the functional currency. For this reason, the current rate method of translation is used. The exhibit also shows the computation of the translation adjustment for the year which results from the impact of rate changes on the net monetary position (total assets minus total liabilities) during the year. The translation adjustment arises because assets and liabilities are translated at the current rate while stockholders' equity accounts (net assets) are translated at the historical rate and income statement accounts at

Exhibit F-7
Temporal Method—Remeasurement under FASB Statement No. 52

	Canadian Dollars	Exchange Rate	U.S. Dollars
Balance Sheet:			
Assets			
Cash	C$ 77,555	.80	US$ 62,044
Rent Receivable	25,00	.80	20,000
Building (net)..............	475,000	.90	427,500
	C$ 577,555		US$ 509,544
Liabilities and Equity			
Accounts Payable............	6,000	.80	4,800
Salaries Payable	4,000	.80	3,200
Common Stock..............	555,555	.90	500,000
Retained Earnings	12,000	See below.	1,544
	C$ 577,555		US$ 509,544
Income Statement:			
Rent Revenue	C$ 125,000	.85	US$ 106,250
Operating Expenses	(28,000)	.85	(23,800)
Depreciation Expense	(25,000)	.90	(22,500)
Translation Exchange Loss	—		(10,406)
Net Income.................	C$ 72,000		US$ 49,544
Retained Earnings Statement:			
Balance, January 1, Year 1	C$ —		US$ —
Net Income.................	72,000	See above.	49,544
Dividends	(60,000)	.80	(48,000)
Balance, December 31, Year 1 .	C$ 12,000		US$ 1,544

continued on next page

Exhibit F-7—Continued

Computation of Translation Exchange Loss for S for Year 1

	Canadian Dollars	Exchange Rate	U.S. Dollars
Net Monetary Position January 1, Year 1	C$ —		US$ —
Plus:			
Cash Invested by P	555,555	.90	500,000
Cash and Receivable from Rents..............	125,000	.85	106,250
Less:			
Cash Disbursed for Building .	(500,000)	.90	(450,000)
Cash Disbursed and Liabilities Incurred for Operating Expenses ...	(28,000)	.85	(23,800)
Cash Disbursed for Dividends	(60,000)	.80	(48,000)
Subtotal			84,450
Net Monetary Position, December 31, Year 1	C$ 92,555	.80	74,044
Translation Exchange Loss			US$ 10,406

Source: Belcher, Finley E., and Stickney, Clyde P., *Business Combinations and Consolidated Financial Statements* (Richard D. Irwin, Homewood, Ill.).

an average rate. The net assets (equity) of the investor in the foreign subsidiary are at risk to exchange rate fluctuations and not merely the net monetary assets.

Proponents of the current rate method maintain that the use of this method will reflect most clearly the true economic facts since presenting all revenue and expense items at current rates reflects the actual earnings (those that can be remitted to the home country) of a foreign operation at that time. Also, stating all items at the current rate retains the operating relationships after the translation intact with those that existed before the translation; e.g., the current ratio would be the same after translation as before translation. Critics of the current rate method claim that since fixed assets are translated at the current rate and not at the rate that existed when they were acquired, the translated amounts do not represent historical (acquisition) costs and therefore are not consistent with generally accepted accounting principles, which are based to a great extent upon the application of the historical cost principle.

Exhibit F-8

Translation of Foreign Financial Statements—All Current Methodology

	Canadian Dollars	Exchange Rate	U.S. Dollars
Balance Sheet:			
Assets			
Cash	C$ 77,555	.80	US$ 62,044
Rent Receivable	25,000	.80	20,000
Building (net)...............	475,000	.80	462,044
	C$ 577,555		US$ 509,544
Liabilities and Equity			
Accounts Payable...........	6,000	.80	4,800
Salaries Payable	4,000	.80	3,200
Common Stock..............	555,555	.90	500,000
Translation Adjustment.......			(59,156)
Retained Earnings	12,000	See below.	13,200
	C$ 577,555		US$ 462,044
Income Statement:			
Rent Revenue	C$ 125,000	.85	US$ 106,250
Operating Expenses	(28,000)	.85	(23,800)
Depreciation Expense	(25,000)	.90	(21,500)
Net Income	C$ 72,000		US$ 61,200
Retained Earnings Statement:			
Balance, January 1, Year 1	C$ —		—
Net Income	72,000	See above.	US$ 61,200
Dividends	(60,000)	.80	(48,000)
Balance, December 31, Year 1 .	C$ 12,000		US$ 13,200

continued on next page

Exhibit F-8—Continued

Computation of Translation Adjustment for S for Year 1

	Canadian Dollars	Exchange Rate	U.S. Dollars
Net Asset Position			
January 1, Year 1	C$ —		US$ —
Plus:			
Cash Invested by P	555,555	.90	500,000
Net Income	72,000	.85	61,200
Less:			
Dividends	(60,000)	.80	(48,000)
Subtotal			513,200
Net Asset Position,			
December 31, Year 1	C$ 567,555	.80	454,044
Translation Adjustment.			US$ 59,156

Source: Belcher, Finley E., and Stickney, Clyde P., *Business Combinations and Consolidated Financial Statements* (Richard D. Irwin, Homewood, Ill.).

Since the temporal method states monetary assets at the current rate, proponents of this method claim that this reflects the foreign currency's ability to obtain U.S. dollars. Since historical rates are used for long-term assets and liabilities, the historical cost principle is maintained for balance sheet accounts. This reflects generally accepted accounting principles; generally accepted accounting principles are not changed by the translation process. However, the use of the temporal method distorts financial statement relationships that exist before and after remeasurement.

Reference:

Hoyle, Joe Ben, *Advanced Accounting* (Plano, TX: Business Publications, Inc., 1987).

See also: EXCHANGE RATE
FOREIGN TRADE
FOREIGN EXCHANGE STRATEGIES
MONETARY ASSETS AND LIABILITIES

FOREIGN TRADE

Trade among nations is a common occurrence and normally benefits both the exporter and the importer. In many countries international trade accounts for more than 20 percent of their national incomes. Foreign trade can usually be justified on the principle of comparative advantage. According to this economic principle, it is economically profitable for a country to specialize in the production of that commodity in which the producer country has the greater comparative advantage and to allow the other country to produce that commodity in which it has the lesser comparative disadvantage. For example, a doctor should practice medicine in which he specialized instead of performing office typing tasks because the doctor has a greater comparative advantage over a typist in this situation; the typist should perform that service in which she has the lesser comparative disadvantage (typing).

Major obstacles to international trade include tariffs imposed upon imports. A tariff is a duty or tax levied on foreign imports. Tariffs are usually specific tariffs (30 per pound of a commodity) or ad valorem tariffs (15 percent of the value of the imported commodity). Tariffs are usually imposed to provide revenue or to protect a home industry. These two objectives are normally incompatible. Arguments suggested to support free (or freer) trade include the following: tariffs deny individuals and nations the benefits of greater productivity and a higher standard of living; tariffs eliminate or reduce the advantages of specialization and exchange among nations and prevent the best use of scarce world resources. Basic arguments for tariffs are grouped as follows:

1. protect infant industries.
2. equalize costs of production between domestic and foreign producers.
3. protect U.S. jobs.
4. protect high U.S. wages.
5. keep money at home
6. develop and protect defense industries.

Import quotas are also used to set the maximum absolute amount of a particular commodity that can be imported. Export subsidies are used to encourage exportation of certain goods or to prevent discrimination against U.S. exporters who sell in a foreign market at a world price lower than the domestic price. Exchange controls are also used to control the flow of international trade. Some controls are used to ration a country's scare foreign exchange. Some countries use different exchange rates for different commodities to encourage or discourage imports. The United States has granted tariff concessions on thousands of commodities (automobiles, steel, chemicals) to promote world trade as well as economic and political harmony. The Trade Act of 1974 gave the president a wide range of measures that could be used to open trade doors around the world. This act also allowed the president to extend most-favored-nation treatment to various nations.

The United States and other nations have organized international financial institutions to provide various forms of foreign aid. The International Bank for Reconstruction and Development (the World Bank) is intended "to supplement private investments in foreign countries by nations and individuals having capital to lend." The World Bank issues and sells bonds and uses the proceeds for loans to "any business, industrial, or agricultural enterprise in the territory of a member," and guarantees loans by private investors. The major purpose of the World Bank is to stimulate world production, trade, and investment. The International Finance Corporation (IFC) is affiliated with the World Bank. The IFC attempts to stimulate economic development by encouraging the growth of private productive enterprises, especially in lesser developed areas. It can invest in private enterprises but without government guarantees of repayment. The International Development Administration, also affiliated with the World Bank, was organized to allow underdeveloped nations to borrow funds. The Inter-American Development Bank was organized to stimulate the economic development of the Latin American nations. The United States makes major contributions to these international organizations.

External, foreign financing sources for international trade transactions include commercial bank loans within the host country and loans from international lending agencies. Foreign banks can be used to discount trade bills to finance short-term financing. Eurodollar financing is another method for providing foreign financing. A Eurodollar is a dollar deposit held in a bank outside the United States. An active market exists for these deposits. Banks use Eurodollars to make dollar loans to borrowers; the interest rate is usually in excess of the deposit rate. Such loans are usually in very large amounts, are short-term working-capital loans, and are unsecured. U.S. firms frequently arrange for lines of credit and revolving credits from Eurodollar banks. No compensating balances are required.

The Eurobond market is widely used for long-term funds for multinational U.S. companies. A Eurobond is a long-term security issued by an internationally recognized borrower in several countries simultaneously. The bonds are denominated in a single currency. Such bonds are usually fixed-income bonds or floating-rate bonds; some bonds are convertible into common stock.

Many countries have organized development banks that provide intermediate- and long-term loans to private enterprises. Such loans are made to provide economic development within a country. The Export-Import Bank (Exim Bank) is an independent agency of the U.S. government organized to facilitate the financing of exports from the United States. It makes long-term loans to foreigners, enabling such parties to purchase U.S. goods and services. The bank often participates with private lenders in extending credit and guarantees payment of medium-term financing incurred in the export of U.S. goods and services.

International trade procedures differ in some respects from those used in domestic trade. Three key documents include the trade draft (an order to pay); a bill of lading (a shipping document used in transporting goods from the exporter to the importer); and a letter of credit (issued by a bank on behalf of the importer to guarantee the creditworthiness of the purchaser). The trade draft, or bill of exchange, is a written statement (an unconditional order) by the exporter ordering the importer to pay a specific amount of money at a specific time. A sight draft is payable on presentation to the party to whom the draft is addressed (the drawee). A time draft is payable a certain number of days after presentation to the drawee. If the draft is accepted by the drawee, it represents a trade acceptance. If a bank accepts the draft, it is referred to as a bankers' acceptance; such instruments are highly marketable. The bill of lading gives the holder title to the goods. The bill of lading accompanies the draft.

U.S. citizens, resident aliens, and domestic corporations generally receive the same tax treatment for the income they earn. U.S. citizens who work in foreign countries for extended periods of time are provided a special exception. Currently, such individuals can exclude up to $70,000 of income earned from performing personal services in foreign countries. A U.S. citizen satisfies the bona fide resident test if the individual (1) has been a resident of a foreign country for an uninterrupted period which includes an entire tax year and (2) has maintained a tax home in a foreign country during the period of residence. Generally, nonresident aliens and foreign corporations are taxed only on their U.S. investment income. However, if such parties conduct a trade or business in the United States at some time during the year, the parties are taxed on both their U.S. investment income and their income that is attributable to the conduct of the U.S. trade or business.

A foreign tax credit permits U.S. taxpayers to avoid double taxation by crediting income taxes paid or accrued to (1) a foreign country or (2) a U.S. possession against the U.S. tax liability.

See also: EUROBONDS
EURODOLLARS
EURO MARKET
EUROPEAN COMMUNITY
FOREIGN EXCHANGE
FOREIGN EXCHANGE STRATEGIES
FOREIGN OPERATIONS AND EXCHANGES
IMPORT-EXPORT BANK
TARIFF

FORWARD CONTRACTS

A cash contract by which two parties agree to the exchange of an asset (for example, foreign exchange) to be delivered by the seller to the buyer at some specified future date.

Forward contracts are especially important in the foreign exchange markets because they allow individuals and firms to protect themselves against foreign exchange risk. Suppose a company is going to import electronic parts from a French manufacturer in three months time at a price fixed in terms of francs. If the company waits for three months to buy the francs that it knows it is going to need, it assumes foreign exchange risk: the dollar price of the franc may appreciate, raising the dollar price of the electronic parts. Instead of assuming this risk, the company may choose to purchase a forward contract today for the delivery of francs three months from now. Then even if the price of francs appreciates, the company has guaranteed that it will be able to purchase the electronic parts at a price in dollars that it is willing to pay.

In the foreign exchange market, the forward price and the spot price are linked by the interest parity condition. This condition says that the percentage difference between the forward rate (F) and the spot rate (S), called the forward premium, will equal the difference between the real (inflation adjusted) foreign interest rate (i_f) and the real domestic interest rate (i_d):

$$(F - S)/S = i_f - i_d$$

If, for example, the real foreign interest rate is 10 percent and the real domestic rate is 8 percent, the interest parity condition implies that the forward rate will be 2 percentage points higher than the spot rate.

This condition holds because rational investors who need foreign currency in the future always have the option of buying the currency now on the spot market and investing it in an interest-earning foreign bank account until needed, or buying a forward contract for the future purchase and delivery of the foreign currency and investing the funds in an interest-earning domestic bank account until the foreign currency is delivered. The normal operations of efficient markets and rational investors ensures that the expected cost of these two alternatives will always be equal; therefore, the difference between the spot rate and the forward rate reflects differences in real interest rates.

A forward contract is very similar to a futures contract, but there are two important differences. First, forward contracts are negotiated between two parties so that they may reflect individualized terms and conditions. In contrast, a futures contract is traded on an exchange. The exchange sets all of the terms of the contract except price, including size of the contract, delivery date, grade of commodity, etc. Second, forward contracts are not marked to market each day by an exchange as is the case with futures contracts. As a result, gains and losses on forward contracts are recognized only when the contract matures, while holders of future contracts must recognize the rise or fall in the value of their contracts as they are marked to market by the exchange.

FRAUD

Fraud is a legal concept that requires a conscious knowledge of the falsity with deliberate intent to deceive. Fraud includes intentional deception, misappropriation of an enterprise's assets, and the manipulation of financial data to benefit the perpetrator (management or employee). Constructive fraud is a deceit that involves a false representation of a material fact without reasonable ground for belief that is relied on by another and results in his damage.

The adequacy of performance by an auditor relates primarily to the professional skill, judgment, and knowledge generally required of professional auditors. Ranges of misrepresentation include negligence (belief without adequate basis), constructively fraudulent (without belief in a position taken), and fraudulent (known to be false). The auditor's reliance on a company's internal control procedures makes the discovery of certain types of fraud more difficult. Furthermore, the concept of materiality can also affect fraud detection because items that are not material to the financial statements are not always examined or are merely sampled.

Kiting is a form of fraud that has been used to conceal weak cash positions and to increase the current ratio (current assets divided by current liabilities). For example, if an interbank transfer is added to one cash account on December 31 and subtracted from another account on January 2, the cash balance as of December 31 would be overstated as would be a liability account which made the fraud possible. Lapping is another form of fraud which involves misappropriating a customer's remittance. The customer's account is credited when cash is collected from another customer at a later date. Lapping requires continued misappropriations and delays in posting to customers' accounts.

In tax law, tax fraud falls into two categories: civil and criminal. Under civil fraud, the IRS can impose as a penalty an amount equal to 50 percent of the underpayment. Under criminal tax fraud, fines and/or imprisonment are prescribed for conviction of various types of fraud. Conviction under civil and criminal fraud requires a specific intent on the part of the taxpayer to evade the tax. Negligence alone is not sufficient. Criminal fraud also requires willfulness (deliberately and with evil purpose). The IRS has the burden of proving fraud.

The Report of the National Commission on Fraudulent Financial Reporting, April 1987, offered recommendations for public companies which dealt with (1) the tone set at the top by management that influences the corporate environment within which financial reporting occurs (2) the internal accounting and audit functions, (3) the audit committee, (4) management and audit committee reports, (5) the practice of seeking second opinions from independent public accountants, and (6) quarterly reporting. The total package of recommendations is designed to:

1. Improve the financial reporting environment in the public company in several important respects and thus to reduce the incidence of fraudulent financial reporting.

2. Improve auditing standards, the standard-setting process, and the system for ensuring audit quality, to detect fraudulent financial reporting earlier and perhaps thus deter it.

3. Enhance the regulatory and law enforcement environment to strengthen deterrence.

4. Enhance the education of future participants in the financial reporting process.

Major deterrents to fraudulent activities are fear of detection and punishment and the moral effect of unethical actions on the perpetrator. The fear factor is associated with the threat and effect of detection and punishment.

A reliable fraud deterrence program should be built around these barriers to fraudulent acts:

1. a well-designed organizational structure

2. sound and comprehensive internal control policies and procedures

3. competent, responsible, and alert management and supervision

4. aware and concerned corporate directors, audit committees, and corporate officers

5. competent, creative, and aggressive audit surveillance

6. comprehensive policies and procedures for dealing with fraud

7. high moral and ethical standards of officers, employees, and auditors.

The discovery of fraud can be approached logically from a search for the perpetrator's:

1. *motive*—reason or incentive that moves a person to action;

2. *method*—plan, prodedure, process; and

3. *opportunity*—circumstances favorable for the purpose.

The Commission on Auditors' Responsibilities addressed the question of an auditor's responsibility to a client for fraud of client personnel as follows:

> Under generally accepted auditing standards the independent auditor has the responsibility, within the inherent limitations of the auditing process . . . to plan his examination . . . to search for errors or irregularities that would have a material effect on the financial statements, and to exercise due skill and care in the conduct of the examination. The auditor's search for material errors or irregularities ordinarily is accomplished by the performance of those auditing procedures that in his judgment are appropriate in the circumstances to form an opinion on the financial statements; extended auditing procedures are required if the auditor's examination indicates that material errors or irregularities may exist . . . An independent auditor's standard report implicitly indicates his belief that the financial statements taken as a whole are not materially misstated as a result of errors or irregularities.

In tax law, tax fraud falls into two categories: civil and criminal. For civil fraud, the Internal Revenue Service can impose as a penalty an amount equal to 50 percent of the underpayment. For criminal tax fraud, fines and/or imprisonment is prescribed for conviction of various types of fraud. Conviction of civil and criminal fraud requires a specific intent on the part of the taxpayer to evade the tax. Negligence alone is not sufficient. Criminal fraud also requires willfulness (deliberately and with evil purpose). The IRS has the burden of proving fraud.

See also: CONTROL FUNCTION

FOREIGN CURRUPT PRACTICES ACT
FRAUDULENT FINANCIAL REPORTING
INTERNAL CONTROL

Reference:

Burton, John C., et al., eds., *Handbook of Accounting and Auditing* (Warren, Gorman & Lamont, Boston, 1981).

FRAUDULENT FINANCIAL REPORTING

The Treadway Commission was organized to identify causal factors which can lead to fraudulent financial reporting and to make recommendations to reduce the incidence of such reporting. This commission prepared an important document: The Report of the National Commission on Fraudulent Financial Reporting. Significant conclusions from this document relating to fraudulent financial reporting are summarized in this entry.

Fraudulent financial reporting refers to the intentional or reckless conduct, whether act or omission, that results in materially misleading financial statements. The cause of fraudulent financial reporting are often associated with the following factors:

Incentives:

Desire to obtain higher price from stock or debt offering.
Desire to meet the expectations of investors.
Desire to postpone dealing with financial difficulties
Personal gain, additional compensation, promotion or
escape from penalty for poor performance.

Pressures:

Sudden decreases in revenue or market share.
Unrealistic budget pressures.
Financial pressure from bonus plans based on short-term
economic performance.

Opportunities:

Absence of board of directors or audit committee that
oversees process.

Weak or nonexistent internal accounting controls.
Unusual or complex transactions.
Accounting estimates requiring significant subjective
   judgment by management.
Ineffective internal audit staffs.

Effect sought: smooth earnings or overstate company assets.

Auditors assess the overall level of risk of an engagement as it relates to irregularities and illegal acts. Various factors are considered when evaluating the risk level including the following:

	Lower Risk	**Higher Risk**
Management attitude on financial reporting	Oversight group	One person
Management turnover	Nominal	High
Emphasis on meeting earnings projections	Little	Very high
Reputation in business community	Honest	Improper
Profitability relative to industry	Adequate	Inadequate
	Consistent	Inconsistent
Rate of change in industry	Stable	Rapid
Status of industry	Healthy	Distressed
Organization of operations	Centralized	Decentralized
Going-concern problems	Small	Substantial
Contentious accounting issues	None	Many
Difficult-to-audit transactions	Few	Many
Misstatements detected in prior audit	Few	Many
Relationship	Return audit	New audit

Source: D.R. Carmichael, "The Auditor's New Guide To Errors, Irregularities and Illegal Acts, *Journal of Accountancy*, September 1988.

Among the many recommendations made by the commission, emphasis was placed upon improving the tone of the top management of the company to discharge its obligation to oversee the financial reporting process. This requires that companies should maintain effective internal controls that provide reasonable assurance that fraudulent financial reporting will be prevented or detected. Written codes of corporate conduct were highly recommended as techniques for improving financial reporting. The commission also approved the establishment of mandatory independent audit committees. All public companies would be required to include in their annual reports to stockholders management reports signed by the chief executive officer and the chief accounting officer and/or the chief financial officers. The report should acknowledge management's responsibilities for the financial statements and internal control, discuss how these responsibilities were fulfilled, and provide management's assessment of the effectiveness of the company's internal controls. The chairman of the audit committee should be required to have included in the annual reports to the stockholders a letter describing the committee's responsibilities and activities during the year.

Independent public accountants should recognize their responsibility for detecting fraudulent financial reporting, especially by taking affirmative steps in each audit to assess the potential for fraudulent financial reporting and to design tests to provide reasonable assurance of detection.

The committee recommended that the SEC be given additional enforcement remedies, such as to impose civil money penalties in administrative proceedings and to seek civil money penalties from a court directly in an injunctive proceeding. The SEC should pursue criminal prosecution of fraudulent financial reporting cases and should conduct an affirmative program to promote increased criminal prosecution of fraudulent financial reporting cases by educating and assisting government officials with criminal prosecution powers.

Educators were advised to incorporate throughout the curricula knowledge and understanding of the factors that can cause fraudulent financial reporting and the strategies that can lead to a reduction in its incidence.

See also: FRAUD
FOREIGN CORRUPT PRACTICES ACT

Reference:

Treadway Commission, The Report of the National Commission on Fraudulent Reporting.

FREE ENTERPRISE SYSTEM

In the United States, the free (or private) enterprise system is the basic economic system. In a free enterprise system:

1. private citizens are free to own and operate a business,

2. the means of production (land, factories, equipment) are privately owned, although government does own and operate some enterprises such as the postal system.

3. incentive for investors and business is the profit motive, and

4. competition is a characteristic of the marketplace.

The terms capitalism and free enterprise are often used interchangeably. Accounting serves the free enterprise economic system by providing financial data that can be used to make the economic choices that an enterprise or person must make, especially as these choices relate to the allocation of an enterprise's or investor's economic resources. Accounting also serves other economic systems.

See also: ANTITRUST POLICY
ECONOMICS

Reference:

Baumol, W.J., and Alan S. Blinder, *Economics: Principles and Policy* (Harcourt Brace Jovanovich, San Diego, Calif., 1986).

FULL DISCLOSURE

Full or adequate disclosure is an accounting concept which requires that information provided in financial accounting reports be sufficiently complete to avoid misleading users of the reports by omitting significant facts or information. The disclosure concept also refers to revealing information that would be useful in the decision-making processes of informed users. Full disclosure is required for the fair presentation of financial statements. Examples of items usually included in financial statements include accounting policies, depreciation and inventory methods, contingencies, related-party transactions, and lease and pension details.

The Accounting Principles Board in APB Statement No. 4 stated that fair presentation is met when:

a proper balance has been achieved between the conflicting needs to disclose important aspects of financial positions and results of operations in accordance with conventional aspects and to summarize the voluminous underlying data into a limited number of financial statement captions and supporting notes.

Many disclosures are made in the body of the financial statements and in notes (footnotes), schedules, and supplementary statements. Significant accounting policies are usually disclosed in the first note to the financial statements or in a summary of significant policies preceding the first note.

See also: ACCOUNTING ASSUMPTIONS
ACCOUNTING PRINCIPLES
EFFICIENT MARKET THEORY
MATERIALITY
OFF-BALANCE SHEET ITEMS
SUBSEQUENT EVENTS

FUTURE VALUE

The future value (amount) of a single sum at compound interest is the original amount plus the compound interest thereon, stated as of a specific future date. For example, what will be the amount in a savings account on December 31, 1990, if $10,000 is invested at 14 percent interest on December 31, 1986? Using a Future Amount of 1 Table (see Exhibit F-9 on the following page) for i = 14 percent and n = 4, the future amount can be computed as follows:

$$\$10,000 \times 1.68896 = \$16,889.60.$$

See also: ANNUITY
INTEREST
PRESENT VALUE

Exhibit F-9

Future Value (Amount) of 1 Table

n	8.0%	9.0%	10.0%	12.0%	14.0%	16.0%	18.0%
1	1.080000	1.090000	1.100000	1.120000	1.140000	1.160000	1.180000
2	1.166400	1.188100	1.210000	1.254400	1.299600	1.345600	1.392400
3	1.259712	1.295029	1.331000	1.404928	1.481544	1.560896	1.643032
4	1.360489	1.411582	1.464100	1.573519	1.688960	1.810639	1.938778
5	1.469328	1.538624	1.610510	1.762342	1.925415	2.100342	2.287758
6	1.586874	1.677100	1.771561	1.973823	2.194973	2.436396	2.699554
7	1.713824	1.828039	1.948717	2.210681	2.502269	2.826220	3.185474
8	1.850930	1.992563	2.143589	2.475963	2.852586	3.278415	3.758859
9	1.999005	2.171893	2.357948	2.773079	3.251949	3.802961	4.435454
10	2.158925	2.367364	2.593742	3.105848	3.707221	4.411435	5.233336
11	2.331639	2.580426	2.853117	3.478550	4.226232	5.117265	6.175926
12	2.518170	2.812665	3.138428	3.895976	4.817905	5.936027	7.287593
13	2.719624	3.065805	3.452271	4.363493	5.492411	6.885791	8.599359
14	2.937194	3.341727	3.797498	4.887112	6.261349	7.987518	10.147244
15	3.172169	3.642482	4.177248	5.473566	7.137938	9.265521	11.973748
16	3.425943	3.970306	4.594973	6.130394	8.137249	10.748004	14.129023
17	3.700018	4.327633	5.054470	6.866041	9.276464	12.467685	16.672247
18	3.996019	4.717120	5.559917	7.689966	10.575169	14.462514	19.673251
19	4.315701	5.141661	6.115909	8.612762	12.055693	16.776517	23.214436
20	4.660957	5.604411	6.727500	9.646293	13.743490	19.460759	27.393035
21	5.033934	6.108808	7.400250	10.803648	15.667578	22.574481	32.323781
22	5.436540	6.658600	8.140275	12.100310	17.861039	26.186398	38.142061
23	5.871464	7.257874	8.954302	13.552347	20.361585	30.376222	45.007632
24	6.341181	7.911083	9.849733	15.178629	23.212207	35.236417	53.109006
25	6.848475	8.623081	10.834706	17.000064	26.461916	40.874244	62.668627
26	7.396353	9.399158	11.918177	19.040072	30.166584	47.414123	73.948980
27	7.988061	10.245032	13.109994	21.324881	34.389906	55.000382	87.259797
28	8.627106	11.167140	14.420994	23.883866	39.204493	63.800444	102.966560
29	9.317275	12.172182	15.863093	26.749930	44.693122	74.008515	121.500541
30	10.062657	13.267678	17.449402	29.959922	50.950159	85.849377	143.370638

Reference:

Woelfel, Charles J., *Financial Managers Desktop Reference to Money, Time, Interest and Yield* (Probus, Chicago, 1986).

FUTURES MARKET

A futures market enables buyers and sellers to exchange contracts for the future delivery of commodities or financial instruments. If a commodity producer wishes to sell a commodity in the future, he or she can assure the ability to do so by selling a futures contract today. Alternatively, if a commodity user needs to buy a commodity in the future, he or she can make certain that it can be done by buying a futures contract today. Futures markets, therefore, make it possible for producers and consumers to act today to make sure that they will be able to do what they want to do in the future.

In the early part of the last century, it was common in the United States for farmers to bring their products to market at a set time of the year. Often this resulted in a glut during market season, and farmers found prices very depressed when they came to sell their products. At other times, prices could be very high because of shortages. Some farmers and merchants began to make contracts for future delivery, assuring the farmers at least a minimum price for their crops.

After the Civil War, there evolved the formal practice of futures trading at commodity exchanges (like the Chicago Board of Trade and elsewhere) as traders began to exchange contracts for future delivery that were standardized as to grade, size, and time of delivery. Standardization was important to the growth of futures trading because it made trading on futures contracts for a specific commodity identical, and thus interchangeable with other contracts for delivery of the same commodity during the same time period.

It is contract standardization that distinguishes a futures contract from a forward contract. A forward contract is tailored to the needs of the individual buyer and seller, and is an agreement between the two of them directly. A futures contract is a standardized agreement that takes place under rules prescribed by the futures exchange on which the contract is traded. Each buyer or seller deals through the exchange clearing house, and each is insured against default by the exchange itself.

Today, organized futures markets for the exchange of standardized contracts for future delivery exist for a large number of items, including grains and feeds (wheat, corn, soybeans), livestock (cattle, hogs, porkbellies), metals (copper, silver, gold), lumber, and financial assets (foreign currencies, stocks, and debt instruments). The prices of futures contracts for these items are published daily in the *Wall Street Journal* and elsewhere.

Exhibit F-10 on the following page shows a set of quotations for futures contracts traded during a typical day. The exchange where the contracts are traded is shown in parentheses next to the name of the commodity or financial instrument. Each row of price quotes reflects the day's trading in a particular futures contract. The delivery date of the contracts is listed as the first item on each row. For example, July corn traded on the Chicago Board of Trade (CBT) or gold for delivery in August sold on the Commodity Exchange in New York (CMX).

Exhibit F-10

Futures Prices

Tuesday, May 26, 1987

Open Interest Reflects Previous Trading Day.

	Open	High	Low	Settle	Change	Lifetime High	Lifetime Low	Open Interest
–GRAINS AND OILSEEDS–								
CORN (CBT) 5,000 bu.; cents per bu.								
July	188½	191	186	190¾	– ¼	227	154	51,789
Sept	189	190½	186	190¼	– 1¼	205½	157¼	17,871
Dec	191	191¾	186½	191¾	– 3	212	163¼	44,266
Mr88	198¾	199	194	198¾	– 3¼	218	171	8,708
May	201	202	198	201¼	– 3½	221	174	2,438
July	201	203¼	200	202½	– 3	222	181½	1,175
Est vol 40,000; vol Fri 26,106; open int 126,258, +460.								
OATS (CBT) 5,000 bu.; cents per bu.								
July	153	155	150	152	– 4¾	173½	113¾	2,032
Sept	143	144½	140	142	– 5¼	164	116	1,442
Dec	149½	151	147	148	– 5	169½	121½	1,391
Est vol 1,000; vol Fri 733; open int 4,970, +187.								
SOYBEANS (CBT) 5,000 bu.; cents per bu.								
July	549	553	537	545	–13½	592½	477	33,167
Aug	552	552½	540	546¾	–14¼	597	475¼	9,851
Sept	545	548	539	546	–13¾	600	466½	3,672
Nov	547	555	543	550½	–17	612	460¼	40,680
Ja88	558	561	552	558¾	–16½	618	466½	4,342
Mar	568	568½	560	566¾	–17¼	628	474	1,832
May	575	575	567	572½	–17½	634	476	651
July	568	574	568	573¼	–17¾	633	488½	255
Est vol 42,000; vol Fri 27,361; open int 94,457, –943.								
SOYBEAN MEAL (CBT) 100 tons; $ per ton.								
July	163.00	165.50	161.50	164.10	– 3.60	177.80	134.50	27,658
Aug	163.50	165.00	161.50	163.40	– 4.80	178.50	134.10	10,329
Sept	165.50	166.00	162.00	164.50	– 4.70	181.00	133.00	6,735
Oct	165.00	165.00	162.50	164.50	– 4.70	182.50	131.50	5,200
Dec	166.00	167.00	163.50	165.80	– 4.90	185.50	132.00	11,183
Ja88	165.00	167.50	165.00	167.50	– 4.20	187.00	132.50	898
Mar	168.00	169.80	167.00	169.80	– 4.60	188.00	135.00	746
May	168.00	169.00	167.80	169.00	– 5.00	188.00	155.00	133
Est vol 17,000; vol Fri 15,160; open int 62,971, –1,058.								
SOYBEAN OIL (CBT) 60,000 lbs.; cents per lb.								
July	16.45	16.60	16.10	16.32	– .57	18.70	14.55	31,823
Aug	16.40	16.72	16.32	16.53	– .56	18.40	14.65	16,368
Sept	16.60	16.91	16.28	16.71	– .57	18.25	14.68	8,267
Oct	16.80	17.10	16.75	16.90	– .55	18.45	14.82	9,243
Dec	17.10	17.42	16.95	17.23	– .53	18.75	15.52	14,006
Ja88	17.30	17.55	17.26	17.30	– .55	18.85	15.57	1,830
Mar	17.75	17.90	17.60	17.60	– .55	19.00	16.75	370
May	17.90	18.10	17.80	17.85	– .52	19.25	18.15	143
Est vol 24,000; vol Fri 8,619; open int 82,196, +512.								
WHEAT (CBT) 5,000 bu.; cents per bu.								
July	284	290¾	282	289¾	+ 2	316½	223¼	19,152
Sept	288	295	285½	295	+ 2¾	318¾	233	5,725
Dec	295	304	293½	303¾	+ 5	325	247½	6,195
Mr88	298½	306	295	306	+ 4½	324	253	870
May	290	293	287	293	+ 2	315	264½	167
Est vol 10,000; vol Fri 4,718; open int 32,180, +47.								

	Open	High	Low	Settle	Change	Lifetime High	Lifetime Low	Open Interest
COTTON (CTN)–50,000 lbs.; cents per lb.								
July	70.95	73.35	70.40	73.18	+ 1.16	74.20	32.32	7,738
Oct	70.75	72.70	70.15	72.70	+ .75	73.50	33.50	3,126
Dec	69.45	71.90	69.45	71.88	+ .72	72.90	68.40	12,573
Mr88	71.00	72.70	70.35	72.60	+ .90	73.30	47.50	2,466
May	71.50	73.20	71.10	73.20	+ .90	73.75	53.40	587
July	72.00	72.00	71.80	73.45	+ .95	73.60	53.90	154
Est vol 8,000; vol Fri609; open int 26,710, +268.								
ORANGE JUICE (CTN)–15,000 lbs.; cents per lb.								
July	131.10	131.50	130.85	131.40	+ .35	137.40	84.75	3,934
Sept	127.75	128.35	127.75	128.35	+ .10	135.00	107.50	2,200
Nov	125.80	125.80	125.05	125.05	– 1.15	135.50	108.00	1,006
Ja88	125.00	125.00	125.00	124.75	– 1.25	135.90	115.00	537
Mar	....	....	....	124.75	– 1.25	135.00	121.00	492
Est vol 300; vol Fri 473; open int 8,291, –125.								
SUGAR–WORLD (CSCE)–112,000 lbs.; cents per lb.								
July	6.95	6.98	6.53	6.55	– .48	9.92	6.17	32,010
Sept	7.20	7.20	6.80	6.85	– .36	8.70	6.24	226
Oct	7.32	7.34	6.93	6.99	– .42	9.60	6.41	45,865
Mr88	7.75	7.75	7.40	7.44	– .38	8.95	7.04	16,654
May	7.86	7.86	7.61	7.62	– .39	8.86	7.45	753
July	7.86	7.86	7.70	7.70	– .40	8.88	6.83	1,533
Oct	7.94	7.99	7.80	7.87	– .38	8.40	7.80	639
Est vol 32,126; vol Fri 7,252; open int 97,753, –402.								
SUGAR–DOMESTIC (CSCE)–112,000 lbs.; cents per lb.								
July	22.15	22.18	22.15	22.17	....	22.19	20.65	1,252
Sept	21.97	21.97	21.96	21.97	....	21.97	20.93	1,948
Nov	....	....	....	21.85	....	21.85	20.26	2,065
Ja88	....	....	....	21.65	....	21.65	21.25	293
Mar	....	....	....	21.70	+ .05	21.70	21.51	185
Est vol 457; vol Fri 798; open int 5,766, +82.								
–METALS & PETROLEUM–								
COPPER (CMX)–25,000 lbs.; cents per lb.								
May	66.90	66.90	65.10	65.20	– 2.10	70.00	58.20	835
July	66.20	66.25	64.60	64.90	– 1.80	70.00	58.20	40,387
Sept	65.20	65.20	63.75	64.10	– 1.55	70.35	59.40	17,796
Dec	65.10	65.10	63.70	64.10	– 1.50	69.50	60.05	11,836
Mr88	65.35	65.35	63.85	64.25	– 1.45	68.00	60.70	2,908
May	65.00	65.00	64.50	64.50	– 1.45	68.35	60.90	768
July	64.30	65.00	64.25	64.75	– 1.45	68.65	62.30	384
Est vol 9,000; vol Fri 5,199; open int 74,979, –1,145.								
GOLD (CMX)–100 troy oz.; $ per troy oz.								
May	450.00	450.50	450.00	451.40	–12.60	480.00	414.00	4
June	448.50	458.50	445.50	451.80	–12.80	481.50	350.50	51,863
Aug	463.50	464.50	451.00	457.50	–13.00	488.00	356.00	33,434

	Open	High	Low	Settle	Change	Lifetime High	Lifetime Low	Open Interest
Nov	.5130	.5130	.5130	.5155	+ .0020	.5200	.4800	601
Dec	.5020	.5100	.5020	.5095	+ .0024	.5150	.4750	1,079
Ja88	....	....	....	.5095	+ .0035	.5125	.4826	364
Feb	.5075	.5075	.5075	.5135	+ .0040	.5100	.4750	165
Est vol 6,318; vol Fri 6,006; open int 37,665, –687.								
–WOOD–								
LUMBER (CME)–130,000 bd. ft.; $ per 1,000 bd. ft.								
July	180.30	181.20	177.60	181.70	+ 1.90	190.30	155.10	3,470
Sept	172.00	173.10	170.00	172.90	+ 2.00	184.00	159.50	1,311
Nov	165.90	167.00	165.00	166.70	+ 1.10	175.00	156.70	692
Ja88	165.00	166.50	164.80	166.10	+ .90	173.00	156.00	362
Mar	166.00	166.20	165.00	165.60	+ .50	169.10	156.00	235
Est vol 961; vol Fri 1,036; open int 6,075, –27.								
–FINANCIAL–								
BRITISH POUND (IMM)–25,000 pounds; $ per pound								
June	1.6475	1.6485	1.6250	1.6255	– .0430	1.6895	1.3600	40,607
Sept	1.6400	1.6420	1.6150	1.6180	– .0465	1.6860	1.3420	6,073
Dec	1.6300	1.6390	1.6090	1.6155	– .0475	1.6850	1.3675	472
Est vol 16,080; vol Fri 10,573; open int 47,175, –162.								
CANADIAN DOLLAR (IMM)–100,000 dlrs.; $ per Can $								
June	.7435	.7445	.7425	.7436	+.0018	.7681	.6995	16,982
Sept	.7418	.7424	.7408	.7416	+.0020	.7673	.6950	5,885
Dec	.7400	.7406	.7390	.7396	+.0022	.7667	.6980	1,779
Mr88	....	....	....	.7376	+.0024	.7655	.7052	372
Est vol 3,005; vol Fri 1,861; open int 25,097, –303.								
JAPANESE YEN (IMM) 12.5 million yen; $ per yen (.00)								
June	.7000	.7018	.6954	.6956	–.0156	.7283	.6121	48,823
Sept	.7055	.7077	.7010	.7014	–.0166	.7347	.6160	3,678
Dec	.7125	.7140	.7075	.7080	–.0176	.7430	.7110	582
Est vol 42,246; vol Fri34,830; open int 53,119, +4,016.								
SWISS FRANC (IMM)–125,000 francs-$ per franc								
June	.6781	.6784	.6698	.6703	–.0141	.6953	.5870	32,124
Sept	.6840	.6842	.6756	.6760	–.0144	.7010	.5960	2,663
Dec	.6897	.6910	.6820	.6826	–.0149	.7075	.5970	716
Est vol 28,047; vol Fri 20,501; open int 35,509, –243.								
W. GERMAN MARK (IMM)–125,000 marks; $ per mark								
June	.5575	.5579	.5513	.5516	–.0108	.5692	.4850	46,986
Sept	.5624	.5629	.5562	.5564	–.0116	.5740	.4868	7,655
Dec	.5680	.5680	.5623	.5620	–.0121	.5790	.5604	646
Est vol 31,391; vol Fri 30,558; open int 55,350, –3,000.								
EURODOLLAR (LIFFE)–$1 million; pts of 100%								
June	92.57	92.66	92.55	92.64	+ .19	94.15	90.85	12,574
Sept	91.91	92.03	91.91	92.02	+ .27	94.03	91.56	9,679
Dec	91.52	91.71	91.52	91.70	+ .36	93.88	91.10	4,862
Mr88	91.25	91.50	91.25	91.48	+ .41	93.67	90.84	2,505
June	91.08	91.24	91.07	91.31	+ .43	93.39	90.60	902
Sept	90.93	91.02	90.93	91.16	+ .43	93.13	90.93	339
Dec	90.81	90.81	90.81	91.01	+ .43	92.90	90.81	164

The open price is that of the first transaction during the day. The high and low are the highest and lowest prices during the day. And, the settlement price is an average of the high and low prices during the "closing period" as defined by the exchange, usually the last two minutes of trading.

The open interest reflects the number of outstanding contracts at the end of the previous day's trading. For each commodity or financial instrument, the *Journal* also reports the total volume of trading (number of contracts exchanged) on the day in question and on the previous trading day.

Holders of outstanding contracts must ultimately settle their positions either by liquidation through offsetting purchases or sales, or by receiving or delivering the physical commodity against the contract. The great majority of futures contracts are settled by offset. Only 3 percent of all contracts result in delivery of the actual goods.

See also: FINANCIAL MARKETS
            INVESTING

Gg

GAINS

Gains are increases in equity (net assets) from peripheral or incidental transactions of an entity and from all other transactions and other events and circumstances affecting the entity during a period except those that result from revenues or investments by owners. Gains often arise for events and circumstances that may be beyond the control of an enterprise or its managements. Gains result from such activities as sales of investments in marketable securities, dispositions of used equipment, the settlement of liabilities at other than their carrying amounts, or the winning of a lawsuit.

See also: ELEMENTS OF FINANCIAL STATEMENTS
             EXTRAORDINARY ITEM
             INCOME
             INCOME STATEMENT
             REVENUE

Reference:

SFAC No. 3, *Elements of Financial Statements of Business Enterprises* (FASB, 1981).

GENERALLY ACCEPTED ACCOUNTING PRINCIPLES (GAAP)

Generally accepted accounting principles (GAAP) encompass the conventions, rules, and procedures necessary to define accepted accounting practice at a particular time. The responsibility for developing generally accepted accounting principles in the United States prior to 1973 rested to a great degree with the American Institute of Certified Public Accountants (AICPA). In 1938, the AICPA began issuing authoritative statements through its Committee on Accounting Procedure (CAP). This committee was authorized to issue pronouncements on accounting procedures and practices. It published a series of Accounting Research Bulletins.

CAP was replaced in 1959 by another committee of the AICPA called the Accounting Principles Board (APB). The APB was formed to counteract criticism of CAP and to create a policy-making body whose rules would be binding rather than optional. The APB issued a series of Statements and Opinions. The APB was replaced in 1973 by a new entity—the Financial Accounting Standards Board (FASB).

The FASB currently has the responsibility for setting accounting standards. The FASB is a separate entity from the AICPA. The FASB's authoritative pronouncements are issued in the form of Statements of Financial Accounting Standards and Interpretations. The FASB also issues Statements of Financial Accounting Concepts. Concept Statements do not create generally accepted accounting principles. They establish a theoretical foundation upon which to base financial accounting and reporting standards. The conceptual framework project is discussed elsewhere in this book. The FASB also publishes Technical Bulletins which provide guidance on accounting and reporting problems related to Statements of Standards or Interpretations. The FASB established the Emerging Issues Task Force in 1984 to identify new accounting and reporting issues that arise from new and different types of transactions. If members of the EITF reach a consensus that there is a single preferred treatment, the Chief Accountant of the SEC has stated that he will accept the consensus as authoritative support for practices to be used for SEC reporting. The FASB has not sanctioned the EITF as an authoritative standard-setting body.

In 1984 the Governmental Accounting Standards Board (GASB) was established to determine generally accepted accounting principles for governmental entities. GASB sanctioned NCGA pronouncements and the

AICPA Industry Audit Guide: Audits of State and Local Governmental Units as authoritative.

See also: ACCOUNTING PRINCIPLES
STATEMENTS OF FINANCIAL ACCOUNTING STANDARDS

References:

Financial Accounting Standards Board, *Accounting Standards* (McGraw-Hill, New York, latest edition).

Grady, Paul, "Inventory of Generally Accepted Accounting Principles for Business Enterprises" (AICPA, 1965).

GOALS AND OBJECTIVES

The establishment of useful goals and objectives is the first step in the planning process. Goals are general statements of what an organization seeks to accomplish through its programs; objectives are specific statements which have the same purposes as goals. Successful organizations typically establish a formal process for establishing goals and objectives. The relationship of goals and objectives to the planning and control process is shown in Exhibit G-1.

Establishing goals and objectives serves many purposes: it identifies the basic ends and means to those ends; it provides a sense of direction, decision guidelines, and performance criteria; and it reduces uncertainty within the organization. Goals enable the enterprise to plan, act, evaluate, and revise so that the goals themselves will be realized.

A goal is a statement of where one wants to go or what one wants to achieve. It is the intended result of proposed activity. A goal statement can describe the intended result (make a profit) or indicate the direction that one's activity should take (increase profits; reduce costs). Because goals are general statements of an intended result (point the direction), it is usually necessary to express them more precisely in terms of one or more objectives. Objectives are more specific than goals; they usually specify a performance standard or criteria for results which can be observed or measured. The process of assessing goals and objectives will deal with such issues as:

Exhibit G-1
The Strategic Management Process

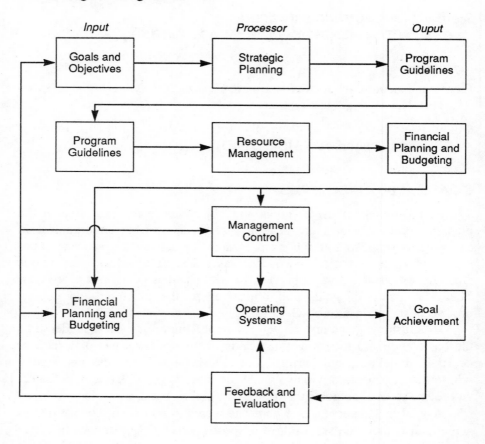

Source: Alan Walter Steiss, *Strategic Management and Organizational Decision Making,* Lexington Books, Lexington, Mass., 1985.

1. What is to be accomplished?

2. Why it is to be undertaken?

3. What is expected of the parties involved?

4. How will one know when it is accomplished?

It is usually beneficial for an organization to have written goals and objectives:

1. to establish what the purpose of an undertaking is and to specify how it is to be accomplished,

2. to serve as a basis for establishing authority and responsibilities,

3. to establish priorities,

4. to determine performance standards, and

5. to communicate effectively the contribution and commitment required of all parties.

Establishing goals and objectives implies that change in some form or other is required. To rationally consider what change is required, one needs to justify the intended result (end). Then one can determine the means (resources and processes) required to attain the end. A practical approach to resolve this issue is to determine what is the current situation and what should be.

Organizations typically have multiple goals which may be in conflict. Managers generally deal with goal conflicts in one of the following ways:

1. Agree to accept a satisfactory rather than a maximum level of performance, i.e., satisficing.

2. Establish a hierarchy among the goals which requires that a satisfactory level of achievement be attained on the more important goals before dealing with less important ones.

3. Continually revaluate and, if necessary, revise goals.

Criteria for effective objectives include suitability, feasibility, acceptability, achievability, measurability, adaptability, cost effectiveness, and commitment by management to the attainment of the objectives.

See also: CONTROL FUNCTION
MOTIVATION
ORGANIZING FUNCTION
PERFORMANCE EVALUATION
PLANNING FUNCTION
SATISFICING

Reference:

Steiss, Alan Walter, *Strategic Management and Organizational Decision Making* (Lexington Books, Lexington, Mass., 1985).

GOING CONCERN

External financial reports are prepared upon the assumption that the business entity will continue to operate indefinitely and will not be liquidated in the foreseeable future. When this is not the case, the going-concern assumption is no longer valid.

An increasing number of businesses are experiencing financial distress. While there are undoubtedly as many causes of financial distress as there are enterprises experiencing distress, the following factors have been identified as usually directly or indirectly involved.

1. Financial problems—difficulties in meeting obligations:
   a. Liquidity deficiency (e.g., working capital deficiencies).
   b. Equity deficiency.
   c. Debt default.
   d. Funds shortage.
2. Operating problems—apparent lack of operating success:
   a. Continued operating losses.
   b. Prospective revenues doubtful.
   c. Ability to operate is jeopardized.
   d. Incapable management.
   e. Poor control over operations.

Specific signs of financial distress in an enterprise include the following: liquidation process began; a declining share of major product markets; deferment of payment to short-term creditors: omission of preferred stock dividends; the filing of Chapter 7 or Chapter 11 bankruptcy; efforts to dispose of a segment of a business; bond default; overdrawn bank account; debt restructuring; externally forced revisions of operations; insolvency and illiquidity. The financially healthy firm usually has an adequate return on investment and a sound balance sheet.

An examination of the financial statements along with evidence obtained from management and other sources can provide the analysts with a basis for evaluating the going-concern condition of an enterprise. Research in business failures indicates that cash flow to total debt ratios, capital structure rations, and liquidity ratios are good predictors of bankruptcy and bond default. Turnover ratios are not particularly helpful in predicting financial distress. Bond rating changes and bond ratings of new issues can frequently be predicted by the use of ratios. Positive cash flows and the ability to obtain cash are the critical events associated with a distressed company's financial viability.

In certain industries, regulatory bodies have been established to monitor financial solvency and stability of companies. State insurance commissioners are usually authorized to evaluate registered insurance companies. The Interstate Commerce Commission evaluates railroads' ability to remain viable economic units. The Federal Deposit Insurance Corporation is deeply involved with the evaluation of commercial banks which come under its jurisdiction.

The auditor's responsibility is to evaluate whether there is substantial doubt for a reasonable period of time about the going-concern condition of the firm. If substantial doubt exists, the auditors obtain management's plans and assess the likelihood of the plans being implemented. If substantial doubt remains, the auditor considers the adequacy of disclosures on the firm's inability to continue and whether to include an explanatory paragraph following the opinion paragraph in the audit report. Auditors are not responsible for predicting future conditions and events.

See also: ACCOUNTING ASSUMPTIONS

GOODWILL

Goodwill is an intangible asset that represents the superior earning power of a business over the normal rate of return on net assets for the industry. Goodwill can also be conceptualized as the excess of the cost of business over the value assigned to the tangible and other identifiable intangible assets of the firm.

Accounting principles require that goodwill not be recorded unless it is acquired in an arm's-length transaction when the net assets of a business, or a substantial portion thereof, are purchased. Goodwill cannot be acquired separately from a related enterprise or group of assets. Any goodwill recorded on the accounting records should be amortized over a period of years not to exceed forty years.

Various methods are available for estimating the amount of goodwill. One method involves capitalizing average net earnings. Capitalizing earnings means computing the principal value that will yield the stated earnings at a specified rate indefinitely. The difference between the amount to be paid for the business and the appraised values of the individual net assets can be considered the price paid for goodwill. For example, assume that an 8 percent return is required on an investment in a business. Earnings of the businesses are estimated at $100,000 per year. The net assets are currently appraised at $1,000,000. The entire business including goodwill would be capitalized at $1,250,000 ($100,000 divided by .08). Goodwill would be valued at $250,000, the difference between the $1,250,000 capitalized value of the business and the $1,000,000 appraised value of the net assets.

See also: BUSINESS COMBINATIONS
            CONSOLIDATED FINANCIAL STATEMENTS
            INTANGIBLE ASSETS

Reference:

Wyatt, Arthur R., "A Critical Study of Accounting for Business Combinations" (AICPA, 1963).

GOVERNMENT OBLIGATIONS

The major marketable securities issued by the United States Treasury are Treasury bills, certificates of indebtedness, notes and bonds. These securities have several important characteristics: they are actively traded, they are considered very safe as to payment of interest and return of principal, and they are excellent collateral for loans. Marketable securities are subject to interest rate risks. If the general level of interest rates rises, the prices of securities held by investors decline in price. Government obligations are also subject to risks associated with a decline in purchasing power of the dollars (inflation) in which interest and principal are payable.

Treasury bills are non-interest-bearing obligations sold and quoted on a discount basis. Bills are issued with maturities of 90 and 180 days, and one year. Certificates of indebtedness have maturities of from one to five years. Treasury bonds have maturities of more than five years. Treasury bonds are usually callable by the Treasury at par at an option date several years prior to their maturity.

Treasury bills are auctioned each Monday, one issue maturing in 13 weeks and another in 26 weeks. Allotments are made to the highest bidders down to the price at which sufficient subscriptions have been received to sell the bills offered by the Treasury. Coupon obligations, including certificates of indebtedness, notes, and bonds, are offered through a Treasury announcement at auction. The Treasury offers the holders of maturing issues the right to exchange their securities for new issues. Various opportunities for advance refundings are made available to holders of government securities (for example, prerefundings in which holders of Treasury issues with a maturity of under one year are given the right to exchange their holdings for longer date issues usually with a maturity from one to five years).

Federal agencies also issue securities. The Federal Land Banks, Federal Intermediate Credit Banks, Federal Home Loan Banks, the Federal National Mortgage Association, the Bank for Cooperatives and the Tennessee Valley Authority issue securities. However, these securities are not guaranteed by the Treasury. These securities are generally considered to be of high quality, are readily marketable, and typically have relatively attractive yields.

United States Savings Bonds are designed primarily for individual investors. These bonds are not transferable and cannot serve as collateral for bank loans. They are considered very safe investments and have a moderately attractive rate of return if held to maturity. Series E bonds mature in seven years, nine months, and pay income at maturity or earlier redemption. The bonds are redeemable on demand according to a fixed schedule of prices. Owners may extend the maturity date of the bonds for an additional ten years. Series H bonds mature in ten years, are purchased at par, and bear interest paid semi-annually by the Treasury to the registered owner. The bonds are redeemable on demand at par.

Interest on most government obligations, including all marketable securities issued since March 1, 1941, and all savings bonds and notes currently issued, are fully taxable under federal tax law. All government securities are exempt from state and local taxes, except estate, inheritance, gift, and excise taxes. The increment on Series E bonds from year to year is taxable as interest either from year to year, or at maturity or prior redemption.

Municipal bonds are issued by counties, cities, towns, villages, special tax districts, authorities. They are usually classified as general obligations bonds supported with the full faith and credit of the municipality pledged and limited obligations which are special assessment and revenue bonds. The quality of municipal bonds is affected by the economics of the municipality, its population, wealth, income, and financial administration.

The process of marketing state and local government issues is described by a publication of the National Bureau of Economic Research as follows:

> Once a state or local governmental unit has completed the necessary legal steps that authorize it to borrow money, the marketing process follows a fairly standardized pattern. If, as is usual, the issue is to be sold by competitive bidding, then the interest to borrow is announced formally (informal news has already been circulated in most cases and bids are invited). In the somewhat rarer case of a negotiate when offering an investment banking house acts as the adviser, it may also organize the underwriting syndicate. This dual role, however, is frowned upon by some critics. In the more common case of a competitive sale, the second phase is that of the organization of groups for the purpose of bidding on the issue. The third stage, which almost always follows hard upon the award of the bid to the group offering the lowest borrowing cost, is the reoffering of the securities by the successful bidders to ultimate investors.

Municipal bonds are sold primarily in the over-the-counter market. Commercial banks and dealers specialized in making a market in these securities are directly involved in the marketing process. Major investors in state and local obligations include commercial banks, fire and casualty companies, life insurance companies, mutual savings banks, state and local retirement funds and nonfinancial corporations.

Municipal bonds are repaid either through a sinking fund or by serial (single issue divided into a number of different maturities) or installment repayments. In certain cases, payment is made from current municipal revenues or by refunding through a sale of a new issue.

GOVERNMENT REGULATION OF BUSINESS

The regulatory trend during the history of the United States has been toward both social and economic regulation. Social regulators include the Environmental Protection Agency, the Occupational Safety and Health Administration, the Consumer Product Safety Commission, and others. Economic regulators include the Federal Trade Commission, Civil Aeronautics Board, Federal Communications Commission, the Interstate Commerce Commission, and others. Public policy issues related to regulation cluster around antitrust policies, equality of economic opportunity, equality of employment opportunity, occupational safety and health, consumerism, and the physical environment.

The State Governmental Affairs Committee described a federal regulatory office as "one which (1) had decision making authority, (2) establishes standards or guidelines conferring benefits and imposing restrictions on business conduct, (3) operates principally in the sphere of domestic business activity, (4) has its head and/or members appointed by the president . . . and (5) has its legal procedures generally governed by the Administrative Procedures Act."

Congress has passed major antitrust laws which have for their purpose the maintenance of competition and the prevention of restraint of trade. This legislation also restricts unfair competitive practices.

The Sherman Antitrust Act declared that "every contract, combination . . . or conspiracy in restraint of trade or commerce among the several states is hereby declared to be illegal"; and "every person who shall monopolize, or . . . combine or conspire to monopolize any part of the trade or commerce among the several states . . . shall be deemed guilty of a misdemeanor . . . ." Courts have generally held that the restraint must be "undue" and "unreasonable" before it is considered to be illegal. The courts have held that bigness in and of itself is not proof of violation. The "principle of reason" has to be applied to such cases. Specifically, the Sherman Act prohibited price discrimination when it tends to lessen competition in any line of commerce. The Act also forbids sellers from requiring buyers to refrain from buying the goods of their rivals when such a policy tends to create a monopoly (for example, certain tying arrangements and exclusive dealing arrangements).

The Clayton Act, passed in 1914, was directed at the tendency toward corporate combinations which restrained trade or commerce. As it relates to antitrust matters, the Clayton Act states the "Unfair methods of competition in or affecting commerce, and unfair or deceptive acts or practices in or affecting commerce are hereby declared unlawful." Specifically, the act prohibits price discriminations that would result in a lessening of competition or tend to create monopoly; tying clauses in contracts which required buyers of products not to use the product of a competitor of the seller; the acquisition of the stock of one corporation by a competing corporation for the purpose of lessening competition; and interlocking directorates. Recent developments in 1977 in antitrust legislation raised the penalty for violations from misdemeanors to a felony punishable by fines not exceeding $1 million for a corporation or $100,000 for an individual and imprisonment not exceeding three years.

The Clayton Act was amended in 1936 when the Robinson-Patman Act was passed. The Robinson-Patman Act was designed to prevent "unfair" competition in trade by giving or receiving discounts or services when such acts amounted to discrimination and in a substantial reduction of competition. Price discrimination can occur when a supplier sells the same product to two different competitive wholesalers at different prices, when the effect may be to injure competition. The Act also makes it illegal for a buyer to knowingly induce or receive a discriminatory, lower price. Price differentials can be legal if they do not injure competition, they result from cost differences in selling to different customers, they are used to sell obsolete products, they are offered in good faith to meet a competitor's price, and they are offered to noncompeting customers. The Act also prohibits sellers from offering various types of advertising or promotional allowances unless they offer them to all customers "on proportionately equal terms."

The Robinson-Patman Act was amended in 1950 by the Anti-Merger Act, or the Celler-Kefauver Amendment, which makes it illegal for one corporation to acquire the assets of another company where the acquisition would substantially lessen competition, restrain commerce, or tend to create a monopoly.

The Federal Trade Commission Act of 1914 declares "that unfair methods of competition in commerce are hereby declared unlawful. The commission is hereby empowered and directed to prevent persons, partnerships, corporations, except banks, and common carriers subject to the acts which regulate commerce, from using unfair methods in commerce." The Wheeler-Lea Act of 1938 empowered the Commission to restrain business practices that it considers harmful to the public interest, especially false advertising and the adulteration of manufactured products.

Alternatives to government regulation would include greater freedom in allowing businesses to attain social objectives, increased cooperation between business and government in establishing realistic performance standards, a willingness on the part of business to acknowledge the legitimacy of social objectives, and let the marketplace bring about desired changes in business behavior.

See also: PRICING POLICY

Reference:

Buchholz, Rogene A., *Business Environment and Public Policy: Implications for Management* (Prentice-Hall, Englewood Cliffs, N.J., 1982)

GROSS MARGIN ANALYSIS

Gross margin (or gross profit) is the excess of sales over cost of goods sold. Gross margin represents the dollar amount of financial resources produced by the basic selling activity of the firm. On an income statement, gross margin appears as follows:

	1991	**1990**	**Change**
Sales	$225,00	$ 100,000	$125,000
Cost of goods sold	90,000	50,000	40,000
Gross Margin	135,000	50,000	85,000
Operating expenses	90,000	35,000	55,000
Net income	$ 45,000	$ 15,000	$ 30,000

Changes in gross margin from period to period may be due to any one or any combination of the following variables:

1. Change in sales caused by:
    a. change in selling price (sales-price variance);
    b. change in volume of goods sold (sales-volume variance).
2. Change in cost of goods sold caused by:
    a. change in unit cost (cost-price variance);
    b. change in volume of goods sold (cost-volume variance).

The four gross margin variances can be computed for year-to-year data using the following formulas and the following data which relate to the income statement shown earlier. The analysis which results from interpreting these variances is referred to as gross margin analysis.

	1991	1990
Number of units sold	150,000	100,000
Sales price per unit	$1.50	$1.00
Cost per unit	0.60	0.50

1. Sales-price variance   = Current year's units sold × Change in sales price per unit
                          = 150,000 × $0.50
                          = $75,000 favorable variance
2. Sales-volume variance = Change in units sold × Last year's prices
                          = 50,000 units × $1.00
                          = $50,000 favorable variance
3. Cost-price variance   = Current year's units sold × Change in cost per unit
                          = 150,000 × $0.10
4. Cost-volume variance   = Change in units sold × Last year's cost per unit
                          = 50,000 units × $0.50
                          = $25,000 unfavorable variance

When the four variances are combined, the $85,000 change in gross profit from 1990 to 1991 is identified:

Sales-price variance	$75,000
Sales-volume variance	50,000
Cost-price variance	(15,000)
Cost-volume variance	(25,000)
Change in gross margin	$85,000

For a multiproduct firm, a sales-mix variance is usually computed. This variance identifies the change in gross margin attributable to shifts in the sales mix for the company. This approximates the effect of changing the sales mix at a constant volume. This variance can be computed using the following formula:

Sales-mix variance	=	Current year's sales × Change in gross margin rate
	=	$225,000 × (.60 − .50)
	=	$22,500 favorable variance

GNP DEFLATOR

Real GNP is calculated by dividing nominal GNP by an average price level, thereby correcting for changes in the average price of all goods and services in the economy. Economists use the word *deflate* for this conversion of a nominal value to a real value. The aggregate price level is based on a price index called the GNP deflator.

The GNP deflator is always referenced to a base year, which is now 1982. By definition, the GNP deflator is defined to equal 100 in the base year. The average price level for any year is calculated by dividing that year's deflator by 100. Thus, the average price level for the base year is 1.0. Based on the values of the GNP deflator on the following page, the average price level for 1986 was 1.141, meaning that prices in 1986 were 14.1 percent higher than their 1982 level.

Year	GNP Deflator (1982 = 100)
1950	23.9
1960	30.9
1970	42.0
1980	85.7
1981	94.0
1982	100.0
1983	103.9
1984	107.7
1985	111.2
1986	114.1
1987	117.5

Source: *Economic Report of the President*, 1988.

See also: GROSS NATIONAL PRODUCT

Hh

HORIZONTAL MERGER

One method of increasing profit is for a firm to expand their share of the market. This can be accomplished by a merger with a firm producing a similar product. Such a merger is called a horizontal merger. These types of mergers were most common in the early history of our industrial economy. Most mergers over the so-called first wave of merger activity, 1887 to 1904, were horizontal mergers. Today, such mergers are closely scrutinized owing to the fact that they may impede competition.

See also: MERGER

HUMAN CAPITAL

Just as a firm invests in productivity-increasing capital equipment, individuals also invest in themselves through increased education, job training, and other similar productivity-enhancing activities. Economists refer to such investments as investments in human capital.

Just as firms calculate an expected rate of return on a capital investment to assist them in their decision making, many economists believe that individuals follow a similar analysis when contemplations investments in themselves. For example, those attending college perceive that there will be a positive return on their investment of funds, time, and foregone income.

HUMAN RESOURCE ACCOUNTING

Human resource accounting refers to accounting for the cost of recruiting, familiarizing, and developing personnel in a manner somewhat similar to procedures relating to manufacturing inventories or acquiring plant and equipment. Human resource accounting makes an effort to measure more accurately the cost of employee-personnel practices, turnover, and similar matters. Human resource accounting attempts to report the importance of human resources (knowledge, skill, training, loyalty, etc.) in relation to the enterprise's earning process. Treating the costs normally associated with human resource accounting as assets and subsequently depreciating them does not currently represent generally accepted accounting principles.

Reference:

Flamholtz, Eric, *Human Resource Accounting* (Dickerson, Encino, Calif., 1974).

Ii

IMPLICIT COSTS

See Imputed and Implicit Costs.

IMPORTS

U.S. imports are foreign goods and services purchased by consumers, firms, and governments in the United States. As the data in the table on the following page indicate, the U.S. has been importing more goods and services in recent years than it has been exporting. Thus, the U.S. has been experiencing a trade deficit (the value of imports is greater than the value of exports).

The United States imports many products for which it does not have a comparative advantage, such as crude petroleum, compact automobiles, tropical fruits, shoes, and many other labor-intensive products.

IMPUTED AND IMPLICIT COSTS

Expenditures that are attributable to the use of one's own factor of production, such as the use of one's own capital, are imputed costs. In accounting, imputed costs are often ignored when recording transactions.

317

Year	Imports ($billions)	Net Exports ($billions)
1950	$ 12.3	2.2
1960	24.0	5.9
1970	60.5	8.5
1980	318.9	32.1
1981	348.9	33.9
1982	335.6	26.3
1983	358.7	-6.1
1984	442.4	-58.9
1985	449.2	-79.2
1986	481.7	-105.5
1987	546.7	-119.9

Interest imputation is the process that estimates the interest rate to be used in finding the cash price of an asset. An imputed interest rate is similar to an implicit interest rate in that it equates the present value of payments on a note with the face of the note, but it can also be established by factors not associated with the note transaction or underlying contract. The imputed rate approximates a negotiated rate (a fair market interest rate) between independent borrowers and lenders. The imputed rate takes into consideration the term of the note, the credit standing of the issuer, collateral, and other factors. For example, an investor is considering the purchase of a large tract of undeveloped land. The offering price is $450,000 in the form of a non-interest-bearing note that is to be paid in three yearly installments of $150,000. There is no market for the note or the property. When the investor considered the current prime rate, his credit standing, the collateral, other terms of the note, and rates available for similar borrowings, a 12 percent interest rate was imputed.

Implicit interest (versus imputed interest) is interest implied in a contract. Implicit interest is interest that is neither paid nor received. The implicit interest rate is the interest rate that equates the present value of payments on a note with the face of the note. The implicit rate is determined by factors directly related to the note transaction. For example, assume that a dealer offers to sell a machine for $100,000 cash or $16,275 per year for ten years. By dividing the cash price by the annual payments (an annuity), a factor of 6.144 is computed ($100,000/$16,275). By referring to a Present Value of an Annuity of 1 in Arrears table, 6.144 appears in the 10 percent interest column when ten payments are involved. Therefore, the implicit interest rate in this offer is 10 percent.

Reference:

APB Opinion No. 21, *Interest on Receivables and Payables* (1971).

INCOME

Income has been defined in various ways according to authoritative sources:

1. "Income and profit . . . refer to amounts resulting from the deduction from revenues, or from operating revenues, of cost of goods sold, other expenses, and losses . . ." (Committee on Terminology, 1955).

2. "Net income (net loss)—the excess (deficit) of revenue over expenses for an accounting period . . ." (Accounting Principles Board, 1970).

3. "Comprehensive income is the change in equity (net assets) of an entity during a period of transactions and other events and circumstances from nonowner sources" (Financial Accounting Standards Board, 1980).

The measuring and reporting of income and its components are among the most significant accounting problems. Income as reported on the income statement can be conceptualized as follows:

$$\text{Revenues} - \text{Expenses} + \text{Gains} - \text{Losses} = \text{Net income}$$

Income determination is based upon the matching of efforts (expenses and losses) and accomplishments (revenues and gains). Two approaches are used to compute net income: the net assets approach and the transaction approach. Under the net assets approach, the net assets (total assets − total liabilities) of an enterprise are compared at the beginning and ending of a period. If there have been no investments or withdrawals of assets by owners during the period, the increase in net assets represents net income. A decrease represents a net loss. The net assets approach to computing net income can be conceptualized as follows:

Net income = Ending net assets – Beginning net assets + Asset withdrawals – Asset investments.

For example, assume that a company's net assets at the beginning of a period were $100,000 and at the ending, $150,000. Owners invested $10,000 and withdrew $5,000 during the period. Net income is computed as follows:

Ending net assets	$150,000
Deduct: Beginning net assets	100,000
Change in net assets during the period	50,000
Add: Asset withdrawals	5,000
Deduct: Asset investments	10,000
Net income for the period	$ 45,000

The transaction approach to measuring income measures and reports revenues and expenses relating to the enterprise that result in net income. This information is especially useful for decision making. For example, the accounting records could provide the following information:

Revenues	$150,000
Deduct: Expenses	105,000
Net income	$ 45,000

The term profit is generally used to refer to an enterprise's successful performance during a period. Profit has no technical meaning in accounting and is not displayed in financial statements. The term has no significant relationship to income or comprehensive income. The term gross profit is sometimes used to indicate the excess of sales over cost of goods sold.

See also: CAPITAL
EARNINGS PER SHARE
EXPENSES
GAINS
INCOME STATEMENT
MATCHING PRINCIPLE
RETAINED EARNINGS
REVENUE

References:

SFAC No. 6, *Elements of Financial Statements* (FASB, 1985).

SFAC No. 5, *Recognition and Measurement in Financial Statements of Business Enterprises* (FASB, 1984).

INCOME STATEMENT

An income statement presents the results of operations for a reporting period. The income statement provides information concerning return on investment, risk, financial flexibility, and operating capabilities. Return on investment is a measure of a firm's overall performance. Risk is the uncertainty associated with the future of the enterprise. Financial flexibility is the firm's ability to adapt to problems and opportunities. Operating capability relates to the firm's ability to maintain a given level of operations.

The current official view expressed by the Accounting Principles Board is that income "should reflect all items of profit and loss recognized during the period," except for a few items that would go directly to retained earnings, notably prior period adjustments. The following summary illustrates the income statement currently considered to represent generally accepted accounting principles:

Revenues	$XXX
Deduct: Expenses	XXX
Gains and losses that are not extraordinary	XXX
Income from continuing operations	XXX
Discontinued operations	XXX
Extraordinary gains and losses	XXX
Cumulative effect of change in accounting principle	XXX
Net income	$XXX

Generally accepted accounting principles require disclosing earnings per share amounts on the income statement of all publicly reporting entities. Earnings per share data provide a measure of the enterprise's management and past performance and enable users of financial statements to evaluate future prospects of the enterprise and assess dividend distributions to shareholders. Disclosure of earnings per share effects of discontinued operations and extraordinary items is optional but is required for income from continuing operations, income before extraordinary items, the cumulative effect of a change in accounting principle, and net income.

See also: ACCOUNTING CHANGES
DISCONTINUED OPERATIONS
EARNINGS PER SHARE
EXPENSES
EXTRAORDINARY ITEM
GAINS
INCOME
INCOME TAX
LOSSES
MEASUREMENT
OBJECTIVES OF FINANCIAL REPORTING BY
BUSINESS ENTERPRISES
PRIOR-PERIOD ADJUSTMENTS
RECOGNITION
REVENUE
STATEMENT OF EARNINGS AND
COMPREHENSIVE INCOME
STATEMENT OF RETAINED EARNINGS

Reference:

APB No. 30, *Reporting the Results of Operations* (APB, 1973).

INCOME TAX

The Tax Reform Act of 1986 is the most sweeping federal tax legislation since the wartime Revenue Act of 1942. The 1986 act dramatically lowered marginal tax rates which will require many taxpayers to reorient their thinking about taxes when making decisions.

Income taxes can have a major impact on many business decisions: the form of business organization, financing methods, sale or exchange of capital assets, investment incentives, accounting methods, revenue recognition, pension funding, and others.

Companies should establish a framework for dealing with income taxes. The process should involve the following broad steps:

1. develop tax objective(s),

2. identify strategies available for accomplishing these objective(s), and

3. develop specific applications of these strategies.

Tax objectives for most companies include (1) permanent saving of tax dollars, (2) reduction of tax liabilities, and (3) deferring tax liabilities to some future period.

Basic strategies relating to effective income-tax policies include (1) the direct method, (2) avoidance of traps and pitfalls, and (3) tax evasion (an unacceptable strategy). The direct method requires that tax strategies be structured around income opportunities, expenditure opportunities, deferral opportunities, a timing approach, and a tax provision approach. These strategies and applications can be summarized as follows:

Objective	Strategies	Applications
Avoiding taxes	I. The Direct Method 1. income approach	Tax-free income; the dividends exclusion
Reducing taxes	2. expenditure approach	Deductions: R&D, charitable, and other expenditures
Deferring (postponing) taxes	3. deferral approach	Tax deferral arrangements; tax deferred investments
All of the above	4. timing approach	Postponing income; early payment of expenses; taking advantage of tax changes
All of the above	5. tax provision	Tax credits; special tax rates
	II. Avoidance of Traps and Pitfalls	Knowledge of tax laws regulations, and court decisions; advice of accountants and lawyers
	III. Tax Evasion (not acceptable)	Not reporting taxable income; claiming deductions not allowed

INCOME TAX ALLOCATION

Federal, state, and local governments impose taxes against individuals, businesses, and other entities. Taxable income is determined by applying the tax rules and regulations. Since tax rules and regulations are used to compute taxable income while accounting principles are used to compute income reported on financial statements, taxes payable can differ from the provision for income taxes (income tax expense) reported on the income statement. This difference can result in a special liability or deferred charge item being reported on the balance sheet. Accounting for these differences is generally accomplished by a process referred to as income tax allocation.

It is possible for some revenue and expense items to be included in accounting and taxable income in different accounting periods. Some items may be recognized earlier or later for accounting purposes than for tax purposes. These differences are called temporary differences (formerly referred to as timing differences), and result in establishing deferred credits or deferred charges in the financial statements. When the item reverses in subsequent periods, the deferred balance is eliminated. For example, a company may use straight-line depreciation for accounting purposes and use accelerated depreciation when preparing its income tax return. The accounting procedures developed to deal with these timing differences is called interperiod tax allocation. Comprehensive income tax allocation requires allocation for all timing differences.

Generally accepted accounting principles require companies to recognize a current or deferred tax liability for the tax consequences of all events recognized in the financial statements. Deferred taxes are based on the difference between the tax bases of assets and liabilities and their amounts for financial reporting purposes. Companies are required to recompute their tax liabilities if the tax rates change and to recognize the effect in net income. This procedure is referred to as the liability method of income tax allocation (versus the deferred method, which was income statement oriented). The basic objective of the liability method is to present the estimated actual taxes to be payable in future periods as the income tax liability reported on the balance sheet. To accomplish this objective, it is necessary to consider the effect of certain future changes in tax rates in the computation of the current period's tax provision. The computation of the deferred taxes is based on the rate expected to be in effect when the timing differences reverse. The amount computed is viewed as a tentative estimate of the liability (or asset) which is subject to change as the tax rate changes or as the taxpayer moves into a different tax rate bracket.

The computation involves multiplying the aggregate unreversed timing differences including those originating this period by the expected future tax rate to determine the expected future tax liability. This estimated liability is the amount reported on the balance sheet at the end of the accounting period. The difference between this amount and the amount on the books at the beginning of the period is the deferred taxes for the period.

This approach is referred to as the asset and liability approach in accounting for temporary differences between taxable income and financial net income. Proponents of this view argue that ultimate realization of the amount of the tax deferral will depend upon the tax rates in effect when the temporary differences reverse (and not to the rates when the differences originate). The Financial Accounting Standards Board's Statement No. 96 requires this treatment and supersedes Accounting Principle Board's Opinion No. 11 which required the deferral method of accounting for tax timing differences. This method is effective for years beginning after December 15, 1988.

Permanent differences are distinguished from timing differences. A permanent difference is one that enters into accounting income but never into taxable income or vice versa. For example, interest received on state and municipal obligations is never a part of taxable income but is included in accounting income.

The components of income tax expense are separately reported on the income statement by intraperiod income tax allocation. Intraperiod income tax allocation matches a portion of the total income tax expense against the pretax (1) income from continuing operations, (2) income (loss) from the operations of a discontinued segment, (3) gain (loss) from the disposal of a discontinued segment, (4) gain (loss) from an extraordinary item, and (5) the cumulative effect of a change in accounting principle. The portion of the income tax expense for continuing operations is shown as a separate item on the income statement and is reported as a deduction from pretax income from continuing operations or, if there are no additional components of net income, from income before income taxes.

Reference:

Financial Accounting Standards Board, Statement No. 96, *Accounting for Income Taxes,* (FASB, 1987).

INCREMENTAL COST ANALYSIS

Incremental, or differential, costs are the differences in cost between two alternatives. Incremental cost analysis can be applied to most decisions that involve alternative courses of action where financial factors are involved. For example, incremental cost analysis is useful when determining the most profitable stage of production at which to sell a product, accepting or rejecting orders, make-or-buy decisions, increasing or abandoning operations, and capital budgeting decisions.

Incremental costs are usually variable or semivariable in nature. Variable costs increase or decrease as volume increases or decreases and in the same proportion. Semi-variable, or mixed, costs increase or decrease as volume increases or decreases but not in the same proportion because they contain some fixed costs. Fixed costs can be included in incremental cost analysis when a change in capacity of the operation is anticipated.

To be useful for decision-making purposes, a cost must be a relevant cost. To be relevant, a cost must pertain to the future and must vary among alternatives being considered. Historical costs are irrelevant; amounts already invested are sunk costs and are ignored when assessing new investments. For example, when choosing between two pieces of equipment and the material costs required for each machine is the same, the material cost is irrelevant for decision-making purposes.

Incremental, or differential, costs are the differences in cost between two alternatives. Incremental cost analysis can be applied to most decisions that involve alternative courses of action where financial factors are involved. For example, incremental cost analysis is useful when determining the most profitable stage of production at which to sell a product, accepting or rejecting orders, make-or-buy decisions, increasing or abandoning operations, and capital budgeting decisions.

Incremental costs are usually variable or semivariable in nature. Variable costs increase or decrease as volume increases or decreases and in the same proportion. Semivariable, or mixed, costs increase or decrease as volume increases or decreases but not in the same proportion because they contain some fixed costs. Fixed costs can be included in incremental cost analysis when a change in capacity of the operation is anticipated.

To be useful for decision-making purposes, a cost must be a relevant cost. To be relevant, a cost must pertain to the future and must vary among alternatives being considered. Historical costs are irrelevant; amounts already invested are "sunk" costs and are ignored when assessing new investments. For example, when choosing between two pieces of equipment and the material costs required for each machine is the same, the material cost is irrelevant for decision-making purposes. Several cases will be developed to illustrate the application of incremental cost analysis.

Case 1. Replacement of equipment. A manager purchases a computer for $100,000 on January 1, 19X1. The cash cost of operating the computer for the next ten years is expected to be $50,000 per year. At the end of ten years, the computer will be worthless. On January 2, 19X1, a salesman for a competing computer firm offers to sell a computer that can handle the same work at a cash operating cost of only $25,000 per year. The second computer would cost $200,000 and would have an expected life of ten years with no salvage value at the end of that period. maintenance and repair costs of $1,000 per year are expected for both machines. The manager learns that he can get a $10,000 trade-in for the computer he purchased on January 1.

Using incremental cost analysis, the manager prepares a schedule of the future costs that differ between the alternate courses of action (income tax considerations are ignored).

Relevant incremental costs	Cash Outflows Over 10 Years	
	Keep Computer	Replace Computer
Cash operating costs	$500,000	$250,000
Cash savage value if traded today		(10,000)
Cost of new computer		200,000
Total relevant costs	$500,000	$440,000

The analysis shows that the company will obtain cash savings of $60,000 over the ten-year period if the equipment is replaced. The $60,000 difference in total costs between the two alternatives is called the incremental cost.

Case 2. The make-or-buy decision. A manufacturer purchases certain parts used in the production of radios. The firm has idle capacity sufficient to manufacture these parts. The estimated cost of material, labor, and variable overhead expenses required to manufacture the parts total $100,000. No other use of the idle facilities is feasible. The cost to purchase these items from outside sources totals $90,000. Should the firm make or buy the parts?

The cost to purchase from outsiders is lower than the variable cost of manufacturing the parts with the idle plant capacity. The fixed costs of the available plant capacity (rent, insurance, etc.) are sunk costs and are irrelevant to the decision. The parts should be purchased from outside sources.

Management would want to consider other factors in addition to cost considerations when making a make-or-buy decision. Working capital requirements may be changed, morale problems may develop, production schedules might be disrupted, or relations with suppliers or customers might be affected. These factors could affect the decision.

Case 3. Possibility of additional sales. A factory is operating at 90 percent of capacity (45,000 units). Fixed expense is $100,000; variable expense is $6 per unit. The product is currently selling for $10 per unit. A customer in a foreign country has offered to buy 5,000 additional units at $7 per unit. If the order is accepted, total expense per unit is $8 ($100,000 fixed plus $300,000 variable expense divided by 50,000 units). It would appear that the firm will lose money if it sells the 5,000 units at $7 per unit.

	Current Volume	Additional Order	Volume of Order Accepted
Sales			
Current (45,000 @ $10)	$450,000		$450,000
Additional (5,000 @ $7)		$35,000	35,000
Less variable costs (@ $6)	270,000	(30,000)	(300,000)
Contribution margin	$180,000	$ 5,000	$185,000

The additional order will add a total of $5,000 towards the net income of the firm. The $100,000 fixed costs are not relevant to this decision because they do not vary among the two alternatives.

See also: CONTRIBUTION MARGIN ANALYSIS

Reference:

Montgomery, A. Thomas, *Managerial Accounting Information* (Addison Wesley, Reading, MA, latest edition).

INDEXING

Indexing refers to the tying of payment increases to some economic index. For example, certain wage contracts are written in such a way that workers will receive an agreed upon amount per hour plus an additional amount for each point increase in the Consumer Price Index. This type of wage arrangement is often called an escalator clause. Social Security payments are also indexed. This indexing assures that recipients' real incomes will not fall with inflation.

INDIFFERENCE CURVE

An indifference curve represents graphically alternative combinations of two products for which a consumer is indifferent. In Figure 9 on the following page, the individual would be indifferent between the combination of goods X and Y denoted by point A and that denoted by point B. The individual would prefer any combination of these goods that is to the right of the indifference curve, and would not choose to be to the left of the indifference curve.

An indifference curve is a theoretical construct used in economics to illustrate certain theoretical propositions, such as the law of demand.

INDUSTRIAL POLICY

In the late 1970s and early 1980s, there were calls for the United States to adopt an industrial policy which would select certain industries for preferential treatment (tax policies and protectionist policies) in order to stimulate their competitiveness in world markets. This notion was patterned after the Japanese strategy of government subsidization to selected industries, such as semiconductors.

Figure 9

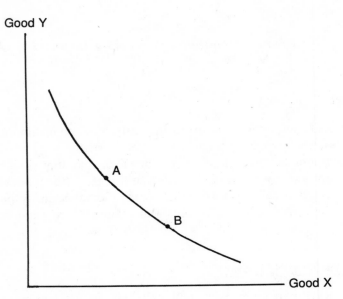

Robert Lawrence describes the argument for an industrial policy as: "There are fundamental deficiencies in the U.S. industrial system . . . managers are myopic . . . workers lack discipline . . . trade protection, granted unconditionally, has slowed adjustments to international competition . . . the government has failed to plan and coordinate its industrial evolution. It ought to have policies that promote industries with potential and assist those in decline." Advocates for an industrial policy suggested there being a central agency to formulate the policy operating with advice from industry and from labor. Arguments against having an industrial policy point to the need for the government to strengthen instead the natural forces for increased productivity within the economy by alleviating excessive governmental controls and regulations.

References:

Economic Report of the President, 1984.

Lawrence, Robert Z., *Can America Compete?* (Washington, D.C.: Brookings Institution, 1984).

INFLATION

Inflation is a persistent increase in the price level. Inflation is primarily demand-pull inflation or cost-push inflation. Demand-pull inflation arises when the demand for goods and services exceeds the available supply in the short run. This type of inflation frequently occurs in a fully employed economy and it leads to competitive bidding for economic resources. Cost-push inflation usually begins with increased costs of factors of production (wages, material costs) or increased prices of consumer goods (wage-price spiral).

There are two types of price changes:

1. Specific price levels: price changes of a specific commodity or item, such as a car or house; and

2. General price level: price changes of a group of goods and services.

In a technical sense, inflation refers to changes in the general price level. When the general price level increases, the dollar loses purchasing power—the ability to purchase goods or services. The opposite situation is referred to as deflation. Holding monetary assets and liabilities during periods of inflation or deflation results in purchasing power gains or losses. Monetary items are assets and liabilities that are fixed in terms of current dollars and cannot fluctuate to compensate for the change in the general price level. Monetary assets include cash, receivables and liabilities.

Changes in the general price level can affect, adversely or otherwise, almost every business decision. Changes in the general price level can affect organizational planning, controlling, and evaluating functions:

1. Is any of the budgeted or reported net income due to inflation?

2. Did the company lose or gain purchasing power from inflation due to holding monetary assets and liabilities?

3. How did inflation affect the financial statements during the period?

4. Were changes in the general price level taken into consideration when budgets were prepared? When dividend policy was determined? When analyzing financial statements? When evaluating performance

of investment centers? When selecting a source or method of financing?

A price index is used to measure changes in price levels. A price index is a series of numbers, one for each period, representing an average price of a group of goods and services, relative to the average price of the same group of goods and services at a base period. The Consumer Price Index for All Urban Consumers, published by the Bureau of Labor Statistics of the Department of Labor in *Monthly Labor Review,* is perhaps the most widely used price index.

Current cost information is needed to deal with changes in specific prices. Replacement costs are commonly used in current cost systems and for decisions involving specific prices.

See also: CONSUMER PRICE INDEX
COST-PUSH INFLATION
DEMAND-PULL INFLATION

INFORMATION SYSTEMS

A management information system (MIS) is a process which organizes and communicates relevant information on a timely basis to enable management to perform its functions properly. The term system refers to the components or subsystems that interact and interrelate to accomplish a goal or objective.

The activities of an information system include collection, processing, and communication of information. A management information system (MIS) includes the means by which information is provided to decision makers so that they may effectively attain the organization's goals and objectives. The major attributes of an MIS include the following: relevance, accuracy, timeliness, completeness, conciseness, economy, and flexibility. Subsystems of a typical business organization include the following: personnel subsystems, purchasing subsystems, production subsystems, marketing subsystems, order-processing subsystems and financial subsystems. A primary subsystem is one that impacts the entire structure of an organization. A secondary subsystem is one that is limited to a single functional part of an organization.

Developing an MIS involves the following steps:

1. Establish the goals of the system.

2. Identify the information needed to attain the goal.

3. Design the system.

4. Test the system.

5. Implement the system.

6. Monitor and control the system.

These steps can be expanded in terms of a feasibility assessment and system design:

1. *Feasibility assessment*—Preliminary analysis of current system; identification of reporting needs; requirements in terms of people, equipment, and forms; preliminary assessment of costs and benefits.

2. *System design*—Complete description of the system; testing design to ensure that it can accomplish what it is supposed to accomplish.

A management accounting system should be designed to provide timely and accurate information to assist management develop product costs, control costs, improve productivity, increase efficiency and effectiveness, and motivate and evaluate performance. The system should serve as a communications channel between various levels of management, especially as they relate to (1) organizational goals and objectives and (2) product performance and production efficiencies. Sophisticated electronic technology is available to develop reporting and control systems that are accurate, timely, and effective.

References:

Johnson, H. Thomas, and Robert S. Kaplan, *Relevance Lost: The Rise and Fall of Management Accounting* (Harvard Business School Press, Boston, 1986).

Maciariello, Joseph A., *Management Control Systems* (Prentice-Hall, Englewood Cliffs, N.J., 1984).

Wu, Frederick H., *Accounting Information System: Theory and Practice* (McGraw-Hill, N.Y., 1983).

INSIDER TRADING SANCTIONS ACT OF 1984

The Insider Trading Sanctions Act of 1984 increased the penalties against persons who profit from illegal use of insider information. The Act allows the SEC to seek fines of up to three times the profits gained or losses avoided by those insiders who improperly use material nonpublic information. The Act also increases from $10,000 to $100,000 the criminal penalties for market manipulation, securities fraud, and certain other violations. The Act does not define "material inside information" or limit its prohibitions to corporate insiders. Anyone who assists another person to violate the insider trading rules can be held liable.

See also: FRAUD

INSTALLMENT SALES METHOD

The installment sales method of accounting recognizes revenue as cash is collected when receivables are collectible over an extended period of time, rather than at the time of sale. The installment sales method of recognizing revenue is a modification of the cash collection method.

The installment sales method should be used only when there is a significant uncertainty concerning the ultimate collection of the sales proceeds. In such situations, revenue recognition is postponed. For example, a company sold for $100,000 land which cost $60,000. The rate of gross profit on this transaction is 40 percent ($40,000/$100,000). It is assumed that there is considerable uncertainty concerning the collectibility of the receivable resulting from the transaction. During the first year, the company collected $20,000. Income (gross profit) in the amount of $8,000 ($20,000 × 40%) is recognized. As can be noted, payments are prorated between recovery of the cost of the property and profit to be recognized on the sale.

INSURANCE

Insurance is a contract between an insurer and the insured whereby the insurer indemnifies the insured against loss due to specific risks, such as from fire, storm, death, etc. Insurance is an integral part of most enterprises' risk management. Insurance contracts require an agreement, consideration, capacity, legality, compliance with the Statute of Frauds and delivery. Liability insurance protects the insured from claims by third parties for damages resulting from actions or events that are the responsibility of the insured. Casualty insurance protects the insured from a variety of insurable events such as fire, storm, theft, explosion, and other casualties.

Insurance policies usually contain a deductible clause that excludes a fixed amount of the loss from recovery. Casualty insurance policies frequently contain a coinsurance clause in the contract. A coinsurance clause provides that the insurance company shall be liable for only a portion of any loss sustained by the insured unless the insured carries insurance which totals a certain percent, frequently 80–90 percent of the fair value of the asset. In the event of a loss, the insured recovers from the insurance company that portion of the loss which the face of the insurance policy bears to the amount of insurance that should be carried as required by the coinsurance clause.

The coinsurance indemnity is expressed as follows:

$$\frac{\text{Face amount of policy}}{\text{Coinsurance percentage} \times \text{Fair value of property at date of loss}} \times \text{Fair Value}$$

To illustrate, assume a company purchases a $20,000 insurance policy on some equipment; the policy has an 80 percent coinsurance clause. A fire loss occurs at a time when the fair value of the equipment was $30,000. The amount of the loss was $6,000:

$$\frac{\$20,000}{(80\%)\ (\$30,000)} \times \$6,000 = \$5,000 \text{ recoverable from insurer}$$

The insured can recover the lowest of the face of the policy, the fair value of the loss, or the coinsurance indemnity.

See also: CASH SURRENDER VALUE

Reference:

Huebner, S.S., et al., *Property and Liability Insurance* (Prentice Hall, Inc., Englewood Cliffs, N.J., 1982).

INTANGIBLE ASSETS

Intangible assets are special rights, grants, privileges, and advantages possessed by a business which can benefit future operations by contributing to the enterprise's earning power. Intangible assets do not possess physical substance. Intangible assets include patents, copyrights, trademarks, trade names, franchises, licenses and royalties, formulas, and processes, organization costs, leasehold and leasehold improvements, and goodwill.

Intangible assets may be acquired from other enterprises or individuals, or the company may develop intangible assets. Intangible assets can be classified as unidentifiable and identifiable intangible assets. An unidentifiable intangible is one that cannot exist independent of the business as a whole. Goodwill and organization costs are unidentifiable intangible assets. Identifiable intangible assets have a separate identity and existence of their own, independent of the business as a whole. Patents, copyrights, and medical patient charts are examples of identifiable intangible assets. If acquired by purchase, the intangible item is recognized as an asset. If developed by the enterprise, the research and development costs are expenses when incurred.

The life of an intangible asset may be determinable if fixed by law, regulation, agreement, contract, or by the nature of the asset. The cost of an intangible asset having a determinable life should be amortized in a rational and systematic manner over the term of its existence, but not to exceed 40 years. If the life of the intangible asset is indeterminate, as might be the case for goodwill and trade names, the cost of the assets should be written off over a period of years established by management, but not to exceed forty years. The straight-line method of amortization should be used to write off the cost of intangible assets over future periods to be benefited by the assets unless another systematic method is considered more relevant and reliable.

A patent has a legal life of 17 years. Copyrights are granted for a period of years covering the life of the creator of the copyright plus an additional 50 years. Franchises may be granted for a limited time or for an unlimited period. Organization costs are incurred during the formation of a corporation and prior to income-producing operations. Such costs include expenditures incurred relating to promoters, attorneys, accountants, underwriters' charges as well as registration and listing fees, and printing costs associated with the issuance of securities. Such costs should be written off over a period of time not to exceed 40 years. Leasehold improvements should be written off over the term of the lease.

Reference:

APB No. 17, *Intangible Assets* (APB, 1970).

INTEREST

Interest is money paid for the use of borrowed funds or money earned from capital invested. Interest (I) depends on three factors: (1) the amount of capital that is borrowed or loaned, called the principal (P), (2) the rate of interest (R), and (3) the amount of time (T) for which the principal is borrowed or lent. *Simple interest* is calculated as follows:

$$I = P \times R \times T \tag{1}$$

The interest rate (R) is the ratio of the amount of interest (I) paid or earned, during a certain period of time, to the amount of principal (P). If time (T) is equal to one year, then the *simple interest rate* (R) is:

$$R = I / P / 1 \tag{2}$$

For example, if the principal is $1,200 and interest earned is $150 per year, then the interest rate is 0.125, or $150/$1,200/1. The interest rate is usually stated as a percentage. In this example, the interest rate is 0.125, or 12.5 percent.

The amount of time (T) for which interest is earned or paid is usually stated in years. In the above example, if the funds were lent for six months, time would be equal to 1/2, or 0.5. In this case, the *simple interest rate* would be 0.25, or 25 percent. The rate would be calculated as:

$$R = \$150/\$1,200/0.5 = 0.25.$$

Sometimes funds are borrowed or loaned only for a certain number of days. In this case, time in the interest formula is expressed as a fraction of days per year, that is, as time (T) = days/year. Bankers often employ a 360-day year when calculating interest. At other times, a 365-day calendar year is used. Using a calendar year, if funds are borrowed for 20 days, then time (T) would be equal to 20/365, or 0.0548.

The federal Truth in Lending Act requires that interest rates on consumer loans be stated in annual percentage rate (APR) terms. In APR terms, the interest rate measures the cost of funds on a yearly basis, that is, what the rate would be if the funds were used for one year. The law also requires that the lender disclose to the borrower not only the APR rate of interest but also any finance charges or other fees connected with the loan.

When interest on a loan or investment is not actually paid out to the lender each period, it accumulates or compounds. *Compound interest* is the amount paid or earned on the original principal plus accumulated interest. On a one-year loan where interest is paid at the end of the year, simple interest and compound interest are the same because there is no accumulated interest. However, if the loan is extended for two years and the interest is not paid out until the end of the second year, then it is necessary to include the first year's accumulated interest together with the principal when computing the interest for the second year.

The basic formula for the future value (FV) of a principal sum invested at compound interest is

$$FV = P \times (1 + R)^T \tag{3}$$

As an example, assume the Indians who sold Manhattan in 1626 for $24 had invested their money at 6 percent, with interest compounded annually. At the end of 1986, they would have

$$FV = \$24 \times (1 + .06)^{360} = \$30,926,000,000$$

In this example, time (T) is equal to 1986 − 1626 = 360 years. The above example assumes *annual* compounding; that is the interest accumulates once at the end of each year. In many cases, however, interest is accumulated *semiannually*, *quarterly*, or even *daily*. In such cases, the formula in equation (3) can still be used to calculate future value, but the value for time (T) must be changed to reflect not the number of years but the number of compounding periods. And the value for the interest rate (R) must reflect the rate paid per compounding period. As a general rule, to calculate interest with *multiyear* compounding, divide the annual rate of interest by the number of compounding periods per year and multiply the number of years by the number of annual compounding periods. Use these values for *R* and *T* respectively in the above formula.

In the example above, if the Indians had invested their money at 6 percent interest with *semiannual* compounding, they would have

$$FV = \$24 \times (1 + .06/2)^{360 \times 2} = \$41,977,000,000$$

Some financial institutions pay interest on deposits on a daily basis. With daily compounding, it is normally assumed that there are 360 compounding periods per year when calculating the rate per period, but a calendar year is used in computing the value for time. The formula for future value with *daily* compounding becomes

$$FV = P \times (1 + R/360)^{T \times 365} \qquad (4)$$

Using this formula, a saver depositing $1,000 in a certificate of deposit for two years with daily compounding at 6 percent would have when the certificate matures

$$FV = \$1,000 \times (1 + .06/360)^{2 \times 365} = \$1,127.49$$

The *effective rate of interest* (ER) on a loan or investment with multi-year compounding can be calculated as

$$ER = (FV / P)^{1/T} - 1 \qquad (5)$$

In the above example, the effective rate of interest on the certificate of deposit with daily compounding is

$$ER = (\$1,127.49/\$1,000)^{1/2} - 1 = 0.06183 \text{ or } 6.183\%$$

The difference between simple interest and compound interest is illustrated in Exhibit I-1 on the following page.

See also: ANNUITY
CAPITALIZATION OF INTEREST
FEDERAL RESERVE SYSTEM
FUTURE VALUE
PRESENT VALUE
YIELD TO MATURITY
RULE OF 69
RULE OF 78
U.S. RULE AND MERCHANTS RULE

Reference:

Woelfel, Charles J., *Financial Managers Desktop Reference to Money, Time, Interest and Yield* (Probus, Chicago, 1986).

Exhibit I-1
Simple Interest and Compound Interest Compared

End of year	Interest Earned	Cumulative Interest	Balance
		SIMPLE INTEREST	
1	$1,000(.10) = $100	$100	$1,100
2	$1,000(.10) = 100	200	1,200
3	$1,000.(10) = 100	300	1,300
4	$1,000(.10) = 100	400	1,400
		COMPOUND INTEREST	
1	$1,000(.10) = $100.00	$100.00	$1,100.00
2	$1,100(.10) = 110.00	210.00	1,210.00
3	$1,210(.10) = 121.00	331.00	1,331.00
4	$1,331(.10) = 133.10	464.10	1,464.10

INTEREST RATE SWAP

An interest rate swap (sometimes called a rate swap) is an agreement between two parties to exchange a series of interest payments based on an agreed principal amount (often termed the "notional" amount). Because the parties exchange only the interest payments without exchanging the underlying debt, interest rate swaps do not appear on the balance sheets of the participants, although the inflows and outflows from swap transactions show up on the income statements.

Early interest rate swaps began to be popular in the Euromarkets starting around 1981. At that time, the typical swap transaction involved a firm with a high credit rating (usually a financial institution) with a desire for short-term funds and a lower-rated company needing longer-term, fixed-rate funds. Although the better-rated company could usually raise both short- and long-term funds at a lower rate, it normally had a comparative advantage in raising longer-term funds because investors tend to require a higher risk premium for securities with longer maturities.

For the purpose of illustration, assume that Company X is the high-rated firm and Company Z is its lower-rated partner. Suppose X can borrow long-term in the Eurobond market at 10 percent and short-term at the London interbank offered rate (LIBOR) plus 0.5 percent. Firm Z can borrow at 12 percent in the bond market and at the LIBOR plus 1.0 percent in the short-term market. Firm X thus has a comparative advantage relative to Firm Z in obtaining long-term funds, even though it can borrow in both markets more cheaply than can Firm Z. Similarly, Firm Z has a comparative advantage in raising short-term funds. A swap transaction allows each firm to gain from a trade in which each borrows in the market where it has a comparative advantage and then swaps interest payments with its partner.

Company X could issue Eurobonds for an agreed principal amount at 10 percent and pledge to pay Company Z interest on the set amount of principal at a rate equal to the LIBOR each quarter. Company Z in turn could issue short-term debt at the LIBOR plus 1.0 percent and agree to pay Company X a fixed rate of 10.5 percent on the notional principal.

The effect of this transaction on each company is as follows:

	Firm X	Firm Z
Cost of Borrowed Funds	(10%)	(LIBOR + 1%)
Swap Inflow	10.5%	LIBOR
Swap Outflow	(LIBOR)	(10.5%)
Original Cost of funds	LIBOR + 0.5%	12%
Cost of funds after Swap	LIBOR – 0.5%	11.5%
Advantage from Swap	1.0%	0.5%

By trading interest payments through the swap transaction, both companies are able to reduce their cost of funds below what it would have been before the swap. Company X is able to borrow at a variable rate equal to the LIBOR minus 0.5 percent, cutting its cost of funds by 1.0 percent. And Company Z is able to obtain long-term funds at a cost of 11.5 percent, instead of the 12 percent that it would normally have had to pay.

Through the swap transaction, Company X transforms a fixed-rate contract with an interest rate of 10 percent into a floating-rate obligation with an effective rate of the LIBOR minus 0.5 percent. Likewise, Company Z turns a floating-rate contract into a fixed-rate obligation with a rate of 11.5 percent. Both participants thus gain from the swap arrangement.

The largest market for interest rate swaps is denominated in U.S. dollars, although swaps in other currencies are available. Swaps normally are executed over the telephone and may begin immediately.

The parties to a swap transaction sign a legal contract that governs the exchange of cash flows. The risk to each party in the transaction is that the other will default on his obligation. Should this occur, the other party stops payment immediately, but is still obligated to pay the interest on its original debt and may suffer an increase in its cost of funds.

Sometimes parties to a swap transaction may insist on the extra protection of a letter of credit, collateral, or some other form of guarantee. There has been an increase in the use of third-party insurers who guarantee against default by the participants of a swap.

Many swap transactions now are arranged through commercial or investment banks acting as intermediaries. Typically, the financial intermediary will enter into offsetting swaps with both parties and earn a fee from the spread between the two swap agreements. The fee compensates the bank for assuming the credit risk stemming from possible default by either party.

The size of the market in swaps has grown dramatically from an estimated $3 billion in 1982 to more than $200 billion by the end of 1985. It is reported that from 50 to 75 percent of the volume of new Eurobond issues is now swap related. Because of the great growth in the demand for swaps, there has been an increase in the use of brokers who attempt to locate counterparties desiring a particular swap specified by the customer. And large commercial and investment banks have begun to make a market in swaps by booking one side of the transaction before an actual counterparty is found, in effect "warehousing" swap transactions.

It has become common for companies to use the swap market to transform floating-rate debt into fixed-rate obligations. This kind of transaction is particularly attractive to institutions such as savings and loans that traditionally have had substantial gaps between the duration of their assets and that of their liabilities. Other companies are able to use swaps to "unlock" high coupon debt by swapping it for lower variable-rate debt.

Besides the normal fixed-rate/floating-rate swap, some firms have begun to exchange floating-rate debt based on one index for floating-rate debt based on a different index (what is termed a "basis" swap). There also are exchanges of fixed-rate debt in one currency for floating-rate debt denominated in another currency as well as forward contracts and options on swaps.

As a financial innovation, swaps offer financial managers an effective device of liability management and interest rate hedging. Using swaps, managers can easily transform the financial characteristics of their liabilities.

References:

Bicksler, James, and Chen, Andrew H., "An Economic Analysis of Interest Rate Swaps," *Journal of Finance* (July 1986), pp. 645–655.

Arnold, Tanya S., "How to Do Interest Rate Swaps," *Harvard Business Review* (September/October 1984), pp. 96–101.

INTERLOCKING DIRECTORATE

An interlocking directorate is one means by which two or more companies can have ties without there being any financial arrangements between the companies. One example is that the same individual could sit on the board of directors of two companies. While the Clayton Act of 1914 forbade such arrangements between competing companies, this regulation was not enforced until the late 1960s with any meaningful degree of force.

INTERNAL CONTROL

Internal control refers to the systems, procedures, and policies employed by an enterprise to help assure that transactions are properly authorized and are appropriately executed and recorded. Internal control applies to both administrative controls and accounting controls. Administrative (operating) controls include a plan of organization, procedures, and records that lead up to management's authorization of transactions. Accounting (financial) controls deal with the plans, procedures, and records required for safeguarding assets and producing reliable financial records.

Auditing standards require that accounting controls be designed to provide reasonable assurance that:

1. Transactions are executed in accordance with management's general or specific authorization.

2. Transactions are recorded as necessary to permit preparation of financial statements in conformity with generally accepted accounting principles or any other criteria applicable to such statements and to maintain accountability for assets.

3. Access to assets is permitted only in accordance with management's authorization.

4. The recorded accountability for assets is compared with the existing assets at reasonable intervals and appropriate action is taken with respect to any difference.

Broad categories of control procedures that apply to both financial and administrative controls include the following:

1. Organizational:

    a. Separation of duties.

    b. Clear lines of authority and responsibility.

    c. Formal policies.

2. Procedures:

    a. Accounting checks.

    b. Proper documents and records.

    c. Error detection and correction procedures.

    d. Physical control over assets and records.

3. Competent, trustworthy personnel (bonded where appropriate).

4. Performance goals and objectives:

    a. Periodic reviews of performance.

    b. Comparisons of recorded accountability with assets.

5. Independent review of the system.

The Foreign Corrupt Practices Act, passed in 1977, had a major impact on internal control applications in that it requires public companies to maintain reasonably complete and accurate financial records and a sufficient system of internal accounting controls. A major reason for this legislation was that Congress believed that public companies had inadequate controls to detect bribes and improper payments.

A review of internal accounting controls is essential to an audit of financial statements. A study of internal accounting controls enables the auditor to make a judgment concerning the reliance that can be placed on the records and for determining the nature, extent, and timing of various tests of the accounting data that the system has produced.

See also: AUDIT
              BANK RECONCILIATION
              FOREIGN CORRUPT PRACTICES ACT

Reference:

Burton, John C., et al., eds. *Handbook of Accounting and Auditing* (Warren, Gorham & Lamont, Boston, 1981).

INTERNAL RATE OF RETURN

The internal rate of return (or time adjusted rate of return) is defined in various ways:

a. IRR is the discount rate that equates the present value of a project's cash inflows with the present value of the project's cash outflows.

b. IRR is the minimum rate that could be paid for the funds invested in a project without losing money.

c. IRR is the discount rate that results in a project's net present value equalling zero.

By definition, IRR is the rate when Net Present Value (NPV) = 0. Therefore, IRR is the rate at which cash inflow multiplied by present value of annuity of $1 = cash outflow. In a problem with uniform expected annual cash inflows, the discount factor is simply equal to initial outlays divided by annual cash inflows. The discount factor is then located in a table of present values for an annuity of $1. If annual cash inflows are not uniform, a trial-and-error method can be used to calculate the internal rate of return. Select a reasonable interest rate and compute the present value of the cash inflows. If this present value does not equal the initial outlay, continue selecting rates until they are equal. The interest rate at which the net present value of future cash inflows equals the initial outlay for the project is its internal rate of return. Many calculators and computers are available to compute the IRR easily.

See also: CAPITAL BUDGET

INVENTORY

Inventory is a term used to identify material or merchandise owned by the enterprise that eventually will be sold to customers or used in the process of production. Merchandise inventory is a term used for goods held for sale by retail or wholesale firms. Goods held for resale by manufacturing firms are referred to as finished goods. Manufacturing firms may also have work-in-process inventories which represent partially completed products still in the production process. Manufacturing firms may also have raw materials inventories which consist of materials which will become part of goods to be manufactured.

The more common methods of assigning cost to inventory include the following:

1. *Specific identification method.* Each item in inventory is individually identified, and a record is kept of its actual cost. The actual flow of goods is monitored and recorded exactly. Each item in the ending inventory can be identified, and its cost is assigned to the item.

2. *First-in, first-out method (FIFO).* The flow of goods is assumed to be such that the oldest items in the inventory are sold or used first. Inventory items on hand at the end of the period are assumed to have been acquired in the most recent purchases.

3. *Last-in, first-out method (LIFO).* The flow of goods is assumed to be such that the items most recently purchased are sold or used first. The ending inventory is assumed to have come from the earliest purchases.

4. *Weighted average method.* The flow of goods is assumed to be such that all items available for sale during the period are intermingled randomly, and items sold or used are picked randomly from this intermingled inventory. The weighted average cost per unit is computed according to this formula:

$$\frac{\text{Beginning inventory} + \text{Purchases}}{\text{Units in beginning inventory} + \text{units purchased}} = \text{Average cost per unit}$$

5. *Moving average method.* The flow of goods is assumed to be such that the items in the inventory are intermingled randomly after each addition to the inventory; items sold or used are picked randomly from those items in the inventory at the time. Under this method, an average cost per unit for the items in the inventory is computed after each purchase according to this formula:

$$\frac{\text{Total cost of inventory on hand after each purchase}}{\text{Total number of units in the inventory on hand after each purchase}} = \text{Average cost per unit}$$

Major impacts of FIFO and LIFO inventory costing methods on financial statement items in times of rising prices are shown here:

	FIFO	LIFO
Ending inventory in balance sheet	Higher	Lower
Current assets	Higher	Lower
Working capital	Higher	Lower
Total assets	Higher	Lower
Cost of goods sold in income statement	Lower	Higher
Gross margin	Higher	Lower
Net income	Higher	Lower
Taxable income	Higher	Lower
Income taxes payable	Higher	Lower

INVENTORY MODEL

The control of inventory involves two major considerations:

1. What is the optimal size for a purchase order?
2. When should the order be placed?

When considering the optimal order size, a manager knows that:

1. certain expenses tend to increase with an increase in order size; for example, storage-space cost, insurance, taxes, risk of spoilage or theft, interest on money invested to finance the inventory, etc.; and

2. other expenses tend to decrease with an increase in order size; for example, cost of clerical work associated with purchasing and receiving and paying bills, freight expense, etc.

As order size increases, the cost of ordering inventory decreases while the cost of carrying inventory increases. Exhibit I-2 illustrates the relationship between order size and inventory-handling costs. The optimal order size is the order size at which the ordering-cost and carrying-cost curves intersect. This relationship can be expressed in the following formula:

$$\text{Economic order size} = \sqrt{2AP/S}$$

where A = annual quantity used, in units; P = cost of placing an order; and S = annual cost of carrying one unit in stock for one year. To illustrate this concept, assume that a company uses 3,600 units of inventory each year. The cost of placing an order is $8, and the cost to carry one unit in inventory for one year is $1:

$$\text{Economic order size} = \sqrt{(2)(3,600)(8)/\$1}$$
$$= 240 \text{ units.}$$

The next issue to consider is when should inventory be ordered. If the lead time (the time between placing an order and receiving delivery), the economic order size, and the average usage are known, the time issue can

Exhibit I-2

Economic Order Model for Inventory

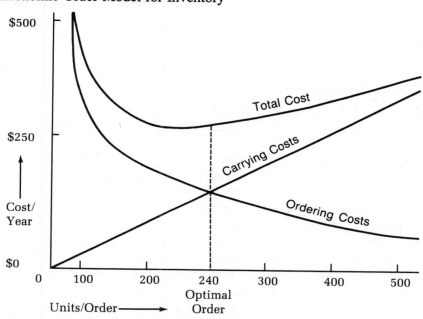

be resolved. For example, in the illustration the demand is 3,600 units per year or approximately 10 units per day. One order of 240 units will last for about 24 days. The time between orders will have to be about 24 days. The order should be placed so that the new order will arrive just as the last one is used up. Suppose it takes 14 days from the time an order is placed until the goods arrive. In this case, each order should be placed 10 days after the last one has arrived, so that the new goods will arrive on the 24th day after the arrival of the previous order.

See also: CONTROL FUNCTION
            INVENTORY
            INVENTORY PROFIT
            PLANNING FUNCTION

Reference:

Moscove, Stephen A., et al., *Cost Accounting* (Houghton Mifflin, Boston, 1985).

INVENTORY PROFIT

The Securities and Exchange Commission recommends that publicly owned companies disclose the amount of profit included in the income statement which will not recur due to increased replacement cost of inventories caused by inflation. Such profits are normally referred to as inventory profits (paper profits). The SEC supported this recommendation with the following arguments:

> The most significant and immediate impact of price fluctuations on financial statements is normally felt in cost of goods sold in the income statement. In periods of rising prices, historical cost methods result in the inclusion of "inventory profits" in reported earnings. "Inventory profits" result from holding inventories during a period of rising inventory costs and is measured by the difference between the historical cost of an item and its replacement cost at the time it is sold. Different methods of accounting for inventories can affect the degree to which "inventory profits" are included and identifiable in current income, but no method based upon historical cost eliminates or discloses this "profit" explicitly. Such "profits" do not reflect an increase in the economic earning power of a business and they are not normally repeatable in the absence of continued price-level increase. Accordingly, where such "profits" are material in income statements presented, disclosure of their impact on reported earnings and the trend of reported earnings is important information for investors assessing the quality of earnings.

Inventory profit comes from holding inventory in periods of rising prices rather than from selling inventory. The reported net income under FIFO during periods of rising prices is usually larger than under LIFO because LIFO charges the latest, higher cost of inventory to cost of goods sold. The excess of FIFO's net income attributable to this factor over LIFO's net income represents inventory profit. The cost of goods sold under LIFO approximates the replacement cost of the inventory sold and thus minimizes inventory profit. Inventory profit arises primarily when old, low inventory costs (FIFO costs) are matched against current selling prices. It is the difference between the old, low inventory costs and current replacement cost of inventory that creates inventory profit.

See also: CONTROL FUNCTION
INVENTORY
PLANNING FUNCTION

INVESTING

Investing refers to committing capital with the expectation of profit. The expected profit may be in the form of dividends, interest, or capital appreciation. Speculation refers to an attempt to make profit from short-term changes in the price of an asset.

Investments are classified in financial terms as fixed income and equity investments. Fixed income investments include bonds, real estate mortgages, and preferred stock. Equity investments include common stock and real estate. Tne major classifications of stocks include industrial, financial, public utility, and railroad stocks. The major classes of bonds are U.S. government, state and municipal government, and corporate obligations.

Major types of investments include:

1. Nonmarketable:
    Savings accounts
    Certificates and time deposits
    Money market accounts
    U.S. savings bonds

2. Money market
    Treasury bills
    Municipal bonds
    Negotiable certificates of deposit
    Commercial paper
    Repurchase agreements (RP or repo; an agreement between a borrower and a lender to buy and repurchase securities)
    Bankers acceptances

3. Capital market
    Fixed income:
    Treasury securities
    Federal agencies securities

Municipal bonds
Corporate bonds
Preferred stock
Equities (common stock)

4. Options and futures contracts
Equity-related securities:
Options:
1. corporate created (rights, warrants, convertibles)
2. investor created (puts and calls)
Futures contracts:
Commodities
Financial futures (e.g., T-bills, T-bonds, CDs)
Foreign currency futures
Energy futures
Stock market index futures
Options on futures

5. Investment companies
Open end:
Money market
Capital market
Closed end

In a broad sense, the investment decision takes into consideration the investor's situation and the characteristics of possible investments. The investor's situation typically involves such matters as their expectations, motives, income, cash requirements, capital, time horizon (short, intermediate, or long-term), safety and other considerations, as well as proper evaluation of the risks they are willing to assume.

The basic matters to consider when evaluating different investments are yield, risk, duration, liquidity, and tax impact. Yield is required to compensate the investor for the impact of inflation and for risk taking. The total yield on an investment is the increase in the value of the investment, usually stated as a percent of invested capital per year. When inflation is taken into consideration, the yield is referred to as the real yield. Risk is the probability that the investment will be worth less in real dollars than when it was made, taking into consideration the investment's cumulative yields. Beta is a measure of the risk of an individual stock relative to the stock market as a whole. Risks associated with bonds are typically based on the probability of default on principal or interest. As a general rule, the higher the yield, the higher the risk, and vice versa. Risk can sometimes be avoided through diversification of investments. Risks can also be avoided in some situations by taking into consideration the duration of the investment. Certain stocks are extremely risky over a period of time shorter than the economic cycle which is considered to be three to five years and less risky in the long run. Liquidity of an investment refers to whether the investor can withdraw the invested funds on demand. The degree of required liquidity will affect the type of investment an investor should consider.

Investment instruments are usually either equity or debt, or a combination thereof. Equity, or ownership, entitles the investor to a share in the profit and capital appreciation. Debt instruments provide a return in the form of interest and capital appreciation. Preferred stock is legally an equity interest but has some of the characteristics of a bond with an infinite term. Convertible bonds, convertible preferred stock, and participating preferred stock also contain elements of equity and debt.

Characteristics of various types of investments are summarized in Exhibit I-3 on the following pages.

The purpose of bond analysis is to evaluate the ability of the debtor to pay interest and principal as they fall due. The purpose of common stock analysis is to determine the probable future value of a share of stock. Many factors are involved in determining the value of common stock, especially earnings per share and the price-earnings ratio at which the shares sell. Factors affecting investment evaluations include the trend of earning per share, the quality of reported earnings and corporate assets, dividend policy, demand for the stock, and the quality and performance of management. Major factors affecting the quality of earnings include depreciation practices, research and development expenditures, and inventory policies.

Exhibit I-4 presents a glossary of major terms related to securities trading on exchanges.

Exhibit I-3
Characteristics of Selected Investment

Type	Purpose	Characteristics
Annuity	Provide income for life or for a determinable number of years. Available at life insurance companies.	Annuities are relatively safe investments and usually have a minimum guaranteed rate of return. Variable annuities often provide a higher rate of return than do regular annuities. Many annuities carry a lower rate of interest than do other available investment opportunities with similar risks.
Asset Management Accounts	Provide a financial service that accumulates into a single account a variety of investment and transaction services, e.g., brokerage services, a money-market fund, and and a credit card. Available at commercial banks, brokerage houses, insurance companies, and mutual funds.	Coordinates investment and banking activities, simplifies record-keeping, provides market rates of return on cash balances, makes available margin loans at competitive rates, etc. Many asset management accounts require a relatively large initial investment. The account may not be federally insured. Annual fees can be substantial.
Bankers Acceptances	Negotiable time drafts drawn typically to finance the import, export, transport, or storage of products. Available from banks and brokerage firms.	Relatively safe, short-term investments backed by the credit of the borrowing company. Penalties often imposed for early demand for funds.
Certificate of Deposit	Instrument represents a sum of money left at a bank for a period of time; at the end of the period, the bank pays the deposit plus interest. Available at banks, brokerage firms, savings and loan associations, and credit unions.	Depositor can "lock in" yield for a specified time. Higher rate of return than on savings account. Little risk to principal. Penalty often imposed for early withdrawal.
Common Stock	An ownership interest in a corporation. Available at brokerage firms, some banks and savings and loan associations, and financial-services companies.	Equity investments with potential for relatively high returns and capital appreciation. Some participation in management through right to vote for board of directors. Exposure to market risk. Broker's commissions when buying and selling.
Corporate Bonds	Debt typically issued by large corporations. Available at brokerage firms, investment bankers, and corporations.	Pays a fixed investment return over a relatively long period of time. Relatively safe if held to maturity. Less safe than government bonds of similar maturity. Some can be called before maturity.

Exhibit I-3—Continued

Type	Purpose	Characteristics
GNMA-Mortgage backed government securities (Ginnie Maes)	A GNMA investment is made up of a pool of FHA and VA residential mortgages. After the Government National Mortgage Association gives its approval to the mortgages, a GNMA mortgage-backed certificate is issued. GNMA securities are available through brokerage firms, commercial banks and unit investment trusts.	GNMA securities provide monthly principal and interest payments, guaranteed by the U.S. government. Yields are competitive with government and federal agency securities and high grade corporate bonds. The value of the security can fluctuate with changes in interest rates. The securities are very liquid.
Revenue Bonds	Bonds the interest and principal of which is to be paid from a specific source, e.g., tolls, electric or water revenues, etc. Available at banks and brokerage firms.	Relatively high yields as compared with general obligation bonds. Narrow revenue base can increase risks.
Mutual Funds	Pooled resources of many investors; funds invest in a variety of securities, e.g., stocks, bonds, and money-market securities. Available at mutual-fund companies, brokerage firms, financial-services companies and insurance companies.	Provide for diversification of portfolio at a relatively low cost, thereby reducing risk. Professional management. "Switching" privilege from one type of fund to another is typically available. Wide selection of funds. Minimum initial investment. Not federally insured. Subject to market and credit risks. Management fees and sales charges are typical.
NOW Accounts	A savings account that allows checking activity. Available at banks and savings and loan associations.	Deposits earn interest and can be withdrawn readily. Record-keeping reduced for investor. Interest is earned on funds in the account, assuming a minimum balance is maintained.
Options (puts/call, straddles, etc.)	The right to buy (call) or sell (put) a fixed amount of a given stock at a specified price within a limited period of time. Available at brokerage firms.	Provide leverage for investment. Risk limited to amount invested in the option. Speculative. Entire investment can be lost.
Preferred Stock	Corporate stock with a fixed dividend and a priority claim over common stock if the company is liquidated. Available at brokerage firms, banks, savings and loan associations, and financial-service companies.	Preference over common stock in distribution of dividends and assets, if the corporation is liquidated. Usually lower return than for common stock of the same company. Risk/yield usually will not as attractive as bonds.

Exhibit I-3—Continued

Type	Purpose	Characteristics
Real Estate Investment Trusts (REITS)	A business trust or corporation that operates by acquiring or financing real estate projects. Available at brokers, banks, and financial planners.	Provide for capital appreciation and liquidity. Centralized management. Limited liability. Typical risks associated with investment in real estate.
Repurchase Agreement ("repo")	An interest in a security at a specified price with the agreement that the seller will repurchase the interest in the security at a specified time and price plus interest. Available at banks and brokerage firms.	Provide short-term investment opportunities with "locked-in," relatively high interest return. Agreements often provide that investment will be replaced in a day or two at a predetermined rate. Typically requires an established relationship with a bank or dealer. Relatively complex. Large dollar amounts.
Treasury Bills, treasury bonds and treasury notes	Bills have maturities of 13, 26 and 52 weeks. Sold in minimum amounts of $10,000 and in multiples of $5,000 above the minimum. Treasury bills have maturities of more than 10 years; $1,000 minimum. Notes are medium term securities; minimum usually $5,000. Available at Federal Reserve Banks and branches, Bureau of Public Debt, U.S. Treasury Department, banks and brokerage firms.	U.S. Treasury securities are backed by the full faith and credit of the U.S. government. Very liquid. Exempt from state and local taxes. Risks associated with interest-rate fluctuations exist.
Unit Investment Trust	Fixed portfolio of securities accumulated by a sponsor and offered in units to the investor. Available through the sponsor, brokerage firms and banks.	Provide for diversification and professional selection. Sponsor typically quotes bid prices on a daily basis. Long maturity.
Unit Investment Trusts	A unit investment trust is a fixed portfolio of securities designed to attain specific investment goals, principally monthly income and preservation of capital through diversification. Unit investments trusts are assembled and administered by professionals. The portfolio is held in trust on behalf of the investors by a bank trustee. Ownership interests in the trust can be purchased through brokerage firms and commercial banks.	These securities offer diversification, monthly income, high current returns, professional selection, reinvestment options and liquidity.

Exhibit I-3—Continued

Type	Purpose	Characteristics
Futures	Goods, articles, rights, services, and interests in which contracts for future delivery may be traded. Available on a registered exchange.	Potential to accumulate many contracts on a relatively small investment. Very speculative.
Individual Retirement Accounts (IRA)	Long-term, tax deferred account that enables a person to accumulate retirement funds. Available at mutual-fund companies, banks, brokerage firms, and insurance companies.	No taxes paid until withdrawals, typically after retirement when investor is in a lower tax bracket. Withdrawals made before age 59½ are usually subject to a penalty.
Keogh Plan	A retirement plan for self-employed persons and their employees. Earnings of plan and new funds deposited are exempt from income taxes until withdrawn, subject to certain specified limits. Available at mutual funds, banks, brokerage firms, credit unions, and insurance companies.	Plan deposits and earnings are available for growth; untaxed until withdrawal. Restrictions are present; withdrawals made prematurely can be penalized.
Money-market Mutual Fund	Pooled money of many investors in a variety of short-term money market securities issued by the federal government, "blue-chip" corporations, and banks. Available at mutual-fund companies, brokerage firms, and financial service companies.	High, short-term interest rates available. Professional management. Diversification of investment. Initial minimum investments may be required. Usually not insured.
Municipal Bond	A contractual obligation between an authorized political subdivision (e.g., state, county, city, school district) and an investor. Available at banks and brokerage firms.	Interest is exempt from federal taxation: frequently exempt from state and local taxes in the state of origin. Good safety record. Many issues available. Subject to interest-rate risks, e.g., as rates change so does the principal value of outstanding bonds. Market risks related to changes in credit rating exist. Prices respond negatively to inflation.
General Obligation Bonds	Bonds of political subdivisions that are to be repaired from taxes on property in the particular subdivision. Available at banks and brokerage firms.	Backed by taxing power of the political subdivision. Yields are relatively lower than yields on revenue bonds of similar rating and maturity.

Exhibit I-4
Glossary of Securities Trading on Exchanges

Account—Record of client's transactions and credits/debits balances of cash and/or securities with a firm.

Arbitrage—Arbitrage refers to the simultaneous purchase and sale of the same or equivalent money, commodity, or security, to take advantage of a price discrepancy. Place arbitrage attempts to take advantage of price discrepancies in different markets (for example, New York and London). Time arbitrage attempts to take advantage of price discrepancies between intermediate delivery or spot prices and future delivery or future quotations. Kind arbitrage seeks to take advantage of discrepancies in price between securities and other instruments that will become equivalent, such as convertible securities, split-up shares, etc.

Asked price—Lowest price at which a dealer is willing to sell a security.

Basis point—01% of yield on a fixed-income security. For example, if a bond yield to maturity changed from 9.10 to 10.45, there was a 130 basis points change.

Bid—Price at which someone is willing to purchase a security.

Block trading—Block trading involves transactions of at least 10,000 shares of stock bought and sold by institutional investors.

Blue-chip stocks—A blue-chip stock is a common stock representing ownership of a major company with a long history of profitability and constant or increasing dividends. Blue-chip stocks are considered to be financially strong and capable of surviving severe economic downturns without significantly affecting their dominant position in the industry, profitability or dividend-paying ability.

Clearing—The clearing process refers to the settlement of security transactions. The clearing process offsets transactions so that the actual delivery of securities and money can be reduced. The Stock Clearing Corporation is organized to conduct the clearing process for the New York Stock Exchange. Transactions in stocks, rights, and warrants are cleared through the Corporation. Odd lots and bonds are delivered by the Central Delivery Department.

Charting—Charting is a practice of graphically presenting stock price indices or individual stock prices to present a picture of price behavior over a period of time. Charting is used primarily to provide information about price trends and for forecasting.

Cyclical stocks—Cyclical stocks are stocks of corporations whose earnings fluctuate with the business cycle. Such companies have relatively low earnings per share during periods of recession and sharply increasing earnings during the recovery phase of the business cycle. Cyclical stocks are generally considered to include basic manufacturing industries, such as machinery and automobile manufacturing.

Dollar averaging—Dollar averaging is an investment strategy where an investor purchases a fixed dollar amount of a particular common stock periodically. The investor hopes to accumulate a large number of shares when the price of the stock is low and a smaller number of shares when the price is high. Hopefully, the average price for all the shares will be substantially lower than the average price the investor would pay if he purchased a constant number of shares periodically.

The Dow Jones Averages—The Dow Jones Averages are market indicators published by the financial publishing house of Dow, Jones & Co. Stock averages are computed for 30 industrial, 20 rails, and 15 utility common stocks, and a composite of the three groups. All stocks include in the averages are listed on the New York Stock Exchange. The averages are widely issued to reflect the trend of common stock prices over short and/or long periods of time.

Dow theory—An interpretation of the primary market trend which holds that there is no primary market trend (upward or downward for a year of more) unless there is simultaneous correlation between the movement of the Dow industrial, transportation, and utility averages.

Efficient market—The term efficient market refers to a market in which it is assumed that all known information about a security is fully reflected in its price (that is, a price efficient market). In an efficient market, mispriced securities do not exist. The market price of a security equals its fair intrinsic value. The investor trades only because he/she has excess cash, needs cash, or want to attain a tax advantage.

Ex-dividend—A stock is purchased ex-dividend when the purchaser acquires the shares without the right to receive a recently declared dividend. An investor who purchases a share of stock on or after the ex-dividend date is not entitled to receive the scheduled dividend. The ex-dividend date is four days prior to the date of record. The date of record is a date established when dividends are declared and is used to obtain a record of all stockholders of record as of the record date, which is usually several weeks prior to the payment date. A transfer of stock ownership prior to the ex-dividend date is said to be cum dividends or dividends on because the new owner of the shares will receive the dividend payment.

Form 10-K—A report filed annually with the Securities and Exchange Commission by a company that issues a separate annual report to shareholders. The company must report the following information in the report: financial statements; supplementary financial information; selected financial data for five years; management's discussion and analysis of financial condition and results of operations; market for the registrant's common stock and related security holder matters, a brief description of the business of the company and its subsidiaries, information for three years relating to industry segments, classes of similar products or services, foreign and domestic operations and export sales; and identity of company's directors and officers, their principal occupation or employment, and the name and financial business of their employer, and an offer in the annual report or proxy statement to provide without charge a copy of the Form 10-K along with the name and address of the person to write to for this material.

Growth stocks—Growth stocks are stocks of corporations whose earnings have demonstrated rapid growth in comparison with the economy and which are expected to grow at above-average rates in the future.

Income stocks—Income stocks are stocks of corporations with relatively constant earnings and dividends along with a high dividend yield in comparison with other stocks. Stocks of utility companies are often considered income stocks.

Junk bonds—Speculative bonds with a credit rating of BB or lower; such bonds usually have a high risk and high yield.

Margin trading—In margin transactions, the investor purchases securities and pays only a percentage of their cost; the balance is paid by the broker and is treated as a loan to the investor. For example, an investor purchases on margin 100 shares of stock at a price of 90. The investor might be asked to maintain a 60 percent margin—that is, he must pay 60 percent of the cost, or $5,400. This amount is his equity in the stock. The broker pays the remaining $3,600 as a loan to the investor, keeping the stock as collateral. The investor is thus able to purchase stock worth $9,000 while putting down only $5,400 of his own funds. The broker charges a commission on the full $9,000 purchase price, and also collects monthly interest on the loan. The investor expects the price of the stock to rise. Buying stock on the margin provides the investor with considerable leverage.

Over-the-counter markets—The over-the-counter markets are composed of security trading outside organized securities exchanges. These markets bring buyers and sellers together and increase the marketability for the large number of securities not traded on the organized exchanges. Unlisted stocks, government, municipal, and corporate bonds, and new issues are usually traded in the over-the-counter markets. Dealers in this market typically communicate by telephone with other dealers when negotiating (versus auctioning) transactions. The National Quotation Bureau, Inc. collects quotations and distributes a list to subscribers—pink stock sheets and yellow bond sheets divided geographically, Eastern, Central, and Pacific.

Odd-lot trading—Buying or selling in other than the established unit or round lot. In an odd-lot transaction, one-eighth of a point is added to (or deducted from) the price of each share purchased (or sold).

Options—Options are privileges acquired to buy or sell a security at a specified price within a specified period of time. Options include puts, calls, straddles, spreads, strap and strip. A put is a contract giving the holder the privilege to deliver a given number of shares of a specific stock to the maker within a certain time and at a certain price. The holder expects to make a profit from a decline in the stock. A call is a contract whereby the holder obtains the privilege of purchasing stock. The purchaser expects to profit from an increase in the price of the shares. Straddles and spreads are combinations of one put and one call. In a straddle, the put and call are at the market when the options are written. When prices are points below the market for the put and above the market for a call, the result is a spread. A strap is a combination of two calls with one put; a strip is two puts with one call. The option price is at the market when the options are written. Put and call brokers publish lists of prices on options from time to time.

Orders—An order describes the terms and conditions relating to the execution of an order by a broker for a customer. Market orders to buy and sell at the market are the major type of orders used in securities trading. Limited orders are orders placed by customers to place a limit on the order as to price. A limited buying order must be executed at the limit price or less. A selling order limited to a specific price must be executed at that price or more. Day orders are automatically cancelled if not executed on the same day the order is placed. Open, or GTC (good till cancelled) orders are good until executed or specifically cancelled by the customer. Stop-loss orders can be placed to limit losses. Stop-loss orders become market orders when the price of the stock reaches a specified quotation.

Point—Market prices are listed in points. A point is equal to a market price of $1 per share. Listings normally are given to the nearest one-eighth of a point.

Round lot—Trading on the New York Stock Exchange is done in standard numbers of shares, called round lots. A round lot is usually 100 shares or a multiple thereof. For bonds, the standard unit is one $1,000 bond. Lots smaller than round lots are called odd lots.

Securities Exchange Act of 1934—The Exchange Act is designed to make available more reliable information to the public, to prevent and provide remedies for fraud, manipulations, and other abuses in security trading, to ensure fair and orderly markets, to regulate the securities markets, brokers, and dealers to see that just and equitable principles of trading are observed, to regulate the use of credit in securities trading, and to regulate trading by insiders.

Settlement—Settlement refers to when and how a transaction on the Exchange must be settled. Except for specific agreements, every transaction must be settled by 12:30 P.M., delivery time, of the fourth following full business day. A cash settlement involves delivery of securities and payment of money on the same day.

Short selling—Short selling involves selling securities that are not owned by the seller. A short sale can occur where the seller does not possess the securities sold; a sale against the box occurs if the seller owns the securities sold but does not intend to deliver them at the time of the sale. A short seller expects the price of the security sold short to decline and to be able to buy back or cover the short sale at a lower price at a future date.

Stock purchase warrants—Stock purchase warrants, or option warrants, are instruments attached to other securities which entitle the holder to purchase shares of common stock at a specified price per share within a given period or for an indefinite time. Warrants can be issued separately or attached to other securities.

Transfer taxes—Transfer taxes are an excise tax levied by the State of New York on all transfers of beneficial ownership of securities within the state. The federal government also levies an excise tax based on the market value of stocks, rights, or warrants sold.

When-issued or when-distributed basis—New securities issues are traded on a when-issued basis before the delivery of the securities can be made.

Secondary markets for securities in the United States include:

Securities	Markets

Equity markets (stock, rights, warrants)	Organized exchanges:
	  New York Stock Exchange
	  American Stock Exchange
	  Regional Stock Exchanges
	Over-the-counter market
	Third markets
	Fourth markets

Bond markets governmentals, municipals, corporate	Over-the-counter markets Organized exchanges
Options and warrants	Organized exchanges

See also: INVESTMENT METHODS AND STRATEGIES

Reference:

Jones, Charles P., *Investments: Analysis and Management* (John Wiley & Sons, New York, 1985).

INVESTMENT BANKING

An investment bank is a financial intermediary that engages in originating, underwriting, and distributing of new securities. The principal clients of investment bankers are business firms and governments who want to raise funds in the money and capital markets.

Investment bankers advise clients concerning the nature of the securities that should be issued, their price, and the timing of the sale. Working together in underwriting *syndicates* investment banking firms normally will contract to buy the securities from a client at a fixed price, and then resell the securities to institutions and private investors. Investment bankers make money on the spread between the price they pay for a security (the *bid* price) and the price they sell the security to the public (the *asked* price). If the client issuing the security is guaranteed a fixed price for the security by the investment banking firm, the deal is said to be an *underwritten issue.* When the investment banker does not guarantee the client a fixed price, the sale of the securities is said to be undertaken on a *best efforts* basis.

In a typical public security sale, a company will contact its investment banker to decide how much money to raise, the type of security to issue, the price to charge, and the timing of the sale. The investment banker will help the company prepare and file a registration statement with the Securities and Exchange Commission (SEC) and a prospectus. Usually, about 20 days are required for the SEC to approve a new issue. The price of the stock or the coupon rate on the bond is set on the day the SEC approves the issue, and the securities are offered to the public the following day.

Typically, the investment banker who sets up the deal will organize an underwriting syndicate in order to lay off some of the risk of financing the new issue. In addition to the firms that actually participate in the syndicate, there also usually are a larger number of investment bankers who form a selling group, to market the securities to individual investors. The selling group is made up of members of the underwriting syndicate plus a large number of security dealers who take responsibility for marketing relatively small shares of the issue. In some large underwriting deals, the number of firms in the selling group may be as many as 300 or more.

The standing of an individual investment banking firm in the issuance of a particular security is shown in the "tombstone" advertisements that are published in the *Wall Street Journal* and elsewhere in the financial press. The tombstone ads, like the underwriting pyramids they represent, divide participants into several categories. At the top are the "special bracket" firms which are the lead underwriters. Below this apex group are the "major bracket" firms and then the "major-out-of-order" firms. Last are the lesser firms which are included in the selling group because of their retailing ability, but which have very small shares of the total issue.

The practice of investment banking originated in Europe in the late 1700s. During this period, it became common for a few large firms to organize syndicates of investment firms composed of several large firms and many smaller underwriters. The firms in a syndicate cooperated in the financing and sale of new issues to the public and profited according to their share in the total effort. Major investment banking houses during this time included the Barings and the Rothschilds.

The practice of investment banking spread to the United States from Europe. All of the early American firms had ties to Europe, which provided capital and technical skill. After the Civil War, the industry came to be dominated by a few large firms like J. P. Morgan, Kuhn Loeb, Lehman Brothers and others, but the syndicate system, involving a few large firms at the apex of the underwriting pyramid and many smaller firms at the base, survived. The strength of the largest firms depended on their ability to effectively put together large groups of investors to absorb the ever-larger issues of new securities.

By the 1920s, commercial banks had become heavily involved in the underwriting of stocks and bonds. Many attributed the widespread failure of commercial banks in the early 1930s to their involvement in investment banking activities. The demand for reform culminated in the passage of the Glass-Steagall Act of 1933 which effectively separated commercial and investment banking. As a result of this law, established bankers had to choose whether to give up their depository or their underwriting business. Morgan, for example, decided to remain in commercial banking, but several partners left to form the investment banking firm of Morgan Stanley. First Boston Corporation was created out of the underwriting department of the First National Bank of Boston.

Throughout the post–World War II period, investment banking has remained for the most part a relatively concentrated industry. A few large firms dominate syndicate systems made up of many smaller firms. In 1984, the top 15 firms underwrote 96 percent of all new public security issues, and the top 4 firms underwrote 61 percent. Among the top firms in the industry in 1984 were Salomon Brothers, Drexel Burnham Lambert, First Boston, Merrill Lynch, Goldman Sachs, Shearson Lehman/American Express, Morgan Stanley, Kidder Peabody, and Prudential-Bache.

Despite its relatively concentrated structure, the investment banking industry continues to be subject to change from new competitive pressures and financial innovations. The development of the Eurosecurities market has drawn corporate clients overseas, heightening competitive pressures. The introduction of shelf registration by the SEC in 1982 increased underwriting competition and reduced traditional underwriting profits. The development of the junk bond market pioneered by Drexel Burnham Lambert and the use of junk bond funds to finance mergers, tender offers, and leveraged buyouts has expanded dramatically the involvement of the industry in the financing of mergers and acquisitions. In this area and others, the industry has been subject to increased competition from commercial banks, which continually have sought to lower the legislative barriers separating commercial and investment banking. Finally, the industry has been rocked by a series of insider trading scandals which threaten it with a new series of governmental regulations.

See also: FINANCIAL MARKETS
SECURITY MARKETS
SHELF REGISTRATION

References:

Auerbach, Joseph, and Hayes, Samuel L., *Investment Banking and Diligence: What Price Deregulation?* (Boston, MA: Harvard Business School Press, 1986).

Carosso, Vincent P., *Investment Banking in America: A History* (Cambridge, MA: Harvard University Press, 1970).

INVESTMENT COMPANIES

An investment company, or trust, is defined by the Investment Company Act of 1940 as one engaged in the business of investing, reinvesting, owning, holding, or trading in securities having a value exceeding 40 percent of its total assets. Exceptions provided by law include security underwriters, distributors and brokers, banks, insurance companies, savings and loan associations, small loan companies, public utility holding companies, charitable corporations, and others. An investment trust fund is an agency by which funds of a number of participants are combined and invested in securities to enhance the safety of the principal and increase the yield to the participants. The trust arrangement makes it possible to distribute the investment risk through diversification and expert management.

An investment company raises capital by issuing shares or certificates of beneficial interest. The trust also borrows by issuing bonds. Available funds are invested. Trusts generally do not attempt to obtain controlling interests which would limit efforts at diversification. Each investment company arranges its portfolio with its specified purpose or goal in mind. Investment companies hope to realize capital gains on their investments, as well as interest and dividends from securities.

Investment companies are classified by the SEC as follows:

1. Management investment companies, both closed-end and open-end, commonly referred to as mutual funds.

2. Unit or fixed and semifixed trusts.

3. Periodic payment plans.

4. Companies issuing face amount installment certificates.

Closed-end companies have a fixed amount of capital. Shares in the company are bought and sold in the market through brokers, and are usually listed on the stock exchange. Open-end company's shares are sold to investors through authorized investment dealers at asset value, less a nominal redemption fee in certain cases. The net asset value of open-end shares is typically computed twice daily. One organization may sponsor several companies.

Open-end funds are classified as common stock funds, balanced funds (hold bonds as well as stocks), group funds (such as chemical or natural gas securities), and bonds and preferred stock funds. Investment trusts offer the investor diversification, selection, and administration of securities. The investors may be charged a loading charge that is added to the price at the time of purchase and/or an annual deduction from the investment income for the services of a management or sponsoring organization.

The Investment Company Act describes a diversified company as a management company at least 75 percent of whose assets are represented by cash and cash items, government securities, securities of other investment companies, and other securities in which holdings of the securities of one issuer do not exceed 10 percent of the outstanding securities of the issuer or 5 percent of its own total assets. A nondiversified company adopts a policy of placing a major portion of its assets in special situation investments.

Common trust funds combine a number of small trusts to bring about efficiency in management, to effect diversification, and to attain a larger yield on the investment at a lower cost. Commercial banks frequently use common trust funds to attract small investment accounts.

The Investment Company Act of 1940 regulates companies that do not come under the Securities Act of 1933 or the Securities Exchange Act of 1934. The general purposes of the Investment Company Act are to obtain honest and unbiased management for the company, to obtain greater participation in management by security holders, to review the adequacy and feasibility of the capital structures of the companies, to prescribe the financial statements and accounting of the companies, and to regulate selling practices, especially by requiring registration under the Act.

The Investment Advisers Act of 1940 was passed to arrange for the supervision of investment advisers. The Act requires the registration of investment advisers with the SEC. Under the Act, the investment adviser cannot act as principal for his own account, or as broker for another, in a transaction with his client without first disclosing the fact to the client and obtaining the client's consent.

See also: INVESTING

INVESTMENT METHODS AND STRATEGIES

Exhibit I-5

Investment Types Matched with Investment Objectives

x = Generally Applicable
o = Depends on Specific Investment

	Certificates of Deposit	Money Market Funds	Corporate Bonds	Municipal Bonds	Zero Coupon Bonds	Government Securities	GNMA	Common Stocks	Utility Stocks	Preferred Stocks	Convertible Securities	Mutual Funds	Unit Investment Trusts	Stock Options	Stock Warrants	Tax-Deferred Annuity—Fixed	Tax-Deferred Annuity—Variable	Limited Partnerships	Real Estate Investment Trusts	Precious Metals	Commodity Futures
1. Income Needs																					
Liquidity	x	x	x	o	x	x	x	x	x	x	x	x	x	x	x	o	o		x	x	x
Monthly Income		o					o	o			o	x				x	x				
Quarterly Income	o	o	x	x		o		o	x	o	o	o						o	o		
High Yields	o	o	x			x	x	o	x	o	o	o	x			x	o	o	x		
Predictable Income	x		x	x	x	x	o	o	x	x	x	o	x			x			o		
2. Growth Needs																					
Long-Term Appreciation								o	o		o	o			x			o	o		
Short-Term Growth								o			o	o		x	x					x	x
Suitable for IRA/Keogh	x	x	x		o	x	x	o	x	x	x	o	o	o		x	x	o	x		o
3. Reducing Taxes																					
Tax-Free Income		o		x	o							o	o								
Tax-Deferred Income																x	x	o	o		
Tax Write-offs																		o			
4. Investment Temperament																					
Security of Income	x	o	x	x	x	x	x		x	x	x	o	x			x				o	
Security of Principal at Maturity	x		x	x	x	x	x				o		o			x					
Professional Management		x										x						x	x	x	
Speculation								o				o		x	x				o	x	x
5. Market Conditions																					
Diversification		x										x	x					x	o	x	
Anticipate Stock Market Volatility								x		x	x			x	o						o
Anticipate Inflation		o						o			o	o	o					x	o	o	x
Anticipate Rising Interest Rates		x						o			o	o							o	o	o
Anticipate Falling Interest Rates	x		x	x	x	x	x	o	x	x	o	o	o			x	o	o	o		o

Source: Dean Witter Reynolds, Inc.

INVESTMENT METHODS AND STRATEGIES

Various theories have been advanced to determine the best method of selecting securities. The theories differ primarily in the distinction drawn between speculative and investment strategies. These theories can be concisely described in the following terms:

Theory	Strategy	Analysis
Technical selection	Speculative	Price and trading volume charts
Fundamental selection	Mixed	Valuation of future cash flows and cash assets
Efficient market selection	Investment	None—hold widely diversified portfolio with acceptable risk

Technical selection assumes that security prices usually move in identifiable patterns which can be determined through chart techniques to extrapolate trends. Fundamentalists rely heavily upon an analysis of discounted future cash flows to estimate the intrinsic worth of securities. Those who accept the efficient market theory hold that all important information associated with securities is already reflected in existing prices. Hence, analysis is not required.

Exhibit I-5 identifies various investment instruments with specific investment objectives. A variety of investment methods are defined in Exhibit I-6.

Exhibit I-6
Glossary of Investment Methods and Strategies

Advance-decline—Breadth of market. If advances consistently outnumber declines, the market is considered to be in a bullish phase. When declines are more numerous than advances, the market is considered to be in a bearish phase. When the Dow Jones Average advances and the advance-decline ratio either does not advance or levels off, the advance is probably false. If the advance-decline ratio is strong but the Dow levels off, the Dow should begin to rise.

Averaging up—The technique of buying additional shares of a particular stock as the price of the stock rises to reduce the average cost of the stock.

Bear market—A down market; a stock market after it has developed a downward trend. A bear market will usually not last as long as a bull market; declines more rapidly than a bull market goes up. When the Dow Jones Industrial Average fails to penetrate the peak of the preceding intermediate advance, a bear market is signaled. A bear market is confirmed when the next intermediate dip penetrates the low point of the preceding decline. The bear market will continue as long as these conditions exist. Chartists look for broad movement and increasing volume before they signal a primary trend. Can use effectively short selling, selling against the box, buying bonds, and options.

Blue chips—The common stock of well-established, profitable, and large U.S. companies, such as IBM, GE, GM, and many others.

Bond—Strategies include switching back and forth between stocks and bonds, depending upon market levels.

Breadth-momentum index—A comparison of the amount of movement up or down of the advance-decline line with the movement of the New York Stock Exchange Index of stock prices. See advance-decline.

Breakouts—Sharp and strong upward or downward stock price movements from previously horizontal pattern. Breakouts signal a significant move in the price of the stock. False breakouts are common.

Bull market—An up market; the market in an established upward movement. Bull markets typically last longer than do bear markets. Many signals are available to supposedly determine the end of a bull market, (for example, low dividend yields on common stock and the floating of many new stock issues). When the Dow Jones Industrial Average fails to penetrate the low point of the preceding intermediate decline, a reversal of the bear (down) trend is possible. The bull market is confirmed when the next intermediate rise in the Dow penetrates the preceding peak. As long as these conditions keep recurring, the bull market continues.

Buy-and-hold—The strategy of buying common stock and holding it for an indefinite period. Investor ignores market fluctuations. Can be justification for selling the security if there are major changes in the corporation or in the security.

Cash flow per share—Net income plus expenses such as depreciation that do not involve actual cash outlays. Some analysts consider this ratio to be more significant than earnings per share; others maintain that it can be very misleading.

Cash position—Some investors hold large amounts of cash or Treasury Bills during a bear market or during the last stages of a bull market, anticipating more favorable opportunities in the future. During periods of declining market prices, investors hold a cash cushion to invest at a later date. A fully invested position, usually less than 3 percent cash, is a bearish signal; a strong cash position, over 10 percent, is bullish. Companies having strong (weak) cash positions, can make (cannot make) substantial purchases and help the market rise.

Charts—Graphic presentation of stock prices and volume of trading frequently used to forecast the market. Examples of charting include simple-line charts, trend-line charts, moving-average charts, point-and-figure charts, and many others. Used frequently in technical analysis.

Climax—Sudden, sharp price trend changes on stock charts along with great increases in the volume of trading that signal immediate concern or opportunity.

Concept stocks—Stocks to which a big idea can be associated, such as a scientific breakthrough, a new drug discovery, and a new merchandising approach. Sharp price fluctuations are often associated with concept stocks.

Confidence index—Investor optimism and pessimism. A ratio of the yield on *Barron's* High-Grade Bond index to the yield on the Dow-Jones Composite Bond Average. Suggests the confidence of experienced investors in medium-grade corporate bonds relative to high-grade bonds. When lower-grade bond issues outperform high-grade bonds, the confidence index rises, which is an optimistic sign for stock prices. Investors are not worrying about safety and are willing to purchase a lower-quality bond. The converse is also true.

Consensus of indicators—An averaging by various statistical methods of many stock market price indicators (for example, volume, short sales, free credit balance, advance-decline line at market tops and total short interest at market bottoms, and the odd-lot short sales ratio at market tops).

Constant-dollar plan—A plan which keeps a fixed number of dollars in stock with a fluctuating amount in bonds or other defensive instruments. If stocks rise, some shares are sold and the extra money beyond the previously decided fixed amount is used to buy bonds. If stocks go down, bonds are sold and the money is used to buy shares to bring the dollars in the stocks up to the desired amount.

Constant-ratio formula—A plan which keeps a fixed ratio of money in stock and bonds (for example, 50 percent in stocks and 50 percent in bonds). As the market fluctuates, stocks are sold and bonds bought, or vice versa, so as to keep the ratio constant. This plan is supposed to work well in a complete market cycle that includes some wide swings.

Contrary opinion—Action that differs from what the general investing public does at a certain time. Its purpose is to outsmart the market. The underlying idea of this theory is that what a majority of investors know is not worth knowing.

Convertible bonds—Convertibles may offer the stability of a bond in down markets and the capital gains opportunity of common stock in up markets. Provides some downside protection.

Divergence analysis—Analysis of the difference between the actions of sophisticated and unsophisticated investors (for example, short-sellers and specialists (sophisticated) versus odd-lot investors (unsophisticated).

Diversification—Holding more than one stock of a security to reduce overall risk, especially to spread risk among various counterbalancing industries and among different corporations within each industry. Diversification can presumably be attained for an individual investor by holding between five to fifteen different securities. Diversification can also be achieved through investing in mutual funds.

Dollar averaging—Investing an equal amount of money at stated intervals (monthly, quarterly) in a particular security or group of securities.

This practice should result in buying at low price levels to balance buying at higher prices. Dollar averaging is sometimes modified to allow increasing the amount of periodic investment when stock prices are low and decreasing the amount when stock prices are high.

Federal Reserve Board actions—Noting actions taken by the Board of Governors of the Federal Reserve System which can influence business and the stock market (for example, discount (interest) rates, margin requirements, and member bank's reserves (money supply) to serve as an indicator of stock market behavior.

Gold stock price—Observe the prices of gold mining companies stocks which tend to move in a direction opposite to that of the stock averages.

Government bonds—Purchase government bonds on margin when a business recession is due because the government will undoubtedly adopt easy money policies which will result in a drop in interest rates and an increase in bond prices. Government securities are usually purchased for the safety factor.

Graham formula—An investment timing plan which involves computing a normal or central value for earnings on the Dow Jones Industrial Average and the yield on Moody's Corporate Aaa Bond Average. The formula involves a fundamental approach to investing.

Growth stocks—Stocks of companies with earnings above the average at an annual rate are assumed. Growth stocks tend to become overvalued and to move in comparatively wide swings.

Hedging—A sale or purchase of a contract for future delivery against a previous purchase or sale of an equal quantity of the same commodity or an equivalent quantity of another commodity that has a parallel price movement, and when it is expected that the transaction in the contract market will be cancelled by an offset transaction at the time the contemplated spot transaction is completed and before the futures contract matures; or, the practice of buying or selling futures to counterbalance an existing position in the trade market, thus avoiding the risk of unforeseen major movements in price. Hedging may be accomplished in different ways in the stock market (for example, using options, to have a long position in stocks viewed favorably along with short positions in stocks viewed unfavorably; 50 percent long, 50 percent short; stable convertible bond and a common stock that fluctuates with the market in a bear market).

High-low index—A measure of the difference between the number of stocks making new highs in price for the year and those making new lows. Considered a good indicator of bull market tops; provides early warning signal for the market in general.

Income stocks—Stocks of companies that pay liberal and reliable dividends. However, the higher the yield, the higher the risk. Growth prospects should usually be considered.

Insider transactions—The buying and selling activities of directors, officers, and large stockholders, reported monthly in the Official Summary of Security Transactions and Holding (the *Insider's Report,* compiled by the SEC. Insider transactions can provide clues to stock prices.

Institutional investing—The investing activities of funds and other large investors of other people's money that dominate the stock market which sometimes can provide clues concerning the volatility of stocks, diversification, risk, and other factors.

Investment advisory services—Advice about stock and bond markets, typically made available in newsletter form (for example, Value Line Investment Survey).

Investment clubs—Groups who agree to pool investment funds which meet regularly to determine jointly investment opportunities and decisions.

Leadership—Stocks leading the advance or decline in a market. The quality of the stocks providing market leadership is important. Following a long advance, if low-priced stocks are attracting the most value, the investor understands that the public is heavily invested. This could indicate a top. If the volume leaders are the blue chip stocks, the advance has further to go.

Leverage—The advantage (or disadvantage) obtained by the use of borrowed money. In a rising market, the practice causes the asset value of the common stock to appreciate more rapidly percentage-wise than investing without the use of borrowed funds. Gains and losses are magnified through the use of leverage. Leverage in the stock market can be obtained through the use of margin, warrants, margined warrants, options, and convertibles.

Low-priced stocks—Stocks selling below a relative low amount (for example, $10), which are frequently noted for price volatility. One theory suggests buying such stocks toward the bottom of a typical yearly price range and selling toward the top of the range. When a preponderance of low-priced stocks among the leaders exists, the market is nearing the end of a rally. The beginning of an upswing reflects an investor preference for quality stock; after they have been bid up in price, the investor turns to the lower-quality issues. If the Dow Jones Industrial Average is rising and the average price of the leaders is high, the bull market should continue.

Margin credit—A strategy which requires the investor to be willing to accept considerable losses. Margin requirements imposed by the SEC can also be used as an indicator of stock price movement.

Money supply—The expansion or contraction of the money supply has a relationship to stock prices, interest rates, and other factors affecting the market. Monetary indicators include net free bank reserves, member banks' borrowings, Treasury bill rates, the federal funds rate, the discount rate, interest rates, and others.

Monthly investment plan—An investment strategy which requires small investors to buy individual stocks in small dollar amounts on a periodic basis. Such plans are supposed to develop a habit of thrift in individuals.

Most active stocks—Stocks showing the largest volume of trading during a certain period (for example, daily, weekly, annually) can provide clues to market trends. For example, an increasing number of negative price movements in lists of most active stocks is often a signal of a bear market.

Moving average—An arithmetic means that changes according to a specified period of time (for example, a three- or five-year moving average). Moving averages have been used to determine market trends and the rate of change of stock prices.

Municipal bonds—Debt issues of cities, states, and other local governments. Interest income is usually free of federal income tax and some state and local taxes. Municipals usually provide safety and a reasonable after-tax yield comparison with taxable securities, especially for taxpayers in a higher tax bracket.

Mutual funds—Companies which pool investment money from individuals and others which provide diversification and professional management.

New issues—Common stock issues of companies that are going public and are selling stock to the public for the first time. The term is also applied to new issues of corporate or municipal bonds. Studies indicate that the odds against new common stock issues are unfavorable.

New York Stock Exchange seat prices—The cost of membership on the Exchange is considered by some investors to reflect optimistic or pessimistic expectations for the market in general.

Normal-value plans—Formula investment plans which rely on determining a normal stock market level that should exist at a particular time. The formula typically relates a stock market average to fundamental values, such as earnings, dividends, or interest rates.

Odd-lot short sales—Short sales in less than one hundred shares are sales by unsophisticated investors who are considered by some to be losers. A significant rise in the volume of odd-lot short selling interpreted to mean that the stock market will improve, thus providing the odd-lot short seller a typical loss. The odd-lot short sales ratio is the ratio of odd-lot short sales to regular odd-lot sales.

Options activity ratio—A speculative index based on the level of options activity compared with the volume of trading in the stock market.

Over-the-counter stocks—Unlisted stocks which sometimes offer the possibility of finding young and relatively small corporations that show promise.

Price-earnings ratio—A ratio of the market price of a stock to the stock's annual earnings per share. This ratio can indicate whether a particular stock is properly priced. A very high price-earnings ratio suggests high expectations for the future which can be disabling and may be based merely on psychology. For some investors, the price-earnings ratio establishes a relationship between the intrinsic value, or justified price, of a stock and its current market price.

$$\text{Intrinsic value} = \text{Earnings per share} \times \text{P/E ratio}$$

The P/E ratios are inversely related to interest rates because interest rates are directly related to rates of return.

Psychology—The emotional and behavioral patterns of investors and speculators is a factor in determining stock prices and trends.

Scale trading—An investment strategy involving buying a specified number of shares of a particular stock whenever the price of the stock moves downward by a certain amount (for example, a half point), and selling the same number of shares each time the price of the stock rises by a greater amount (for example, a full point).

Seasonal variations—Stock prices fluctuate according to the hour, the day, the month, the season, the year, a series of years, and other periods. Experts often expect short-term price changes for stocks to be random movements. Cyclical movements involve longer times and reflect stock movements through periods of recession, depression, recovery, and inflation. Industries that tend to resist recession include health and food.

Selling strategy—An investment plan established to suggest a point when a security should be sold. Many investors suggest that one should sell a stock if he or she would not want to buy more of the stock. Many share signals have been proposed (for example, a decline in the price-earnings ratio of a stock).

Short interest—The number of shares that have been sold short of a particular stock or of the market as a whole. The short interest ratio is the ratio of total short interest on the New York Stock Exchange to daily average stock volume. A ratio of more than approximately 2.00 is considered bullish; a ratio of less than 2.00 is considered bearish. This ratio is commonly considered to be a contrary opinion indicator (short sellers are usually wrong). A falling short interest is considered to be bullish. The greater the number of shares sold short, the stronger the technical position. Speculators must back the securities they sold. A market with a large short position is in a strong position to rally rapidly if the market remains strong. Short sellers become anxious during a rally and cover their short positions.

Short selling—A strategy which generally goes against the market. Short selling is generally considered to be speculative and risky. Folklore says that one should never stay short after the short interest becomes very large. Relatively active short selling by members of the New York Stock Exchange tends to reflect sophisticated selling and indicates a possible negative stock market.

Special situations—Conditions which give promise of large capital gains with limited risk accompanied by an uncertain time factor. Special situations include mergers and reorganizations, large liquid assets, liquidations, stocks with high volatility, litigations, changes in law, management changes, technological innovations, marketing innovations, turnaround situations and many more.

Speculation index—A ratio of lower quality stocks to activity in higher quality stocks. A high level of volume on the American Stock Exchange (considered speculative) compared with the volume on the New York Stock Exchange could indicate considerable speculative interest in the market.

Stock-Bond yield spread—The difference between the average dividend yield on common stocks and the average yield from interest on high grade corporate bonds. A stock yield of 10 percent and a bond yield of 8 percent would be considered a negative spread and could indicate that stocks are overvalued.

Stock-loss orders—An order left with a broker to sell a stock if it drops to a certain price in order to stop the loss.

Support and resistance levels—A support level is a price level that a stock or the market has difficulty in breaking through on the downside; a resistance level is the same on the upside. Buying activity increases support levels; selling pressures increase resistance levels. Levels of support and resistance can indicate a major change in the market.

Tape trading—Reading the stock market tape is a very short-term method of forecasting stock movements, often used by professional traders. Through a careful examination of the tape as transactions occur, the astute tape reader hopes to anticipate price changes and to take advantage of such changes when they occur.

Tax investing—Investing strategy in which the tax consequences are the major considerations.

Trends—Strategies based on the tendency of stock prices to follow established trends or directions (for example, bull or bear markets). Matters to consider are how steep is the trend, has the trend been tested, and similar questions.

Undervalued and overvalued securities—Stocks or bonds which are priced below or above what is a reasonable or normal value as related to underlying net assets, earning power, or other securities may offer opportunities for profitable investment. Searching for undervalued securities is a form of bargain hunting.

Upside-downside volume—A comparison of the trading volume of stocks with rising prices with those of stocks with falling prices can provide clues of the market direction.

Volume of trading—The number of shares of stock traded during a particular period of time can provide a basis for trading or not trading. The volume of trading typically slows before the top of a bull market and before the bottom a bear market.

Warrants—Warrants giving the holder the right to buy a specified amount of a particular common stock at a certain price within a specified period of time can be attractive securities where leverage is a factor.

See also: BOND
CAPITAL STOCK
INVESTING
OPTION
PREFERRED STOCK

Reference:

Radcliffe, Robert C., *Investing: Concepts, Analysis, and Strategy* (Scott, Foresman and Company, Glenview, Ill., latest edition).

INVISIBLE HAND

Adam Smith in *The Wealth of Nations* explained that individuals will act in a way that promotes their own self-interest. But, by doing so, as if "led by an invisible hand to promote an end which was no part of his intention," he is also promoting the general welfare. Because of this, according to Smith, government interference in the economy is unnecessary. This belief underscored Smith's view of the virtues of free markets and free trade.

ISOQUANT

An isoquant is a graphical device used in the teaching of economics to illustrate that different combinations of inputs can be used to produce the same amount of output. As illustrated in Figure 10, an output level of Q^* can be produced either by using K_1 amount of capital and L_1 amount of labor, or by using K_2 amount of capital and L_2 amount of labor. Many combinations of inputs are possible in the production of the same level of output, but only one combination will be preferred. To determine the optimal combination of inputs, the price of each input must be known.

See also: PRODUCTION FUNCTION

Figure 10

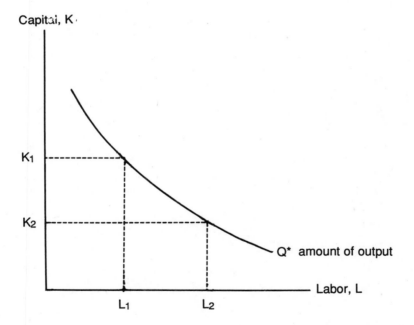

JOINT PRODUCTS AND BY-PRODUCTS

Joint costs are costs of simultaneously producing or acquiring two or more products (joint products) that are produced or acquired together. Joint products resulting from the single-production process usually require further processing. Typically, none of the joint products have a relative value of such a size that it can be designated a major product. To illustrate the allocation problem associated with joint products, assume that the joint cost of producing Product A and Product B in a common manufacturing process is $90,000 (the joint costs up to the split-off point). It is now necessary to determine the inventory value of Products A and B. The relative sales value method of allocating the $90,000 to Products A and B is widely used. Assume that the 20,000 units of Product A have a sales value of $100,000, and Product B a sales value of $200,000. The $90,000 would be allocated to Products A and B in the amounts of $30,000 (one-third) and $60,000 (two-thirds), respectively. This can be illustrated as follows:

Joint cost, $90,000 | Product A, $30,000

Product B, $60,000

Split-off point

Joint costs are sometimes allocated on a physical measure basis. Under this method, total joint costs are allocated to the joint products on the basis of some unit of product output, such as units, pounds, tons, or square feet.

By-products are those products emerging at the split-off point that have minor sales value as compared with those of the major products. In many operations, by-products are the same as scrap. By-products frequently are not allocated to any of the total joint costs incurred in the process. If additional costs are incurred after the split-off to process further the by-products, these costs are usually assigned to the by-product.

See also: ALLOCATION
                COST ACCOUNTING

JOINT VENTURE

The combination of two or more firms into a single activity is known as a joint venture. Generally, these relationships are short lived, formed for the production of a specific product. Also, the relationships are generally informal in nature, although they can be formal. When formal in nature, the new enterprise formed by the joint venture is called the child. While public statistics are not available, it has been estimated that the incidence of joint ventures has been increasing steadily during the 1980s. One reason for this trend is the necessity for firms to bring new products to market faster than in the past in an effort to meet more effectively foreign competition.

Reference:

Harrigan, Kathryn R. *Strategies for Joint Ventures* (Lexington Books, Lexington, Mass., 1985).

JOURNAL

A journal is a chronological record of events and transactions. The process of recording events and transactions in a journal is called journalizing. A journal is often referred to as a book of original entry because events and transactions are typically initially recorded therein using the double-entry system of accounting.

All events and transactions could be recorded in a general journal. A general journal entry consists of the transaction date, the accounts and amounts to be debited and credited, and an explanation of the event or transaction. A typical general journal entry is shown here:

Jan.15   Cash (debit)   500
                    Sales (credit)   500
                            Sold merchandise for cash.

In addition to the general journal, special journals are often used to facilitate the recording of a large number of similar transactions. Typical special journals are described here:

Type of Special Journal	Nature of Transactions Recorded
Sales journal	Sales of merchandise on credit
Purchases journal	Purchases of merchandise on credit
Cash receipts journal	All receipts of cash from any source
Cash payments journal	All payments of cash for any purpose

The general journal would be used to record any event or transaction that could not be recorded in a special journal.

See also: ACCOUNT
                    ACCOUNTING SYSTEM
                    DOUBLE-ENTRY SYSTEM
                    LEDGER

JUNK BOND

The term junk bonds was first used to denote outstanding bonds issued by firms suffering current financial troubles. Many times these firms (often referred to as fallen angels) had been financially strong when the bonds were originally issued, but for one reason or another had encountered difficulties which made bond default a strong possibility.

As used today, junk bonds refer to all speculative-grade debt, regardless of the financial condition of the issuing firm. Speculative-grade bonds are those with ratings below BBB- (from Standard & Poor's) or Baa3 (from Moody's). In recent years, these ratings frequently have been assigned to bonds issued by new firms that do not have an established performance record. In the past, such new firms may have been denied access to the bond market because of their low ratings and forced to rely solely on equity finance or bank borrowings. Thus, the development of the market for junk bonds has provided such firms with a new financing alternative.

The investment banking firm of Drexel Burnham Lambert is generally credited with making junk bonds acceptable by creating an active secondary market in these securities. When interest in takeovers and leveraged buyouts increased dramatically in the early 1980s, the demands of both corporate raiders and management swelled the demand for debt capital. Drexel Burnham Lambert worked actively to persuade certain institutions (including some mutual funds) and others to invest in high-yield, low-rate debt securities (that is, junk bonds). Drexel developed substantial expertise in putting together deals which proved attractive to both investors and issuers, and this success catapulted Drexel to the top of the investment banking business.

See also: BOND
          BOND RATINGS

KITING

An embezzlement scheme involving the overstatement of cash by recording a deposit without a corresponding withdrawal at year end. An example of kiting follows:

12/15 Bookkeeper writes herself a $5,000 check on First Bank and cashes it. No journal entry is made.

12/16 Bookkeeper is robbed or gambles it away.

12/31 Bookkeeper covers the shortage by (1) writing a $5,000 check on Second Bank account and deposits in First Bank account; bookkeeper does not record check in cash disbursements journal until after year end and not listing check as outstanding on 12/31 bank reconciliation.

Kiting might be discovered by reviewing all bank transfers before and after year-end to determine that the book entry is recorded in the same year that the check is dated and the deposit in the bank is made. Interbank transfer checks in transit at year-end should also be traced to the outstanding check list and to deposits in transit in the bank reconciliation process.

The deposit date of all transfers should be verified by tracing the deposit to the cutoff bank statement (a bank statement for the first 8–10 business days after year end) of the receiving bank. The traditional four-column bank reconcilation (or proof of cash) would probably expose the fraud.

See also: BANK RECONCILIATION
FRAUD
LAPPING

Ll

LABOR MARKET

Separate labor markets exist for individuals with different skills and career objectives. Most individuals acquire a professional or technical background in order to compete in a select number of markets. Within these narrowly defined markets, the supply of labor is positively related to the wage rate. An increase or decrease in the wage rate increases or decreases the quantity of workers willing to offer their labor services to that market. The demand for labor is a derived demand. It is derived from the market demand for the firm's final product. A change in the demand for a firm's final product causes a corresponding change in the demand for inputs, including labor. Given this demand, quantity demanded is inversely related to the wage rate.

In the figure on the following page is a graphical representation of a generic labor market. This market is in equilibrium at the wage rate, w*, and the quantity of labor, L*.

See also: DEMAND FOR LABOR

Figure 11

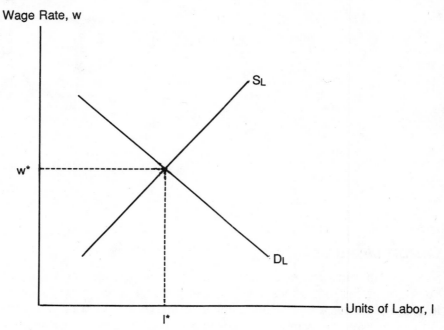

LABOR PRODUCTIVITY

Labor productivity refers to the amount of output produced by a worker. Generally, it is measured as the ratio of total output per unit of labor, where the units of labor could be in terms of number of workers or number of man-hours. Estimates of output per worker are published in the *Economic Report of the President,* among other places.

See also: FACTOR PRODUCTIVITY

LABOR THEORY OF VALUE

The labor theory of value states that the value of a good or service is proportional to the amount of labor used to produce that good or service. Karl Marx exposed this view, but its origins can be traced to the English philosopher John Locke. Economists rely on markets to determine value.

LABOR UNION

A labor union is an organization of workers from a similar occupation. A union represents its members' interests in such areas as contract negotiations with management. These contractual agreements include wage and fringe benefits, working conditions, job retraining, and length of the work week. In 1988, less than 17 percent of the labor force belonged to a union, and this percentage is falling. Unionized workers are in mostly clerical, operative, or teaching-related professions.

Typically, union workers' contracts are multi-year agreements. Although employers may want to respond to market pressure by lowering wages, they often do not have the ability because of a prior contractual agreement with union members and other workers under contract.

LAFFER CURVE

The diagram below illustrates a nonlinear relationship between tax rates and tax revenues for an economy. Such a relationship was popularized by Arthur Laffer and is commonly known as the Laffer curve.

Figure 12

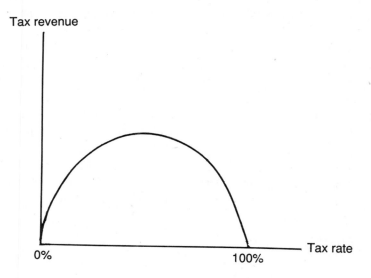

The Laffer curve shows that for either a zero tax rate or a 100 percent tax rate (measured on the horizontal axis) no tax revenues (measured on the vertical axis) will be collected by the government. Tax revenues only will be positive at tax rates between 0 percent and 100 percent. As illustrated, there is some tax rate at which tax revenues will be a maximum. The value of such a tax rate is not known for the U.S. economy.

LAGGING ECONOMIC INDICATORS

See Economic Indicators

LAISSEZ FAIRE

See Libertarianism

LAPPING

An embezzlement scheme in which cash collections from customer's are stolen. Lapping occurs in an environment in which one person has both recordkeeping responsibilities and custody of cash. To avoid discovery, the embezzler corrects the customers' accounts within a few days by posting other cash receipts to the accounts from which the proceeds have been embezzled.

Auditing techniques used to detect lapping include (1) confirmation of old accounts and written off accounts; analytical review of the average age of receivables and receivable turnover (lapping increases the average age and decreases turnover); examine authenticated deposit slips from bank and compare names, dates, and amounts on remittance advices to information on deposit slips; and review internal control procedures. Remittance advices should also be compared with information recorded in the accounts. Noncash credits to accounts receivable should be verified. Monthly statements of customers should be compared with their accounts. Customers accounts should be reconciled individually with the account receivable control account.

See also: FRAUD
            KITING

LAW OF DEMAND

The quantity of a product consumers are willing to purchase is referred to in economics as quantity demanded. Economists believe that there is a predictable negative relationship between price and quantity demanded, and they call this relationship the law of demand.

The law of demand states that the quantity of a product that individuals demand increases when the price of the product decreases, assuming all other factors which could influence purchasing decisions remain constant. Conversely, the law of demand predicts that the quantity demanded of a product decreases when the price increases, assuming all other factors which could influence purchasing decisions remain constant. The law of demand is graphically represented by a downward sloping relationship, a demand curve, between price and quantity demanded, as shown below in Figure 13.

Figure 13

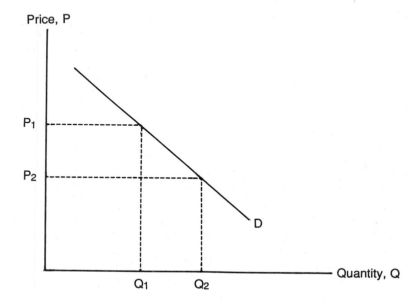

This inverse relationship between price and quantity demanded can be derived mathematically and graphically from certain fundamental axioms in economics; however, there is also an intuitive explanation. At higher prices, less quantity is demanded because the sacrificed opportunities from having to pay the higher price are greater than they would be at lower prices. These sacrificed opportunities generally involve the ability to purchase a substitute product.

LAW OF DIMINISHING RETURNS

In economics, the short run is defined as a period of time when at least one factor of production is fixed, generally capital. Labor, then, is the variable factor. The law of diminishing returns states that as increasing units of a variable factor (labor) are added to a fixed factor (capital), the output produced by the additional units of the variable factor will increase but eventually at a decreasing rate. Stated alternatively, when diminishing returns set in, output will begin to increase at a decreasing rate as more units of the variable factor are used. Output will eventually decline absolutely. If diminishing returns were not a characteristic of production, then the world's supply of wheat (the output) could be grown in a flower pot (the fixed factor) by simply adding more and more seed (the variable factor).

THE LAW OF SUPPLY

There is no law of supply in economics. From the consumer side, there is the law of demand that leads to a graphical illustration of a downward sloping demand curve. However, the accompanying upward sloping supply curve comes from the theory of cost. From this theory, it follows that the marginal cost of production will increase (as a result of diminishing returns) and that firms make their short-run output decisions based on marginal cost. From this, it follows that supply curves are drawn upward sloping.

LEADERSHIP FUNCTION

Leadership is a major function of management. Basic functions of leadership include providing structure and ensuring motivation and compliance. Leadership is required if organizational goals and objectives are to be achieved. Leadership influences persons to act for a common objective. It is a quality of managers which involves getting subordinates (followers) to assist in the attainment of organizational ends. The skill of a leader relates to traits of the leader; the leader's knowledge of the personality, character, and needs/wants of followers; behavior patterns and interrelationships; situational dimensions (position power, task structure, leader-member relations); organizational requirements; and other factors. More specifically, successful leadership depends on:

1. the confidence that subordinates have in their leader

2. the nature of the subordinates' jobs (routine, nonroutine)

3. the authority or power placed in the leadership position (rewards, punishments).

To be successful, a leader should:

1. have expertise in the planning, organizing, and control functions of management

2. have confidence in his or her ability to lead

3. possess communication skills

4. understand persons, tasks, organizational structure, motivation, personalities, the art of persuasion, etc.

Leadership theories are many and varied. Older forms of leadership theory are based on an understanding of the traits of a leader: maturity, character, decisiveness, intelligence, and others. Research generally confirms that no single trait or set of traits can assure effective leadership. Behavioral theories of leadership styles have been proposed to explain leadership. Behavioral theories include the following:

1. Autocratic vs. participative (democratic) styles

2. A "hands-on" management style

3. A two-dimensional model

The autocratic style of leadership is essentially leadership centered in the manager. The manager makes and announces the decision. The area of freedom for subordinates is limited and the use of authority by the manager is considerable. The participative leadership style is primarily subordinate-centered leadership where subordinates have considerable freedom and the use of authority by the manager is limited. A "hands-on" management style requires a high degree of involvement in operations by a manager. Two-dimensional models of leadership are behavior-oriented. In two-dimensional models, one dimension focuses on people and the other dimension focuses on tasks (assignments, production). For example, a leadership style could be one in which the manager had a high concern for people and a low concern for tasks. Another style would be the opposite. A third style could be a moderate concern for people and tasks. A fourth could be high concern for both people and tasks. Other combinations are possible.

Leadership has been described by Robert Blake and Jane Mouton in *The New Managerial Grid* in terms of The Managerial Grid (see Exhibit L-1). The two-dimensional Grid identifies combinations of concern for production and concern for people. Concern for people is represented on the vertical axis of the grid; concern for production (tasks) represented on the horizontal axis. The four corners of the grid and the center describe various management styles:

Corner	Leadership Style
1.1	Low concern for both people and production.
1.9	High concern for people and low concern for production; democratic leadership.
9.1	High concern for production and low concern for people; autocratic leadership.
9.9	High concern for both people and production; Blake and Mouton believe that this style is the most effective leadership style.
5.5	Equal concern for people and production (that is, a balanced approach to leadership).

Exhibit L-1
The Managerial Grid

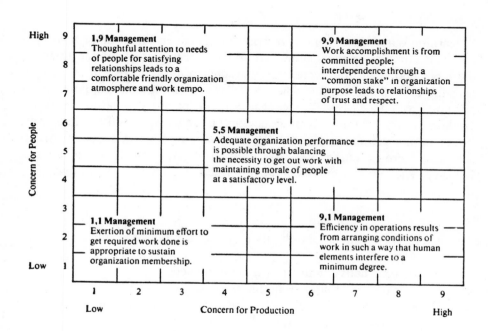

See also: CONTROL FUNCTION
GOALS AND OBJECTIVES
ORGANIZATIONAL BEHAVIOR
PERFORMANCE EVALUATION

Reference:

Pennings, Johannes M., ed., *Decision Making: An Organizational Behavior Approach* (Markus Wiener, New York, 1983).

LEADING ECONOMIC INDICATORS

See Economic Indicators

LEARNING CURVE

A learning curve describes the relationship between direct labor hours per unit and cumulative units produced. When accumulated volume doubles, the labor hours per unit decreases by a constant percentage. An 80 percent learning curve indicates that when cumulative volume doubles, labor hours per unit are reduced by 20 percent to 80 percent of the previous level. As workers become familiar with a specific task, their productivity increases. This learning process is particularly noticeable in new products or processes. The learning curve was first used in World War II in the aircraft industry. The learning curve can be described algebraically as follows:

$$y(x) = ax - b$$

where $y(x)$ = direct labor hours required to produce x unit

x = cumulative number of units produced
a = number of hours required to produce first unit
b = function the rate at which $y(x)$ decreases as cumulative production increases

Edward L. Summers and Glenn A. Welsch list activities most subject to learning curve analysis:

1. Activities which have not been performed or not performed in their present operational form.

2. Activities being performed by new employees and others not familiar with the operations.

3. Activities which involve the use of a stated raw material for the first time or which involve a change in the way the material is used.

4. Production runs of short duration, especially if these runs are repeated.

To illustrate an application of the learning curve, assume that a ship builder estimates that it takes 4,000 labor hours to produce a yacht. The company expected to build eight yachts for various customers. The company estimates that its learning curve is 80 percent after the first yacht is built. The effect of the learning curve on labor hours is computed as follows:

Cumulative Quantity A	Cumulative Average Hours Per Yacht B	Cumulative Hours C
1	4,000	4,000
2	3,200 (4,000 × .80)	6,400
4	2,560 (3,200 × .80)	10,240
8	2,048 (2,560 × .80)	16,384

Column A = Double the cumulative quantity.
Column B = Multiply the cumulative averages by the learning curve percentage.
Column C = Multiply the cumulative average by the cumulative quantity.

A learning curve chart is illustrated in Exhibit L-2 on the following page.

A firm that accumulates experience the fastest can benefit competitively over a long-run period. A knowledge of how the experience curve operates can help companies develop strategies for new products and processes, pricing, expansion, and other plans.

See also: PRICING POLICY

Reference:

Buffa, Elwood S., *Modern Production/Operations Management* (John Wiley & Sons, New York, 1983).

LEASES

A lease is a contract whereby real or personal property is provided by a lessor/owner to a lessee/renter for a specified period of time in exchange for compensation in the form of rent. Leases are usually entered into by a lessee primarily to acquire the right to use or control an asset.

Exhibit L-2

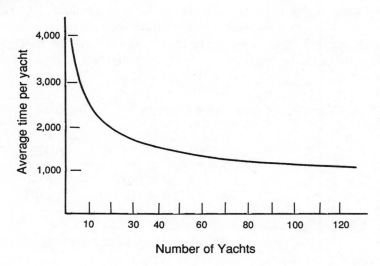

Lease classifications for financial accounting and reporting purposes can be summarized as to type and accounting method by lessee and lessor:

Type	Lessee	Lessor
Noncapitalized (no sale or purchase of asset assumed)	Operating lease	Operating lease
Capitalized (sales and purchase of asset assumed)	Capital lease	Sales-type lease Direct-financing lease Leveraged lease

The lessee classifies a lease as a capital lease if the lease meets any one of the following criteria:

1. The lease transfers ownership of the property to the lessee by the end of the lease term.

2. The lease contains an option to purchase the leased property at a bargain price.

3. The lease term is equal to or greater than 75 percent of the estimated economic life of the leased property.

4. The present value of rental and other minimum lease payments equals or exceeds 90 percent of the fair value of the leased property less any investment tax credit retained by the lessor.

If none of these criteria is met, the lease is an operating lease.

For the lessor, a lease must meet one of the four criteria specified for the lessee and both of the following criteria:

1. Collectibility of the minimum lease payments is reasonably predictable.

2. No important uncertainties surround the amount of nonreimbursable costs yet to be incurred by the lessor under the lease.

If these criteria are not met, the lease is an operating lease.

An operating lease requires the recognition of the rental agreement requiring periodic payments for the use of an asset during that period. Rent expense or rent income is recognized on the income statement of the lessee and lessor, respectively. No new assets or liabilities are recorded.

A capital lease is, in substance, the purchase of an asset and the incurrence of a liability. A capital lease transfers substantially all of the ownership privileges, including the benefits and risks of property ownership, and represents in economic substance but not in legal form a purchase or sale of an asset. Such leases should be accounted for by the lessee as the acquisition of an asset and the incurrence of a liability.

A leveraged lease is a three-party lease involving a lessee, a lessor, and a long-term creditor, usually a bank or other financial institution. The long-term creditor provides nonrecourse financing to the lessor. The financing provides the lessor with substantial leverage in the transaction. For example, a contractor might agree to build an office building and lease it to a company. To finance the construction of the building, a bank lends money to the contractor (lessor). The contractor uses a relatively small amount of his own funds. The lessor-owner's return on the investment comes from lease rentals, investment tax credit, and income tax benefit from depreciation on the total cost of the property and interest expense deductions on the debt, and other expenses. The lessor classifies the leveraged lease as a direct financing lease.

A sale-leaseback occurs when an owner sells property and then leases the same property back. The seller-lessee usually has a tax advantage in that the entire lease payment can be deducted, which can include interest and amortization of the cost of land and partially depreciated other real property. The sale-leaseback is often used when financing is a problem. From an accounting point of view, any profit or loss incurred by the seller-lessee from the sale of the asset under a capital lease is deferred and amortized over the lease term or the economic life of the asset. If the lease is an operating lease, any profit or loss on the sale should be deferred and amortized in proportion to the rental payments over the period the asset is used by the lessee.

See also: LIABILITIES
    SUBSTANCE OVER FORM

Reference:

Seidler, Lee and D.R. Carmichael, eds., *Accountants' Handbook* (John Wiley & Sons, N.Y., 1981).

LEDGER

A ledger (or general ledger) is a book or file of ledger accounts which are usually numbered to provide easy access and cross-referencing uses. Typical ledger accounts include cash, accounts receivable, inventory, and accounts payable. A list of a firm's general ledger accounts with their corresponding numbers is called a chart of accounts. In an accounting system, events and transactions are initially recorded chronologically in a journal and then are transferred (or posted) to a ledger account. At the end of an accounting period, a trial balance is taken from the general ledger from which financial statements are prepared.

In addition to a general ledger, many firms have subsidiary ledgers which are used to record details of certain general ledger accounts. For example, a company having many credit customers may have an accounts receivable account in the general ledger and may maintain a subsidiary accounts receivable ledger to record data about individual customers. The accounts receivable account in the general ledger is called a control account because its balance should equal the total of the individual account balances in the subsidiary ledger. A subsidiary account is often used to support accounts receivable, accounts payable, inventory, plant assets, capital stock, selling expenses, and general and administrative expenses. A subsidiary ledger could be created for any general ledger account.

The use of subsidiary ledgers and control accounts can reduce substantially the number of general ledger accounts, reduce the probability of errors, improve the probability of locating errors that do occur, and allow for the division of labor where persons can be assigned to the various subsidiary ledgers.

See also: ACCOUNT
ACCOUNTING SYSTEM
CHART OF ACCOUNTS
JOURNAL
TRIAL BALANCE

LEGAL CAPITAL

Many state laws require corporations to maintain a minimum level of stockholders' equity to prohibit the corporation from distributing assets to shareholders to the extent that it would impair this minimum. Legal capital is defined by state law. The par value of shares issued and outstanding of par value stock is often the legal capital. If a corporation issues no-par stock, legal capital may be (1) total consideration paid in for the shares, (2) a minimum amount required by state incorporation laws, or (3) an amount established by the board of directors. Legal capital does not refer to the market value or book value per share.

See also: CAPITAL
CAPITAL STOCK

LETTER OF CREDIT

A letter of credit is a financial instrument issued by a bank to an individual or to a company that substitutes the credit of the bank for that of the individual or company. It is frequently used by companies ordering goods from foreign suppliers with whom they have not established credit. The foreign recipient can sell or transfer the letter of credit to another party if it is addressed to the beneficiary "and/or transferee(s)." Such a letter of credit is considered a negotiable instrument.

Sometimes a letter of credit is issued to individuals as a source of funds while traveling. Correspondent institutions of the issuing bank will advance cash to the holder of the letter and post the amounts of the advances on the letter. This kind of arrangement although widely used in the past has largely been replaced by the use of traveler's checks.

See also Banker's Acceptances

LEVERAGE

Leverage is used to explain a firm's ability to use fixed-cost assets or funds to magnify the returns to its owners. Leverage exists whenever a company has fixed costs.

There are three types of leverage in financial management: operating, financial, and total leverage. Financial leverage is a financing technique that uses borrowed funds or preferred stock (items involving fixed financial costs) to improve the return on an equity investment. As long as a higher rate of return can be earned on assets than is paid for the capital used to acquire the assets, the rate of return to owners can be increased. This is referred to as positive financial leverage. Financial leverage is used in many business transactions, especially where real estate and financing by bonds or preferred stock instead of common stock are involved. Financial leverage is concerned with the relationship between the firm's earnings before interest and taxes (EBIT) and the earnings available to common stockholders or other owners. Financial leverage is often referred to as "trading on the equity." Operating leverage is based on the relationship between a firm's sales revenue and its earnings before interest and taxes. Operating leverage arises when an enterprise has a relatively large amount of fixed costs in its total costs. Total leverage reflects the impact of operating and financial leverage on the total risk of the firm (the degree of uncertainty associated with the firm's ability to cover its fixed-payment obligations).

Financial leverage arises as a result of fixed financial charges related to the presence of bonds or preferred stock. Such charges do not vary with the firm's earnings before interest and taxes. The effect of financial leverage is that an increase in the firm's earnings before interest and taxes results in a greater than proportional increase in the firm's earnings per share. A decrease in the firm's earnings before interest and taxes results in a more than proportional decrease in the firm's earnings per share. The degree of financial leverage (DFL) can be measured by the following formula:

$$\text{Degree of Financial Leverage (DFL)} = \frac{\text{Percentage change in earnings per share}}{\text{Percentage change in earnings before interest and taxes}}$$

The degree of financial leverage indicates how large a change in earnings per share will result from a given percentage change in earnings before interest and taxes. Whenever the degree of financial leverage is greater than one, financial leverage exists. The higher this quotient, the larger the degree of financial leverage.

To illustrate the application of financial leverage, assume that an investor is considering the purchase of real estate with a selling price of $100,000. The investment will produce a net income of $15,000 annually. The investor has the option of acquiring the investment for cash or borrowed funds obtainable at the rate of 14 percent interest to leverage the investment. The effect of several leveraged options is illustrated in Exhibit L-3.

The example illustrates an investment where the financial leverage was positive. When the after-tax cost of borrowing exceeds the cash return that can be earned on the asset, negative financial leverage results. At this point, leverage cannot increase the rate of return to common stock equity.

Since debt financing incurs fixed interest charges, the ratio of debt to equity is considered a measure of financial leverage. This ratio indicates the relationship between the funds on which fixed financial charges must be paid and the total funds invested in the firm. The higher the debt to equity ratio, the higher the financial leverage and the greater the increase of operating profits and losses on earnings per share.

When an investor uses borrowed funds to acquire real estate or any other asset, any increase in property value belongs to the equity investor. The investor's equity which increases substantially with only a modest increase has an option to purchase real estate for $100,000 cash or by using

Exhibit L-3
Financial Leverage

	Option 1 Cash purchase (100% equity)	Option 2 Leverage 1:1 (50% borrowed; 50% equity)	Option 3 Leverage 4:1 (80% borrowed; 20% equity)
Acquisition price of asset	$100,000	$100,000	$100,000
Equity in investment	100,000	50,000	20,000
Income from invest- ment before interest	15,000	15,000	15,000
Less: Interest on borrowed funds at 14%		(7,000)	(11,200)
Cash return	15,000	8,000	3,800

$$\frac{\text{Cash return}}{\text{Equity investment}} \qquad \frac{15,000}{100,000} = 15\% \qquad \frac{8,000}{50,000} = 16\% \qquad \frac{3,800}{20,000} = 19\%$$

90 percent financing. The investor holds the property for 10 years and the property increases at 4 percent per year. The percentage increase in equity growth differs dramatically when borrowed funds are used:

	Cash Purchase	**90% Financing**
Acquisition price	$100,000	$100,000
Equity investment	100,000	10,000
Investment value at end of 10 years	140,000	140,000
Percentage increase in equity growth:		
$\dfrac{\text{Equity growth}}{\text{Original equity}}$	40%	400%

Operating leverage refers to the extent that fixed costs are utilized in the production process during an operating cycle. Operating leverage can also be used to measure the impact on earnings per share of having different levels of fixed to variable costs in manufacturing products. Earnings before interest and taxes are related to changes in the variable cost to fixed cost relationship. As fixed operating costs are added by the firm, the potential operating profits and losses are magnified, and are ultimately reflected in the variation in earnings per share of stock. For example, a book publisher's cost of producing another book is below the average cost of producing the book; hence, the gross margin (sales less cost of goods sold) per book is relatively large. An enterprise with a large percentage increase in income relative to its increase in unit sales can expect to have large operating leverage. The degree of operating leverage (DOL) can be measured by the following formula:

$$\text{Degree of Operating Leverage (DOL)} = \frac{\text{Percentage change in earnings before interest and taxes}}{\text{Percentage change in sales}}$$

The degree of operating leverage indicates how large a change in operating profit will result from a given percentage change in sales. As long as the degree of operating leverage is greater than one, there is positive operating leverage.

The degree of total or combined leverage (DTL) is computed as follows:

$$\text{Degree of Total Leverage (DTL)} = \frac{\text{Percentage change in earnings per share}}{\text{Percentage change in sales}}$$

Whenever the percentage change in earnings per share resulting from a given percentage change in sales exceeds the percentage change in sales, total leverage is positive. The total or combined leverage for a company equals the *product* of the operating and financial leverages (DTL = DOL × DFL). Total leverage indicates a firm's ability to use both operating and financial fixed costs to magnify the effect of changes in sales on a firm's earnings per share.

Exhibit L-4 illustrates the application of leverages to a firm's income statement. In this illustration, note that fixed expenses and interest expense remain unchanged. Note the section of the statement involved in the computation of operating leverage, financial leverage, and total leverage. Also note that what provides the leverage is fixed expenses and interest expenses which remain unchanged. When operating, financial, and total leverages increase, the risks the firm assumes also increase since the total risk of the firm is related to the firm's ability to cover fixed operating and financial costs. In the illustration, note that the total or combined leverage of 2.0 is the result of multiplying 1.2 (DOL) by 1.67 (DFL). For this illustration, if sales increase by 1 percent, EBIT will increase by 1.2 percent. If EBIT increases by 10 percent, net income will increase by 18.7 percent. With total leverage of 2.0, to increase net income by 10 percent, sales must increase by 5 percent. Leverage analysis is an extension of break-even analysis and uses the same basic information: price, quantity, variable expenses, and fixed expenses.

Exhibit L-4
Financial, Operating, and Total Leverage

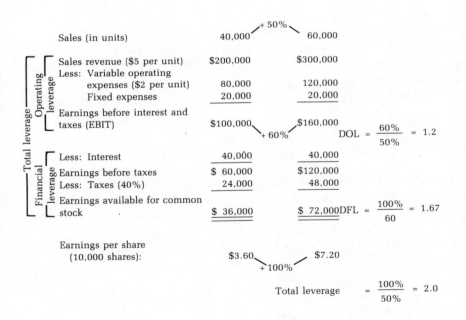

See also Cost of Capital

LIABILITIES

Liabilities are probable future sacrifices of economic benefits arising from present obligations of a particular entity to transfer assets or to provide services to other entities in the future as a result of past transactions or events. This definition makes a distinction between owners' equity and liabilities and emphasizes economic obligation rather than legal debt. Three essential characteristics of an accounting liability include the following:

1. A duty or obligation to pay exists.
2. The duty is virtually unavoidable by a particular entity.
3. The event obligating the enterprise has occurred.

Liabilities are usually classified as either current or noncurrent liabilities. Current liabilities are those obligations whose liquidation is reasonably expected to require the use of existing resources properly classified as current assets, or the creation of other current liabilities. This definition of current liabilities emphasizes a short-term creditor's claim to working capital rather than to the due date for classification purposes. Accounts payable, dividends payable, salaries payable, and taxes payable are examples of current liabilities. Liabilities which are not current liabilities are referred to as noncurrent or long-term liabilities. Bonds payable and mortgages payable are examples of long-term liabilities.

Contractual liabilities arise from events which are either expressly or implicitly contractual in nature. Some obligations are imposed on business enterprises by government or courts (such as taxes and fines), while others relate to nonreciprocal transfers from a business enterprise to owners or others (such as cash dividends and donations). A constructive liability is one which is implied from an arrangement, such as vacation pay and bonuses. Equitable obligations are neither contractual nor constructive obligations, but obligations arising from fairness, ethical and moral principles, or equity. An example of an ethical obligation is the responsibility of a monopoly supplier to deliver goods or services to dependent customers. Equitable liabilities are not currently recognized in financial statements. Contingent liabilities arise from an existing situation, or set of circumstances involving uncertainty as to possible gain or loss to an enterprise that will ultimately be resolved when one or more future events will occur or fail to occur. Only contingent losses are recognized. A contingent liability is accrued if (1) it is probable that a liability has occurred, or an asset has been impaired, and (2) it can be reliably measured. Examples of contingent liabilities include product warranties and pending litigation. Deferred liabilities are often found on financial statements. Deferred credits include (1) prepaid or unearned revenue involving a contractual obligation to provide a future good or service, such as for rent or interest received in advance, and (2) obligations arising from accounting principles which defer income recognition of the item, such as investment tax credits and deferred tax credits. The second type of deferred liabilities imposes no duty on the firm to transfer assets in the future. Such items arise from past transactions and are currently deferred from the income statement.

See also: CONTINGENCIES
CURRENT LIABILITIES

References:

SFAC No. 3, *Elements of Financial Statements of Business Enterprises* (FASB, 1981).

SFAC No. 5, *Recognition and Measurement in Financial Statements of Business Enterprises* (FASB, 1984).

LIBERTARIANISM

The school of thought advocating individual freedom as the cornerstone of the economic system is known as libertarianism. The belief is that individuals should be permitted to do as they like and that free markets will regulate such an economy. Associated with this laissez faire school of thought is Nobel Lauraute Milton Friedman.

LICENSING

To insure that certain business and professional practices maintain accept-able levels of services, states (and sometimes the federal government) re-quire that licenses be obtained in order to operate. For example, medical doctors must pass a state medical board examination before practicing. Lawyers must also pass a board examination. Real estate agents have to obtain a license before engaging in transactions. Restaurants must meet health standards in order to operate, and so on.

From an economic perspective, licensing provides information to con-sumers as to which practitioners have met a preestablished minimum level of acceptance.

LIQUIDATION

Liquidation is one relief procedure available to an insolvent debtor. Liqui-dation has as its basic purpose the realization of assets and the liquidation of liabilities rather than the continuation of the business as in a reorganiza-tion. Insolvency refers to the inability of a debtor to pay its obligations as they come due. Chapter 7, Bankruptcy Reform Act of 1979, outlines the procedures for corporate liquidation. Chapter 7 is the basic liquidation pro-cedure and is sometimes referred to as ordinary bankruptcy. Chapter 7 is available to most debtors other than a government unit, a bank, insurance company, or a railroad.

Liquidation can be started by a voluntary petition (debtor initiates the petition) or involuntary petition (creditors initiate the petition). In a liqui-dation, an interim trustee is appointed. Unsecured creditors have a right to elect a permanent trustee. In most cases, the interim trustee becomes the permanent trustee. The trustee liquidates the debtor's nonexempt property as soon as possible "with the best interests of parties in interest." The trustee proceeds to distribute the available proceeds to the debtor's creditors according to priorities assigned in Chapter 7. After the property of the debtor has been converted into cash and a proper distribution has been made to creditors and others, the debtor receives a discharge. The court will grant the debtor a discharge unless certain conditions are present. Nonindividuals do not receive a discharge in a Chapter 7 case. Nonindividual debtors normally file a voluntary Chapter 7 petition to provide for an orderly liquidation of their assets and distribution of proceeds to their creditors.

The term liquidation is sometimes used to refer to a situation where a business, such as a partnership, liquidates, winds up, or settles the affairs of the partnership with the partnership terminating when the liquidation has been completed. In partnership liquidations, partnership assets are realized, liabilities paid, and distributions of cash, if any, are made to the partners.

Liquidation is sometimes used to refer to the settlement of liabilities while realization refers to the process of converting noncash assets into cash.

See also: BANKRUPTCY
PARTNERSHIP
REORGANIZATION
SOLVENCY AND INSOLVENCY

Reference:

Ginsberg, Robert E., *Bankruptcy* (Prentice-Hall, Englewood Cliffs, N.J., 1985).

LIQUIDITY

Liquidity describes the amount of time required to convert an asset into cash or pay a liability. For noncurrent assets, liquidity generally refers to marketability. Cash is a highly liquid asset. Property, plant, and equipment would ordinarily be very nonliquid assets. Liquidity is important in evaluating the timing of cash inflows and outflows. The liquidity of an enterprise is a major indicator of its ability to meet its debts when they mature.

Liquidity ratios are often used to measure a firm's liquidity. These ratios typically relate to the enterprise's working capital—its current assets and current liabilities. Current assets include cash, short-term marketable securities, receivables, inventories, and prepaid items. Current liabilities include such items as accounts payable, taxes, interest payable, and other such short-term payables. Major liquidity ratios include the current ratio and acid-test ratio computed as follows:

$$\text{Current ratio} = \frac{\text{Current Assets}}{\text{Current Liabilities}}$$

$$\text{Acid–test ratio} = \frac{\text{Quick Assets}}{\text{Current Liabilities}}$$

Quick assets include cash, short-term marketable securities, and accounts receivable. Inventories are excluded because there may be some delay in converting them into cash. Prepaid expenses are excluded because they cannot be converted into cash. The acid-test ratio is a more severe test of a company's short-term ability to pay its debts than is the current ratio.

See also: FINANCIAL STATEMENT ANALYSIS
RATIOS
WORKING CAPITAL

LIMITED PARTNERSHIP

A limited partnership has two types of partners: general partners and limited partners. The general partners are the active managers of the enterprise. They organize and operate the partnership and accept full financial liability. Limited partners are passive participants in the venture. They contribute capital to the organization but are not active in its operation. The limited partners have no liability for the debts of the organization beyond their original investment.

Much investment in real estate has been carried on through limited partnerships. Often the general partner in a real estate limited partnership is the developer who has planned the project and often will manage it once it is developed. This form of organization gives the developer the ability to raise capital by selling limited partnership shares to investors in much the same way as if the enterprise were a corporation.

From the standpoint of the limited partners, a limited partnership combines the legal advantages of limited liability with the tax benefits of partnership ownership. The limited partnership is not subject to corporate income tax. Therefore, the depreciation expenses and other tax benefits can be passed through to the individual limited partners in proportions specified by the partnership agreement. This is what has given the limited partnership its appeal as a vehicle for real estate investment. The tax losses of the partnership can flow through to the limited partners giving them the benefit of a tax shelter without the risk of unlimited liability should the enterprise fail.

Forty-nine states plus the District of Columbia have passed the Uniform Limited Partnership Act which recognizes limited partnerships as a legal form of business organization and requires that a limited partnership be formed by a written document. Louisiana is an exception and has its own limited partnership laws.

Limited partnerships fall into two major categories: private and public. Private limited partnership need not be registered with the Securities and Exchange Commission (SEC) if all the partners, the syndicator, and the property are in one state, or if there are no more than 35 investors involved. Public partnerships which are offered for sale in more than one state must be registered with the SEC as an interstate security offering.

Typically, public limited partnerships are underwritten by major securities brokerage houses such as Merrill-Lynch, E. F. Hutton, etc. They are offered for sale by agents and brokers across the country. Sales of public real estate limited partnerships are reported to have exceeded $8 billion in 1985.

A substantial disadvantage of investment in limited partnerships is that partnership shares are relatively nonliquid. There is no active secondary market in partnership shares, although some are beginning to develop. In some cases, the general partners may offer to buy back the shares of limited partners wishing to sell out, but usually they are not required to do so.

The 1986 Tax Reform Act made several changes that substantially reduced the appeal of real estate investment in general and limited partnership investment in particular. First, the top marginal tax bracket was lowered, reducing the value of passive tax losses. Second, limitations were placed on interest deductions and on the size of tax losses from passive investments such as real estate limited partnerships. Finally, the depreciation period for real estate was lengthened considerably.

See also: MASTER LIMITED PARTNERSHIP

Reference:

Jarchow, Stephen P., *Real Estate Limited Partnership Syndications* (New York, NY: John Wiley and Sons, 1985).

LOANABLE FUNDS THEORY

The loanable funds theory of interest rates is a supply and demand theory of the determination of nominal interest rates. Very simply, the nominal rate of interest is assumed to be determined by the demand and supply of loanable funds in the financial market.

The demand for loanable funds arises from the demands of individuals, businesses, and government. In each of these sectors of the economy, loanable funds (that is, borrowed money) are desired because the current spending plans of some individuals, businesses, and governments are greater than their current incomes. These deficit spenders need to borrow funds to bridge the gap between their spending plans and their current incomes.

The demand of individuals, businesses, and governments for loanable funds is assumed to be sensitive to the rate of interest they must pay on borrowed money. The higher the rate of interest, the less they are likely to want to borrow. Their demands are also affected by their level of income: the higher their income, the more they are likely to want to borrow.

On the other side of the market, the supply of loanable funds is influenced by the decisions of individual savers—persons, businesses, and governments. The separate decisions of these individual saving units regarding the amount they will save is a principal determinant of the supply of loanable funds in the market.

Their decisions to supply loanable funds in the market (that is, to save and lend money) are influenced by the rate of interest and their levels of income. The higher the rate of interest, the more funds are likely to flow into the market as individuals, businesses, and governments curtail their spending plans to reap the rewards of higher interest rates.

Savings and thus the supply of loanable funds is sensitive also to the level of income. The higher the level of income the higher the level of savings and thus the supply of loanable funds.

The supply of loanable funds also is influenced by the amount of new money creation on the part of the banking system. The supply of new money is affected by the decisions of the central bank as well as the actions of individual commercial banks. When the Federal Reserve expands the nation's monetary reserves through its open market operations, for example, it tends to expand the level of excess reserves in the banking system as a whole. Since excess reserves are not profitable, rising excess reserves encourage private banks to increase their lending, and as bank lending expands, the supply of loanable funds and the money supply rise.

The supply and demand for loanable funds interact in the market to determine the nominal rate of interest. This interaction is illustrated in Exhibit L-5, panels I and II. An increase in the propensity of individual economic units to save will shift the supply of loanable funds in panel I from S to S', resulting in a fall in the nominal rate of interest. Similarly, a rise in new money creation brought on by a change in Federal Reserve policy also will shift the supply schedule in panel I outward from S to S', lowering the nominal rate of interest at least in the short run.

The effects of inflation on the supply and demand for loanable funds is illustrated in panel II of Exhibit L-5 on the following page. Inflation tends to increase the demands of borrowers as they try to spend to beat the next round of price increases. Accordingly, this effect is shown as a shift in the demand for funds from D to D'. Inflation also reduces the level of savings that flow into the financial system because individuals and businesses tend to invest their excess funds in real assets such as land, art, gold, and foreign currency. This effect is shown as a shift inward in the supply of loanable funds from S to S'. The net effect of the shifts in both demand and supply is to increase the nominal interest rate from r to r'.

The loanable funds theory provides an easy way to understand and assess the impact of certain specific changes in such variables as the level of savings, new money creation, and inflation on financial markets. But as with any economic theory it is highly abstract, and in its simple form it does not properly allow for interaction and feedback effects from the rest of the economy. In its current state of development, it is not possible to use the theory to forecast actual changes in interest rates consistently or with precision.

Exhibit L-5

Panel I

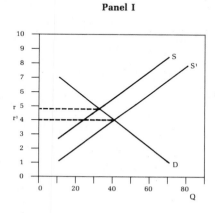

Panel II

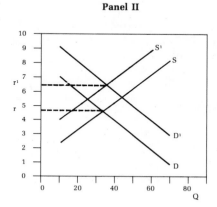

Reference:

Cooper, S. Kerry, and Fraser, Donald R., *The Financial Marketplace* (Reading, MA: Addison-Wesley, 1986), Ch. 6.

LONG RUN

In economics, activities are classified as long-run and short-run events. The distinction can not be quantified in terms of calendar time. Rather, the short run is a time period in which at least one factor of production is fixed, usually capital. The long run is a time period where all factors of production are variable.

See also: SHORT RUN

LORENZ CURVE

A Lorenz curve is a graphical device used by economists for illustrating the distribution of incomes (or similar data) for an economy, or the like. As seen from Figure 14 below, 60 percent of all U.S. families account for 40 percent of all earned income. If incomes were equally distributed, 40 percent of all families would account for 40 percent of earned income. The area between the 45-degree line and the Lorenz curve illustrates income inequality.

Figure 14

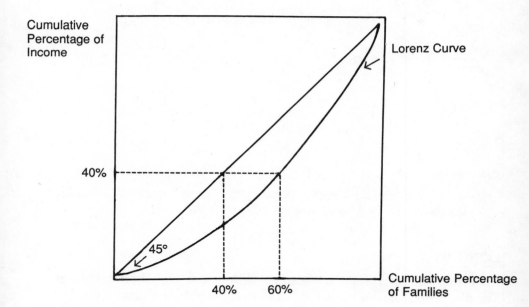

LOSSES

Losses are decreases in equity (net assets) from peripheral or incidental transactions of an entity and from other transactions and other events and circumstances affecting the entity during a period, except those that result from expenses or distributions to owners. Losses can arise from such transactions and events as the sale of investments in marketable securities and from the disposition of used equipment. Losses can be classified as "operating" or "nonoperating," depending on their relation to the enterprise's major ongoing or central operations.

See also: ELEMENTS OF FINANCIAL STATEMENTS
EXPENSES
EXTRAORDINARY ITEM
INTERIM FINANCIAL REPORTS

Reference:

SFAC No. 1, *Elements of Financial Statements of Business Enterprises* (FASB, 1981).

LOWER OF COST OR MARKET

Inventory and equity marketable securities are frequently valued in the financial statements at lower of cost or market. In applying the lower-of-cost-or market method, the cost of the ending inventory or portfolio of marketable equity securities is determined by an appropriate method and compared with market value at the end of the period. If market value is less than cost, an adjusting entry is made to record the loss and restate the inventory or securities. For inventory applications, market in "lower cost or market" is interpreted as replacement cost with upper and lower limits that cannot be exceeded. For example, market or replacement cost should not exceed the net realizable value (that is, estimated selling price in the ordinary course of business less reasonably predictable costs of completion and disposal); and market should not be less than net realizable value reduced by an allowance for an approximately normal profit margin.

When applied to marketable equity securities, the lower-of-cost-or-market method is applied separately to short-term and long-term portfolios of securities. Losses in market value related to the short-term portfolio are reported as part of income from continuing operations for the period. Losses in market value related to the long-term portfolio are reflected directly in the shareholders' equity section of the balance sheet in an owners' equity contra account.

The lower-of-cost-or-market method is a conservative accounting method that avoids valuing inventory or marketable equity securities on the balance sheet at more than replacement cost. The method is somewhat inconsistent in that market decreases are recognized, while market increases are not recognized. However, most accountants prefer to reflect the loss in the utility of an asset in the period the impairment is first recognized and can be estimated while gains should be recognized only when realized.

See also: INVENTORY

Mm

MACROECONOMICS

It is common practice to divide the study of economics into two parts, microeconomics and macroeconomics. Microeconomics is the study of the allocation of scarce resources among alternative uses. The units of analyses in microeconomics are the consumer and the firm. In contrast, macroeconomics (macro meaning large) is the study of the entire economy. Of interest in the study of macroeconomics is how the economy responds to alternative government policies or to changes in its environment (such as changes in trade policies in foreign countries). Regardless of the level, the same basic economic tools are fundamental to the analysis.

See also: ECONOMICS
              MICROECONOMICS

MANAGEMENT

Management is the process by which human efforts are coordinated and combined with other resources to accomplish organizational goals and objectives. Management has been defined as "the art of getting things done

421

through people" (Mary Parker Follett). Management requires an understanding of the economic principle of division of labor, which breaks tasks down into subtasks, and the coordination of effort, which reorganizes the subtasks in an efficient and effective whole.

Managers perform five basic functions: planning, organizing, directing, leading, and controlling as noted in Exhibit M-1 below.

Planning is the means of coordinating an idea into a reality, that is, determining the goals and objectives of the organization and the means of attaining them. Planning involves making decisions about a course of action and establishing priorities relating to the action.

Organizing and directing an enterprise requires that managers establish patterns of relationships (structures, hierarchies) among people and other resources that work to produce an output or to accomplish a common goal or objective. Organizing and directing relate to the flow of work through the organization under guidance.

Exhibit M-1
The Management Process

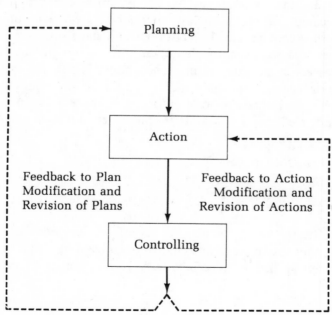

Leadership is required if organizational goals are to be achieved. Leadership influences persons to act for a common end or purpose. The skill of the leader relates to his/her knowing the personality, character, wants of subordinates, behavior patterns, organizational requirements, and other factors.

Controlling is primarily taking appropriate actions to ensure that organizational goals and objectives are planned and carried out (that is, that the firm attain maximum effectiveness).

Management by objectives (MBO) is a relatively recent innovation in management that often improves performance and morale. MBO involves the joint establishment of objectives and performance review procedures in an effort to improve productivity. This principle is based on the theory that people find satisfaction in their work and accept responsibility for their performance. To be effective, MBO should have the approval and commitment of top management and provide a means for participation by subordinates in the setting of objectives, a degree of self-determination in implementing plans, and a periodic review of performance.

See also: CONTROL FUNCTION
DIRECTING
INFORMATION SYSTEMS
LEADERSHIP FUNCTION
MANAGEMENT THEORIES
ORGANIZING FUNCTION
PLANNING FUNCTION

MANAGEMENT THEORIES

Cultural values and technological developments are primary elements of most management theories. Several major theories include:

1. classical organization theory
2. scientific management
3. modern behavioral organization theory
4. information systems theory
5. quantitative management science

Modern management theory includes elements of each of these theories and, in that sense, can be considered eclectic.

Classical organization theory focused attention on the functions or processes of management. Some principles of management frequently associated with the classical theory include authority, discipline, unity of command, chain of command, unit of direction, centralization, order and equity.

Scientific management had its origins with Frederick W. Taylor who applied principles of engineering to designing financial incentive systems to motivate workers. Time and motion studies were outgrowths of Taylor's scientific management theory. Such studies contributed to improvements in the utilization of human and natural resources, primarily at the shop level.

Modern behavioral organization theory focuses on human behavior: individual, group, organizational and environmental. With the oncoming of the computer age, management theory began to deal with management information systems as they impacted on management practice and thought. Organizations are conceptualized as a set of interrelated systems, each with its set of inputs, processing, and outputs.

How systems operate and how systems interface (with each other and with the external environment) are major interests of information systems theories.

Quantitative management science focuses on decision making and uses economic effectiveness criteria, measured in terms of costs, as a major objective. Mathematical models and computers provide powerful analytical tools and techniques which are widely used in a quantitative management science approach to management.

See also: EFFICIENCY AND EFFECTIVENESS
MANAGEMENT
QUANTITATIVE METHODS

Reference:

Baker, Kenneth R. and Dean H. Kropp, *Management Science* (John Wiley & Sons, New York, 1985).

MARGINAL ANALYSIS

Marginal analysis is the single most pervasive concept in economics. Decision making is described in terms of marginal benefits and marginal costs, that is the additional (marginal means additional) benefits associated with a decision and the additional costs associated with that same decision.

This marginal rule is applicable to a number of important economic questions. Marginal benefits and costs are considered when deciding how to allocate scarce resources (land, labor, air, water, etc.). Similarly, firms seeking to maximize profits do so by producing a level of output where marginal revenue equals the marginal cost of production. Also, decisions between alternative investments are made on the basis of the marginal return from each.

MARGINAL BENEFITS

In economics, the word marginal means additional. Marginal benefits are the additional benefits received from a particular action. For example, the marginal benefits from an additional year of education may include an X percent higher salary, Y times greater job flexibility, and W percent more knowledge. Marginal benefits are usually compared to marginal costs when making decisions.

See also: MARGINAL ANALYSIS
            MARGINAL COST

MARGINAL PRODUCT

Marginal product refers to the additional output produced by an additional unit of input. The marginal product of labor is the additional output produced by adding one additional unit of labor to the production process, holding capital fixed. The marginal product of capital is the additional output produced by adding one additional unit of capital to the production process, holding labor fixed.

MARGINAL PRODUCTIVITY THEORY OF INCOME DISTRIBUTION

John Bates Clark (1847–1938) advocated in *The Distribution of Wealth* (1899) that factors of production should be paid according to their marginal product. Those factors contributing more to output should be rewarded accordingly. While this proposition is the basis for much of modern microeconomic theory, it is difficult to translate Clark's prescription into practice owing to the difficulty in measuring marginal products precisely.

MARGINAL PROPENSITY TO CONSUME OR SAVE

The marginal propensity to consume refers to the portion of each additional dollar earned that consumers allocate to consumption as opposed to savings. Thus, the marginal propensity to consume (mpc) plus the marginal propensity to save (mps) sum to unity:

$$mpc + mps = 1.$$

In the U.S. economy, the mpc has historically been about .90. It has averaged slightly higher than .90 during the 1980s.

MARGINAL REVENUE

Marginal revenue refers to the additional revenue earned by a firm from selling one additional unit of its product. If a product can always be sold at the same price, then the additional revenue earned from selling one additional unit of the product equals the product's price. In general, however, a firm will have to lower its price to increase its quantity demanded (according to the law of demand); therefore, marginal revenue will decrease as additional units are sold. For a firm to maximize profit, economics teaches that the firm should produce to the point where marginal revenue equals marginal cost.

MARKET STRUCTURE

The composition of firms in a market determine the structure of that market. There are four distinct market structures discussed in economics:

perfect competition, monopolistic competition, oligopoly and monopoly. With perfect competition, there are numerous sellers of a homogeneous product (oats): no barriers to entry exist. With monopolistic competition, there are many sellers of a differentiated product (breakfast cereal): there are some minor barriers to entry. With an oligopoly, there are a few sellers of a product that may be identical (steel) or differentiated (toothbrushes): there may be barriers to entry. And, with a monopoly, there is only one seller: entry barriers may be severe.

MARX, KARL

Karl Marx (1818–1883), author of *Das Kapital,* may be the most influential social philosopher of the past century. The central theme in Marx's writings is that society can achieve its highest level through a communist system. Such a system, guided by social planning, would stress the equality of resources. This system, in theory, would be void of political hierarchial structures. No communist society today parallels Marx's vision.

MATCHING PRINCIPLE

The matching principle is an accounting principle that requires that revenues generated and expenses incurred in earning those revenues should be reported in the same income statement. In other words, total expenses involved in obtaining the revenues are recorded in the period. In this way, sacrifices (expenses) are matched against benefits or accomplishments (revenues). Revenues are recognized according to the realization principle. Expenses are determined in accordance with the matching principle.

General guidelines associated with applying the matching principle include the following:

1. Associating cause and effect.

2. Systematic and rational allocation.

3. Immediate recognition.

See also: ACCOUNTING ASSUMPTIONS
　　　　　　 ACCOUNTING BASIS
　　　　　　 EXPENSE

REALIZATION
RECOGNITION
REVENUE

MATERIALITY

Materiality refers to the magnitude or significance of something that would be of interest to an informed investor or creditor in making evaluations and decisions. Materiality implies significance, substance, importance, and consequence. Although materiality is primarily quantitative in nature, it is not exclusively so. Magnitude alone, without considering the nature of the item and the circumstances surrounding the decision being made, generally is not a sufficient basis for making a materiality decision. An item is material for accounting purposes if the omission or misstatement of it, in light of surrounding circumstances, makes it probable that the judgment of a reasonable person relying on the information would have been changed or influenced by the omission or misstatements.

Materiality judgments are concerned with levels or thresholds. Immaterial items which have little or no consequences to statement users can be handled as expediency, fairness, and professional judgment require. The Financial Accounting Standards Board decided not to establish materiality rules in Statement of Financial Accounting Concepts No. 2, but rather left the decision on materiality to the judgment of those who have all of the facts. The FASB stated that "no general standards of materiality could be formulated to take into account all the considerations that enter into an experienced human judgment," and that when the Board imposes materiality rules, it is "substituting generalized collective judgments for specific individual judgment, and there is no reason to believe that collective judgments are always superior." The FASB did qualify the above by stating that materiality rules may be written into some standards, which, in fact, has been done.

See also: ACCOUNTING ASSUMPTIONS
ACCOUNTING PRINCIPLES
QUALITATIVE CHARACTERISTICS OF
ACCOUNTING INFORMATION

Reference:

SFAC No. 2, *Qualitative Characteristics of Accounting Information* (FASB, 1981).

MAXIMAX CRITERION

Uncertainty is a situation in which the decision maker does not have information about the outcomes of his or her actions, and no estimates can be made about the probabilities associated with alternative outcomes. One criteria for guiding managers in such a situation is the maximax criterion.

The rule is to select the alternative (such as an investment opportunity) that will yield the maximum possible outcomes under the best (maximum) of all possible situations. This is a criterion of optimism.

See also: MAXIMIN CRITERION

MAXIMIN CRITERION

Uncertainty is a situation in which the decision maker does not have information about the outcomes of his or her actions, and no estimates can be made about the probabilities associated with alternative outcomes. One criterion for guiding managers in such a situation is the maximin criterion.

The rule is to select the alternative (such as an investment opportunity) that will yield the maximum possible outcomes under the worst (minimum) of all possible situations. This is a criterion of pessimism.

See also: MAXIMAX CRITERION

MEASUREMENT

Measurement is the assignment of numbers to objects, events or situations in accord with some rule or guideline. The property of the objects, events, or situation which determines the assignment of numbers is called the measurable attribute (or magnitude). The number assigned is called its measure (the amount of its magnitude). The rule or guideline defines both the magnitude and the measure.

In accounting, assets and liabilities currently reported in financial statements are measured by different attributes, depending on the nature of the item and the relevance and reliability of the attribute measured. Five different attributes of assets and liabilities are used in present accounting practice:

1. The historical cost of an asset is the amount of cash or its equivalent paid to acquire it. Historical cost for a liability is the historical proceeds received when the liability is incurred.

2. Current cost of an asset is the amount of cash or other consideration that would be required today to obtain the same asset or its equivalent. For liabilities, current proceeds are the amount that would be received today if the same obligation were incurred.

3. Current exit value is the amount of cash or its equivalent that would be received currently if an asset were sold under conditions of orderly liquidation. For liabilities, current exit value is the amount of cash that would have to be paid currently to eliminate the liability.

4. Expected exit value is the nondiscounted cash flows associated with the expected sale or conversion of an asset at some future date. For liabilities, expected exit value is the amount of cash expected to be paid to settle the liability in the due course of business.

5. Present value of expected cash flows is the cash flows associated with the expected sale or conversion of an asset at some future date discounted at an appropriate rate of interest. For liabilities, the present value is the discounted amount of cash expected to be paid to settle the liability in the due course of business.

Historical cost (or historical exchange price) method underlies the conventional accounting system. Inventories, property, plant, and equipment are often recorded at historical or acquisition cost. Current cost is also used in measuring inventories. Current exit value is usually used for marketable equity securities. Expected exit value is often used for accounts receivable and accounts payable. Present value of expected cash flows is frequently used for long-term receivables and payables.

The monetary unit of measurement used in current practice is nominal units of money, unadjusted for changes in purchasing power of money over time.

See also: ASSETS
COST PRINCIPLE
CURRENT VALUE ACCOUNTING
LIABILITIES
STATEMENT OF FINANCIAL POSITION

References:

SFAC No. 5, *Recognition and Measurement in Financial Statements of Business Enterprises* (FASB, 1984).

Staubus, George J., "An Induced Theory of Accounting Measurement" (*The Accounting Review,* Vol. LX, No. 1, January 1985).

MEDIUM OF EXCHANGE

In economic transactions money serves as a medium of exchange. Without money (a unit of account), all exchanges would take place through barter. With money, exchanges occur more efficiently.

The most important characteristic of any medium of exchange is that it is widely accepted. Gold, silver and bank notes were, at one time, acceptable mediums of exchange. Confederate money also had its period of acceptance. Today, the U.S. currency is the accepted unit of account for exchanges in this country.

See also: MONEY

MERGER

Firms will merge with one another if it is profitable for them to combine their activities. Sellers may have an incentive to merge if their companies appear to be in financial trouble or if there is a lack of future leadership (as in the case of a family-operated enterprise). Buyers may have an incentive to merge for several reasons: the buyer thinks that he or she can turn around a nonprofitable firm and enjoy the resulting financial benefits, the buyer wants to expand his or her share of a market (horizontal merger), the buyer seeks to ensure a reliable flow of inputs into its production process (vertical merger), or the buyer perceives that it would be profitable (through economics of scale) to diversify and become larger (conglomerate merger).

In 1982, and again in 1984, the Department of Justice, at the urging of President Ronald Reagan, relaxed their antitrust criteria regarding mergers. This policy intensified the trend of increased merger activity that began in the early 1970s. During the Reagan administration there have been more than 250,000 merger-related activities valued at over $2 trillion. Critics suggest that this rash of mergers will reduce domestic competition, but proponents point to the fact that there is little empirical evidence in support of that argument. There is some evidence that merger activity has slightly reduced private research and development (R&D) activity in the United States owing to the fact that post-merger firms extinguish the smaller firm's R&D program.

See also: HORIZONTAL MERGER
            VERTICAL MERGER

MICROECONOMICS

It is common practice to divide the study of economics into two parts, microeconomics and macroeconomics. Macroeconomics is the study of the aggregate economy. In contrast, microeconomics (micro meaning small) is the study of the allocation or exchange of scarce resources among market participants—consumers and producers (firms). Many argue that microeconomics is the foundation for macroeconomics because within microeconomic theory the fundamentals of exchange are developed.

See also: ECONOMICS
            MACROECONOMICS

MONETARY ASSETS AND LIABILITIES

Monetary assets and liabilities are items whose balances are fixed in terms of number of dollars regardless of changes in the general price level. All other items not representing a right to receive or an obligation to pay a fixed sum are nonmonetary items. Monetary items include cash, receivables, certain marketable securities, accounts payable and bonds payable. In periods of inflation (periods of rising prices), persons holding monetary assets tend to lose purchasing power, while persons holding monetary liabilities tend to gain purchasing power.

See also: FOREIGN OPERATIONS AND EXCHANGES

MONETARY POLICY

One important function of the Federal Reserve System (Fed) is to control the growth of the money supply in order to maintain a steady rate of economic growth. Monetary policy refers to the Fed's ability to change the money supply in order to influence economic activity.

See also: FEDERAL RESERVE SYSTEM

MONEY

Money is what money does. Money provides a uniform way to measure the value of goods and services. Therefore, money serves as a unit of account. Money also serves as a medium of exchange. Money makes exchanges more efficient. Finally, money is a store of value. Money is one form in which wealth can be maintained. It represents present and future purchasing power for those who hold it.

Money is measured in several ways. The narrowest definition of money, referred to as M1, consists of all currency (paper money and coins) plus demand deposits (checking accounts with unlimited check-writing privileges). A broader measure of money is M2. It consists of M1 money plus money market deposit accounts, money market mutual funds, overnight repurchase agreements, passbook savings accounts and small-denomination time deposits. The broadest measure of money is M3. M3 is M2 money plus large-denomination time deposits and specialized money market mutual funds for institutional investors. M1 is the most liquid measure of money and M3 is the least liquid.

Figures for M1, M2 and M3 are published in the *Economic Report of the President* each year, and are also published in the *Wall Street Journal* on a regular basis.

See also: FIAT MONEY

MONEY MARKET

Money markets refer to financial markets in which short-term debt instruments, such as Treasury bills, commercial paper, and certificates of deposit are traded. Money market certificates are a special type of certificate of deposit issued by banks, savings and loans, mutual savings banks, and credit unions. Money market funds are portfolios of liquid short-term securities in which shares or interests can be acquired. They usually operate like a passbook savings account or a checking account. Investors usually receive interest at rates higher than the federally-restricted rates paid by banks, savings and loans, mutual savings banks and credit unions.

See also: DEMAND FOR MONEY
               FINANCIAL MARKETS

MONOPOLISTIC COMPETITION

Monopolistic competition refers to a market structure in which there are many sellers of a differentiated product (such as breakfast cereal) and in which there are minor barriers to entry. Generally, competition in this type of industry is not in terms of price, as in a competitive market, but rather in terms of product attributes. Firms will advertise appealing characteristics of their product in an effort to attract new customers.

See also: COMPETITION
               MARKET STRUCTURE

MONOPOLY

A monopoly is a market structure in which there is only one supplier of a product. There are significant barriers to entry into such an industry. Having no competition from producers of identical or closely substitutable products, the monopolist will set price in such a way so as to maximize profits. This price will be greater than the price that would prevail under perfect competition, and the corresponding output level will be less than that which would prevail under perfect competition.

Monopoly is a theoretical construct used in economics to illustrate the opposite extreme to perfect competition, thereby demonstrating the economic efficiencies associated with competition. There are no pure monopolies in the United States, by law.

See also: NATURAL MONOPOLY

MONOPSONY

Monopsony refers to a situation in which there is only one buyer of a product. One example of such a situation relates to mill towns wherein the mill is the dominant employer of labor. In such a situation, the monopsonist has significant control over the offer wage.

See also: BILATERAL MONOPOLY

MORAL SUASION

The Federal Reserve (Fed) can control the money supply using three tools: open market operations, changes in reserve requirements, and changes in the discount rate. To reinforce the efficiency of changes in the discount rate, the Fed will often exert moral suasion on member banks. This is an informal, yet forceful, request to member banks to curb borrowing activity.

See also: DISCOUNT RATE

MORTGAGE

A mortgage is a pledge of property as security for the payment of a debt. Analytically, a mortgage is separate from a promissory note. Whereas a note provides evidence of a debt and a promise to repay, a mortgage provides collateral that may be sold if the note is not paid as promised.

Typically, a mortgage refers to the pledge of real estate as security for the repayment of a loan. A mortgage loan may take on any one of a variety of forms mutually agreeable to the borrower and lender. Beginning in the 1930s, however, long-term amortized mortgage loans for residential real estate were popularized by the Federal Housing Administration (FHA) and the Federal Home Loan Bank Board. Since that time, nearly all real estate mortgages include an amortization provision.

With a traditional amortized mortgage loan, the interest rate is fixed over the life of the loan, and a level monthly payment that includes both principal and interest is calculated so as to fully pay off the loan at maturity. The monthly payment necessary to amortize the principal balance on a mortgage loan can be calculated from the following formula for the present value of an annuity:

$$P = PMT / (1 + i) + PMT / (1 + i)2 + \ldots PMT / (1 + i)m \qquad (1)$$

where

P	=	principal balance outstanding (that is, the present value of the annuity)
PMT	=	monthly payment
i	=	monthly interest rate
m	=	number of months to maturity

The formula in equation (1) reduces to:

$$PMT = P \times [i / (1 - (1 + i) - m)] \qquad (2)$$

Equation (2) may be used to calculate the monthly payment if the principal balance, interest rate, and maturity of the mortgage loan are known. The monthly payment increases with the rate of interest and falls with increases in the term to maturity.

The interest component of each monthly payment can be calculated as:

$$In = i \times Pn \qquad (3)$$

where In is the dollar amount of interest paid each period and Pn is the principal amount outstanding at the beginning of the period. The amount of each payment that is applied to reduce the principal balance each month is:

$$Rn = PMT - In \qquad (4)$$

The loan balance outstanding (Pn) at the end of any period is equal to the present value of the remaining monthly payments discounted at the mortgage rate of interest. That is,

$$Pn = PMTn+1/ (1 + i) + PMTn + 2/ (1 + i) 2 \ldots PMTm / (1 + i)m-n$$

Over time, as the loan balance (Pn) falls, the interest component (In) of each monthly payment also declines and the principal component (Rn) increases.

Exhibit M-2 shows loan balance outstanding over the life of a 30-year $100,000 mortgage loan at various rates of interest. It also shows the proportion of each monthly payment devoted to interest during the term of the loan. At higher rates of interest, the fraction of each payment consumed by interest increases, and thus the outstanding loan balance falls more slowly. Even after 25 years, the loan balance on the 14-percent loan in Exhibit M-2 is still $50,922, while the balance on the 8-percent loan is only $36,188.

Exhibit M-2
$100,000 Mortgage for 30 Years (360 payments)

Interest Rate	Montly Payment	Loan Balance After ___ Years				
		5	10	15	20	25
8.0%	$733.76	95069.85	87724.70	76781.55	60477.96	36188.11
10.0%	$877.57	96574.32	90938.01	81664.56	66406.86	41303.22
12.0%	$1,028.61	97663.21	93417.99	85705.71	71694.83	46241.31
14.0%	$1,184.87	98430.81	95283.62	88971.60	76312.16	50922.25

Interest Rate	Percent of Payment as Interest After ___ Years					
	0	5	10	15	20	25
8.0%	90.86%	86.38%	79.70%	69.76%	54.95%	32.88%
10.0%	94.96%	91.71%	86.35%	77.55%	63.06%	39.22%
12.0%	97.22%	94.95%	90.82%	83.32%	69.70%	44.96%
14.0%	98.46%	96.92%	93.82%	87.60%	75.14%	50.14%

Beginning with the inflation of the 1970s, mortgage lenders began to develop a number of alternatives to the traditional fixed-rate mortgage, such as the adjustable rate mortgage (ARM) and the graduated payment mortgage (GPM), which have become popular. With these alternative mortgage instruments, the interest rate or the payment level may change over the life of the mortgage, but the basic mathematics of mortgage finance shown in equations (1) through (4) above is still essentially the same.

Like bonds, mortgages may trade on the secondary market after they have been issued. In recent years, there has been a dramatic growth in the use of mortgages as security for financial instruments which are bought and sold on financial markets. These securities are commonly referred to as mortgage-backed securities (MBS) and include collateralized mortgage obligations (CMO) and pass-through securities, such as those sold by the Government National Mortgage Association (GNMA).

Also like bonds, mortgages often include certain option features that affect their value in the secondary market. Most mortgages permit the borrower to prepay his loan when he moves or chooses to refinance, and lenders are forbidden to charge explicit prepayment penalties in many states. A mortgage *prepayment privilege* is like a call option on a bond. Some mortgages also contain the equivalent of a put option for the lender. This option is called a *due-on-sale clause*. It permits the lender to "put" the loan to the borrower (that is, require that the borrower pay off his debt) whenever the property is sold by the borrower. This cancels the loan and requires that the new buyer find his own financing. Other mortgages (for example, those insured by the Federal Housing Administration) are *assumable*. With an assumable mortgage, a new buyer may simply assume the equity of the original buyer and continue paying on the original mortgage at the original rate of interest.

See also: AMORTIZATION
ADJUSTABLE RATE MORTGAGE
GRADUATED PAYMENT MORTGAGE

MOTIVATION

Motivation is an internal pressure which encourages, urges, or prompts a person or group to act or not act in a certain manner. Classical motivation theory relates to the concept that humans maximize their own self-interest. This conceptualization is reflected in Adam Smith's economic philosophy expressed in *The Wealth of Nations*. Humans are motivated primarily by economic concerns. Economics incentives in the industrial setting are under the control of the organization; employees are to be controlled and motivated by the organization. As rational economic creatures, humans must not allow their emotions and feelings to interfere with economic activities, including motivation.

Advances on the classical theory suggested that basic human needs were the source of motivations and these needs were structured in a hierarchy: physiological satisfaction, safety and security, social needs, self-esteem and the respect of others, and self-actualization. The unsatisfied needs motivate human behavior. Individuals satisfy their lower level needs before proceeding to a higher level of need satisfaction which influences behavior. If a lower-level need is threatened, individuals will revert to that level.

Douglas McGregor developed the well-known theories of human behavior commonly referred to as Theory X and Theory Y. Individuals respond differently under the two theories of behavior. Theory X assumes a negative/passive approach to employees' motivation; Theory Y assumes a positive/active approach. Theory X focuses on external direction and control factors, and Theory Y focuses on integration and self-actualization as major behavior determinants. Theory X-type individuals dislike work, prefer directions, require control, and respond to threats; they are not ambitious, desire security above other needs, and are irresponsible. Theory Y-type people look for meaning in their work, possess initiative, are self-directing and problem-solving, and are committed to a job if it is satisfying; they are ambitious and seek responsibilities. According to many behaviorists, tasks could be structured to motivate, supervise, and direct people according to Theory X or Theory Y.

As might be expected, a Theory Z was proposed. William G. Ouchi undertook a study of the philosophy underlying Japanese business practice which concluded that Western businesses would probably be more successful, healthier, and happier work places if they adopted policies and practices found in Japanese industry. Qualities found desirable in Japanese organizations include: lifetime employment, equality of worth, mutual respect, job flexibility, loyalty to the company, and nonspecialization.

See also: CONTROL FUNCTION
            GOALS AND OBJECTIVES
            PERFORMANCE EVALUATION
            STOCK COMPENSATION PLANS

Reference:

Dessler, Gary, *Organization Theory: Integrating Structure and Behavior* (Prentice-Hall, Englewood Cliff, N.J., 1985).

MULTINATIONAL CORPORATION (MNC)

A multinational corporation (MNC) is a business firm that operates in more than one country. Since World War II, both the size and sophistication of multinational business activity has increased substantially, and a new and fundamentally different format for international business activity has developed. The distinguishing characteristic between the new form of commercial endeavor and earlier activities is that firms now very often make direct investments in fully integrated operations abroad, rather than merely buying resources or selling manufactured products. Many companies have become worldwide entities operating in many different countries and controlling all phases of the production and distribution process—from extraction of raw materials, through manufacturing, to marketing and delivery to consumers throughout the world.

The evolution of the multinational corporation has greatly increased global economic and political interdependence. For the most part, multinational corporations are free to pursue profit opportunities and allocate resources across international boundaries. Thus, they may borrow in the capital markets of one country to finance expansion in another, or transfer products and personnel from one overseas subsidiary to another.

In the chase for global profit opportunities, the actions of multinational corporations often come into conflict with the goals of the nation states in which they operate. Countries may want multinational corporations operating within their borders to produce more products domestically, to hire more local labor, and to export more. But such demands by host countries may conflict with global corporate profit strategies. When this happens, political tensions rise, and nation states may seek to impose certain controls on the operations of multinational corporations. Yet despite these inevitable stresses, multinational corporations have become an important force for global economic integration.

Reference:

Streeten, Paul, "Multinations Revisited," *Finance and Development* (June 1979), pp. 39–42.

MUTUAL FUNDS

Mutual funds are investment companies that obtain money from investors through the sale of shares and invest the funds thereby obtained in financial assets (e.g., stocks, bonds, commercial paper, etc.). The value of a share in a mutual fund can be calculated at any time by taking the total market value of all assets owned by the fund, net of any liabilities, and dividing the result by the number of shares outstanding. This is called the fund's *net asset value per share.*

The shareholders are the owners of the fund. They elect the board of directors who hires the manager of the fund. The manager is responsible for looking after the assets of the fund, within the limits established by the board of directors. Mutual funds provide investors the advantages of investment diversification and professional management.

Most mutual funds do *not* allow the managers of the fund complete discretion to invest in any kind of assets they choose. Instead, most will specialize in particular sectors of the financial market. Some invest only in equity securities, while some purchase only bonds. Some purchase both. Some, known as "money market mutual funds," invest only in money market instruments.

Mutual funds can be categorized according to their investment objective. For example, some known as "growth funds" invest in growth stocks. Others, known as "income funds," invest in stocks that pay high dividends and in bonds.

In recent years, there has been an explosion in the number and variety of special-purpose mutual funds. There are now a wide array of special-purpose funds for investors to choose from. Sector funds invest only in certain sectors of the economy such as technology, health care, real estate, metals, etc. International or global funds may invest in securities outside the United States. And tax exempt funds invest in tax-exempt municipal securities.

The managers of a mutual fund are paid a management fee. Annual fees range from 0.25 percent of the value of net assets to more than 1 percent of net assets. Often fund managers will receive additional fees depending on the investment performance of the fund as an incentive for above average performance. Funds are often managed by investment advisers, independent management companies, firms associated with securities brokers, and insurance companies.

Other costs of the fund, such as administrative and custodial expenses, also must be paid by fund investors. Often these services are provided by the management company but are charged to the fund. Total expenses including the management fee usually range from 1 to 2 percent of the net asset value of the fund.

Mutual funds can be divided into two broad categories: *closed-end* and *open-end* funds. Closed-end funds neither sell nor redeem shares of the fund after they have been originally issued to investors. Once the original shares in the fund have been sold, investors who want to sell their shares or buy additional ones must do so on the secondary market. The shares of closed-end funds trade, for example, on the New York Stock Exchange and over the counter.

Like the price of any security traded in the market, the price of closed-end mutual funds is established by demand and supply. Closed-end funds thus may sell at a price that is either above or below the per share net asset value of the fund.

In efficient markets, the price of closed-end fund shares should be close to the net asset value of the fund, and it is hard to understand why investors would ever pay a substantial premium above the net asset value of a fund. Nevertheless, substantial discounts and premiums are often observed. No convincing explanation for the existence of large discounts and premiums has been offered except market inefficiency.

Some investment analysts recommend the purchase of closed-end funds selling below their net asset value as a good way for investors to buy the market at a discount. However, because of the uncertainties of market valuation, closed-end mutual funds have not been as popular as open-end funds.

In an open-end fund, investors may redeem their shares from the fund at their net asset value. The management of the fund also may continually issue additional shares to new investors at their net asset value. When old shares are redeemed, securities in the fund's portfolio may be sold to raise the necessary cash. Alternatively, when new shares are issued, the funds may be used to make additional investments. To make the process of redeeming and issuing shares easier, most funds will maintain a small cash balance to cushion the day-to-day inflow and outflow of funds.

Open-end funds can be divided into two classes: *load funds* and *no-load funds*. Load funds are sold to investors through security brokers or other marketing organizations which add a load charge to the net asset value of the shares which they sell. The difference between the net asset value and offer prices of open-end funds quoted in financial newspapers reflect the load, or sales charge. These charges may vary from 2 percent to as high as 10 percent. A few funds charge redemption fees when shares are sold back to the fund. No-load funds are sold to investors at their net asset value. In financial newpapers, these funds are indicated with the letters "N. L." in the offer price column.

Today, most open-end mutual funds offer investors a wide range of investor services including automatic reinvestment of dividends and capital gains, contractual purchase plans, telephone redemption, check writing, and other services.

Many funds are organized into mutual fund families. Within a fund family there may be a money-market fund, an income fund, a growth fund, and many others. The Fidelity Fund family is an extreme example, offering investors more than 50 different funds to choose from. Family funds like Fidelity usually allow investors to switch their investments from one fund to another simply by calling a toll-free number.

Investors in mutual fund families are able to personally diversify their fund holding in any way to meet their own special investment needs and objectives. For example, investors wishing to take on additional risk might increase their holdings of the fund family's growth stock fund, while more conservative investors might place a larger portion of their assets in the money market fund.

Mutual funds are not subject to corporate income tax as long as they pay out to shareholders in the form of dividends and capital gain distributions at least 90 percent of the taxable income of the fund. Federal tax law allows shareholders to be taxed as if they held their portion of the assets of the fund directly.

Mutual funds are governed by the provisions of the Investment Company Act of 1940, which mandates rules for organization, operation, and disclosure. During the postwar period, open-end mutual funds have proven to be exceedingly popular with investors. The number of open-end funds has grown from 68 in 1940 with assets of only $448 million to 1,246 funds in 1984 with assets totalling $371 billion.

A number of academic studies have attempted to measure the performance of mutual funds relative to various measures of the performance of the overall market. Most have concluded that the great majority of mutual funds do not consistently outperform the overall market. Nevertheless, mutual funds still offer small investors the substantial advantages of portfolio diversification and ease of investment that are very difficult for the typical small investor to obtain elsewhere.

See also: INVESTMENT COMPANY
REAL ESTATE INVESTMENT TRUST.

References:

Radcliffe, Robert C., *Investment Concepts, Analysis, and Strategy* (Glenview, IL: Scott, Foresman & Company, 1987), Ch. 17.

Wiesenberger Investment Companies Service, Inc., *Investment Companies* (Boston, MA: Warren, Gorham & Lamont, 1986).

Nn

NATIONAL LABOR RELATIONS ACT

An important step in the history of the labor movement in the United States came in 1935 with the passage of the National Labor Relations Act, known also as the Wagner Act. This legislation permitted the formation of labor unions that could represent workers in collective bargaining activities. One aspect of this act was the establishment of the National Labor Relations Board (NLRB) to oversee the establishment of unions and their activities.

NATURAL MONOPOLY

Under certain circumstances it may be efficient for there to be only one supplier of a product. Such circumstances exist when the minimum efficient scale of production is very large. Because the technical nature of such a production process suggests that it is natural for the firm to be a sole supplier, the term natural monopoly is used.

In most local areas there is only one electric power company providing electricity to residential and commercial users. It is not cost efficient for there to be more than one owing to the fact that the minimum level of output needed to achieve economies of scale is so large. In the case of electric power, there is also a public service commission to regulate the price of the electricity.

See also: ECONOMIES OF SCALE
              MINIMUM EFFICIENT SCALE

NATURAL RESOURCES

Natural resources are those resources that are exhausted as the physical units representing these resources are removed, processed, and sold. Natural resources include oil and gas reserves, timber, coal, sulphur, iron, copper and silver ore. Natural resources are also considered long-term inventories acquired for resale or use in production over a period of years.

Natural resources are initially recorded in the accounts at their acquisition cost. The periodic allocation of the cost of a natural resource to the income statement is called depletion. Depletion reflects the physical exhaustion of a natural resource. Depreciation reflects the exhaustion of the service potential of a tangible fixed asset, such as property, plant, and equipment.

The cost of a natural resource minus any residual value is systematically depleted as the natural resource is transformed into inventory. The depletion charge is usually computed by the unit-of-production method as follows:

Step 1   Compute the depletion charge per unit:

$$\frac{\text{Cost} - \text{Salvage value of the natural resource}}{\text{Estimated number of units in the natural resource}}$$

Step 2   Compute the depletion charge for the period:

Unit depletion charge × Number of units converted during the period

The Internal Revenue Code authorizes the use of percentage depletion for income tax purposes. According to the Code, a percentage of gross income from the property is charged against operations when arriving at taxable income. Percentage depletion is a function of gross income rather than of production. Percentage depletion is allowable even after the cost of the asset has been fully recovered.

See also: ALLOCATION

              AMORTIZATION

              DEPRECIATION

              SUCCESSFUL-EFFORT ACCOUNTING

Reference:

Touche Ross & Co., *Oil and Gas Accounting: What Producers Must Know* (Touche Ross & Co., N.Y., 1980).

NEGATIVE INCOME TAX

A negative income tax is an alternative to our present welfare system. Under a negative income tax scheme, a family would receive a guaranteed income subsidy. As gross earnings of the family increase from $0, the negative income tax payments would decrease, but at a rate less than 100 percent. Therefore, recipients have a financial incentive to earn additional income.

NEGOTIABLE INSTRUMENTS

Negotiable instruments are written orders or promises to pay money that may be transferred from one person to another by delivery, or by endorsement and delivery, the full legal title thereby becoming vested in the transferee. The negotiation of such an instrument to a *holder in due course* gives such holder the same rights as held by the original payee (promisee), free from defenses (except real defenses) which might defeat them. Article 3 of the Uniform Commercial Code, entitled "Commercial Paper," is concerned with notes drafts, checks, and certificates of deposit. Most such instruments are negotiable in form. Other types of negotiable property interests which are not commercial paper (e.g., stock and bond certificates, order or bearer bills of lading and warehouse receipts) are covered in other sections of the Code, primarily Article 7.

    Laws relating to commercial paper developed among traders and merchants in Europe through customs and practices considered to be appropriate for the fair and efficient conduct of business. The body of common law provided a legal basis for the form and structure of commercial paper. At a later time, the rules of law relating to commercial paper were codified by legislation. The Uniform Negotiable Instruments Law was the first of the uniform business statutes drafted under the guidance of the Commissioners on Uniform State Laws. The Uniform Negotiable Instruments Law has been adopted by all the states and is the basic pattern for Article 3 of the Uniform Commercial Code.

A negotiable instrument is commercial paper (promissory notes, checks, drafts or bills of exchange, and certificates of deposit). A promissory note is an unconditional promise in writing made by one person to another, signed by the maker, engaging to pay on demand or at a fixed or determinable future time a sum certain in money to order or to bearer. A bill of exchange is an unconditional order in writing addressed by one person to another, signed by the person giving it, requiring the person to whom it is addressed to pay on demand or at a fixed or determinable future time, a sum certain in money to order or to bearer. A check is a bill of exchange drawn on a bank payable on demand. A certificate of deposit is an acknowledgment by a bank of a receipt of money with an engagement to repay it.

A negotiable instrument must meet the following four requirements:

1. It must be in writing and signed by the maker or drawee.

2. It must contain an unconditional promise or order to pay a certain sum in money and no other promise, order, obligation, or power except such as is authorized by Article 3 of the Uniform Commercial Code.

3. It must be payable on demand, or at a definite time.

4. It must be payable either to order or to bearer.

There is no express requirement concerning the materials with which or on which a negotiable instrument must be written. "Signed" includes any symbol executed or adopted by a party with present intention to authenticate a writing. A conditional promise or order (unnegotiable) is evident (1) if it states that it is subject to or governed by any other agreement or (2) if it states that it is to be paid only out of a particular fund or source (with some exceptions). For a sum to be certain, the amount must be capable of being calculated from data on the face of the note. To be payable in money requires that it be paid in the medium of exchange adopted by the government as its currency.

A promise is an undertaking to pay and must be more than an acknowledgment of an obligation. An order is a direction to pay and must be more than an authorization or request. Instruments payable on demand include those payable at sight or on presentation and those in which no time for payment is stated. Order paper is negotiated by the transferor's indorsing the paper and delivering it to the new holder. It is possible to negotiate bearer paper by delivery without an indorsement; however, a transferee will usually ask for an indorsement so as to obtain the advantage of the broader contract liability.

A holder in due course is a holder who has taken the instrument under the following conditions:

1.   That it is complete and regular upon its face.

2.   That he became the holder of it before it was overdue, and without notice that it has been previously dishonored, if such was the fact.

3.   That he took it in good faith and for value.

4.   That at the time it was negotiated to him, he had no notice of an infirmity in the instrument or defect in the title of the person negotiating it.

It is generally held that a holder in due course holds the instrument free from any defect of title of prior parties, and free from defenses available to prior parities among themselves, and may enforce payment of the instrument for the full amount thereof against all parties liable thereon. The holder of a note is presumed to be the owner thereof, and he may sue thereon in his own name.

Various forms of endorsement include the following:

1.   Special endorsements   Pay to the order of John Doe
                                    Signed: Bill Doe

2.   Blank endorsement   Signed: Bill Doe

3.   Restrictive endorsement   Pay to John Doe only
                                    Signed: Bill Doe

4. Qualified endorsement	Pay without recourse to order of John Doe Signed: Bill Doe
5. Conditional endorsement	On the election of the mayor in Greensboro, NC, Pay to the order of John Doe Signed: Bill Doe

An unqualified endorser, who receives consideration, warrants to the transferee and to any subsequent holder who receives the instrument in good faith:

1. That he has good title to the instrument, or represents a person with title, and that his transfer is otherwise rightful.

2. That all signatures are genuine or authorized.

3. That the instrument has not been materially altered.

4. That no defense of any prior party is good against him.

5. That he has no knowledge of any insolvency proceeding involving the payor.

A transferor without endorsement, who receives consideration, warrants to his transferee only who receives the instrument in good faith the same warranties.

Unless the instrument specifies otherwise, two or more persons (multiple signers) who sign as maker, acceptor, drawer, or endorser and as a part of the same transactions are jointly and severally liable. An accommodation party is one who signs the instrument in any capacity for the purpose of lending his name to another party to it. When the instrument has been taken for value before it is due, the accommodation party is liable in the capacity in which he has signed.

An unqualified endorser is released from liability on his endorser's promise if the holder failed to make due presentment to the payor or to give the endorser prompt notice of the payor's dishonor. The liability of a person on commercial paper may be discharged by (1) cancellation or renunciation and (2) discharge of secondary liability by changing primary contract.

An instrument is dishonored when a necessary or optional presentment is duly made and due acceptance or payment is refused or cannot be obtained within the prescribed time.

The Uniform Negotiable Instrument Act states "that where a signature is forged or made without authority of the person whose signature it purports to be, it is totally inoperative, and no right to retain the instrument, or to give a discharge, or to enforce payment thereof against any party thereto, can be acquired through or under such signature, unless the party, against whom it is sought to enforce such right, is precluded from setting up the forgery or want of authority."

The Act also states "that an instrument is not invalid for the reason only that it is ante-dated or past-dated, provided this is not done for an illegal or fraudulent purpose. The person to whom an instrument so dated is delivered, acquired title thereto as of the date of delivery."

The Act states that "where a negotiable instrument is materially altered without the assent of all parties liable thereon, it is voided, except as against a party who has himself made, authorized or assented to the alteration and subsequent endorser. But when an instrument has been materially altered and is in the hands of a holder in due course, not a party to the alteration, he may enforce payment thereon according to its original tenor." However, any person who by his negligence substantially contributes to a material alteration of the instrument or to the making of an authorized signature is precluded from asserting the alteration or lack of authority against a holder in due course or against a drawee or other payor who pays the instrument in good faith and in accordance with the reasonable commercial standards of the drawee's or payor's business.

Banks have a debtor-creditor relationship with depositors. Even though a depositor has funds in the bank, a payee cannot force a drawee bank to make payments. The drawer could possibly have an action against a bank-drawee for wrongfully dishonoring a check. Generally, banks are not obligated to pay on a check presented more than 6 months after date but can pay in good faith and charge customer's account. Banks are liable to a drawer for payment on bad checks unless the drawer was negligent. Drawer is required to promptly examine returned checks for irregularities or be held liable for bank's losses resulting from insufficient care and vigilance. A bank is considered to know the signature of endorsers and can collect from the party that cashed the check. Generally, oral stop payment orders are good for 14 days; written stop payment orders are good for six months and are renewable. A bank is entitled to a depositor's endorsement on deposited checks. If the endorsement is missing, the bank can supply it.

Contradictions sometimes appear in negotiable instruments. Generally the following rules apply: words control over figures; handwritten terms control over typewritten and printed terms; typewritten terms control over printed terms; an instrument stating "I promise to pay" and signed by two persons results in joint and several liability for both parties.

See also: COMMERCIAL PAPER.

NEGOTIATING PROCESS

Negotiating is a basic form of decision making. Many different and conflicting theories of negotiating exist. Most theories contain one or more of the strategies of organizational influence identified by David Kipnis and Stuart M. Schmidt:

Strategy	Behavior
Reason	The use of facts and data to support the development of a logical argument. *Sample tactic:* "I explained the reasons for my request."
Coalition	The mobilization of other people in the organization. *Sample tactic:* "I obtained the support of co-workers to back up my request."
Ingratiation	The use of impression management, flattery, and the creation of goodwill. *Sample tactic:* "I acted very humbly while making my request."
Bargaining	The use of negotiation through the exchange of benefits or favors. *Sample tactic:* "I offered an exchange (if you do this for me, I will do something for you)."

Assertiveness	The use of a direct and forceful approach. *Sample tactic:* " I demanded that he or she do what I requested."
Higher authority	Support of higher levels in the organization to back-up requests. *Sample tactic:* "I obtained the informal support of higher-ups."
Sanctions	The use of organizationally-derived rewards and punishments. *Sample tactic:* "I threatened to give him or her an unsatisfactory performance evaluation."

Success in negotiating involves many factors, including the following:

1. Negotiate strategically: focus on corporate goals and objectives, and culture; external environment; ethical position.
2. Develop personal characteristics and skills: trust, coping, confrontation, assertiveness, stress-handling capacity, leadership, interacting and interpersonal skills, exercise of power and authority, persuasive skills, logical reasoning, networking, and others.

Research into traits of successful negotiators suggest that the following traits are important:

1. the ability to plan and prepare for negotiations,
2. the ability to reason clearly under stressful conditions,
3. the ability to listen carefully and express oneself clearly and persuasively,
4. high self-esteem and personal integrity, and
5. high level of aspiration and expectation, high level of negotiating skills, and high level of perceived power.

See also: COMMUNICATION FUNCTION
CONTROL FUNCTION
LEADERSHIP FUNCTION
MANAGEMENT

References:

Bazerman, Max H., and Roy J. Lewicki, *Negotiating in Organizations* (Sage Publications, Beverly Hills, Calif., 1983).

Steers, Richard M., and Lyman W. Porter, *Motivation and Work Behavior* (McGraw-Hill, New York, 1983).

NET ASSETS

Net assets of an enterprise are the excess of total assets over total liabilities as reported on the balance sheet. Net assets also equal owners' equity. Equity is defined as the residual interest in the assets of an entity that remains after deducting its liabilities. In a business enterprise, the equity is the ownership interest. The relationship between net assets and ownership interest can be illustrated as follows:

$$\text{Assets} - \text{Liabilities} = \text{Net assets}$$
$$\text{Assets} - \text{Liabilities} = \text{Equity (or ownership interest)}$$

Therefore,
$$\text{Net assets} = \text{Equity (or ownership interest)}$$

See also: ACCOUNTING EQUATION
CAPITAL

NETWORK ANALYSIS

Various methods have been devised to plan and control a project having multiple steps or stages which are interdependent and sequential. Program Evaluation and Review Technique (PERT) is one such method. PERT was developed by the U.S. Navy Special Projects Office and was used to plan, schedule, and control the development of the Polaris submarine and other projects.

To employ PERT, it is necessary:

1. to list all the tasks (steps, activities) required by a project,
2. to arrange tasks in sequence, and
3. to estimate the time to perform each task.

For each task, an estimate of the time required to complete the task should be made:

1. an optimistic estimate: the shortest possible time required to complete the task,
2. a pessimistic estimate: the longest possible time required to complete the task, and
3. an estimate of what is considered most likely.

To illustrate PERT applications, assume that a warehouse is to be constructed according to the schedule shown in Exhibit N-1. A graph can be used to facilitate the analysis. In preparing PERT networks, each task can be shown as an arrow. The expected time to complete each task is placed on the PERT network as shown in Exhibit N-2. The completion of a task (called an event) can be shown as a circle.

Exhibit N-1
Construction Schedule for a Warehouse (in months)

	Activity	Expected time	Minimum time	Maximum time	Preceding activities
A	Start planning	0	—	—	—
B	Blueprints completed	3	2	3	A
C	Site preparation	5	4	6	B
D	Foundation laid	8	7	10	C
E	First floor completed	9	10	12	D
F	Storage area completed	8	10	12	E
G	Inspection completed	1	1	2	A, B, C, D, E, F

Exhibit N-2

A PERT Network for the Construction of a Warehouse

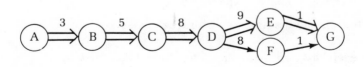

Critical path: 26 months shown by the double arrows

The next step is to identify the *critical path*, i.e., the longest set of adjoining tasks through the network. In the illustration, the critical path is A, B, C, D, E, G, which takes 26 months. The critical path is shown as double arrows. Any delay in this critical path delays the entire project. Delays along other paths are not as important, The amount of time by which an activity can be delayed without becoming a part of the critical path is called "slack." There is no slack along the critical path.

PERT can be modified to take into consideration any uncertainty in the time it takes for jobs in the project to be completed. PERT analysis can also be developed to include cost data. The estimated cost of a project is determined by summing the cost of each task. In certain cases, it may be possible to expedite the completion of a project (to earn a bonus or to meet a deadline) by reducing time required for a task along the critical path. The extra cost incurred in expediting the project can be compared to the original cost established to determine the cost of buying time in the critical path.

Once a PERT plan has been started, efforts should be made to maintain the time and cost schedules established for the project. Corrective action should be taken when needed to keep on schedule.

Critical path analysis has many advantages:

1. All activities are identified and planned.

2. Planning, performance, and control activities are coordinated (e.g., objective completion dates are established; potential bottlenecks are identified).

3. Scheduling is facilitated (e.g., the earliest and latest completion dates for network events can be specified).

4. Responsibilities and goals are established.

5. Project costs can be controlled and often reduced.

See also: PLANNING FUNCTION
CONTROL FUNCTION
DECISION MAKING

NONMONETARY EXCHANGES

A nonmonetary exchange is a reciprocal transfer between an enterprise and another entity in which the enterprise acquires nonmonetary assets by surrendering nonmonetary assets. Nonmonetary exchanges can also include services and liabilities. Monetary assets are fixed in terms of dollars and are usually contractual claims to a fixed amount of money. All other assets are nonmonetary. Nonmonetary assets include inventory, property, plant and equipment. The cost of a nonmonetary asset acquired in a nonmonetary exchange is the fair value of the asset surrendered to obtain it, and a gain or loss should be recognized on the exchange. The gain or loss is computed by comparing the fair value of the asset surrendered to its book value. If a small amount of monetary consideration (referred to as boot) is given or received, the cost of the asset acquired can be computed as follows:

Cost = Fair value of asset surrendered + Boot given or − Boot received

When the nonmonetary exchange involves similar productive assets, the general rule stated above for recognizing gains and losses is modified. Similar productive assets are ones that are of the same general type, that perform the same function, or that are employed in the same line of business, such as a delivery truck for another delivery truck. When similar productive assets are exchanged, the exchange is not essentially the culmination of the earning process—the earnings expected from the original asset have not been completely realized but will be continued by the acquired asset. When similar productive assets are exchanged, the assets acquired are recorded at the book value of the asset surrendered, unless boot is involved in the exchange. The payor of the boot recognizes no gain on the exchange (losses are always recognized). The recipient of the boot recognizes gain on the exchange to the extent that the boot exceeds a proportionate share of the book value of the asset surrendered (losses are always recognized). Because boot has been received, the earning process is considered to have been completed to that extent and some gain can be recognized. When boot is received or paid, the book value of the similar productive asset acquired can be computed as follows:

Payor of boot:
    Cost = Lower of book or fair value of asset surrendered – Boot paid

Recipient of the boot:
          Lower of book or fair value of asset surrendered –
          Boot received + Gain recognized

See also: COST PRINCIPLE
              PROPERTY, PLANT, AND EQUIPMENT

NORMATIVE ECONOMICS

Normative economics refers to the use of personal preferences and value judgments to argue for what ought to be.

See also: POSITIVE ECONOMICS

NOTES RECEIVABLE

A negotiable promissory note is an unconditional promise in writing made by one person to another engaging to pay on demand or at a fixed or determinable future time a sum of money to order or to bearer. Negotiability of the note makes the instrument readily transferable and increases its usefulness since the seller can discount it or use it as collateral for a loan. The person promising to pay is the maker of the note; the person to be paid is the payee. Promissory notes may be either interest- or noninterest-bearing.

If a note is not paid at maturity, it is said to have been dishonored. If the payee of a note sells it prior to maturity, the transaction is referred to as discounting a note. The note can be discounted either "with recourse" or "without recourse." When a note is discounted "with recourse," the payee is contingently liable for the payment of the note if it is dishonored at maturity by the payee. To illustrate the discounting of a note receivable, assume that a $1,000, 90-day, 4 percent note dated September 3 is discounted at a bank on October 3 (60 days from maturity). The bank discount rate is 8 percent. The cash proceeds from the discounting is computed as follows:

1. Compute the maturity value of the note:

$1,000 × 0.04 × 90/360 = $10 interest plus $1,000 face value = $1,010

2. Calculate the discount charged by the note buyer on the maturity value of the note for the number of days from the date of discount to the date of maturity:

$$\$1,010 \times 0.08 \times 60/360 = \$13.47$$

3. Calculate the proceeds that the company receives from the discounted note:

$$\$1,010 - \$13.47 = \$996.53$$

If a "with recourse" discounted note is dishonored by the maker at maturity, the endorser is required to make good on the note, pay any interest due at maturity, and pay a protest (collection) fee.

See also: NEGOTIABLE INSTRUMENTS
              RECEIVABLES

NOTES TO FINANCIAL STATEMENTS

Notes or footnotes to financial statements are procedures used to present additional information not included in the accounts on the financial statements. Generally accepted accounting principles consider notes to be an integral part of financial statements. Accounting principles require that certain information be disclosed in notes, such as narrative discussion, additional monetary disclosures, and supplementary schedules. One of the notes typically describes the major accounting policies used in preparing the financial statements (for example, inventory cost-flow assumptions, depreciation method). The notes to financial statements are usually factual rather than interpretative.

See also: ACCOUNTING POLICIES AND PROCEDURES
                  FINANCIAL STATEMENTS
                  FINANCIAL STATEMENT ANALYSIS

Oo

OBJECTIVES OF FINANCIAL REPORTING BY BUSINESS ENTERPRISES

SFAC Concepts Statement No. 1, Objectives of Financial Reporting by Business Enterprises, describes the broad purpose of financial reporting, including financial statements. The objectives in Statement No. 1 apply to general purpose external financial reporting and are directed toward the common interests of many users. The objectives arise primarily from the needs of external users who lack the authority to obtain the information they want and must rely on information management communicates to them. According to Statement No. 1, financial reporting should provide:

Information that is useful to present and potential investors and creditors and other users in making rational investment, credit, and similar decisions.

Information to help investors, creditors, and others assess the amounts, timing, and uncertainty of prospective net cash inflows to the related enterprise because their prospects for receiving cash from investments, from loans to, or from other participation in the enterprise depend significantly on its cash flow prospects.

461

Information about the economic resources of an enterprise, the claims to those resources (obligations of the enterprise to transfer resources to other entities and owners' equity), and the effects of transactions, events, and circumstances that change resources and claims to those resources.

Concepts Statement No. 1 also gives specific guidance about the kinds of information the financial reporting should provide:

Information about an enterprise's economic resources, obligations, and owners' equity.

Information about an enterprise's performance provided by measures of earnings and comprehensive income and their components measured by accrual accounting.

Information about how an enterprise obtains and spends cash, about its borrowing and repayment of borrowing, about its capital (equity) transactions, including cash dividends and other distributions of enterprise resources to owners, and about other factors that may affect an enterprise's liquidity or solvency.

Information about how management of an enterprise has discharged its stewardship responsibility to owners (stockholders) for the use of enterprise resources entrusted to it.

Statement No. 1 emphasizes that earnings information is the primary focus of financial reporting. According to this statement, earnings should be measured with accrual accounting. This requires that the financial effects of economic transactions, events, and circumstances should be reported in the period when they occur instead of when cash is received or paid.

The statement indicates that management is responsible for the custody and use of the entity's resources and that financial reporting should provide information concerning that stewardship function. Financial reporting also requires that reports should include management's explanations and interpretations that would be of benefit to external users in addition to quantitative information.

See also: FINANCIAL ACCOUNTING
                FINANCIAL ACCOUNTING STANDARDS BOARD
                FINANCIAL REPORTING

Reference:

SFAC No. 1, *Objectives of Financial Reporting by Business Enterprises*
   (FASB, 1978).

OBJECTIVITY

Objectivity or verifiability is the ability to perform an accounting function
without bias. The measurement that results from an objective application
of accounting principles and methods should be capable of duplication by
another person. In auditing, objectivity refers to an auditor's ability to be
impartial in the performance of an audit. Where there is considerable uncertainty in the measurement process, the measurement method that is
most objective (least subjective) should usually be followed. For example,
the cost of a building arrived at in an arm's-length transaction is usually
more objective than an appraisal value by a real estate appraiser.

See also: ACCOUNTING ASSUMPTIONS
                ARM'S-LENGTH TRANSACTION

OFF-BALANCE SHEET ITEMS

Off-balance sheet items generally refer to the application of procedures
that provide financing without adding debt on a balance sheet, thus not
affecting financial ratios or borrowing capacity of an enterprise. Accounting for leases by a lessee sometimes enables the lessee to disguise what is
in fact a long-term borrowing to finance the purchase of a leased asset as
an operating lease, thereby avoiding having to report a long-term liability
on the financial statements.

Many companies prefer to keep liabilities off their balance sheets.
Some of the advantages claimed to companies from off-balance-sheet
financing include the following:

1. Improvement in the company's debt-to-equity ratio for borrowing purposes and to improve the market value of the company's stock.

2. Borrowing capacity enhanced, especially if there are contractual limits or restrictions related to balance sheet items.

3. Borrowing costs reduced from an improved balance sheet resulting from the off-balance-sheet financing.

4. Management compensation plans improved if they are related to ratios or earnings that are favorably affected by off-balance-sheet financing.

5. Risk sharing and tax management opportunities can be created through the use of limited partnership arrangements and in-substance debt defeasance.

See also: DEFEASANCE
FULL DISCLOSURE
LIABILITIES
PRODUCT FINANCING ARRANGEMENTS

OPERATING CYCLE

The operating cycle of a business is the time between the acquisition of inventory and the conversion of the inventory back into cash. The operating cycle of a business is also referred to as the cash cycle and the earnings cycle. For some industries, such as a distillery, the operating cycle may extend 10 years or longer. For a grocer, the operating cycle would be measured in days. The normal operating cycle of a business is crucial to what determines whether assets and liabilities are current or noncurrent. For example, current assets include cash and other assets that are expected to be turned into cash, sold, or exchanged within the normal operating cycle of the enterprise or one year, whichever is longer. Current liabilities are liabilities that come due within the normal operating cycle or one year, whichever is longer. Exhibit O-1 illustrates the normal operating cycle of a business.

Exhibit O-1
Normal Operating Cycle of a Business

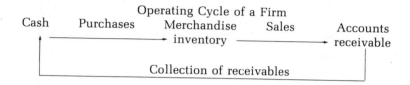

OPINION

See Audit

OPPORTUNITY COST ANALYSIS

Opportunity cost refers to the profit, or contribution, that is lost or foregone by using limited resources for a particular purpose. Opportunity costs arise from diverting an input factor from one use to another. Such costs do not require cash receipts or disbursements. Opportunity costs do not appear in the accounting records because they do not reflect a completed transaction.

Opportunity cost analysis is especially useful when evaluating alternatives. For example, there is an opportunity cost involved in using a machine to manufacture one product instead of another. To illustrate opportunity cost analysis, assume that a company can purchase some parts that it needs for production purposes for $10,000 from a supplier. It can make the parts for $8,000. However, if it makes the parts, it must use plant space that could be rented for $3,000. Opportunity cost analysis proceeds as follows:

	Make	Buy
Cost of obtaining parts	$8000	$10,000
Opportunity cost: rental income lost	3,000	_____
Total	$11,000	$10,000

The company should purchase the parts from the outside supplier at a lower cost than it can make the parts when opportunity costs are considered.

See also: BREAK-EVEN ANALYSIS
GROSS MARGIN ANALYSIS
INCREMENTAL COST ANALYSIS

Reference:

Benston, George J., ed., *Contemporary Cost Accounting and Control* (Dickenson, Encino, Calif., 1977).

OPTIMIZATION

Economic decision making emphasizes the efficient allocation of resources to maximize or minimize an objective, such as maximizing profits or minimizing costs. The mathematical solution to such problems is optimization.

OPTIONS

An option is a marketable security that provides for the future exchange of cash and common shares contingent upon the option owner's choice. An option is created when a seller writes (sells) an option contract to a buyer. A nonreimbursable fee is paid to the individual who sells the right. Option sellers may be corporations or individual traders.

Calls and puts are legal contracts that give the holder the right to buy or sell a specified amount of the underlying interest at a fixed or determinable price (called the exercise or strike price) upon exercise of the options within a specified period of time. A call option conveys the right (but not the obligation) to buy a specified quantity of the underlying interest. A put option conveys the right (but not the obligation) to sell a specified quantity of the underlying interest. For example, the underlying interest might be 100 shares of common stock or a specified amount of a debt obligation or a foreign currency. Buying call (put) options offers the opportunity to make money when a stock's price rises (falls). Options provide significant leverage to trading, (a one-point change in a $5 option is a 20 percent swing). Leverage refers to the ability to gain from the increasing value of a common stock with an investment that is only a percentage of what it would cost you to own the stock.

Each stock option generally covers 100 shares of the underlying stock. The number may be adjusted because of stock splits, stock dividends, and other events. The exercise price of a stock option is stated in dollars per share. No shares are issued by the Options Clearing Corporation (OCC) when an option transaction occurs. Investors rely on confirmations and statements received from brokers which confirm their positions as holders (option buyers) or writers of options.

The exercise (or strike) price is the price at which the buyer of the option has the right to purchase (sell) the underlying interest. Exercise prices are established by the markets on which options are traded at the time trading in an option series begins. Exercise prices are usually set at levels above and below the market price of the underlying interest. The expiration date is the date on which the option expires. If an option has not been exercised prior to expiration, the option ceases to exist. The current expiration date for options, except foreign currency options, is the Saturday immediately following the third Friday of the month in which the options expire. Options may expire in different months and on different cycles (monthly, quarterly, or a combination thereof).

A premium is the price that the buyer of an option pays and the writer of an option receives for the rights conveyed by the option. Premiums change in reaction to the relationship between the exercise price and the current market value of the underlying interest, the volatility of the underlying interest, the amount of time remaining until expiration, current interest rates, the prevailing attitude of the investment community, supply and demand, and other factors related to the underlying interest. A put premium reflects a bearish attitude; a call reflects a bullish attitude. Premiums are expressed in different units, such as in dollars or in basis points, for different types of options.

The intrinsic value of an option reflects the amount by which an option is in-the-money (the amount of the intrinsic value). At a time when the current market price of ABC stock is $56 a share, an ABC $50 call would have intrinsic value of $6 a share. If the price of the stock drops below $50, the call has no intrinsic value. Time value refers to whatever value the option has in addition to its intrinsic value. For example, when the market price of the ABC stock is $50 a share, an ABC $50 call may command a premium of $4 a share. The $4 is time value and reflects the expectation of an investor that, prior to expiration, the price of ABC stock will increase by an amount which would enable him/her to sell or exercise the option at a profit. An option may have both intrinsic value and time value (its premium may exceed its intrinsic value). For example, with the market price of the ABC stock at $55, an ABC $50 call may command a premium of $6 a share—an intrinsic value of $5 a share and a time value of $1 a share.

A "spread" occurs in a situation where the investor is both the buyer and writer of the same type of option (puts or calls) on the same underlying interest, with the options having the same exercise price and expiration date. Purchasers are betting on considerable stock-price variability to earn a profit; sellers are counting on small stock-price variability. For the purchaser to break even, the stock's price must increase or decrease by an amount equal to the premium on both a put and a call. A strip is two puts and one call on the same security with identical expiration dates and striking price. The purchaser of a strip believes the probability of a price decline is larger than the probability of a price increase. A seller of a strip believes that the opposite will occur. A strap is two calls and one put. Purchasers believe the probability of a stock price increase exceeds those of a price decline. The seller believes the opposite will occur.

Common stock index options are options on an index of many stocks. For example, the S&P 100 index was constructed by the Chicago Board Options Exchange to resemble the S&P 500 stock index. The exercise of a stock index does not result in a settlement of both cash and securities. The settlement is in cash. Stock indexes can be used to hedge or leverage market risk.

See also: INVESTING

References:

Major brokerage firms have publications explaining options and options trading.

ORGANIZATIONAL BEHAVIOR

Planning, control, budgeting, and pricing activities of management are influenced by and have influence on the behavior of people who work in the organization. There are many aspects to organization behavior. Major areas in organizational behavior have been identified:

1. *Organizational theory and decision making*—This area deals with such matters as organizational structure (centralized/decentralized; functions of organizations; line and staff structures).

2. *Motivation and perception*—Human needs, levels of needs, and relationships.

3. *Communications*—Formal and informal communication structures and networks.

4. *Behavioral science*—Behavioral impacts of management and managerial activities.

5. *Ethical issues*—Competence, independence, integrity, and fairness (equity).

Behavior in organizations is conditioned by many factors including organizational structure, management styles, control systems, and others.

See also: BUDGET
COMMUNICATION FUNCTION
CONTROL FUNCTION
CONTROLLER
DELEGATION
DIRECTING

ETHICS
GOALS and OBJECTIVES
MANAGEMENT
MANAGEMENT THEORIES
MOTIVATION
ORGANIZING FUNCTION
PERFORMANCE EVALUATION
PLANNING FUNCTION
PRICING POLICY
RESPONSIBILITY ACCOUNTING

References:

Dressler, Gary, *Organization Theory* (Prentice-Hall, Englewood Cliffs, N.J., 1986).

Steers, Richard M., *Introduction to Organizational Behavior* (Scott, Foresman, Glenview, Ill., 1984).

ORGANIZATION COSTS

Organization costs are costs related to getting an enterprise started. Organization costs are incurred during the formation of the enterprise and prior to income-producing operations. Expenditures usually classified as organization costs include such items as promoters', attorneys', and accountants' fees, underwriters' commissions, securities registration and listing fees, printing costs, etc. Such costs are ordinarily capitalized as an intangible asset or deferred charge, and amortized (written off) over a period of time not to exceed 40 years. Expenditures relating to the organization of the enterprise are assumed to benefit the future and are considered assets in that without them the company could not have been started. In practice, some accountants treat organization costs as a reduction of contributed capital. This treatment is justified on the grounds that organization charges reflect a reduction of the receipts associated with the financing of the corporation.

See also: CORPORATION
INTANGIBLE ASSETS

ORGANIZING FUNCTION

Organizing is a major function of management. The primary purpose of organization is to provide for the efficient and effective accomplishment of the goals and objectives of the enterprise. The goals and objectives established for an organization which are developed through the planning process serve as the basis of the organizing function.

Organizing an organization requires that managers establish patterns of relationships (structures, hierarchies) among people and other resources that work to produce an output or accomplish a common objective. Organizing is related to how work flows through the organization under guidance. It involves assigning responsibilities through the division of labor and the coordination of the parts into a cohesive whole. The coordination of effort requires the development of effective communications throughout the enterprise. Finally, organization requires the establishment of an authority structure that defines decision-making powers.

Organization theory has identified certain principles that can be used effectively in designing an organization structure:

1. *Specialization*—The tasks assigned to individuals should be limited.

2. *Objectivity*—Activities and functions that are directed towards achieving an enterprise's goals and objectives are to be provided.

3. *Specification*—Authority and responsibilities should be clearly communicated, preferably in writing.

4. *Authority and responsibility*—Authority given should be commensurate (equal) to responsibilities assigned.

5. Unity of command—Subordinates should have only one superior. Exceptions must be appropriately justified.

The organizational chart can also be designed to show line and staff relationships. Line positions involve persons who are directly associated with operations and who are directly responsible for creating and distributing the goods or services of the organization. Line authority is reflected by the typical chain of command that begins with the board of directors and extends down through various levels in the enterprise. Production and sales departments are examples of line activities. Staff refers to persons or groups in an enterprise whose major function is to provide advice and service to the line positions. Personnel and internal auditing departments are staff activities. Exhibit O-2 below shows an organizational chart for a firm which has both line and staff positions. Observe that authority flows from top to bottom. No individual is subject to more than one person with respect to one task. These command relationships reduce or prevent confusion, inefficiencies, and frustration.

Exhibit O-2
Line and Staff Relationships

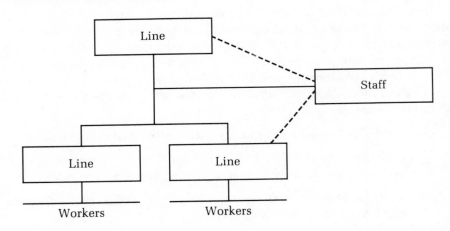

See also: CENTRALIZATION VERSUS DECENTRALIZATION
             CONTROL FUNCTION
             MANAGEMENT
             ORGANIZATIONAL BEHAVIOR
             PLANNING FUNCTION

References:

Dressler, Gary, *Organization Theory* (Prentice-Hall, Englewood Cliffs, N.J., 1986).

Pfeffer, Jeffery, *Organizations and Organization Theory* (Pittman, Belmont, Calif., 1982).

Pp

PARADOX OF THRIFT

More savings may not always be good for the economy. This is a paradox because economics teaches that more savings lead to more investment, which in turn leads to economic growth. However, if everyone increased their savings, consumption activity would decrease and thus national income would fall. As income falls, investment will also fall and this is not good for the economy.

PARETO'S LAW

Vilfredo Pareto in his *Manual of Political Economy* (1906) defined a Pareto optimum exchange as one in which at least one party in the exchange is better off and no one is worse off. This concept of optimality is used in economics to evaluate and compare various income redistribution and resource reallocation schemes.

PARTNERSHIP

A partnership is an association of two or more individuals as co-owners to carry on a business for profit. Written articles of co-partnership are or-

473

dinarily used to identify the rights and responsibilities of the partners, the nature and scope of the partnership, and relationships with outside parties. The partnership agreement usually includes descriptions of the following: asset valuation, admission of new partners, withdrawal of partners, division of profit and loss, liquidation of the business, and related matters.

Partnerships are treated as separate accounting entities from the partners. A partner's capital interest in a partnership is a claim against the net assets of the partnership as reflected in the partner's capital account. A partner's interest in profit and loss determines how the partner's capital interest changes as a result of subsequent operations. Profit-and-loss agreements usually are arranged to reward the partners for their contribution of resources or abilities to the partnership.

In a general partnership, all partners are jointly liable for the debts of the firm. Each partner is an agent of the partnership within the scope of the business and can legally bind the partnership. In most states, the Uniform Partnership Act provides the legal rights and duties of partners and partnerships. A limited partnership consists of at least one general partner and one or more limited partners. The general partner(s) manages the enterprise and has responsibilities as described in the partnership agreement. The limited partner(s) contributes capital to the firm. Their personal liability is generally limited to their investment. They share in the profits and losses but have no voice in directing operations.

Advantages associated with the partnership form of business organization include the ease of formation and dissolution, its ability to pool capital and personal talents and skills, its nontaxable status for income tax purposes, and the relative freedom and flexibility partners enjoy in business matters. Disadvantages associated with partnerships include its limited life, the ability of a partner to commit the partnership in contractual matters, the unlimited personal liability of partners, and the difficulties of raising large sums of capital and of transferring ownership interests as contrasted with the corporate form of business organization.

The admission of a new partner or the withdrawal or death of a partner dissolves the partnership but does not necessarily cause partnership operations to cease. A person may become a partner in an existing partnership by purchasing an interest from one or more of the existing partners and by investing cash or noncash assets in the partnership. A person can be admitted to a partnership only with the consent of all continuing partners in the new partnership enterprise.

A partnership is not assessed an income tax on earnings. Partnership income is allocated to the partners and is reported on the partners' tax returns. The tax bases for assets contributed by the partners to the partnership are the same tax bases that applied to the individual partner making the contribution. The tax basis of a partner's interest in capital of a partnership is the sum of the tax bases of the assets contributed by the partner, increased by the personal liabilities of other partners which the partner assumes, and decreased by the partner's personal liabilities assumed by other partners. The sum of the tax bases of the partnership assets equals the sum of the tax bases of the partners' separate interests in capital.

See also: CORPORATION
              JOINT VENTURE
              PROPRIETORSHIP
              TAX SHELTERS

PATENT

A patent is an exclusive right given to an individual or firm to use a particular process or to make or sell a specific product for a predetermined period of time—17 years in the United States. During that period of time, the patent holder has a monopoly over the patented product or process because the patent gives the inventor the right to prevent others from using his or her patented process or making or selling his or her patented product.

The rationale behind the patent system is based on the belief that innovations benefit society. Therefore, some incentive should be provided to individuals and firms for incurring the risks associated with innovative activity. This rationale is well founded. Innovations often lead to technological improvements, which, in turn, have the benefit of increasing the well-being of society through the development of new or improved products, and through changes in production processes that lower costs or increase efficiency. There is, however, a risk associated with innovative activity because many ideas may never develop into a commercial process or product. Furthermore, new products and processes can easily be stolen before the inventor receives enough final benefits to cover all of the related costs. A patent protects the innovator or innovating firm from some degree of these pressures and thereby helps to encourage the search for new knowledge.

New and useful production processes and products are patentable, but the discovery of basic knowledge is not. The variety of things patentable ranges from a new chemical compound used in producing a drug to a new circuit configuration for high-speed computers, to a new design for a child's toy. The initial cost to obtain a patent may be only a few hundred dollars; however, the cost to firms to retain legal counsel to enforce their patents can run into hundreds of thousands of dollars a year.

See also: CORPORATION
            PROPRIETORSHIP

PAYROLL TAXES

The Federal Social Security Act provides a variety of programs for qualified individuals and families including a federal old-age and survivors' benefits program with medical care for the aged and a joint federal-state unemployment insurance program. Benefits are based upon the average earnings of the worker during the period of employment in covered industries. Funds to support these programs come from payroll taxes imposed under the Federal Insurance Contribution Act (FICA) and the Federal Unemployment Tax Act. Social Security taxes are imposed on both employer, employees, and the self-employed. The tax is collected by the employer who deducts it from the employee's gross pay and remits it to the government along with the employer's share. Both parties are taxed at the same rate based on the employee's gross pay up to an annual maximum limit.

Employers are also subject to another payroll tax which supports a system of unemployment insurance. This tax is levied by the federal government in cooperation with state governments. The federal tax is the Federal Unemployment Tax Act (FUTA). A rate is applied against income earned by covered employees up to a specified amount. The employer is allowed a credit against the federal tax for unemployment taxes paid to the state. In some states, employers with favorable employment records are entitled to a reduction in taxes.

Employers are required to withhold from employees' pay an amount estimated for federal income taxes. Employers remit the withholdings to the federal government. The amount withheld depends primarily upon the employee's earnings and the number of exemptions which the employee is entitled to claim. Many states have income taxes and withholding procedures similar to those used by the federal government.

See also: LIABILITIES

PENSIONS

A pension is an allowance, annuity, or subsidy. A pension plan is an arrangement whereby an employer agrees to provide benefits to retired employees. A pension plan may be either contributory or noncontributory. In a contributory plan, both employer and employee contribute to the fund from which benefits are to be paid. In a noncontributory plan, only the employer makes contributions to the fund.

A single-employer plan is a pension plan established unilaterally by an employer. Multi-employer plans are sometimes established within an industry.

The funding aspect of pension plans are important features of any plan. Funding means to pay to a funding agency. Funding also refers to assets accumulated by a funding agency to provide retirement benefits when they come due. Pension costs that have been paid over to a funding agency are said to have been funded. A funding agency is an organization or individual, such as an insurance company or a trustee, who accumulates assets which will be used for the payments of benefits under the plan and who administers the program. Terminal funding occurs when the benefits payable to a retired employee are funded in full at the time the employee retires; there is no funding for active employees. Pay-as-you-go funding does not provide any prior funding for retirement benefits but provides resources for the pensions as they come due after retirement.

In an insured pension plan, annuities are purchased for employees under individual or group annuity contracts between an employer and an insurance company. The insurance company guarantees the payment of benefits. Noninsured plans are generally funded by a trust agreement between an employer and a trust company.

When pension benefits are no longer contingent on an employee's continued employment, the employee's benefits under the plan are said to be vested benefits. When benefits vest, an employee's pension rights cannot be reduced or taken away.

A defined benefit plan is a plan that states the benefits to be received by employees after retirement or the method of determining such benefits. A defined contribution plan is one in which the employer's contribution is determined based on a specified formula. Future benefits are limited to those that the plan can provide. A defined contribution plan specifies the amount of the periodic contributions to be paid by the plan's sponsor (and not the benefits to be received by a participant). Benefits are usually based on amount credited to an individual's account.

See also: ANNUITY
DEFINED BENEFIT PENSION PLANS
ERISA

References:

FASB, SFAS No. 87, *Employers' Accounting for Pension Plans* (FASB, 1985).

Employee Benefit Research Institute, *Fundamentals of Employee Benefit Programs* (Education and Research Fund, Washington, D.C., 1985).

PERFECT COMPETITION

Perfect competition is the process through which firms adjust to changes in the activities of other firms. The adjective "perfect" in the term perfect competition refers to a theoretical ideal degree of rivalry among firm. This theoretical case is studied in economics in order to establish a bench mark against which the competitive behavior of firms in the real world can be compared.

The assumptions that underlie the perfect competition case are: a large number of homogeneous firms each producing a homogeneous product in the industry and each having only a small portion of total industry output, free entry and exit from the industry, and perfect information on the part of consumers. One important result from the perfect competition case is that in equilibrium all firms will earn zero economic profit.

PERFORMANCE EVALUATION

Performance evaluation is based upon the application of guidelines against which the organization's efforts and accomplishments can be measured. Evaluation implies the existence of a bench mark against which actual performance can be compared. Evaluation can result in the identification of both successes and failures. Comparing actual performance with standard performance is commonly referred to as feedback. Feedback provides a basis for interpreting the results of the evaluation and reinforces the successes and eliminates the failures.

Performance evaluation of profit centers typically focuses upon either net income or contribution toward the firm's income. Performance evaluation usually reflects this relationship:

$$\text{Operation ratio} = \frac{\text{Income}}{\text{Sales}}$$

Performance evaluation of an investment center typically focuses on both the return on investment (ROI) and the residual income. ROI is conceptualized as follows:

$$\text{ROI} = \frac{\text{Income}}{\text{Investment (or Capital employed)}}$$

The residual income approach charges an investment center with an interest charge for the assets employed. The interest charge is usually the company's cost of capital. Performance is evaluated in terms of income earned in excess of the minimum desired rate of return:

$$\text{Residual income} = \text{Investment center income} - \text{Interest charge.}$$

GOALS AND OBJECTIVES
LEADERSHIP FUNCTION
MOTIVATION
ORGANIZATIONAL BEHAVIOR
RATIOS
RESPONSIBILITY ACCOUNTING
RETURN ON INVESTMENT
SEGMENT PERFORMANCE
STOCK COMPENSATION PLANS

Reference:

Daft, Richard L., *Organization Theory and Design* (West, St. Paul, Minn., 1983).

PERSONAL FINANCIAL STATEMENTS

The reporting entity of personal financial statements is either an individual, a husband and wife, or a group of related individuals. Personal financial statements should provide adequate disclosure of information relating to the financial affairs of an individual reporting entity.

For each reporting entity, a statement of financial position (or balance sheet) is now required to present estimated current values of assets and liabilities, a provision for estimated taxes, and net worth. A provision should also be made for estimated income taxes on the differences between the estimated current values of assets, the estimated current amount of liabilities and their respective tax bases. Comparative statements for one or more periods should be presented. A statement of changes in net worth is optional. Such a statement would disclose the major sources of increases and decreases in net worth. Increases in personal net worth arise from income, increases in estimated current value of assets, decreases in estimated current amount of liabilities, and decreases in the provision for estimated income taxes. Decreases in personal net worth arise from expenses, decreases in estimated current value of assets, increases in estimated current amount of liabilities, and increases in the provision for income taxes.

Personal financial statements should be presented on the accrual basis rather than on the cash basis. A classified balance sheet is not used. Assets and liabilities are presented in the order of their liquidity and maturity, respectively. A business interest that constitutes a large part of an individual's total assets should be shown separate from other assets. Such an interest would be presented as a net amount and not as a pro rata allocation of the business's assets and liabilities. An illustration of a personal financial statement is shown in Exhibit P-1.

See also: FINANCIAL STATEMENTS

References:

AICPA, *AICPA Auditing and Accounting Manual* (AICPA, 1982).

Bailard, Thomas E., et al., *Personal Money Management* (Science Research Associates, Inc., Chicago, 1986).

Exhibit P-1
Personal Financial Statements

John and Mary Doe
Statement of Financial Condition
December 31, 1990 and 1991

Assets	1991	1990
Cash	$ 5,000	$ 3,000
Investments		
Marketable securities (Note 1)	20,000	17,000
Clix, Inc., a closely held corporation	100,000	80,000
Residence	200,000	120,000
Personal effects	30,000	25,000
Total assets	$355,000	$245,000

Liabilities and Net Worth	1991	1990
Credit cards	$ 1,500	$ 1,000
Income taxes—current year balance	5,500	4,000
Demand note payable to bank, 16%	10,000	—
Mortgage payable, 10% (Note 2)	100,000	110,000
Total	117,000	115,000
Estimated income taxes on the differences between the estimated current values of assets, the current amounts of liabilities and their tax bases (Note 3)	10,000	5,000
Net worth	228,000	125,000
Total liabilities and net worth	$355,000	$245,000

PETRODOLLARS

Petrodollars is the term applied to Eurodollar deposits held by petroleum-exporting countries or their citizens. Petrodollars are distinguishable from other Eurodollars only by the identity of their owners.

See also: EURODOLLARS

PHILLIPS CURVE

In 1958 A.W. Phillips published an economics article in which he il-lustrated graphically the relationship between the rate of change in wages (vertical axis) and the rate of unemployment (horizontal axis) for the United Kingdom between 1861 and 1913. His data was plotted as an in-verse relationship—higher unemployment rates associated with lower rate of wage increase. Today, the term Phillips curve refers to any graphical relationship between the rate of inflation (vertical axis) in a country and its rate of unemployment. For most economies, a downward sloping relation-ship exists. Some economists contend that no single Phillips curve describes an economy, but rather there is a series of curves that fluctuates around a long run or natural rate of unemployment. This natural rate of unemployment is one to which the economy naturally returns through its own self-correcting mechanisms.

PLANNING FUNCTION

Planning is a major function of management. Planning is a process that establishes goals and objectives and that develops a decision model for selecting the means of attaining those goals and objectives.

The strategic planning model consists of four components:

1. Basic research and analysis of internal and external environments and identification of macro- and micro-level trends.

2. Identification and analysis of alternative goals and objectives.

3. Statement of goals and objectives.

4. Development of policy alternatives and resource utilization.

Planning requires that an organization make choices regarding:

1. its goals and objectives (what the organization wants to do and why), and

2. the means of attaining these ends (when, where, and how to do them).

A hierarchy of planning showing types of planning, levels, and scope is:

Type	Level	Scope
Goals and objectives of the organization	Top management	Broad, company wide and long-term
Policies, departmental	Middle management	Narrow, variable terms, tactical, flexible
Procedures and methods	Line and supervisory	Narrow, variable terms, detailed

See also: DECISION MAKING
GOALS AND OBJECTIVES
MANAGEMENT
ORGANIZATIONAL BEHAVIOR

References:

Fallon, William K., ed., *AMA Management Handbook* (AMACOM, New York, 1983).

Parson, M.J., *Back to Basics Planning* (Facts on File Publications, New York, 1985).

Reinharth, L., H. Shapiro, E. Kallman, *Planning: Strategic, Administrative, Operational* (Van Nostrand Reinhold, Florence, Kentucky, 1980).

POOLING OF INTERESTS

Accounting for a business combination can be accomplished by two methods: pooling of interest method and purchase method. APB Opinion

No. 16 established twelve conditions that must be met before the pooling-of-interest method can be used to account for a business combination.

The concept behind the pooling-of-interests method is that the holders of the common stock in the combining companies continue as holders of the common stock in the combined company. The business combination is accounted for by adding together the book value of the assets and equities of the combined enterprises. The combining corporation records the assets and liabilities received from the combined companies at book values recorded on the books of the combined companies. The equity of the acquired company is combined with the equity of the acquiring company. The allocation of the acquired company's equity among common stock, other contributed capital, and retained earnings may have to be restructured as a result of the differences in the par value of the stock issued and the par value of the stock acquired. The pooling-of-interests method can be contrasted with the purchase method of accounting for a business combination.

See also: CONSOLIDATED FINANCIAL STATEMENTS
PURCHASE ACCOUNTING

Reference:

Accounting Research Bulletin No. 48, *Business Combinations* (AICPA, Committee on Accounting Procedure, 1958).

PORTFOLIO INSURANCE

Portfolio insurance (PI) is a form of hedging that uses stock index futures contracts and index options to limit the downside risk of holding a diversified portfolio of common stocks. PI programs are offered by major banks, brokerage firms, insurance companies, and others. They have attracted many large institutional holders of common stocks like pension funds, mutual funds, and so on.

When the stock market turns down, holders of common stocks traditionally begin to move some portion of their assets out of stocks and into cash to protect themselves against further declines in the market. PI programs attempt to hedge against the possibility of a market decline by selling stock index futures contracts or stock index options (buying stock index put options). The more the market falls, the more futures and options contracts are sold by PI programs. If the market continues to fall, the rise in the value of the portfolio's futures and option positions cushions the decline in the value of the portfolio's common stocks. PI managers believe that such hedging programs using futures and options involve lower transaction costs and provide greater liquidity than the traditional method of actually selling stocks and buying treasury bills.

A recent article in the Federal Reserve Bank of Atlanta *Economic Review* compared the returns to a stock portfolio that matched the S&P 500 Index during 1974-86 with and without portfolio insurance. The article found that in a rising market the uninsured portfolio had a higher return than the insured portfolio; however, in a declining market, the insured portfolio had a higher return. In other words, a PI program reduces downside risk at the cost of upside return. Also, the article found that the cost of the PI program was very sensitive to the degree of downside protection that was desired; that is, the more downside risk that is eliminated, the more potential for upside gain that must be forfeited.

Portfolio insurance differs from true insurance in that it does not guarantee protection in the event of a market downturn. In the stock market crash of October 19, 1987, many PI programs had to be shut down because trading in financial futures and options was suspended. As a result, many portfolio managers were surprised to find that their PI programs provided little or no protection. Following the crash, many PI programs have been discontinued because the increased market volatility raised the cost of PI programs to unacceptable levels by increasing the implicit cost of futures and options premiums. PI programs also have been widely blamed for exacerbating the market's turmoil during and following the October crash.

See also: FUTURES MARKET
             PROGRAM TRADING
             PUT OPTION

Reference:

Abken, Peter A., "An Introduction to Portfolio Insurance," Federal Reserve Bank of Atlanta, *Economic Review* (Nov./Dec. 1987), 2-25.

POSITIVE ECONOMICS

Objective inquiry in economics is called scientific or positive economics. Positive economics is practiced when one predicts that if event A occurs, then event B will follow. This prediction is based on the objective evaluation of facts, that is, that event B is the logical result after event A. The distinguishing characteristic of positive economics is that the predictions are testable if given sufficient information. Thus, positive economics may be either true or false.

See also: NORMATIVE ECONOMICS

PREFERRED STOCK

Preferred stock is a form of capital stock that possesses certain preferences or priorities over common stock. The preferences are usually associated with a prior claim to dividends and the distribution of assets upon the liquidation of the corporation.

Preferred stockholders are usually not given the right to vote in corporate affairs, except under unusual circumstances. Preferred stock is usually par value preferred. Dividends on preferred stock are usually expressed as a percentage of par value: if the preferred is no-par preferred, the dividend is stated as a specific dollar amount. Preferred stock may be noncumulative or cumulative. If the stock is noncumulative, the preferred shareholders are entitled to receive their current year's dividend on dividends declared in that year. However, the Directors do not have to declare and pay dividends on any previous year which has been omitted. In contrast, cumulative preferred stock provides that dividends in arrears (dividends undeclared or passed in prior years) accumulate and must be paid to preferred shareholders before any dividends can be distributed to common stockholders. Dividends ordinarily do not become a liability of the corporation until they are declared.

Preferred stock may be participating or nonparticipating. Participating preferred stock has priority over common stock up to the basic percentage or amount stated for preferred dividends; after an equal percentage or amount is paid to the common, the preferred and common participate in additional dividends. Participating preferred stock may be classified as fully or partially participating preferred stock. If the stock is fully participating, the preferred shareholders are entitled to receive any dividends above the basic rate on a pro rata basis with the common stockholders. The pro rata amount is based on the par or stated value of each class of stock. If the preferred stock is partially participating, the preferred shareholders share the additional dividends with common shareholders only up to the participating amount, with anything above that going entirely to the common shareholders. The following examples illustrate the cumulative and participating features of preferred stock. Assume the following information:

Preferred stock, 6%, $100 par value	$100,000
Common stock, $50 par value, 4,000 shares	$200,000

Case 1
Preferred stock is cumulative and nonparticipating. Dividends on preferred stock are three years in arrears ($100,000 \times .06 \times 3 = \$18,000$). The directors declare a $60,000 dividend. The dividend would be allocated among the common and preferred as follows:

	Preferred	**Common**
Preferred stock:		
Dividend in arrears for three years	$18,000	
Current dividends	6,000	
Common stock:		
Balance available ($60,000 - $24,000)	_____	$36,000
Total dividend	$24,000	$36,000

Preferred stock usually has a preference over common stock as to assets available for distribution upon the dissolution of the corporation. For example, a $100 par value preferred stock may have a liquidating value of $105 per share. The preferred would be entitled to receive $105 per share before the common should the corporation be liquidated. Companies must disclose the aggregate liquidating value of preferred stock on financial statements if one is specified.

Case 2

Preferred stock is cumulative and fully participating. Dividends are three years in arrears. The directors declare a $48,000 dividend.

	Preferred	**Common**
Preferred stock:		
Dividends in arrears for three years	$18,000	
Current dividends	6,000	
Common stock:		
Matching 6% dividend for current year		$12,000
Balance:		
($48,000 − ($24,000 + $12,000) = $12,000)		
100,000/300,000 × $12,000	4,000	
200,000/300,000 × $12,000		8,000
Total dividend	**$28,000**	**$20,000**

Additional features of preferred stock can include convertible rights and callable provisions. Convertible preferred stock provides the option to the preferred shareholder to convert or exchange his preferred shares for other securities of the corporation, generally common stock. The conversion feature is included as a provision in some preferred stock contracts in order to make the purchase of the preferred stock more attractive. The call provision in preferred stock contracts establishes a call price at which the corporation may repurchase the stock from a stockholder.

See also   CAPITAL
CAPITAL STOCK

PREPAID EXPENSE

Prepaid expenses are expenses of a future period that have been paid in advance—for example, prepaid rent or insurance. Prepaid expenses are classified as current assets even though they will never be converted into cash as would be the typical current asset. Current asset classification for prepaid expenses is justified on the basis that if the expenditure for the item had not occurred, cash would have to be expended in the future.

See also: CURRENT ASSET

PRESENT VALUE

Present value is the net amount of discounted expected cash flows relating to an asset or liability. Stated another way, present value is the principal that must be invested at time period zero to produce the known future value. The process of converting the future value to the present value is referred to as discounting. Present value problems can assume this form: if $1,688.96 is to be received four years in the future, what is its present value if the discount rate is 14 percent? Using a formula approach, the present value in this illustration can be computed by using the following formula:

$$pv = f \frac{1}{(1+i)^n}$$

where, pv = present value of any given future amount due in the future

f = a future amount
i = interest rate
n = number of periods.

The present value of $1,688.96 received at the end of four years discounted at 14 percent is $1,000, calculated as follows:

$$pv = (\$1,688.96) \frac{1}{(1+.14)^4} = \$1,000$$

The present value of an annuity is the amount that must be invested now and, if left to earn compound interest, will provide for the receipt or payment of a series of equal rents at regular intervals. Over a period of time, the present value balance increases periodically for interest and decreases periodically for each rent paid or received.

Tables are available that make present value computations relatively easy. Present value of $1 and present value of an annuity of $1 tables are presented in Exhibit P-2 and P-3, respectively.

Exhibit P-2
Present Value of $1

PRESENT VALUE OF 1: $p = \dfrac{1}{(1+i)^n}$

n	1.5%	4.0%	4.5%	5.0%	5.5%	6.0%	7.0%
1	0.985222	0.961538	0.956938	0.952381	0.947867	0.943396	0.934579
2	0.970662	0.924556	0.915730	0.907029	0.898452	0.889996	0.873439
3	0.956317	0.888996	0.876297	0.863838	0.851614	0.839619	0.816298
4	0.942184	0.854804	0.838561	0.822702	0.807217	0.792094	0.762895
5	0.928260	0.821927	0.802451	0.783526	0.765134	0.747258	0.712986
6	0.914542	0.790315	0.767896	0.746215	0.725246	0.704961	0.666342
7	0.901027	0.759918	0.734828	0.710681	0.687437	0.665057	0.622750
8	0.887711	0.730690	0.703185	0.676839	0.651599	0.627412	0.582009
9	0.874592	0.702587	0.672904	0.644609	0.617629	0.591898	0.543934
10	0.861667	0.675564	0.643928	0.613913	0.585431	0.558395	0.508349
11	0.848933	0.649581	0.616199	0.584679	0.554911	0.526788	0.475093
12	0.836387	0.624597	0.589664	0.556837	0.525982	0.496969	0.444012
13	0.824027	0.600574	0.564272	0.530321	0.498561	0.468839	0.414964
14	0.811849	0.577475	0.539973	0.505068	0.472569	0.442301	0.387817
15	0.799852	0.555265	0.516720	0.481017	0.447933	0.417265	0.362446
16	0.788031	0.533908	0.494469	0.458112	0.424581	0.393646	0.338735
17	0.776385	0.513373	0.473176	0.436297	0.402447	0.371364	0.316574
18	0.764912	0.493628	0.452800	0.415521	0.381466	0.350344	0.295864
19	0.753607	0.474642	0.433302	0.395734	0.361579	0.330513	0.276508
20	0.742470	0.456387	0.414643	0.376889	0.342729	0.311805	0.258419
21	0.731498	0.438834	0.396787	0.358942	0.324862	0.294155	0.241513
22	0.720688	0.421955	0.379701	0.341850	0.307926	0.277505	0.225713
23	0.710037	0.405726	0.363350	0.325571	0.291873	0.261797	0.210947
24	0.699544	0.390121	0.347703	0.310068	0.276657	0.246979	0.197147
25	0.689206	0.375117	0.332731	0.295303	0.262234	0.232999	0.184249
26	0.679021	0.360689	0.318402	0.281241	0.248563	0.219810	0.172195
27	0.668986	0.346817	0.304691	0.267848	0.235605	0.207368	0.160930
28	0.659099	0.333477	0.291571	0.255094	0.223322	0.195630	0.150402
29	0.649359	0.320651	0.279015	0.242946	0.211679	0.184557	0.140563
30	0.639762	0.308319	0.267000	0.231377	0.200644	0.174110	0.131367

n	8.0%	9.0%	10.0%	12.0%	14.0%	16.0%	18.0%
1	0.925926	0.917431	0.909091	0.892857	0.877193	0.862069	0.847458
2	0.857339	0.841680	0.826446	0.797194	0.769468	0.743163	0.718184
3	0.793832	0.772183	0.751315	0.711780	0.674972	0.640658	0.608631
4	0.735030	0.708425	0.683013	0.635518	0.592080	0.552291	0.515789
5	0.680583	0.649931	0.620921	0.567427	0.519369	0.476113	0.437109
6	0.630170	0.596267	0.564474	0.506631	0.455587	0.410442	0.370432
7	0.583490	0.547034	0.513158	0.452349	0.399637	0.353830	0.313925
8	0.540269	0.501866	0.466507	0.403883	0.350559	0.305025	0.266038
9	0.500249	0.460428	0.424098	0.360610	0.307508	0.262953	0.225456
10	0.463193	0.422411	0.385543	0.321973	0.269744	0.226684	0.191064
11	0.428883	0.387533	0.350494	0.287476	0.236617	0.195417	0.161919
12	0.397114	0.355535	0.318631	0.256675	0.207559	0.168463	0.137220
13	0.367698	0.326179	0.289664	0.229174	0.182069	0.145227	0.116288
14	0.340461	0.299246	0.263331	0.204620	0.159710	0.125195	0.098549
15	0.315242	0.274538	0.239392	0.182696	0.140096	0.107927	0.083516
16	0.291890	0.251870	0.217629	0.163122	0.122892	0.093041	0.070776
17	0.270269	0.231073	0.197845	0.145644	0.107800	0.080207	0.059980
18	0.250249	0.211994	0.179859	0.130040	0.094561	0.069144	0.050830
19	0.231712	0.194490	0.163508	0.116107	0.082948	0.059607	0.043077
20	0.214548	0.178431	0.148644	0.103667	0.072762	0.051385	0.036506
21	0.198656	0.163698	0.135131	0.092560	0.063826	0.044298	0.030937
22	0.183941	0.150182	0.122846	0.082643	0.055988	0.038188	0.026218
23	0.170315	0.137781	0.111678	0.073788	0.049112	0.032920	0.022218
24	0.157699	0.126405	0.101526	0.065882	0.043081	0.028380	0.018829
25	0.146018	0.115968	0.092296	0.058823	0.037790	0.024465	0.015957
26	0.135202	0.106393	0.083905	0.052521	0.033149	0.021091	0.013523
27	0.125187	0.097608	0.076278	0.046894	0.029078	0.018182	0.011460
28	0.115914	0.089543	0.069343	0.041869	0.025507	0.015674	0.009712
29	0.107328	0.082155	0.063039	0.037383	0.022375	0.013512	0.008230
30	0.099377	0.075371	0.057309	0.033378	0.019627	0.011648	0.006975

Exhibit P-3

Present Value of an Ordinary Annuity

PRESENT VALUE OF AN ORDINARY ANNUITY OF 1: $P_0 = \dfrac{1 - \dfrac{1}{(1+i)^n}}{i}$

n	1.5%	4.0%	4.5%	5.0%	5.5%	6.0%	7.0%
1	0.985222	0.961538	0.956938	0.952381	0.947867	0.943396	0.934579
2	1.955883	1.886095	1.872668	1.859410	1.846320	1.833393	1.808018
3	2.912200	2.775091	2.748964	2.723248	2.697933	2.673012	2.624316
4	3.854385	3.629895	3.587526	3.545951	3.505150	3.465106	3.387211
5	4.782645	4.451822	4.389977	4.329477	4.270204	4.212364	4.100197
6	5.697187	5.242137	5.157872	5.075692	4.995530	4.917324	4.766540
7	6.598214	6.002055	5.892701	5.786373	5.682967	5.582381	5.389289
8	7.485925	6.732745	6.595886	6.463213	6.334566	6.209794	5.971299
9	8.360517	7.435332	7.268790	7.107822	6.952195	6.801692	6.515232
10	9.222185	8.110896	7.912718	7.721735	7.537626	7.360087	7.023582
11	10.071118	8.760477	8.528917	8.306414	8.092536	7.886875	7.498674
12	10.907505	9.385074	9.118581	8.863252	8.618518	8.383844	7.942686
13	11.731532	9.985648	9.682852	9.393573	9.117079	8.852683	8.357651
14	12.543382	10.563123	10.222825	9.898641	9.589648	9.294984	8.745468
15	13.343233	11.118387	10.739546	10.379658	10.037581	9.712249	9.107914
16	14.131264	11.652296	11.234015	10.837770	10.462162	10.105895	9.446649
17	14.907649	12.165669	11.707191	11.274066	10.864609	10.477260	9.763223
18	15.672561	12.659297	12.159992	11.689587	11.246074	10.827603	10.059087
19	16.426168	13.133939	12.593294	12.085321	11.607654	11.158116	10.335595
20	17.168639	13.590326	13.007936	12.462210	11.950382	11.469921	10.594014
21	17.900137	14.029160	13.404724	12.821153	12.275244	11.764077	10.835527
22	18.620824	14.451115	13.784425	13.163003	12.583170	12.041582	11.061240
23	19.330861	14.856842	14.147775	13.488571	12.875042	12.303379	11.272187
24	20.030405	15.246963	14.495478	13.798642	13.151699	12.550358	11.469334
25	20.719611	15.622080	14.828209	14.093945	13.413933	12.783356	11.653583
26	21.398632	15.982769	15.146611	14.375185	13.662495	13.003166	11.825779
27	22.067617	16.329586	15.451303	14.643034	13.898100	13.210534	11.986709
28	22.726717	16.663063	15.742874	14.898127	14.121422	13.406164	12.137111
29	23.376076	16.983715	16.021889	15.141074	14.333101	13.590721	12.277674
30	24.015838	17.292033	16.288389	15.372451	14.533745	13.764831	12.409041

n	8.0%	9.0%	10.0%	12.0%	14.0%	16.0%	18.0%
1	0.925926	0.917431	0.909091	0.892857	0.877193	0.862069	0.847458
2	1.783265	1.759111	1.735537	1.690051	1.646661	1.605232	1.565642
3	2.577097	2.531295	2.486852	2.401831	2.321632	2.245890	2.174273
4	3.312147	3.239720	3.169865	3.037349	2.913712	2.798181	2.690062
5	3.992710	3.889651	3.790787	3.604776	3.433081	3.274394	3.127171
6	4.622880	4.485919	4.355261	4.111407	3.888668	3.684736	3.497603
7	5.206370	5.032953	4.868419	4.563757	4.288305	4.038565	3.811528
8	5.746639	5.534819	5.334926	4.967640	4.638864	4.343591	4.077566
9	6.246888	5.995247	5.759024	5.328250	4.946372	4.606544	4.303022
10	6.710081	6.417658	6.144567	5.650223	5.216116	4.833227	4.494086
11	7.138964	6.805191	6.495061	5.937699	5.452733	5.028644	4.656005
12	7.536078	7.160725	6.813692	6.194374	5.660292	5.197107	4.793225
13	7.903776	7.486904	7.103356	6.423548	5.842362	5.342334	4.909513
14	8.244237	7.786150	7.366687	6.628168	6.002072	5.467529	5.008062
15	8.559479	8.060698	7.605080	6.810864	6.142168	5.575456	5.091578
16	8.851369	8.312553	7.823709	6.973986	6.265060	5.668497	5.162354
17	9.121638	8.543631	8.021553	7.119630	6.372859	5.748704	5.222334
18	9.371887	8.755625	8.201412	7.249670	6.467420	5.817848	5.273164
19	9.603599	8.950115	8.364920	7.365777	6.550369	5.877455	5.316241
20	9.818147	9.128546	8.513564	7.469444	6.623131	5.928841	5.352746
21	10.016803	9.292244	8.648694	7.562003	6.686957	5.973139	5.383683
22	10.200704	9.442425	8.771540	7.644646	6.742944	6.011326	5.409901
23	10.371059	9.580207	8.883218	7.718434	6.792056	6.044247	5.432120
24	10.528758	9.706612	8.984744	7.784316	6.835137	6.072627	5.450949
25	10.674776	9.822580	9.077040	7.843139	6.872927	6.097092	5.466906
26	10.809978	9.928972	9.160945	7.895660	6.906077	6.118183	5.480429
27	10.935165	10.026580	9.237223	7.942554	6.935155	6.136364	5.491889
28	11.051078	10.116128	9.306567	7.984423	6.960662	6.152038	5.501601
29	11.158406	10.198283	9.369606	8.021806	6.983037	6.165550	5.509831
30	11.257783	10.273654	9.426914	8.055184	7.002664	6.177198	5.516806

See also: ANNUITY
FUTURE VALUE
INTEREST

Reference:

Woelfel, Charles J., *Financial Managers Desktop Reference to Money, Time, Interest and Yield* (Probus, Chicago, Ill., 1986).

PRICE ELASTICITY OF DEMAND

The price elasticity of demand is a measure of responsiveness in the quantity demanded of a good or service to a change in the price of that good or service. It is calculated as the percentage change in quantity demanded divided by the corresponding percentage change in price.

Demand is said to be elastic if the elasticity of demand is greater, in absolute value, than −1.0. For example, if the price elasticity of demand for a product were −2.0, then a 1 percent increase (decrease) in that product's price would lead to a 2 percent decrease (increase) in the quantity demanded of that product, everything else remaining the same. If the price elasticity of demand is less, in absolute value, than −1.0 (such as −0.8) then demand is said to be inelastic.

See also: ELASTICITY

PRICE INDEX

A price index is a comparison of the prices of goods and services in the current year to those in a base year. In economics, a number of price indices are used, such as the consumer price index, GNP deflator, producer price index, and wholesale price index.

See also: CONSUMER PRICE INDEX
                GNP DEFLATOR
                PRODUCER PRICE INDEX

PRICE LEADERSHIP

In an oligopoly there is an interdependence among producers. One type of behavior that results from this interdependence is price leadership. Price leadership connotes a behavior where the dominant (leader) firm increases price as a signal for the other firms to follow. Such action, by itself, is not illegal; however, if it comes about as the result of collusion it is illegal just as price fixing is illegal.

See also: MARKET STRUCTURE

PRICING POLICY

Pricing is a profit-planning situation in which management searches for alternative pricing policies and evaluates the profit consequences of the various alternatives before reaching a decision. Pricing policy refers to the principles and practices which determine pricing decisions. Theory and practice vary widely where pricing policies are determined, even within the same industry. Practices range from rule-of-thumb judgments, to conventional practices, to the application of microeconomic principles.

PRICING POLICY: ADMINISTERED PRICING

Administered pricing is a pricing policy in which a seller can exert an influence on the price charged for a product or service because of the absence of competition. Large and powerful producers are occasionally in a position to adopt administered pricing.

PRICING POLICY: CONVERSION COST PRICING

Conversion costs include direct labor and factory overhead costs. Costs of materials used in the product are not considered. Conversion costing is occasionally used when a customer provides the material. Conversion cost pricing requires that factory capacity is limited in terms of labor and overhead cost constraints. When conversion cost pricing is followed, companies direct their efforts to products or services requiring less labor and overhead (scarce resources) because more units can be produced and sold. For example, assume the following information:

	Product X	Product Y
Direct material	$10	$10
Conversion costs:		
Direct labor	5	1
Factory overhead	9	4
Total production cost	$24	$15

If the firm desires a 10 percent markup on conversion cost, the sales price for each product is:

	Product X	**Product Y**
Full cost	$24.00	$15.00
Markup on conversion cost:		
10% × $14	1.40	
10% × $5		.50
Sales price	$25.40	$15.50

More units of Product Y can be produced because Product Y requires less conversion cost. Each product produces the same profit per unit of scarce resource.

See also: BUDGET
            PLANNING FUNCTION

PRICING POLICY: COST-PLUS PRICING

Cost-plus pricing requires a firm to add a predetermined markup to an established or known average cost. The size of the markup depends upon what the firm calculates it can obtain. This form of pricing usually establishes a target rate of return on its investment and uses this rate to establish prices. Cost-plus pricing generally does not take into consideration the elasticity of demand or the relationship of marginal cost to marginal revenue. As a result, the price established may not be the most profitable price attainable. Costs should be used in pricing primarily to forecast the impact on profits of alternative pricing policies. Cost usually refers to full costs. Cost-plus pricing is in essence a backward-cost pricing method. A desired percentage for profit is added to the full cost of the product or service to establish the price. Highway construction, defense, and housing contracts frequently use cost-plus pricing methods. Cost-plus pricing usually involves the difficult task of allocating fixed costs which cannot be traced directly to a project.

A problem with full-cost pricing occurs when two or more products or projects are produced or worked on. How should common costs be allocated to the products or projects and how large should the markup be? In spite of these and other problems, full-cost pricing is widely used because the economic model of pricing is difficult to apply, managers consider full-cost pricing to be safe, and intuitively managers believe that in the long run all costs, fixed and variable, must be recovered if the firm is to survive. However, full-cost pricing cannot guarantee any of these assumptions.

PRICING POLICY: DIFFERENTIAL COST PRICING

A differential cost is the increase in total costs resulting from the production of additional unit(s). A desired markup based as a percentage of differential cost is added to full cost. Differential cost pricing focuses on the contribution to fixed costs and profit that an additional order will produce.

PRICING POLICY: DIRECT COST PRICING

Direct costs include the direct cost of material and labor along with variable factory overhead costs. When direct cost pricing is used, selling prices are set at a percentage above these direct costs incurred in manufacturing or producing the good or service. Direct cost pricing is valid if the cost characteristics of a company's product lines are similar. If the indirect costs that should be allocated to each product line are not essentially the same percentage of direct costs, and if the assets employed by product lines are not similar, direct cost pricing can produce inequities in the pricing process. This method does not base pricing on indirect costs which are often arbitrarily allocated to products.

PRICING POLICY: DISCOUNTS

A discount is a reduction of a stated price. Major types of discounts include quantity, trade, cash, and seasonal discounts.Certain discounts are based on geographical factors (zonal pricing based on delivery distance); delivery methods (discounts for customer collection); trade-in allowances on old equipment. Discounts can be based on physical volume or dollar sales; a percentage discount or a cash difference from a list price; a flat sum rebate or a net price. Discounts can also be published, discretionary, negotiated, or a combination thereof. Major types of discounts and the reasons for using them are outlined here:

Type	Method	Objective
Quantity discount	1. Single order: based on volume purchased at one time.	Relates to individual customer. Encourage large orders. Pass on cost savings and economies in large orders.
	2. Cumulative: based on volume purchased over a fixed period of time.	Discourage small orders. Encourage repeat orders.
Trade discount	Percentage discount from a specific list price which supposedly represents distributors' expenses and profits. Trade discounts may be expressed as a flat rate or combined with a quantity discount.	Assists in controlling final selling price. Discriminating between different types of distributors (retailers, wholesalers). Eliminates need to change catalogues, since discounts can be changed, not list prices.
Cash discount	Deductions offered by seller if payment is within a specified time period.	Encourage early payment of account, reducing credit and collection risks.
Seasonal discount	Different prices depending on the season, day of week, or time of day where demand has a cyclical pattern and supply is fixed.	Encourage spreading of demand, avoidance of peak loading, and increasing demand during low periods (hotels, cinemas, and electricity).

PRICING POLICY: "FAIR" PRICING

"Fair" pricing is an ethical concept of pricing goods and services. Under fair pricing, an organization prices its goods and services at a price that allows the full recovery of all costs plus an equitable profit. Costs incurred for factors of production (land, labor, and capital) are supposed to be in amounts that provide for a fair standard of living for the parties involved. The concept of fair pricing is difficult to apply because what is fair or equitable is difficult to define.

PRICING POLICY: PENETRATION PRICING

Companies have occasionally used penetration pricing in order to gain entrance into a market. In penetration pricing the company introduces a product at a low price and then hopefully moves up to a higher price. Penetration pricing is sometimes used when the competition dictates a price ceiling. Where a high volume of sales is required to make a product profitable, penetration pricing with its low prices might produce the necessary volume.

PRICING POLICY: RETURN ON ASSETS

Some firms establish a price for their product or service based on a desired rate of return on assets employed in the company. The desired markup on cost can be determined according to the following formula and illustration.

The company desires a 10 percent return on $60,000,000 assets employed in the business and annual costs total $45,000,000:

$$\text{Percent markup on cost} = \frac{\text{Assets employed}}{\text{Total annual costs}} \times \frac{\text{Desired rate of return}}{\text{capital employed}}$$

$$\text{Percent markup on cost} = \frac{\$60,000,000}{\$45,000,000} \times 10\%$$

$$\text{Percent markup} = 13.3\%$$

The sales volume would then be computed using this formula:

$$\text{Sales volume} = \frac{\text{Total annual}}{\text{costs}} + (\frac{\text{Total annual}}{\text{costs}} \times \frac{\text{Percentage}}{\text{markup on cost}})$$

$$\text{Sales volume} = \$45,000,000 + (\$45,000,000 \times 13.3\%)$$

$$\text{Sales volume} = \$50,985,000 \text{ (rounded to } \$51,000,000\text{)}$$

If one million units are expected to be sold, the sales price should be $51.00 ($51,000,000/1,000,000 units).

PRICING POLICY: SKIM-OFF-THE-TOP PRICING

If a company's product or service is unique or novel, the company may be able to take advantage of this situation until the market demand declines or competitors enter the field. Pricing under such conditions is referred to as skim-off-the-top pricing, or price skimming. As long as the company maintains an exclusive market for this product, the company could charge a higher than normal price for the product in the early marketing stages. Generally, a higher price will produce a larger dollar volume of sales initially than would a low initial price.

PRICING POLICY: STANDARD COSTS

Standard costs are costs that could be attained with efficient production methods at a normal capacity. In standard cost systems, a standard cost for material, labor, and factory overhead is developed. When a standard costs pricing policy is adopted, the company adds a desired markup to standard costs to establish a price.

PRICING POLICY: STAY-OUT, FLOOR, AND GOING-RATE PRICING

Stay-out pricing refers to low initial pricing which is directed at discouraging potential competitors from entering the market. When stay-out pricing is used, profit margins are low and competitors may find it difficult to compete under such circumstances.

Floor pricing involves lowering prices to meet competitors' prices. A floor-pricing policy frequently results in little or no profit, but is justified on the basis that such pricing is required for the firm to keep its product(s) in the market.

Many firms simply adopt a manufacturer's or wholesaler's suggested retail price as a convenience, or because contracts require it. Going-rate pricing requires a seller to base his prices on prices established by competitors in his market.

PRICING POLICY: TRANSFER PRICING

Divisions of an enterprise frequently buy and sell to one another. A price must be established for these transfers. This price is referred to as the transfer price. Various alternatives to establishing a transfer price include the following:

1. The transfer price should be set equal to the manufacturing cost of the selling division.

2. The transfer price should be the amount the selling division could sell the product to an outside firm.

3. The transfer price should be the amount the buying division could purchase the product from an outside firm.

4. The transfer price should be a negotiated amount agreed upon by the buying and selling divisions.

5. The transfer price should be the costs incurred to the point of transfer plus the opportunity costs for the firm as a whole. The opportunity cost would be the next best alternative for the firm. For example, if the selling division was operating at less than full capacity, the opportunity cost would be zero. If the selling division was operating at full capacity, the opportunity cost would be the lost contribution margin (selling price minus variable costs) resulting from forgoing outside sales to sell to the buying division.

The choice of method depends upon a number of factors, such as the autonomy allowed to divisions, the degree of market competition, the extent to which the goals of the division are expected to correspond to the goals of the firm, short-run supply and demand relationships, and how divisions are evaluated by the firm.

PRICING POLICY: VARIABLE COST PRICING

Variable cost pricing requires that a firm identify its variable and fixed costs. When this distinction can be made, a company's contribution margin (sales minus variable costs) can be computed. The effect on contribution margins of different prices can be related to fixed costs. Assume that a company produces two products and the variable cost of material, labor, and factory overhead for Product X is $20 and for Product Y is $30. If a 25 percent markup on variable cost is used, the sales price is

	Product X	**Product Y**
Full cost (assumed)	$50	$40
Markup on variable cost:		
10% × $20	2	
10% × $30		3
Sales price	$52	$43

A major advantage of variable cost pricing is that the difficult problem of allocating indirect, fixed costs can be avoided. Variable pricing is often useful in pricing a special order at a special price, in a dumping situation, or in a distress case. In difficult times, a company may need to make some revenue above variable cost as an alternative to no revenue. Special-order pricing may involve discriminatory prices which may have to be justified in order not to violate the Robinson-Patman Act.

PRIME RATE

The prime rate is a published rate of interest charged by commercial banks on loans to strong, financially secure organizations and individuals. Rates on other bank loans tend to be scaled up from the prime rate. For example, prime plus 1 percent or prime plus 2 percent.

Every bank sets its own prime rate, but competitive pressures normally force rates to the same level across the country. In changing rates, most banks tend to follow the lead of the large New York City banks. Among these, most banks will follow the example of Citibank, New York's largest bank.

Since the prime rate is not a market-determined rate but an administered rate, it is not directly related to the cost of bank funds. Competition from the Eurobank market and the commercial paper market in recent years has forced most banks to abandon the prime rate in pricing loans to their largest customers. For larger firms, bank lending rates now are normally related to the rate on certificates of deposit, which is an index of the cost of funds to banks. Bank loans to smaller customers who do not have access to the Euromarket or the commercial paper market are still related to the prime rate.

See also: COMMERCIAL BANKS

PRIOR-PERIOD ADJUSTMENTS

A few profit and loss items are reported as prior-period adjustments on financial statements and require a restatement of retained earnings. These items are the corrections of errors of a prior period and adjustments that result from the realization of income tax benefits of preacquisition operating loss carryforwards of purchased subsidiaries.

Material errors in the financial statements of one accounting period that are discovered in a subsequent period usually involve an asset or liability and a revenue or expense of a prior year. In the year of the correction, the asset or liability account balance should be corrected and the related revenue or expense should be made directly to the retained earnings account and should not affect the income statement for the current year. For example, assume that the Blue Company discovered that it failed to record $100,000 of depreciation expense for 1990 and discovered the error in 1991. This error overstated 1990 income before income taxes by a similar amount. Assume that after considering the income tax effect of this error, the error resulted in a net overstatement of income in 1990 of $85,000. The January 1, 1991, retained earnings balance of the Blue Company is assumed to be $500,000. The correction would be disclosed on the December 31, 1991, Statement of Retained Earnings as a prior period adjustment as shown here:

Retained earnings, as previously reported January 1, 1991	$500,000
Less: Correction of overstatement in 1990 net income due to depreciation understatement (net of $15,000 income taxes)	85,000
Adjusted retained earnings, January 1, 1991	$415,000

If comparative financial statements are presented, the prior-year statements should be restated to show the effect on net income, retained earnings, asset or liability balances for all periods reported.

See also: ACCOUNTING CHANGES
          CONSISTENCY
          ERRORS
          INCOME STATEMENT

PRISONER'S DILEMMA

The Prisoner's Dilemma is frequently used to illustrate the impact of non-cooperation in game theory. Two individuals are suspected of jointly committing a crime. Each knows the following information. If, through separate interrogation, neither confesses then only a minor penalty will be imposed; if one confesses and the other does not then the confessor receives no penalty and the accused receives a severe penalty. If both confess, then each receives a moderate penalty (more severe than if neither confesses but less severe that the one given to the guilty non-confessor). If these prisoner's could collectively decide what to do, neither would confess. Independently, their actions cannot be predicted without more information about their gaming strategy.

See also: GAME THEORY

PRO FORMA

A pro forma statement or presentation reports a statement or presentation that would have been shown if a different accounting principle or method had been in effect in an earlier period. For example, for certain accounting changes in the current year that affect a previous year(s), such as a change from straight-line depreciation to an accelerated depreciation method, income before extraordinary items and net income must be computed on a pro forma (as if or for the sake of form) basis for all periods presented as if the newly adopted principle had been applied during all periods affected.

See also: BUDGETING
              EARNINGS PER SHARE

PROGRAM TRADING

Program trading is arbitrage between the market for stock index futures and the stock market itself. Arbitrage traders attempt to profit by buying in one market and selling in another. Program traders try to buy a stock index futures contract, such as the S&P 500 stock index, when it is cheap relative to the prices of the underlying stocks, and sell it when it is high. If the price of the futures contract becomes overvalued, program traders sell the futures and buy the stocks.

To see the relationship between the price of a stock index futures contract and the prices of the underlying stock, assume that an investor has two options for investing his funds over the next 90 days. He may either (1) buy stocks or (2) buy a stock index futures contract. If he buys the actual stocks, the amount of money he will have 90 days from now will be:

$$d \times Ps + ps^x \tag{1}$$

where

d = dividend yield
Ps = current market price of the stock
ps^x = stock price 90 days from now

If, on the other hand, the investor chooses to buy the index futures contract, he may do so and put the amount of money he would have put into stocks into treasury bills instead. His treasury bill account will serve as his margin account and enable him to earn interest at the same time he also holds a stock index futures contract. The amount of money he will have 90 days from now if he buys the futures will be:

$$(1 + i) \times Ps + (Ps^x - Pf) \tag{2}$$

where

i = the interest rate on treasury bills
Pf = the price of the futures contract

If markets function rationally, the return an investor can expect from option (1) will be equal to the return he can expect from option (2). If the returns are not equal, rational investors will choose the option with the highest return. This is what program traders attempt to do. They try to profit from differences between options (1) and (2). In doing so, they increase the efficiency of both markets because their actions tend to force an equality of returns in the stock and futures markets.

Mathematically, if the return from option (1) equals the return from (2), then:

$$d \times Ps + Ps^x = (1 + i) \times Ps + (Ps^x - Pf) \tag{3}$$

Equation (3) implies that:

$$Pf - Ps = (i - d) \times Ps \tag{4}$$

That is, equation (4) states that the difference between the futures price (Pf) and the price of the bundle of underlying stocks (Ps) should be equal to the difference between the interest rate on treasury bills (i) and the dividend rate on the stocks (d) multiplied by the price of the stocks. And this means that:

$$Pf = Ps + (i - d) \times Ps \qquad (5)$$

That is, the futures price should equal the price of the underlying stock plus the difference between the interest rate and the dividend rate multiplied by the price of the stock.

Using computers, program traders constantly track prices on the futures market and prices on the stock exchange. The computers also keep abreast of interest and dividend rates. Then if prices in the futures market get substantially out of line with what traders think they should be based on equation (5), the computers issue buy or sell orders. Thus, computer information is vital in order to quickly identify buying and selling opportunities in the market.

If the price of the futures contract is too high, based on equation (5), program traders will sell the futures contract in the market. At the same time, they may buy the underlying stocks, usually in "baskets" of $5 million to $10 million. By selling the futures and buying the stocks at the same time, they can create a fully hedged position. They also capture a spread, since the futures usually sell at a premium over the value of the stocks (because the interest rate is usually higher than the dividend rate, see equation [4]). When the futures contract expires, the spread goes to zero because the value of the expiring contract must equal the price of the stocks. The traders then "unwind" the programs—selling the stocks and letting the futures expire. When this occurs, they pocket the risk-free profits from the original spread, sometimes far beyond what is available on treasury bills.

In 1985, the spreads were so large that program traders could earn annualized returns which were 400 to 600 basis points above the prevailing three-month treasury bill rate. Since that time, because more and more firms have set up program trading operations, the returns from program trading are reported to have declined.

At the end of every quarter, program traders must unwind their positions because the index futures and options expire. The last hour of trading on the stock exchange during the last day of each quarter has come to be known as the "triple witching hour," the hour at with futures, options, and index option contracts all expire at the same time. Some of these days have been marked by extreme volatility in the market, as program traders have dumped large volumes of stock on the market. This has led to concerns in some quarters as to how this volatility should be managed.

See also: PORTFOLIO INSURANCE.

Reference

"Program Trading Is Really Stock Index Futures Arbitrage," National Investor Relations Institute, *Investor Relations Update* (February 1987), pp. 2–4.

PRODUCER PRICE INDEX (PPI)

The producer price index (PPI) measures the average price change in producer (non-final) goods. In calculating this index, the U.S. Department of Labor, Bureau of Labor Statistics, uses nearly 3,000 producer products ranging from feeds to fibers to fuels. The PPI varies from year to year in a manner similar to the consumer price index (CPI). Listed below are the annual rates of change in the PPI and the CPI from 1980 through 1987.

Year	Annual Percentage Change in	
	PPI	CPI
1980	11.8	12.4
1981	7.1	8.9
1982	3.7	3.9
1983	0.6	3.8
1984	1.7	4.0
1985	1.8	3.8
1986	-2.3	1.1
1987	2.2	4.4

Source: *Economic Report of the President*, 1988.

See also: CONSUMER PRICE INDEX
PRICE INDEX

PRODUCT DIFFERENTIATION

Consumers choose between homogeneous products strictly on the basis of their price. Producers often differentiate their products in order to provide a second dimension through which consumers may make purchasing decisions. The strategy in differentiating one's product is to separate consumer choice from the product's price thereby giving the producer the ability to raise price without loosing many customers, and thus increase revenues. Breakfast cereals, underwear, and shampoos are only a few of the products that are marketed on the basis of differential characteristics.

PRODUCT FINANCING ARRANGEMENTS

Product financing arrangements are transactions in which a company sells a portion of its inventory to another entity with the intent to reacquire that inventory in the future. The purpose of such arrangements is generally a financing arrangement in which one party is able to finance the product and still retain control over its ultimate disposition. For example, Company A sells inventory to Company B and agrees to repurchase the inventory at a specified price and time. Company B uses the inventory as collateral for a bank loan. The proceeds of the bank loan are used by Company B to pay Company A for the inventory. At a later date, Company A repurchases the inventory from Company B plus related holding costs incurred by Company B; Company B uses these proceeds to repay the bank loan. For accounting purposes, Company A is financing its inventory even though legal title has passed to Company B. Company B might be interested in such an arrangement because it may want to work out a similar arrangement with Company A in the future or for other business reasons. Since the economic substance of the transaction did not involve a sale by Company A, the inventory transferred to Company B is included in Company A's inventory even though Company B has legal title. The proceeds from the sale are recognized by Company A as a liability and not as revenue. This treatment requires Company A to report the product and liability (a financing arrangement) on its balance sheet. Exhibit P-4 illustrates a typical product financing arrangement.

See also: REALIZATION
RECOGNITION
REVENUE

Exhibit P-4
Product Financing Arrangement Illustrated

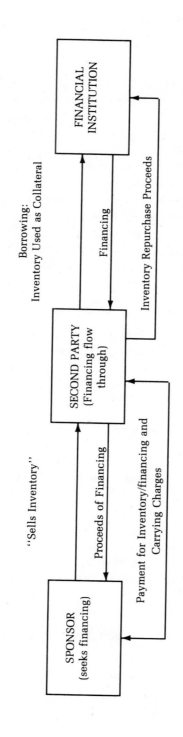

Reference:

SFAS No. 49, *Accounting for Product Financing Arrangements* (FASB, 1981).

PRODUCT LIFE CYCLE

Over time, the sales of a new product will first increase as the product gains market acceptance, and then decrease as competing products are introduced. All products go through such cyclical sales patterns. In Figure 15 on the following page the four phases of a product life cycle are shown along with the pattern of sales that characterizes each stage. During the maturity stage, competitor's are in their growth stage.

PRODUCTION FUNCTION

A production is a relationship between inputs and output. If output is denoted as Q and inputs are denoted as K (for capital) and L (for labor), then:

$$Q = f(K, L)$$

denotes that there is a systematic relationship between these inputs and output. In economics this function is often quantified mathematically. There are many theoretical functions studies in economics. The most frequently studied production function is the Cobb-Douglas production function.

PROFESSION

A profession is an association of individuals engaged in a vocation or occupation that generally is expected to meet the following criteria:

1. It renders essential service to society.

2. It depends upon a body of specialized knowledge acquired through formal education.

3. It has developed a language of its own.

Figure 15

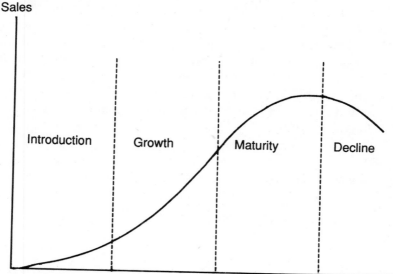

4. It has requirements for admission to the profession which are regulated by law.

5. Its members are governed by ethical principles which emphasize the virtues of honesty, probity, and devotion to the welfare of those served.

6. It has procedures for disciplining those whose conduct violates ethical standards.

The accounting profession is typically subdivided into public accountants who function as independent experts and perform services for clients and internal accountants who work for a particular entity. The profession can be further subdivided as follows:

Public Accountant
External auditor
Tax specialist
Management consultant
Tax accountant
Systems analyst

Internal Accounting
Financial or general accountant
Cost accountant
Internal auditor

A certified public accountant (CPA) is an accountant who has fulfilled certain requirements established by a state law for the practice of public accounting and becomes licensed to practice public accounting in that state. To become a CPA, an accountant must pass a comprehensive examination in accounting theory, practice, auditing, and law. In addition to the CPA examination, other professional examinations have been developed to test the competency level of practitioners. These examinations include the Certificate in Management Accounting (CMA) and the Certified Internal Auditor (CIA).

References:

Previts, Gary John, *The Scope of CPA Services* (John Wiley & Sons, N.Y., 1985).

Carey, John L., *Getting Acquainted with Accounting* (Houghton Mifflin, Boston, 1973).

PROFIT

Profit is a motivating factor behind many managerial activities. Much has been written about the role (as opposed to the method of calculation) of profit. Profit plays three important roles in a capitalistic society. Profit is the financial reward for taking risk; profit is the financial reward for having monopoly power; and profit is the financial reward for having efficient management. The promise of profit provides a strong incentive to owners and managers to act efficiently. Therefore, it is common in economic theory to hypothesize that the guiding criterion by which to evaluate the actions of firms is profit maximization.

See also: ACCOUNTING PROFIT
AGENCY THEORY
CAPITALISM
ECONOMIC PROFIT

PROGRESSIVE TAX

A tax that takes a larger percentage from higher income individuals than from lower income individuals is a progressive tax. The federal individual income tax system is a progressive tax reflecting the ability-to-pay principle of taxation.

PROPERTY

Any legally enforceable right which a person can acquire in something of value is a property right. Property is classified legally as either real or personal property. Real property refers to immovable property, that is, to land and anything permanently attached thereto (such as buildings, equipment, growing trees, etc.). Personal property is all other property, that is, movable property (such as automobiles, money, paintings, etc.). Personal property includes interests evidenced by commercial paper and interests involved in the storage, shipment, sale, and financing of goods.

Eight states have community property systems. The rest are classified as common law jurisdictions. The major differences between the two systems center around property rights possessed by married persons. In a common law system, each spouse owns whatever he or she earns. In a community property system, one-half of the earnings of each spouse is considered owned by the other spouse.

PROPERTY, PLANT, AND EQUIPMENT

Property, plant, and equipment represent long-lived (fixed), tangible (possesses physical substance) assets that are owned by business enterprises for use in operations and are not held for investment or for resale. Property refers to a resource such as land and can include building sites, parking areas, roads, etc. Plant refers to buildings, including structures, facilities, and attached appurtenances (for example, lighting systems, air conditioning or heating systems, docks). Equipment includes such items as office and delivery equipment, machines, furniture and fixtures, motor vehicles, etc.

Property, plant, and equipment are usually presented in financial statements at historical (or acquisition) cost, adjusted for accumulated depreciation. Acquisition cost is the cash or cash equivalent required to acquire the asset, including expenditures required to put the asset into proper condition and location for use. Depreciation is a process that allocates the cost of a tangible long-lived asset, less salvage value, over its useful life in a systematic and rational manner. Except for land, other items included in property, plant, and equipment are subject to depreciation. Property, plant, and equipment are usually classified on the balance sheet after current assets and investments.

PROPERTY TAXES

Governmental authorities such as counties, cities, and school districts levy taxes on real and personal property. Assessed values of property are used as the basis for setting a tax rate sufficient to raise tax revenue that will meet budget requirements. Tax rates usually are determined by using a formula similar to the following:

$$\text{Tax rate} = \frac{\text{Revenue required}}{\text{Assessed property valuation}}$$

Tax rates are usually expressed as a certain number of dollars per $100 of assessed valuation.

Accountants use various methods for accruing real and personal property taxes. The preferable method is monthly accrual using the fiscal period of the taxing jurisdiction. Property taxes are usually recognized as expenses, except where capitalized (as assets), while property is being developed or prepared for use.

See also: LIABILITIES

PROPORTIONAL TAX

A proportional tax is one that takes the same percentage of income from each individual. Advocates of a flat federal income tax system are proponents of proportionalism.

PROPRIETORSHIP

A proprietorship is a firm owned by one individual called a proprietor. In this type of organization the owner makes all of the business decisions and earns all of the profits. Legally, the owner is responsible for all of the firm's debts and liabilities. As one might expect, individual proprietorships are generally small and operate with only a few employees. In comparison with other forms of firm ownership—partnerships and corporations—proprietorships are the largest in terms of numbers, but they have grown in number at the slowest rate (about 2 percent per year).

See also: CORPORATION

              PARTNERSHIP

PROSPECTUS

A prospectus is a document that describes a new security issue. The prospectus is in the form of a circular, letter, notice, or advertisement which offers a security for sale and is filed with the Securities and Exchange Commission (SEC) as part of the registration statement. The Securities Act of 1933 was intended to provide the investing public with full and fair disclosure of information necessary to evaluate the merits of security offerings. The act requires that a registration statement be filed with the Securities and Exchange Commission. To provide the investing public with information included in the registration statements, a prospectus is to be provided potential investors before or at the time of the sale or delivery of the securities.

See also: SECURITIES AND EXCHANGE COMMISSION

PROTECTIONISM

Protectionism refers to federal actions to protect domestic industries from foreign competition. Usually, protectionist measures take the form of tariffs or quotas. Most economists do not advocate a total protectionist trade policy, but some advocate protecting selected industries. One argument for sheltering infant industries (new and expanding industries) is to protect the domestic market from free trade until that industry is capable of competing in international markets. Other arguments are to protect regionally important industries for employment-related reasons. Such industries may include textiles. Advocates of free trade argue that consumers will benefit from open markets in that they will have more and higher quality products available at a lower cost.

See also: QUOTA
          TARIFF

PROXY

A proxy is a document or authorization given by a stockholder to another person that allows that person to vote the stockholder's shares of stock in a corporate meeting. Persons are prohibited from soliciting proxies unless the stockholders have been furnished a written proxy statement or prospectus. A proxy statement discloses matters to be voted on at the next meeting of the shareholders. Proxy solicitations can relate to a variety of matters, especially to obtaining voting power in connection with an annual meeting where directors are to be elected. Special meetings often relate to the authorization or issuance of securities other than for exchange, modification or exchange of securities, stock options to officers and directors, mergers, consolidations, acquisitions, and related matters. Each person solicited by management for a proxy in connection with an annual shareholders' meeting at which directors are to be elected must be furnished with an annual report to shareholders.

See also: FINANCIAL MARKETS

PRUDENT MAN RULE

The prudent man rule is a legal concept of prudence. For example, a prudent man will not invest in speculative securities, will diversify to spread risks and avoid a catastrophic loss, and will remain relatively liquid so that distributions and payments can be made. The prudent man rule has special applications to situations involving estates and trusts.

See also: FIDUCIARY

PURCHASE ACCOUNTING

Purchase accounting is an accounting method that is used under certain circumstances in accounting for a business combination, such as a merger, consolidation, or stock acquisition. Accounting for a business combination by the purchase method follows principles normally applicable under the historical-cost method for acquisitions of assets and issuances of stock. The cost to the purchasing entity of acquiring another company in a business combination treated as a purchase is the amount of cash disbursed or the fair value of other assets distributed or securities issued. The cost of the assets recorded on the acquired company's books is not recorded by the acquiring company as the cost of the purchased assets, as would be the case when the pooling-of-interests method is used. Because the assets acquired are recorded at their fair market value, any excess of cost over these fair values of total identifiable net assets is assigned to intangibles, such as goodwill. Goodwill is amortized over a period not to exceed 40 years. The purchase method of accounting must be used for a business combination unless all conditions prescribed for a pooling of interests are met.

In purchase accounting, postacquisition earnings of the acquired entity are combined with the surviving entity's earnings. Restatement of the financial statements of prior years is not required.

See also: BUSINESS COMBINATIONS
             EQUITY METHOD
             POOLING OF INTERESTS

Reference:

Accounting Research Bulletins No. 51, *Business Combinations* (AICPA, Committee on Accounting Procedure, 1959).

PUT OPTION

Options are contracts between buyers and sellers. Anyone can be a buyer (holder) or a seller (writer) of an option. Two types of options are traded: put options and call options. A put option gives the holder the right to sell the underlying commodity or financial instrument at a specific price during a specific period of time. The writer of the put option is obligated to purchase the commodity or financial instrument from the put holder if the holder wishes to exercise the option. The holder of a put option must pay the writer a sum of money, known as the premium, for the option right. The premium is kept by the writer whether or not the option is exercised.

Options have been traded on financial instruments such as common stocks for many years. There was over-the-counter trading in puts and calls on shares of common stock long before the creation of centralized exchange trading in stock options in the mid-1970s.

Buyers and sellers in the market for common stock options hope to profit from anticipated movements in the prices of the underlying securities on a leveraged basis. For example, the buyer of a put option on common stock hopes to gain from the fall in the price of the associated stock. Because his put option right costs him only a fraction of the value of the underlying securities, any fall in the value of the stock will provide him with a leveraged gain. If, however, the stock rises in value, the value of the put option will fall.

The exercise price (strike price) is the fixed price at which an option may be exercised by its holder. The expiration date is the last day on which the option may be exercised by its holder. If it is not exercised on its expiration date the option ceases to exist and its value becomes zero.

At any given time there are several factors that influence the price (premium value) of a put option. Because an option is a wasting asset, the nearer the exercise date, the less will be the value of the option. Other things equal, options that have longer to run are more valuable than shorter term options.

Price expectations also influence an option's value. When expectations increase, the value of the underlying stock or asset will fall, demand for put options on the stock or asset will grow causing the value of a put option to rise accordingly.

A put option is said to be "in the money" if its exercise price is greater than the market price of the stock. The greater the positive difference between the exercise price of the option and the price of the underlying security, the greater will be the value of the option. For example, if the exercise price on a put option is $60 when the stock is trading for $55, the value of the option will be at least equal to $5. If the market value of the stock falls to $50, the value of the option will increase to at least $10.

A put option is "out of the money" if its exercise price is less than the market price of the stock. Nevertheless, an out-of-the-money option usually still has some value. Its price will not be zero. This is because there is always a chance, however remote, that the market price of the stock may fall, putting the put option "in-the-money" before it expires. The greater the volatility in the price of the stock the more likely this is to happen and, therefore, the greater will be the value of the put option. Accordingly, put options on more volatile securities tend to be more valuable than options on less volatile securities, everything else equal.

See also: OPTIONS

Qq

QUALITATIVE CHARACTERISTICS OF ACCOUNTING INFORMATION

Qualitative characteristics of accounting information are those qualities or ingredients of accounting information that make it useful. The FASB's Statement of Financial Accounting Concepts No. 2, Qualitative Characteristics of Accounting Information, discusses the qualitative characteristics that make accounting information useful and are the qualities to be sought when accounting choices are made. The diagram in Exhibit Q-1 outlines what is referred to as a hierarchy of accounting information qualities. Exhibit Q-2 provides a summary of definitions used in Exhibit Q-1.

The hierarchical arrangement is used to show certain relationships among the qualities. The hierarchy shows that information useful for decision making is the most important. The primary qualities are that accounting information shall be relevant and reliable. If either of these two qualities is completely missing, the information cannot be useful. To be relevant, information must be timely, and it must have predictive value or feedback value or both. To be reliable, information must have representational faithfulness and it must be verifiable and neutral. Comparability, including consistency, is a secondary quality that interacts with

519

Exhibit 9-1
Qualitative Characteristics of Accounting Information

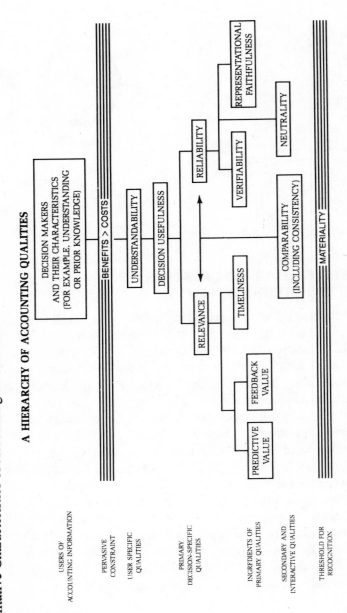

A HIERARCHY OF ACCOUNTING QUALITIES

USERS OF ACCOUNTING INFORMATION

DECISION MAKERS AND THEIR CHARACTERISTICS (FOR EXAMPLE, UNDERSTANDING OR PRIOR KNOWLEDGE)

PERVASIVE CONSTRAINT — BENEFITS > COSTS

USER SPECIFIC QUALITIES — UNDERSTANDABILITY

DECISION USEFULNESS

PRIMARY DECISION-SPECIFIC QUALITIES — RELEVANCE / RELIABILITY

INGREDIENTS OF PRIMARY QUALITIES — PREDICTIVE VALUE, FEEDBACK VALUE, TIMELINESS / VERIFIABILITY, REPRESENTATIONAL FAITHFULNESS

SECONDARY AND INTERACTIVE QUALITIES — COMPARABILITY (INCLUDING CONSISTENCY), NEUTRALITY

THRESHOLD FOR RECOGNITION — MATERIALITY

Source: *Statement of Financial Accounting Concepts No. 2*, "Qualitative Characteristics of Accounting Information" (Stamford, FASB, May 1980). Copyright by Financial Accounting Standards Board, High Ridge Park, Stamford, Connecticut 06905, U.S.A. Reprinted with permission.

Exhibit Q-2
Definitions: Qualitative Characteristics of Accounting Information

Bias Bias in measurement is the tendency of a measure to fall more often on one side than the other of what it represents instead of being equally likely to fall on either side. Bias in accounting measures means a tendency to be consistently too high or too low.

Comparability The quality of information that enables users to identify similarities in and differences between two sets of economic phenomena.

Completeness The inclusion in reported information of everything material that is necessary for faithful representation of the relevant phenomena.

Conservatism A prudent reaction to uncertainty to try to insure that uncertainty and risks inherent in business situations are adequately considered.

Consistency Conformity from period to period with unchanging policies and procedures.

Feedback Value The quality of information that enables users to confirm or correct prior expectations.

Materiality The magnitude of an omission or misstatement of accounting information that, in the light of surrounding circumstances, makes it probable that the judgment of a resonable person relying on the information would have been changed or influenced by the omission or misstatement.

Neutrality Absence in reported information of bias intended to attain a predetermined result or to induce a particular mode of behavior.

Predictive Value The quality of information that helps users to increase the likelihood of correctly forecasting the outcome of past or present events.

Relevance The capacity of information to make a difference in a decision by helping users to form predictions about the outcomes of past, present, and future events or to confirm or correct prior expectations.

Reliability The quality of information that assures that information is reasonably free from error and bias and faithfully represents what it purports to represent.

Representational Faithfulness Correspondence or agreement between a measure or description and the phenomenon that it purports to represent (sometimes called validity).

Timeliness Having information available to a decision maker before it loses its capacity to influence decisions.

Understandability The quality of information that enables users to perceive its significance.

Verifiability The ability through consensus among measures to ensure that information represents what it purports to represent or that the chosen method of measurement has been used without error or bias.

Source: *FASB, Accounting Standards: Statement of Financial Accounting Concepts 1-6.* McGraw-Hill Book Company, New York, N.Y., 1986.

relevance and reliability and contributes to the overall usefulness of information. Two constraints are shown on the chart: benefits must exceed costs and materiality. To be useful and worth providing, the benefits of information should exceed its cost. All of the qualities described are subject to a materiality threshold. Materiality refers to whether the magnitude of an omission or misstatement of accounting information would influence the judgment of a reasonable person relying on the information.

Information provided by financial reporting should be understandable to those who have a reasonable understanding of business and economic activities and are willing to study the information with reasonable diligence.

The hierarchy of qualitative characteristics does not rank the characteristics. If information is to be useful, all characteristics are required to a minimum degree. At times various qualities may conflict in particular circumstances, in which event trade-offs are often necessary or appropriate. For example, the most relevant information may be difficult to understand, or information that is easy to understand may not be very relevant.

See also: CONSISTENCY
             COST-BENEFIT ANALYSIS

Reference:

SFAC No. 2, *Qualitative Characteristics of Accounting Information* (FASB, 1980)

QUANTITATIVE METHODS

Because of the complexity of management, managers have turned to quantitative techniques and models as tools for solving many problems. Such methods are frequently referred to as operations research (OR).

A rational approach to quantitative decision making involves establishing a well-defined objective, selecting a mathematical or logical model, and arranging an optimization process. Quantitative methods include models that:

1. establish equations that can be solved mathematically, and

2. simulation models.

Linear programming is a powerful mathematical procedure designed to assist in planning activities. Most linear programming problems call for the maximization or minimization of some economic objective such as net income, net loss, or costs. These problems often involve the determination of the optimum scheduling routine, product mix, production routing, or transportation route. In such problems, constraints usually exist on available alternatives—for example, constraints on available resources, machine time, manpower, or facilities.

See also: CONTROL FUNCTION
            MANAGEMENT
            PLANNING FUNCTION

Reference:

Bierman, Harold, Jr.. Charles P. Bonini, Lawrence E. Foraker and Robert K. Jaedicke, *Quantitative Analysis for Business Decisions* (Irwin, Homewood, Ill., latest edition).

QUASI-REORGANIZATION

When a corporation encounters financial difficulties, it may attempt to reorganize its capital structure through formal court proceedings. To avoid the problems and expense of court proceedings, a procedure called quasi-reorganization can be undertaken that will accomplish basically the same objective. The purpose of a quasi-reorganization is to absorb a deficit (debit balance in the retained earnings account) and give the enterprise a fresh start. In a quasi-reorganization, a deficit is eliminated against contributed capital. If legal capital is being reduced, state approval is normally required; otherwise, only stockholders' approval is required. Once the deficit is eliminated, the corporation can proceed as though it had been legally reorganized. If the corporation operates profitably after the quasi-reorganization, dividends can be declared which would not have been possible in most states if the deficit had not been eliminated.

Subsequent to the quasi-reorganization, the new retained earnings account shown in the balance sheet must be dated to show it runs from the effective date of the readjustment. This dating should be disclosed in the statements as long as it has special significance, usually until after a post-reorganization earnings pattern has been established. A balance sheet disclosure in the stockholders' equity section could be as follows:

Retained earnings accumulated since October 31, 1992,
    at which time a $500,000 deficit was eliminated
    as a result of a quasi-reorganization $80,000

See also: BANKRUPTCY
                  REORGANIZATION

QUOTA

Quotas are imposed by the federal government to protect domestic producers in selected industries from foreign competition by limiting the supply of certain imported products. There are benefits and costs from the use of quotas as a protectionist device. Economic gains to the producers and employees in the protected industries are often substantial, as measured by increased profitability. Industries wanting to limit foreign competition can exert a great deal of political pressure by lobbying for quotas. Consumers, however, bear the cost of this action because prices for the protected products are higher than they would be if there were freer trade, and the range of product choices to consumers is generally smaller.

See also: PROTECTIONISM

RANDOM WALK

Many economists and financial analysts contend that the price fluctuations of stocks are random, meaning that their movements from one time period to the next are unpredictable. The term used to describe this fact is random walk, meaning that the path of stock prices is random.

RATE OF RETURN ON SECURITIES

The rate of return on a security is a major factor associated with evaluating and selecting an investment. All security-pricing models involve computing the present values of future cash flows which the security is expected to pay. For common stocks, cash flows represent periodic cash dividends. For bonds, cash flows represent periodic coupon payments plus the face value of the bond at maturity.

Various methods are available for computing the rate of return on a security. The single period rate of return is one such measure. This rate is the percentage price appreciation plus the percentage cash return (current yield on a bond; dividend yield on a stock) during a given period. The rate is typically expressed as an annualized value. The single period rate of return can be computed using the following equation:

Single Period Return	=	Percentage Price Appreciation	+	Percentage Cash Return

$$R_t = \frac{P_t - P_{t-1}}{P_{t-1}} + \frac{C_t}{P_{t-1}}$$

where

R_t = the return during the period ending at date t
P_t = security price at date t
P_{t-1} = security price at date t-1
C_t = cash flow received at date t

The equation can also be used to measure future expected single-period returns. The symbol "E" is used to mean expected return, price, etc. The following data can be used to illustrate the computation of the actual rate of return on a stock and the expected rate of return on the stock:

Data	Description	Stock
P_0	Last year's closing price	$20.00
C_1	This year's cash flow	$1.00 dividend
P_1	Today's closing price	$18.00
$E(C_2)$	Next year's expected cash flow	$1.00 dividend
$E(P_2)$	Next year's expected closing price	$22.00

Last year's actual rate of return on the stock:

$$R_1 \text{ on stock} = \frac{\$18 - 20}{\$20} + \frac{\$1}{\$20} = -5.00\%$$

Expected returns for the coming year would be:

$$E(R_2) \text{ on stock} = \frac{\$22 - \$18}{\$18} + \frac{\$1}{\$18} = +27.8\%$$

RATIONAL EXPECTATIONS

Rational expectations theorists believe that households and firms utilize all available information about the economy and public policy when making decisions. Thus, if this prior belief is valid, then demand management policies will have no short-run or long-run effect on real output. Critics of this view point out that the empirical evidence does not support the prediction that the economy does not respond in the short run or long run to policy changes.

See also: POLICY INEFFECTIVENESS PROPOSITION

RATIOS

A ratio is an expression of a mathematical relationship between one quantity and another. The ratio of 400 to 200 is 2:1 or 2. If a ratio is to have any utility, the elements which constitute the ratio must express a meaningful relationship. For example, there is a relationship between accounts receivable and sales, between net income and total assets, and between current assets and current liabilities. Ratio analysis can disclose relationships which reveal conditions and trends that often cannot be noted by inspection of the individual components of the ratio.

Ratios are generally not significant of themselves but assume significance when they are compared with previous ratios of the same firm, ratios of other enterprises in the same industry, and ratios of the industry within which the company operates.

It is helpful to organize ratios in terms of areas to be analyzed and interpreted. At least three major areas can be identified:

1. Short-term liquidity

2. Capital structure (and long-term solvency)

3. Earnings and profitability

Short-term liquidity refers to the ability of a firm to meet its current obligations as they mature. The relationship of current assets to current liabilities is an important indicator of the degree to which a firm is liquid. Working capital and the components of working capital also provide measures of the liquidity of a firm.

The capital structure of an enterprise consists of debt and equity funds. The sources and composition of the two types of capital determine to a considerable extent the financial stability and long-term solvency of the firm. A company's capitalization usually depends on the industry, the financial position of the company, and the philosophy of management. Long-term debt and preferred stock can add "leverage" to a company's capital structure. Capital structure ratios provide information on the debt capacity of the company and its level of financial risk. Financing decisions frequently involve determining the type of arrangements to be used and the amount of indebtedness to be incurred.

Earnings and profitability performance ratios reflect the results of the profit-seeking activities of an enterprise. Much of the data required for evaluating performance is obtained directly from the income statement which summarizes the results of operations. However, performance should be related to the assets which produce the earnings and to the way outsiders (for example, the stock market) perceive the performance and earnings of the enterprise. Measures of operating performance usually provide answers to the following questions: How much profit does the company make on each dollar of investment? How much profit does the company make on each dollar of sales? The profitability of investment usually relates to the following:

1. Return on total assets (total investment)
2. Return on invested capital (debt and equity)
3. Return on owners' investment (shareholders' equity)

The profitability of sales focuses on specific contributions of purchasing, production, administration and overall profitability as reflected in gross profit margin, operating profit margin, and net profit margin.

Several important profitability ratios are referred to as market value ratios. Most of these ratios relate to the valuation of stock and are of considerable importance to financial analysts and stockholders.

These ratios include earnings per share, dividends per share, yield on common stock, dividend payout, and book value per share of common stock. Major financial ratios are illustrated in Exhibit R-3. Data for the problem illustrated is provided in Exhibits R-1 and R-2.

See also: FINANCIAL STATEMENT ANALYSIS
FORECASTING FINANCIAL REQUIREMENTS
LEVERAGE
LIQUIDITY
RETURN ON INVESTMENT
WORKING CAPITAL

References:

Woelfel, Charles, J., *Financial Statement Analysis* (Probus, Chicago, Ill., 1988).

Coleman, Almand, et al., *Financial Accounting and Statement Analysis: A Manager's Guide* (Robert F. Dame, Richmond, Va., 1982).

Exhibit R-1

R. N. Services Company
Balance sheet
December 31, 19X0 and 19X1

	19X1	19X0
Assets		
Current assets:		
Cash	$ 50,000	$ 35,000
Marketable securities	100,000	65,000
Accounts receivable	200,000	250,000
Inventories	80,000	60,000
Total current assets	430,000	400,000
Property, plant, and equipment	1,000,000	800,000
Less accumulated depreciation	(600,000)	(500,000)
	400,000	300,000
Goodwill	100,000	125,000
Total assets	$1,330,000	$825,000
Liabilities and shareholders' equity		
Current liabilities		
Accounts payable	$ 100,000	$100,000
Notes payable	15,000	15,000
Income taxes payable	100,000	85,000
Total current liabilites	215,000	200,000
Long-term debt:		
Bonds and notes payable	500,000	350,000
Total liabilities	715,000	550,000
Stockholders' equity:		
Common stock, 10,000 shares outstanding	250,000	200,000
Contributed capital in excess of par	100,000	100,000
Retained earnings	265,000	25,000
Total equity	615,000	325,000
Total liabilities and shareholders' equity	$1,330,000	$825,000

Exhibit R-2

R. N. Services Company
Income statement
For the years ended December 31, 19X0 and 19X1

	19X1	19X0
Net sales	$625,000	$225,000
Costs and expenses		
Cost of goods sold	100,000	70,000
Selling and administrative expense	150,000	100,000
Interest expense	50,000	30,000
Total costs and expenses	300,000	200,000
Income before income taxes	325,000	25,000
Income taxes	75,000	5,000
Net income	250,000	20,000
Retained earnings at beginning of period	25,000	5,000
Dividends	10,000	0
Retained earnings at end of period	$265,000	$ 25,000

Additional information:
Market price per share of common stock, $75.
Average daily purchases of inventory, $50,000.

REALIZATION

Realization refers to the process of converting noncash resources and rights into money, and this term is used in accounting and financial reporting to refer to sales of assets for cash or claims to cash. The terms realized and unrealized identify revenues or gains or losses on assets sold and unsold, respectively. Accrual accounting recognizes revenue as being realized when it is earned. Under accrual-basis accounting, revenue is usually realized when it is earned. Revenue is generally considered as being earned when the earning process is completed and an exchange has taken place. For example, a manufacturer makes and then sells a product. Revenue is realized when the sale takes place (and not when the product is manufactured) because the earning process is substantially completed and an exchange took place. Revenue from sales of products is often recognized at the date of sale, usually interpreted to mean the date of delivery to customers. Revenue from services rendered is recognized when services have been performed and are billable. Revenue from permitting others to use enterprise resources, such as interest, rent, and royalties, is recognized as time passes or as the resources are used.

Exhibit R-3
Financial Statement Ratios

Ratio	Formula	Solution to case	Interpretation
Liquidity ratios			
a. Current (or working capital) ratio	$\dfrac{\text{Current assets}}{\text{Current liabilities}}$	$\dfrac{\$430,000}{\$215,000} = 2$	Short-term debt-paying ability (i.e., dollar amount of current assets from which to obtain funds necessary to liquidate each dollar of current liabilities).
b. Acid-test (or quick) ratio	$\dfrac{\text{Quick assets, i.e., cash marketable securities, receivables}}{\text{Current liabilities}}$	$\dfrac{\$350,000}{\$215,000} = 1.6$	A more severe test of the short-term debt-paying ability than the current ratio since it excludes inventory (which awaits sale) and prepaid expenses.
c. Cash ratio	$\dfrac{\text{Cash}}{\text{Current liabilities}}$	$\dfrac{\$50,000}{\$215,000} = .23$	The severest test of short-term debt-paying ability.
Measures of the movement or turnover of current assets and liabilities			
a. Receivables turnover	$\dfrac{\text{Sales (net)}}{\text{Average receivables (net)}}$	$\dfrac{\$625,000}{\$225,000} = 2.7$	The efficiency in collecting receivables and in managing credit.
b. Age of receivables	$\dfrac{365}{\text{Receivables turnover}}$	$\dfrac{365}{2.7} = 135$	The number of days it takes on the average to collect accounts receivable: the extent of control over credit and collection.
c. Inventory turnover	$\dfrac{\text{Cost of goods sold}}{\text{Average inventory}}$	$\dfrac{\$100,000}{\$70,000} = 1.4$	Marketability of inventory, efficiency in the management of inventory, and the reasonableness of the quantity of inventory on hand.
d. Days in inventory	$\dfrac{365}{\text{Inventory turnover}}$	$\dfrac{365}{1.4} = 261$	The average number of days required to use or sell inventory (e.g., the average period that an item is held in inventory). For a manufacturing company, the number of days should correspond closely with production time.
e. Working capital turnover	$\dfrac{\text{Net sales}}{\text{Average working capital}}$	$\dfrac{\$625,000}{\$207,500} = 3$	The extent to which a company is using working capital to generate sales.
f. Number of days' purchases in ending accounts payable	$\dfrac{\text{Accounts payable}}{\text{Average daily purchases}}$	$\dfrac{\$100,000}{\$50,000} = 2$	The extent to which the company is paying its bills promptly.
Solvency ratios			
1. Measures of capital structure:			
a. Owners' equity to total assets	$\dfrac{\text{Total owners' equity}}{\text{Total assets (net)}}$	$\dfrac{\$615,000}{\$1,330,000} = .46$	Proportion of firm's assets provided by owner.

Exhibit R-3—Continued

Ratio	Formula	Solution to case	Interpretation
b. Owners' equity to total liabilities	$\dfrac{\text{Total owner's equity}}{\text{Total liabilities}}$	$\dfrac{\$615,000}{\$715,000} = .86$	Relative claims of owners and creditors to rest of firm.
c. Fixed assets to total equity	$\dfrac{\text{Total owners' equity}}{\text{Fixed assets (net)}}$	$\dfrac{\$615,000}{\$400,000} = 1.53$	Relationship of owners' investment to the company investment in fixed assets (i.e. the higher the ratio, the less owners' capital is available for working capital).
d. Book value per share of common stock	$\dfrac{\text{Common stock equity}}{\text{Number of common shares outstanding}}$	$\dfrac{\$615,000}{10,000} = \$61.50$	Net assets reported on financial statement per share of common stock.
2. Measures of debt structure (debt management):			
a. Total liabilities to total assets	$\dfrac{\text{Total liabilities}}{\text{Total assets (net)}}$	$\dfrac{\$715,000}{\$1,330,000} = .53$	Protection available to creditors and the extent to which the company is trading on equity.
b. Total liabilities to owners' equity	$\dfrac{\text{Total liabilities}}{\text{Owners' equity}}$	$\dfrac{\$715,000}{\$615,000} = 1.2$	Relationship between total debt and equity financing. "What is owed to what is owned."
Profitability (earnings) ratios			
1. Net income to sales	$\dfrac{\text{Net income}}{\text{Net sales}}$	$\dfrac{\$250,000}{\$625,000} = .4$	Profit margin per dollar of sales.
2. Operating ratio	$\dfrac{\text{Cost of goods sold} + \text{operating expenses}}{\text{Net sales}}$	$\dfrac{\$100,000 + \$150,000}{\$625,000} = .4$	Profit margin per dollar of sales.
3. Sales to total assets (or asset turnover)	$\dfrac{\text{Net sales}}{\text{Average total assets}}$	$\dfrac{\$625,000}{\$1,077,000} = .57$	Productivity of all assets in generating sales.
4. Earnings per share of common stock	$\dfrac{\text{Net income-preferred dividend requirements}}{\text{Average number of common stock}}$	$\dfrac{\$250,000}{10,000} = \$23$	Return on common shareholders' investment per share of

Exhibit R-3—Continued

Ratio	Formula	Solution to case	Interpretation
5. Price/earnings ratio	Market price per share of common stock / Net income per share of common stock	$75 / $25 = $3	Price paid for stock per dollar of earnings (i.e., the price of earnings). Newspaper include this information in daily stock tables.
6. Dividends yield	Annual cash dividends per share of common stock / Market price per share of common stock	$1 / $75 = .013	Cash yield or return on common stock.
7. Return on investment (or return on assets)	Net income / Average total assets	$250,000 / $1,077,000 = .23	Return on investment in total assets. Sometimes net operating income is used as the numerator while intangibles and investments are excluded from the denominator.
8. Return on common stockholders' equity	Net income / Average common stockholders' equity	$250,000 / $470,000 = .53	Return on the investment by common stockholders.
9. Payout ratio	Cash dividends / Net income	$10,000 / $250,000 = .04	The extent to which a company distributes current earnings to stockholders in the form of dividends i.e. the "generosity" of the Board of Directors.
10. Cash flow from operations per share of common stock	Net income adjusted for noncash items / Average number of shares of common stock outstanding	$395,000 / 10,000 = $39.50	The amount of cash generated from operations for each share of stock.

Modification of the revenue realization principle described above include the following:

1. *Revenue recognized during production.* In long-term construction contracts, contractors can recognize revenue during the construction period using the percentage-of-completion method. This method can be used when the contract price is definite, when a reasonable estimate can be made of progress towards the completion of the project, and the costs incurred or to be incurred are known or can be estimated.

2. *Revenue recognized at the completion of production.* Revenue is sometimes recognized when production is completed. Precious minerals and some agricultural commodities trade in markets which have a readily determinable and realizable market price. Revenue could be recognized for such product when production is completed and before a sale occurs.

3. *Revenue recognized when cash is collected.* When considerable uncertainty exists concerning the collectability of an account, revenue can be recognized as cash is received after the sale. The installment sales method or the cost recovery method would be appropriate for recognizing revenue under these circumstances.

See also: CONSTRUCTION-TYPE CONTRACTS
INSTALLMENT SALES METHOD
MEASUREMENT
RECOGNITION
REVENUE
SALES WITH RIGHT OF RETURN
SERVICE SALES TRANSACTIONS

Reference:

SFAC No. 5, *Recognition and Measurement in Financial Statements* (FASB, 1984).

RECEIVABLES

A receivable is a claim against others for the future receipt of money, goods, or services. Receivables include accounts receivable (sometimes called trade receivables), installment sales receivable, notes receivable, receivables from officers or employees, claims against insurance companies for damages to property, and many other claims.

Accounts receivable arise from the sale of goods or services on account. A major problem associated with accounts receivable is determining what recognition should be given to the possibility that the amount owed may not be collected. The allowance method and the direct write-off method are employed to deal with uncollectible accounts. Under the allowance method, an estimate of uncollectible accounts is made at the end of each accounting period and reported in the income statement as an expense. On the balance sheet, estimated uncollectible receivables are deducted from the gross amount of accounts receivable. This deduction serves as a contra asset or valuation account. The estimated amount of uncollectible accounts is determined as a percentage of credit sales for the period, a percentage of the ending accounts receivable, or by aging the accounts receivable. The allowance method is used when there is high probability that some receivables will not be collected and when the seller can estimate the dollar amount considered to be uncollectible. When the direct write-off method is used, the account is written off and an expense is recognized in the income statement when a customer actually defaults on payment. The write-off method cannot be used when uncollectible amounts are significant and can be estimated.

See also: AGING SCHEDULE
             FACTORING
             NOTES RECEIVABLE

RECOGNITION

Recognition is the process of formally including an item into the financial statements of an entity such as an asset, liability, revenue, or expense. Items are recognized in the statements in both words and numbers. An item and information about the item must meet four fundamental recognition criteria to be recognized, subject to a cost-benefit constraint and a materiality threshold:

1. *Definition*—The item must meet the definition of an element of financial statements.

2. *Measurability*—It has a relevant attribute measurable with sufficient reliability.

3. *Relevance*—The information about it is capable of making a difference in users' decisions.

4. *Reliability*—The information is representationally faithful, verifiable, and neutral.

The amount of revenue recognized in the financial statements is measured by different attributes (for example, historical cost, current cost, current market value, net realizable value, and present value of future cash flows).

Revenues and gains are generally not recognized as components of earnings until realized or realizable and earned. The basic rule is that revenue is recognized when the earning process is completed and an exchange has taken place. This is usually at the point of sale or when a service has been performed. Certain departures from this principle are allowed.

See also: ASSETS
ELEMENTS OF FINANCIAL STATEMENTS
EXPENSES
LIABILITIES
MEASUREMENT
QUALITATIVE CHARACTERISTICS OF ACCOUNTING INFORMATION
REALIZATION
REVENUE

Reference:

SFAC No. 5, Recognition and Measurement in Financial Statements (FASB, 1984).

REFUNDING

Refunding refers to the replacement of an existing debt issue through the sale of a new issue. The issuing of new bonds and the cancellation of the old issue are considered two separate transactions. Retiring the old bonds results in a realized gain or loss equal to the difference between the carrying amount of the bonds and the price paid to retire the bonds. The gain or loss is recognized in the accounting period when the bonds are retired and is not deferred to be amortized in future periods.

See also: BOND

REGRESSION ANALYSIS

It is hypothesized in regression analysis that a variable Y is functionally related to a set of independent variables. In the bivariate (two variable) case, there is only one independent variable, X; therefore, Y = f(X).

In a linear regression model, the observed values of the variable Y are assumed to depend on the observed values of X as:

$$Y_i = a + bX_i + \varepsilon_i$$

for i = 1 . . . n observations and for ε an error term.

For a set of data on the variable Y and X, there will be one straight line that fits the scatter of these data better than any other straight line. That line is called the linear regression line. Ordinary least-squares regression analysis defines the best straight line to be the one for which the sum of the squared error terms is a minimum.

Nearly every statistical software package has a routine for estimating a regression line.

REGRESSIVE TAX

A tax that takes a smaller percentage from higher income individuals than from lower income individuals is a regressive tax. Overall, Social Security is a regressive tax because there is a maximum income limit beyond which no taxes are paid. Therefore, very wealthy individuals pay a lower percentage of their total income to Social Security than do lower income individuals.

RELATED PARTY TRANSACTIONS

For accounting purposes, related parties may be any of the following: affiliates; principal owners and close kin; management and close kin; parent companies and subsidiaries; equity method investors and investees; trusts for the benefit of employees, such as pension or profit-sharing trusts managed by or under the trusteeship of management; or any other party that can significantly influence the management or operating policies of the reporting enterprise, to the extent that it may be prevented from operating in its own best interest. Such other parties could include an officer or director of a corporation, a stockholder, and a partner or joint venturer in a partnership or venture. An affiliate is a party that controls, is controlled by, or is under common control with another enterprise, directly or indirectly. Principal owners are owners of more than 10 percent of an enterprise's voting interest. Management includes persons who have policy-making and decision-making authority within an enterprise and who are responsible for attaining an enterprise's objectives. Next of kin refers to immediate family members whom a principal owner or a member of management might control or influence or by whom they might be controlled or influenced because of the family relationship.

In related party transactions, one party is in a position to control a transaction or the effect of a transaction on another party. In such situations, a conflict of interest or transactions with insiders may occur. Examples of related party transactions that commonly occur in the normal course of business include the following: sales; purchases; transfers of realty and personal property; services received or furnished; use of property and equipment; borrowings and lendings; guarantees. Transactions between related parties cannot be presumed to be arm's-length transactions.

Financial statements must include disclosures of material, related party transactions, except compensation arrangements, expense allowances, and other similar items in the normal course of business. Disclosure shall include the nature of the relationship, a description of transaction(s), dollar amount of transactions, and amounts due to and from related parties. An auditor's responsibility in related party transactions is to make reasonable inquiry to determine that all material relationships are identified and disclosed and that such transactions do not violate fiduciary relationships.

See also: ARM'S-LENGTH TRANSACTION
AUDIT
FRAUD
SUBSTANCE OVER FORM

REORGANIZATION

Reorganization under Chapter 11 of the Bankruptcy Reform Act of 1978 contemplates the continuation of the business enterprise and its eventual rehabilitation, rather than Chapter 7 bankruptcy which has for its purpose the orderly liquidation and distribution of the estate to creditors according to their rank. Chapter 11 is primarily available for businesses although individuals are eligible. The major purpose of this chapter is to allow debtors to adjust their debts, satisfy or modify liens on property, and avoid a liquidation case under Chapter 7. Filing a petition under Chapter 11 effectively stays the debtor's creditors.

A Chapter 11 process involves the following procedures:

1. Proceedings are initiated either voluntarily by the debtor or involuntarily by at least three creditors with claims of at least $5,000 (where more than 12 creditors exist); fewer than three creditors with $5,000 or more in claims where less than 12 creditors exist;

2. the court may appoint a trustee who has custody of the property; a creditors' committee typically comprised of the largest creditors is established;

3. a plan of reorganization is proposed; a debtor in possession has exclusive right to file a plan during the first 120 days after the date of the order for relief; if a trustee has been appointed or if the debtor's plan has not met the 120-day deadline, other parties may file a plan; whoever proposes the plan must come forward with a disclosure statement which provides specific information about the debtor, its history and prospects, and details about the plan;

4. the court may approve or disapprove this informational document;

5. the plan and disclosure statement are submitted to those whose claims and interest are impaired by the plan;

6. finally, if the plan has been accepted by every class of impaired creditors and equity security holders, the court confirms the plan if specified minimum criteria are satisfied (for example, if it is in best interests of creditors and is feasible). Confirmation of the reorganization plan discharges a nonbusiness debtor from most if not all of its debts.

See also: BANKRUPTCY
LIQUIDATION
QUASI-REORGANIZATION
SOLVENCY and INSOLVENCY

Reference:

Ginsberg, Robert E., *Bankruptcy* (Prentice-Hall, Englewood Cliffs, N.J., 1985).

REPURCHASE AGREEMENT

A repurchase agreement, or "repo," is simply a collateralized loan, in which U.S. Treasury bills are used most commonly as the source of collateral. Under a repurchase agreement the borrower will "sell" securities such as treasury bills under an agreement which requires him to buy the securities back from the lender on a fixed date for a fixed price. The lender in this kind of transaction, having "bought" the securities from the borrower, has a corresponding obligation to sell them back to the borrower on the fixed date for the fixed price.

The repurchase price can include an interest component, or the sale and repurchase prices can be the same with interest paid separately for the use of the acquired funds. Usually the repurchase price will be less than the market value of the securities so that the lender has a margin for protection should the borrower default on his obligation to repurchase the securities (that is, repay the loan).

A reverse repo is simply the same transaction from the perspective of the lender. For example, a commercial bank may "buy" government securities from a dealer under a reverse repo. In this case, the bank is the lender, and the dealer is the borrower. Under this kind of arrangement, the bank acquires the obligation to sell the securities back to the dealer (that is, the borrower) at some fixed date for a fixed price.

Repurchase agreements may be done on an overnight basis, for a fixed term, or on the basis of a continuing contract. Fixed-term repos are usually made for less than 30 days. When executed under a continuing contract, repo contracts usually contain a clause to adjust the interest rate on a day-to-day basis.

Interest rates on overnight repurchase agreements usually are lower than the federal funds rate by as much as 25 basis points. The additional security provided by the loan collateral employed with repos lessens their risk relative to federal funds and is responsible for the lower rate. Thus, if a depository institution owns treasury securities, it can raise funds in the repo market more cheaply than borrowing federal funds. Because borrowing in the repo market is a close substitute for borrowing federal funds, the repo rate is closely tied to the federal funds rate. Federal Reserve credit policies largely determine the overnight rate on both repos and federal funds.

Repurchase agreements are usually negotiated in large dollar amounts. Overnight repos and term repos with maturities of one week or less are often arranged in amounts of $25 million or more. Transactions of at least $10 million are common on repos with maturities greater than one week.

The use of repos became common after World War II among a few government security dealers and large money center banks. Since the 1960s, however, the volume of transactions and the number of participants have grown substantially. In 1985, the annual average volume of transactions outstanding on the books of major government security dealers amounted to $320 billion, or almost three times the volume reported in 1981. Repos have proved to be exceedingly popular cash-management vehicles for individuals, firms, and governments with unpredictable cash flows. The popularity of repos stems from the ease with which they can be tailored to specific amounts and maturities to meet the needs of individual market participants.

In recent years, along with the very rapid growth of the repos have come several very widely publicized scandals involving the failure of government security dealers like the Lion Capital Group in New York, ESM in Florida, and BBS in New Jersey, who were heavily involved in the repo market. When these firms went under, a large number of investors

542 RESEARCH AND DEVELOPMENT COSTS

that included financial institutions and local governments sustained heavy losses.

What caused these failures and what investors should do to protect themselves against the possibility of future losses arising from similar failures were explored in the September 1985 issue of the *Economic Review* published by the Federal Reserve Bank of Atlanta. The author of this study concluded that losses can be avoided if investors "(1) operate under the terms of a clearly specified and executed master repurchase agreement, (2) properly assess counterparties including their corporate structure and capital strength, (3) use appropriate procedures for obtaining control of securities, and (4) evaluate securities appropriately and monitor them regularly, making margin calls when necessary."

See also: MONEY MARKET
    TREASURY BILLS

References:

Lumpkin, Stephen A., "Repurchase and Reverse Repurchase Agreements," in Timothy Q. Cook and Timothy D. Rowe, eds., *Instruments of the Money Market* (Richmond, VA: Federal Reserve Bank of Richmond, 1986), pp. 65-80.

Tschinkel, Sheila L., "Repurchase Agreement: Taking a Closer Look at Safety," *Economic Review*, Federal Reserve Bank of Atlanta (September 1985), pp. 4-9.

RESEARCH AND DEVELOPMENT COSTS

According to the FASB, research and development costs are those costs related to developing new products or processes, service, or technique, or modifying existing ones. Research is a planned search or critical investigation aimed at discovery of new knowledge; development refers to bringing research findings into a plan or design for further action. Development includes the conceptual formulation, design, and testing of product alternatives, construction of prototypes, and operation of pilot plants. It does not include routine or periodic alterations to existing products, production lines, manufacturing processes, and other ongoing operations.

All research and development costs should be charged to expense when incurred. This implies that the future expected value of research and development cost does not merit recognition as an asset because of the risks, uncertainties, and estimates involved.

The cost of materials, equipment, and facilities that are acquired or constructed for research and development activities and that have alternative future uses should be capitalized when acquired or constructed. However, when such equipment and facilities are used, the depreciation of such items and the materials consumed should be included as research and development costs. Activities that normally are considered research and development costs include the following:

1. Laboratory research aimed at discovery of new knowledge

2. Searching for applications of new research findings or other knowledge

3. Testing in search for or evaluation of product or process alternatives

4. Modification of the formulation or design of a product or process

See also: INTANGIBLE ASSETS

References:

Link, Albert N., *Research and Development Activity in U.S. Manufacturing* (Praeger, New York, 1981).

SFAS No. 2, Accounting for Research and Development Costs (FASB, 1974).

RESERVE REQUIREMENTS

Reserve requirements are funds that depository financial institutions (commercial banks, savings banks, savings and loans, Edge Act corporations and credit unions) are required by law to set aside as reserves against possible withdrawals by depositors. The Depository Institutions Deregulation and Monetary Control Act of 1980 gave the Federal Reserve System (Fed) the power to set uniform reserve requirements for all depository institutions.

The Fed requires that financial institutions maintain their required reserves in the form of cash in their vaults or as deposits at their regional Federal Reserve Bank. Currently, the Fed pays no interest on funds deposited in reserve deposit accounts. Institutions which are not members of the Federal Reserve System may maintain reserves balances with a regional Federal Reserve Bank indirectly on a pass-through basis with certain approved institutions.

Having the power to set reserve requirements gives the Fed an important tool that can be used to affect the money supply and the profitability of financial institutions. If it raises reserve requirements, the Fed reduces the amount of deposits that financial institutions can maintain, resulting in a decline in the supply of money. In addition, since reserve balances earn no interest, raising the level of required reserves lowers the profitability of depository institutions. Alternatively, a reduction in reserve requirements leads to an expansion of the money supply and an increase in the profitability of banking institutions.

Changing reserve requirements is such a powerful policy instrument and the effects of such changes are so profound that the Fed employs this instrument very seldomly. Instead, it normally uses its open market operations to pursue its monetary objectives. The reserve requirement tool is brought into use only in real financial crises.

Some economists have suggested that reserve requirements be abolished altogether because of their deleterious effects on bank profitability. Others, like Milton Friedman, have argued for 100 percent reserve requirements, asserting that such requirements would give the Fed better control over the money supply. Both of these proposals are extreme and adoption of either appears remote.

See also: FEDERAL RESERVE SYSTEM

RESERVES

Reserve is an accounting term that is used only to describe an appropriation of retained earnings. The major purpose of appropriating retained earnings is to provide more information to the users of the financial statements. Only the board of directors can appropriate retained earnings. Reasons for appropriating retained earnings include contractual agreements requiring such appropriations (for example, a bond indenture may place a limitation on dividends), state law (for example, required by some states when treasury stock is acquired which could impair the capital of the company), and voluntary actions by the board to retain assets in the business for future use. The creation of a reserve is the result of an accounting entry (shown below) and does not set aside cash or any other asset of the company. This term has been used in the past as a valuation account (for example, Reserve for Depreciation) and as a liability whose amount is uncertain (for example, Reserve for Income Taxes). The term should no longer be used for such purposes.

A Reserve account for unspecified contingencies would be created by transferring an amount from Retained Earnings to the Reserve account.

Retained Earnings (Debit)	50,000	
Reserve (or Appropriation) for Contingencies (Credit)		50,000

When the reserve for contingencies is no longer needed, the appropriation can be returned to retained earnings.

Reserve (or Appropriation) for Contingencies (Debit)	50,000	
Retained Earnings (Credit)		50,000

The return of the appropriation to retained earnings increases unappropriated retained earnings without affecting the assets or current position of the company.

If an enterprise desires to set aside cash or other assets to provide for the contingencies, it can do so by establishing a fund (not a reserve). This action would represent a transaction which has economic significance. The establishment of the fund could be made as follows:

Contingency Fund (an asset) (Debit)	50,000	
Cash (Credit)		50,000

See also: RETAINED EARNINGS
                 SHAREHOLDERS' EQUITY

RESPONSIBILITY ACCOUNTING

Responsibility accounting focuses on the collection of data to place responsibility for cost incurrence on managers to achieve cost control. The emphasis is on people—who incurred the costs. Responsibility accounting is also referred to as profit-centered accounting and performance reporting.

Responsibility accounting is based on these assumptions:

1. All spending can be controlled.

2. Responsibility for spending must be assigned and assigned fairly.

Assigning responsibility in an organization requires that authority to act be clearly assigned, and that when responsibilities are assigned, commensurate authority to carry out those responsibilities also be assigned. These relationships are usually presented in the organizational chart and the chart of accounts. The organizational chart should reflect a plan of organization that provides an appropriate segregation of functional responsibilities. Accounting reports should be prepared to summarize the performance of each responsibility center. Such reports should include only those items over which the center has control (see Exhibit R-4 on the following page).

Responsibility accounting requires that costs be collected by responsibility centers so that individuals assigned responsibilities can receive appropriate performance reports. Management practice has accepted four major types of responsibility centers:

1. *Expense (or cost center):* An organizational unit that is held accountable for the incurring of expense.

2. *Revenue center:* An organizational unit that is held accountable only for revenue.

3. *Profit center:* An organizational unit that is held accountable for revenue and expense.

4. *Investment center*: An organizational unit whose management is held accountable for attaining a satisfactory rate of return on capital.

Exhibit R-4
Responsibility Accounting Reports

RESPONSIBLE COMPANY
Assembly Shop A
Foreman Report
March 31, 19☐1

Expense	Budget		Actual		Variances Favorable/(Unfavorable)	
	This Mo.	Year to Date	This Mo.	Year to Date	This Mo.	Year to Date
Direct material	$ 15.000	$ 45.000	$ 16.000	$ 50.000	$(1.000)	$ (5.000)
Direct labor	30.000	90.000	25.000	80.000	5.000	10.000
Supplies	5.000	10.000	5.500	12.000	(500)	(2.000)
Other	100.000	250.000	90.000	295.000	10.000	(45.000)
	$150.000	$395.000	$136.500	$437.000	$13.500	$(42.000)

RESPONSIBLE COMPANY
Plant Superintendent: Plant 1
Plant Expense Report
March 31, 19☐1

Expense	Budget		Actual		Variances Favorable/(Unfavorable)	
	This Mo.	Year to Date	This Mo.	Year to Date	This Mo.	Year to Date
Assembly Shop A	$150.000	$ 395.000	$136.500	$ 437.000	$13.500	$(42.000)
Assembly Shop B						
Assembly Shop C			(Details omitted)			
Assembly Shop D						
Superintendent's office						
	$500.000	$1.300.000	$490.000	$1.280.000	$10.000	$ 20.000

RESPONSIBLE COMPANY
Vice-President Manufacturing
Expense Report
March 31, 19☐1

Expense	Budget		Actual		Variances Favorable/(Unfavorable)	
	This Mo.	Year to Date	This Mo.	Year to Date	This Mo.	Year to Date
Plant No. 1	$ 500.000	$1.300.000	$ 490.000	$1.280.000	$ 10.000	$ 20.000
Plant No. 2						
Plant No. 3			(Details omitted)			
Vice-President's office						
	$3.000.000	$9.300.000	$3.100.000	$9.500.000	$(100.000)	$(200.000)

RESPONSIBLE COMPANY
President
Expense Report
March 31, 19☐1

Department	Budget		Actual		Variances Favorable/(Unfavorable)	
	This Mo.	Year to Date	This Mo.	Year to Date	This Mo.	Year to Date
Manufacturing	$3.000.000	$ 9.300.000	$3.100.000	$ 9.500.000	$(100.000)	$(200.000)
Purchasing						
Sales						
Treasurer			(Details omitted)			
Controller						
President's office						
	$9.000.000	$27.700.000	$9.500.000	$28.300.000	$(500.000)	$(600.000)

See also: CENTERS
CONTROL FUNCTION
DECISION MAKING
GOALS and OBJECTIVES
MANAGEMENT
MOTIVATION
ORGANIZATIONAL BEHAVIOR
ORGANIZING FUNCTION
PERFORMANCE EVALUATION
PLANNING FUNCTION

Reference:

Miller, Elwood L., *Responsibility Accounting and Performance Evaluations* (Van Nostrand Reinhold, Florence, Kentucky., 1982).

RETAIL METHOD

The retail inventory method is a procedure that can be used to estimate inventory on a specific date. The retail method is widely used by department stores and other retail and wholesale enterprises. In order to estimate ending inventory by the retail method, the following information must be available: beginning inventory at cost and at retail; net purchases during the period at cost and at retail values for the period. The following example illustrates the computation of ending inventory which involves computing a ratio of cost to retail of goods available for sale and then applying this ratio to the ending inventory taken at retail to convert it to the ending inventory at cost.

Modifications of this procedure are required for the following situations: additional markups and markup cancellations, and markdowns and markdown cancellations require adjustments to the computations. Markups refer to an additional markup on original sales price; markup cancellations are decreases in prices of merchandise that had been marked up above the original retail price. Markdowns are decreases below the original sale prices; markdown cancellations are decreases of markdowns arising when prices of previously marked down merchandise are increased but not to exceed the markdowns.

	At Cost	At Retail	Ratio
Inventory, January 31	$50,000	$75,000	
Purchases (net) during the period	300,000	450,000	
Goods available for sale	$350,000	525,000	0.6667
Less: January sales		425,000	
Inventory, January 31, at retail		100,000	
Inventory, January 31, at cost:			
$100,000 × 0.6667	$ 66,667		

See also: INVENTORY

RETAINED EARNINGS

Retained earnings are earnings of the corporation which have not been distributed in the form of dividends. The major factors that affect retained earnings include the following:

1. Net income or loss, including income (loss) from continuing operations, discontinued operations, extraordinary gains or losses, and the cumulative effects of changes in accounting principles.

2. Dividends (cash, property, script, stock, liquidating).

3. Prior period adjustments, primarily the correction of errors of prior periods.

4. Appropriations of retained earnings (legal, contractual, and discretionary).

A deficit is a negative retained earnings balance. A deficit is usually the result of accumulated prior net losses or dividends in excess of earnings.

See also: ACCOUNTING CHANGES
CAPITAL
DEFICIT
DIVIDENDS
EXTRAORDINARY ITEM

INCOME
RESERVES
STATEMENT OF RETAINED EARNINGS

RETURN ON INVESTMENT

Return on investment (ROI) is a comprehensive measure of financial performance. The basic formula for computing return on investment involves the following:

ROI = Capital turnover × Margin as a percentage of sales

$$= \frac{\text{Sales}}{\text{Capital employed}} \times \frac{\text{Net income}}{\text{Sales}}$$

The relationship of ROI to balance sheet and income statement items is shown in Exhibit R-2. Note that ROI is computed in this exhibit as follows:

ROI = Turnover × Earning Ratio

where
Turnover   =   Sales/Capital Employed, and
Earning Ratio
   (or Margin) =   Net Income/Sales

Capital turnover is the ratio of sales to capital employed in generating the sales. Capital turnover is a measure of the use of assets in relation to sales. Generally, the larger the volume of sales that management can generate on a given investment in assets, the more efficient are its operations. Margin is the ratio of net income to sales.

Capital employed can be interpreted to mean total assets, total assets less current liabilities (that is, working capital plus noncurrent assets), or stockholders' equity. When management performance is being evaluated, either the first or second concept of capital employed should be used because management should be held responsible for assets available to them.

When stockholders' equity is used as the measure of capital employed, the analysis stresses the long-range ability of the firm to make use of the investments of its owners.

The ROI formula takes into account all of the items that go into the balance sheet and income statement, and so represents a comprehensive overview of performance. Exhibit R-5 shows a structural outline of the relationships that make up ROI.

Various actions that can be taken to improve ROI include the following:

1. Increase total sales by increasing volume, sales price, or some combination thereof, while maintaining or improving the margin on sales.
2. Decrease expenses, thereby increasing net income.

Exhibit R-5
Return on Investment (ROI) Relationships

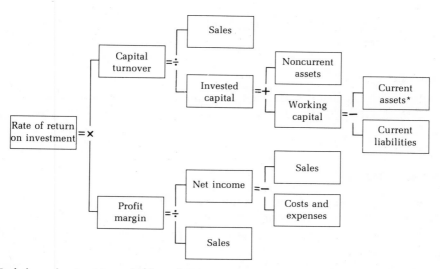

*Includes cash, accounts receivable, and inventory

3. Reduce the amount of capital employed (for example, reduce the inventory level, improve collection of accounts receivable) without decreasing sales.

Advantages claimed for ROI analysis include the following:

1. Focuses management's attention upon earning the best return on total assets.

2. Serves as a measure of management's efficiency and effectiveness.

3. Integrates financial planning, budgeting, sales objectives, cost control, and profit-making activities.

4. Provides a basis for comparing companies.

5. Provides a motivational basis for management.

6. Identifies weaknesses in the utilization of assets.

See also: FINANCIAL STATEMENT ANALYSIS
RATIOS

Reference:

Woelfel, Charles J., and Charles Mecimore, *The Operating Executive's Handbook of Profit Planning Tools and Techniques* (Probus, Chicago, 1986).

REVENUE

Revenue represents actual or expected cash inflows (or the equivalent) that have occurred or will eventually occur as a result of the enterprise's ongoing major or central operations during the period. Gains are not revenue. Gains are increases in equity (net assets) from peripheral or incidental transactions of an entity and from all other transactions and other events and circumstances affecting the entity during a period except those that result from revenues or investments by owners.

Revenue arises primarily from one or more of the following activities:

1. Selling of products.
2. Rendering services.
3. Permitting others to use the entity's assets (leasing, renting, lending).
4. Disposing of assets other than products.

Recognition is the process of formally recording an item in the financial statements of an entity. Revenues are generally recognized when the earning process is complete or virtually complete, and an exchange has taken place. The earning process consists of all those activities that produce revenue, including purchasing, production, selling, delivering, administering, and others.

Revenue is usually recognized at the time of sale of a product or when services have been rendered. Revenue is sometimes recognized before the point of sale. For example, the percentage-of-completion method is sometimes used to recognize revenue from long-term construction contracts. Some long-term service contracts recognize revenue on the basis of proportional performance. Revenue is sometimes recognized after the point of sale where there is great uncertainty about the collectibility of the receivable involved in a sale. Under such circumstances, revenue can be recognized on the installment method or cost recovery method when cash is collected.

See also: CONSTRUCTION-TYPE CONTRACTS
ELEMENTS OF FINANCIAL STATEMENTS
GAINS
INCOME
INCOME STATEMENT
INSTALLMENT SALES METHOD
MEASUREMENT
PRODUCT FINANCING ARRANGEMENTS
REALIZATION
RECOGNITION
SALES
SALES WITH RIGHT OF RETURN
SERVICE SALES TRANSACTIONS

References:

SFAC No. 3, *Elements of Financial Statements of Business Enterprises* (FASB, 1981).

SFAC No. 5, *Recognition and Measurement in Financial Statements of Business Enterprises* (FASB, 1984).

REVERSING ENTRIES

After the accounting records have been adjusted and closed at the end of the accounting period, reversing entries can be made on the first day of the new period to turn around (or reverse) certain adjusting entries. This accounting procedure often simplifies the recording of certain transactions in the new period. For example, assume the following adjusting entry was made to record accrued salaries:

> December 31
> Salaries Expense (Debit)   5,000
> Salaries Payable (Credit)   5,000

The reversing entry on January 1 of the new year is as follows:

> January 1
> Salaries Payable (Debit)   5,000
> Salaries Expense (Credit)   5,000

See also: ACCOUNTING SYSTEM
                ADJUSTING ENTRIES
                CLOSING ENTRIES

REVIEW

A review is defined as "performing inquiry and analytical procedures that provide the accountant with a reasonable basis for expressing limited assurance that there are no material modifications that should be made to the statements in order for them to be in conformity with generally accepted accounting principles or, if applicable, with another comprehensive basis of accounting." The objective of a review is to provide the accountant with a basis for expressing limited assurance that there are no material modifications that should be made to the financial statements.

See also: AUDIT
              COMPILATION

Reference:

Burton, John C., et al., *Handbook of Accounting and Auditing* (Warren Gorham & Lamont, Inc., Boston, 1981).

RISK

Risk is the probability that the actual return on an investment will differ from its expected return. For example, a Treasury bill is considered by many investors to have practically no risk. This cannot be said of a 30-year bond of any major corporation in the United States. Risk is the major constraint on investments; return on investment is the major opportunity or benefit. Other constraints on investments include taxes and the cost of investing. Large potential risks are associated with large potential returns. Small potential risks are associated with small potential returns. Investors are typically risk averse. They will not assume risks for the sake of assuming a risk nor will they incur a given level of risk without being reasonably compensated for doing so. Investors have various risk-return tradeoffs which are reflected in their investing activities.

Risks associated with investing are identified as the interest rate risk, market risk, inflation risk, business risk, financial risk, and liquidity risk. The interest rate risk results from changes in the level of interest rates. Security prices move inversely to interest rates. Interest rate risks are associated primarily with bonds, but they can also affect stocks. The market risk refers to the variability in returns resulting from fluctuations in the market. All investments in securities are subject to the market risk. The inflation risk refers to a loss in purchasing power due to the changes in the general purchasing power of the dollar. The inflation risk is directly related to the interest rate risk. Interest rates tend to rise as inflation increases; lenders demand premiums to compensate them for loss in purchasing power. The business risk refers to the risk of investing in a particular business or industry. The financial risk refers to the risk related to the use of debt financing by companies. Companies that use debt rather than equity to finance their assets typically assume a larger financial risk than those that do not. Financial risk and leverage are closely linked. The liquidity risk is the risk associated with securities which cannot be purchased or sold quickly and without major price concessions. The more uncertainty there is concerning the liquidity of an investment the larger the liquidity risk.

See also: CAPITAL ASSET PRICING MODEL
INVESTING
INVESTING METHODS AND STRATEGIES
RATE OF RETURN ON SECURITIES

RULE OF 69

The rule of 69 states that an amount of money invested at i percent per period will double in 69/i + 0.35 periods. For example, at 10 percent per period, a sum will double in 69/10 + 0.35 = 7.25 periods.

RULE OF 72

The rule of 72 refers to the computation of the time it takes for money at interest to double. It is computed as [72/interest rate]. For example, principal invested at 6 percent will double in approximately 12 years (72/6).

See also: INTEREST

RULE OF 78

The rule of 78 is a procedure followed by some finance companies for allocating interest on loans among the months of a year using the sum-of-the-months'-digits basis when equal monthly payments from the borrower are to be received. For example, the sum of digits from 1 through 12 is 78. Therefore, 12/78 of the year's earnings are allocated for the first month of the contract, 11/78 to the second month, etc.

See also: INTEREST

Ss

SALES

Sales revenue includes the gross charges to customers for the goods and services provided during the accounting period. Net sales are gross sales less any sales returns or allowances available to customers and sales discounts taken by credit customers.

Sales are major business transactions involving the delivery of goods, merchandise, services, properties, and rights in exchange for cash or money equivalents, such as accounts and notes receivable. Most sales represent the normal, ongoing transactions of the enterprise. Other sales may be incidental, unusual in nature, and infrequent in occurrence. For accounting purposes including recording and reporting, sales are usually classified as regular sales, sales from discontinued operations, and extraordinary sales on the income statement. Sales can also be classified according to the outline presented in Exhibit S-1.

See also: REVENUE
SALE-LEASEBACK
SALES WITH RIGHT OF RETURN
SERVICE SALES TRANSACTIONS

Exhibit S-1
Classification of Sales

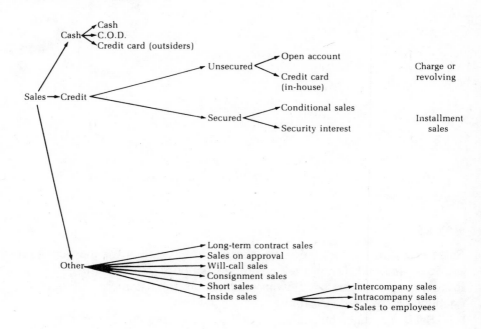

SALE-LEASEBACK

A sale-leaseback transaction is an arrangement whereby an owner sells property and then immediately leases it back from the buyer. The lessee often enters into such a lease to get working capital and to obtain certain tax advantages that might be involved. The lessor usually enters into such an arrangement because it is a profitable investment.

From an accounting viewpoint, the sale and the leaseback are considered as a single transaction involving a secured loan. When certain conditions are met, any profit from the sale is deferred and amortized in proportion to the amortization of the leased asset, if a capital lease is involved, or in proportion to rental payments over the time the asset is used if an operating lease is involved.

See also: LEASES
                SALES

SALES WITH RIGHT OF RETURN

Sales contracts often permit the buyer to return merchandise for a full refund or allow for an adjustment to be made to the amount owed. Such contracts are common in such industries as publishing, records and tapes, and sporting goods.

Where a right to return exists, revenue is not recognized from the sale until all of the following criteria are met:

1. The sales price is fixed or determinable at the date of sale.

2. The buyer has paid or will pay the seller and the obligation is not contingent upon resale of the product.

3. The buyer's obligation to the seller would not be changed by theft or damage to the merchandise.

4. The buyer has an economic substance apart from the seller.

5. The seller does not have sufficient obligations for future performance to bring about directly the resale of the product by the buyer.

6. The amount of future returns can reasonably be estimated.

See also: REALIZATION
RECOGNITION
REVENUE
SALES

Reference:

SFAS No. 48, *Revenue Recognition When Right of Return Exists* (FASB, 1981).

SATISFICING

Managers, like consumers, will allocate their resources—time, talent, energy, etc.—in such a way so as to maximize their overall well being. Thus, the behavior of managers is not always in the best interest of the owners of an organization. For example, a manager may maximize short-term profits (or even something else unrelated to the financial health of the organization) in order to have a list of completed accomplishments. With such a list, a manager may be able to obtain another job at a higher salary. However, the organization in which he or she was originally employed bears the cost of this short-run behavior owing to the fact that it is in their best interest to maximize long-run profits. It is reasonable to ask why the owners of firms allow such myopic managerial behavior to occur, or why they fail to notice that long-run profits are not being maximized. Academic researchers who investigate this issue suggest that managers satisfice owners by performing at a minimum acceptable level, and then, once this level is reached, pursue activities to maximize their own well being.

See also: AGENCY THEORY

SCARCITY

Resources that are limited in quantity (and quality) are called scarce resources. Most resources are scarce. There are very few resources that everyone in the world has in abundance.

Scarcity refers to the limited availability and quantity of resources in relation to the unlimited needs and wants of human beings. Scarcity is a condition that faces every society.

See also: ALLOCATION

SECURITIES AND EXCHANGE COMMISSION

The Securities and Exchange Commission (SEC) is a governmental agency established in 1934 to help regulate the securities market in the United States. The SEC has three major responsibilities: ensuring the provision of full and fair disclosure of all material facts concerning securities offered for public investment, initiating litigation for fraud cases when detected, and providing for the registration of securities offered for public investment.

The SEC is responsible for the administration and enforcement of the following acts: Securities Act of 1933; Securities Exchange Act of 1934; Public Utility Holding Company Act of 1935; Trust Indenture Act of

1939; Investment Company Act of 1940; Investment Advisers Act of 1940.

The SEC's main office is in Washington, D.C., and it has regional and branch officers in major financial centers. The SEC is directed by five commissioners appointed by the President with the approval of the Senate. The SEC is organized as shown in Exhibit S-2 on the following page.

Public accountants deal primarily with the Corporate Finance Division and with the Office of the Chief Accountant. The Corporate Finance Division has primary responsibility to assure that the financial information given to the public in securities offerings is complete and not misleading. The Chief Accountant is the principal advisor to the commission on matters relating to accounting and auditing. Regulation S-X (Form and Content of Financial Statements), the Accounting Series Releases (ASRs), and a recently initiated series called Financial Reporting Releases (FRRs) are the major documents that prescribe the form, content, and methods used in reporting to the SEC. Although the SEC has developed its own rules and procedures, it has generally allowed the private sector to formulate generally accepted accounting principles.

See also: ACCOUNTING PRINCIPLES

References:

Pointer, Larry Gene, and Richard G. Schroeder, *Introduction to the Securities and Exchange Commission* (Business Publications, Plano, Texas, 1986).

Skousen, K. Fred, *An Introduction to the SEC* (South-Western, Cincinnati, Ohio, 1983).

SECURITIES MARKETS

Security transactions take place in either the primary market or the secondary market. In the primary market, the purchaser gives the original issuer of the security cash in exchange for the security. In the primary market, the original security issuer receives cash; the public now holds a security which did not previously exist. Weekly T-bill offerings by the U.S. Treasury and municipal bond sales by a city occur in the primary market. Following the primary offering of a security, the security is said to trade in

Exhibit S-2
The Organization of the SEC

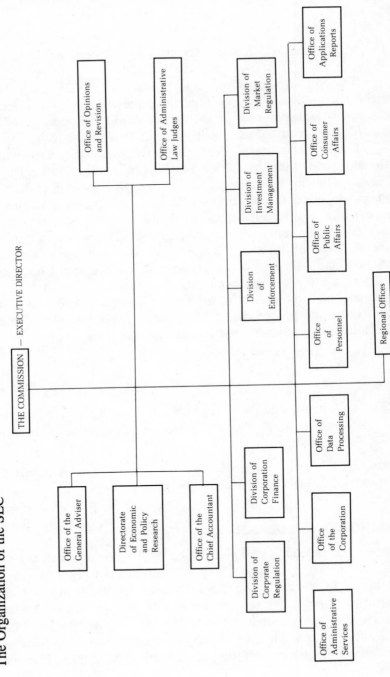

the secondary markets between members of the public. The New York Stock Exchange, the American Stock Exchange, and the Over-the-Counter market are considered secondary markets.

Investment bankers specialize in the creation and placement of securities in the primary market. These organizations provide advice, underwriting, and distribution services to their clients. The advice provided by investment bankers usually relates to the type of security offering (debt or equity), the timing of the offering, the legal characteristics of the issue, and the price at which the security can be sold.

Underwriting refers to the practice of investment bankers to absorb the price risks the issuer is unwilling to accept. Underwriting takes various forms:

1. *Firm commitment*: The underwriter commits to purchase the full amount of the issue from the seller at an agreed upon price. The banker then re-offers the security to the public. The underwriter's spread represents compensation to the underwriter. The investment banker frequently forms a purchase group consisting of other investment bankers who participate in the purchase of the securities. The lead underwriter is primarily responsible for negotiating the agreement with the issuer and maintaining the records.

2. *Stand-by agreement*: The underwriter agrees to help sell the new issue at a given period of time. After this period passes (often 30 days), the underwriter is required to purchase any unsold securities at a predetermined price. Stand-by agreements are frequently used in stock sales which utilize a rights offering.

3. *Best-effort basis*: The banker acts as a broker and returns unsold securities to the issuer. The banker assumes no risk for unsold securities. Best-effort underwriting is often used when the issuer is confident that the issue can be sold or when the issuer is relatively small or not well established.

The distribution of securities is accomplished by various methods. Some issuers market their issues directly to the public (for example, the U.S. government). Common stock offerings using rights can often be marketed directly by the issuer. Syndicates consisting of investment bankers are often formed to assist in the distribution of securities. Members of the purchase syndicate frequently develop a selling group which actively distributes the securities to their clients. The selling group usually consists of members of the purchase group and various retail brokerage houses. A selling group agreement typically establishes the term of the agreement; the division of the underwriter spread among the manager, the purchase group, and the selling group; the accounting procedures; and requires that no member will sell beneath the offering price. During the early days of the offering to the public, the managing underwriter may stabilize the market by purchasing the security at a fixed price—a form of legal price manipulation.

Private placements refer to the distribution of securities to fewer than 25 private buyers. Private placements do not require registration with the SEC. Bond issues are frequently distributed through private placements.

The established stock exchanges and the over-the-counter market represent the secondary markets. On the New York Stock Exchange, members are classified as:

1. *Commission brokers*: Partners in a brokerage firm who execute orders for their clients on the floor of the exchange.

2. *Floor brokers*: Commission brokers who handle overflow transactions with the commission brokers.

3. *Floor traders*: Members who buy and sell solely for their own account.

4. *Specialists*: Members who are assigned a number of stocks in which they act as brokers by maintaining a limit book, and as dealers by selling and buying shares in which they specialize. Specialists provide a continuous and liquid market in securities.

Stock and bond transactions that are not handled on one of the organized exchanges are traded in the over-the-counter (OTC) market. This market is not centrally located but consists of a network of brokers and dealers who communicate by telephone or computer terminal. Mutual fund shares, many bank and finance stock, most corporate bonds, and U.S. government and municipal obligations are traded in the OTC market.

A third market in securities refers to OTC transactions in a security which occur on an organized exchange. Institutional investors often trade large blocks of stock in this market. Negotiated fees are typical in this market.

A fourth market in securities refers to transactions which occur directly between a buyer and a seller of a large block of securities. In the fourth market, brokers and dealers are eliminated. A wire network provides current information that subscribers are willing to buy or sell at specified prices.

Security commissions have been negotiating rates since May 1, 1975. Brokerage firms establish firm-wide rates that relate to types of transactions and classes of customers. Discount brokerage firms offer low commissions but provide little, if any, investment counseling and advice.

A flow chart of a trade execution is shown on the following pages in Exhibit S-3. Exhibit S-4 illustrates a flow chart of the clearing process.

See also: INVESTING
          INVESTMENT METHODS AND STRATEGIES

SEGMENT PERFORMANCE

A segment of a business is a part of an entity whose activities represent a major line of business or class of customer. A segment is a part of an enterprise that sells primarily to outsiders for a profit. Examples of a segment of a business include a subsidiary, a division, a department, a product, a market, or other separations where the activities, assets, liabilities, and operating income can be distinguished for operational and reporting purposes.

Information about segments of a business, especially for diversified companies, is useful to investors of large, complex, heterogenous, publicly-traded enterprises in evaluating risks, earnings, growth cycles, profit characteristics, capital requirements, and return on investments that can differ among segments of a business. The need for segment information is the result of many environmental factors including the growth of conglomerates, acquisitions, diversifications, and foreign activities of enterprises.

A reportable segment is determined by the following procedures:

1. Identifying the enterprise's products and services

2. Grouping the products and services into industry segments

Exhibit S-3

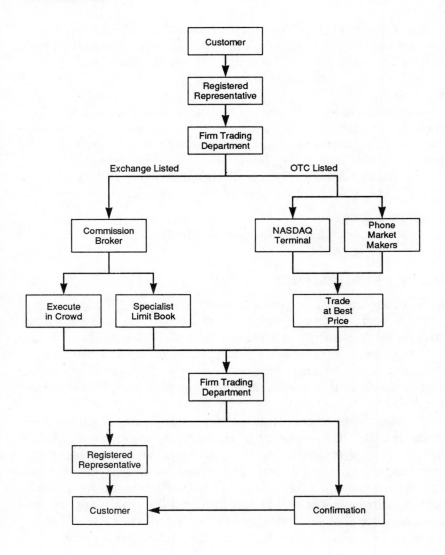

Source: Robert C. Radcliffe, *Investment: Concepts, Analysis, and Strategy,* Scott, Foresman and Company, Glenview, Ill., 1982.

Exhibit S-4

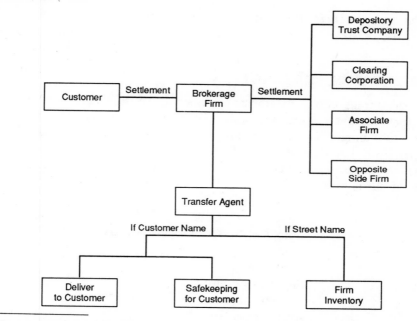

Source: Robert C. Radcliffe, *Investment: Concepts, Analysis, and Strategy*, Scott, Foresman and Company, Glenview, Ill., 1982.

3. Selecting the significant industry segments by applying various tests established for this purpose

Segment information that must be disclosed in financial statements includes an enterprise's operations in different industries, foreign operations and export sales, and major customers. Detailed information relating to revenues, segment's operating profit or loss, and identifiable assets along with additional information must be disclosed. Segment information is primarily a disaggregation of the entity's basic financial statements.

See also: CONTROL FUNCTION
PERFORMANCE EVALUATION
PLANNING FUNCTION

Reference:

SFAS No. 14, *Financial Reporting for Segments of a Business Enterprise* (FASB, 1976).

SERVICE SALES TRANSACTIONS

Service sales transactions are transactions between a seller and a buyer in which, for a mutually agreed price, the seller performs, agrees to perform, or agrees to maintain readiness to perform an act or acts, including permitting others to use enterprise resources that do not alone produce a tangible commodity or product as the principal intended result (FASB). Examples of types of business that offer services include the following:

> Advertising Agencies
> Computer Service Organizations
> Employment Agencies
> Entertainment
> Engineering Firms
> Retirement Homes
> Accounting Firms
> Architecture Firms
> Law Firms
> Travel Agencies

Revenue from service transactions is recognized on the basis of the seller's performance. Performance is the execution of a defined act or acts and occurs with the passage of time. Four methods of recognizing revenue include the following:

1. Specific performance method

2. Completed performance method

3. Proportional performance method

4. Collection method

When performance of services consists of the execution of a single act, revenue should be recognized when that action takes place—the specific performance method. For example, when dental service consists solely of the extraction of a tooth and the tooth is pulled, revenue would be recognized at that point. When services are performed in more than a single act and the final act is so significant in relation to the service transaction taken as a whole that performance cannot be considered to have taken place until the execution of that act, revenue should be recognized only on the completion of the final act—the completed performance method. For example, revenue would be recognized by a moving company when the household furniture was transported to its destination. When performance consists of the execution of more than one act, revenue should be recognized based on the measurement of the sales value of each act—the proportional performance method. For example, recognition of revenue by an accounting firm for stages of work performed in auditing assignments, tax preparations, and related tasks would be on the proportional performance method. If a significant uncertainty exists with regard to the realization of service revenue, revenue should be recognized when cash is collected.

See also: REALIZATION
RECOGNITION
REVENUE
SALES

Reference:

FASB, FASB Invitation to Comment (FASB, 1978).

SHAREHOLDERS' EQUITY

The excess of assets over liabilities (or net assets) of a corporation represents shareholders' equity. This represents the book value of claims of the owners to a share in the entity's assets after debts have been settled. The claims of certain classes of owners may have priority over others, especially where there is common and preferred stock outstanding. The preferred stock would usually have a higher priority but limited rights to share in the net assets and earnings of the corporation. Common stockholders would have a residual interest in the assets and earnings.

Shareholders' equity is increased when shares are issued by the corporation and by additional equity capital arising from earnings, and is decreased by dividends, reacquisition of stock, or losses from operations. Other transactions can also change shareholders' equity.

See also: CAPITAL
CAPITAL STOCK
CORPORATION
PREFERRED STOCK
RESERVES
RETAINED EARNINGS
STATEMENT OF FINANCIAL POSITION

SINKING FUND

A sinking fund is a provision in a bond indenture contract (sometimes it is applied also to preferred stock) that obligates the issuing corporation to pay off a portion of the bond issue each year. Usually a sinking fund does not require that the corporation actually deposit monies in a fund from which the bonds are to be repaid at maturity, although this may be done on very rare occasions.

Typically, a sinking fund requires that the corporation retire a set percentage of the total bond issue each year in one of two ways, either by purchase on the open market or by calling in the bonds from holders to be redeemed at par. The corporation will choose the least-cost option to satisfy the sinking fund requirement. If the bonds are selling on the market at a discount, it will naturally want to try to buy bonds on the market. But if they are selling at a premium, it will want to redeem them at par.

Usually bond issues which require a sinking fund are considered safer for investors than those that do not, and because of this, they normally will carry a somewhat lower interest rate. While sinking funds generally benefit bondholders, the terms of the sinking fund occasionally may work to the detriment of some. For example, a bondholder may find that his bonds are called at par when they may be selling in the market for a premium. In such a case, the bondholder's yield to call may turn out to be substantially less than his expected yield to maturity.

See also: BOND
INDENTURE CONTRACT

SHORT RUN

The short run in economics is defined to be a period of time during which a firm is unable to vary all of its inputs. Generally, labor is variable but capital is not.

SOCIALISM

The hallmark of capitalism is the private ownership of property and the workings of markets. Under pure socialism, all property is owned by the state. Economic activity is not guided by market influences, but rather by a central plan. There are forms of socialism. The Soviet Union's is closer to pure socialism, but England, for example, only has some socialized programs such as medical care.

There are two important distinctions between capitalism and socialism regarding their economic impact. Under capitalism there is less income equality than under socialism. This is due, in part, to the role of profits in a capitalistic society. Also, under capitalism the growth of the economy is determined in large part by the private sector's investment and production activity as opposed to a central plan as under socialism.

See also: CAPITALISM
COMMUNISM

SOLVENCY AND INSOLVENCY

In a popular sense, solvency means that a business is able to pay its debts as they come due. Insolvency means that the business is unable to do so. In Section 101 of the Bankruptcy Reform Act of 1978, insolvency means a financial condition such that the sum of the entity's debts is greater than all of the entity's property at fair valuation. According to this definition, a corporation could be solvent even though it may be temporarily unable to pay currently maturing debts because of the insufficiency of liquid assets.

The ability of a firm to meet its short-term obligations as they come due is usually interpreted to refer to liquidity. Solvency and insolvency usually relate to long-term conditions.

A number of remedies are available to a firm that is in serious financial difficulty, ranging from voluntary agreements with creditors to involuntary arrangements. The courts may also become involved in the process. Nonjudicial and judicial remedies include the following:

Control	Nonjudicial	Judicial
Control by debtor	Extension of maturity date. Composition agreement.	Reorganization (debtor in possession)
Control by others	Creditor committee. Voluntary assignment.	Reorganization (trustee) Liquidation

Composition agreements are arrangements in which creditors accept a certain percentage of their separate claims in full settlement of those claims. Debtor and creditors may enter into a contractual agreement by which control of the debtor's business is given over to a committee formed by the creditors. In a voluntary assignment, a debtor executes a voluntary assignment of property to a trust for the benefit of the creditors. Reorganizations and liquidations are judicial methods for dealing with financially distressed companies.

In liquidations, a statement of affairs is usually prepared when a bankruptcy petition is filed. The statement of affairs outlines the legal status of the various creditors and the realizable value of the assets. A statement of realization and liquidation provides information to the court, debtors, and creditors concerning the progress being made in the liquidation of the business.

See also: BANKRUPTCY
            LIQUIDATION
            LIQUIDITY
            REORGANIZATION
            TROUBLED DEBT RESTRUCTURING

Reference:

Ginsberg, Robert E., *Bankruptcy* (Prentice-Hall, Englewood Cliffs, N.J., 1985).

SOURCES OF FINANCIAL INFORMATION

The nonprofessional investor has many sources of basic financial information available. Most brokerage houses distribute market letters and recommendations to customers. Major newspapers, journals, and periodicals are also available.

1. The Financial Press

   A. Newspapers (current business topics and market price data)

   > *Wall Street Journal* (daily)
   > *The New York Times* (daily)
   > *Commercial and Financial Chronicle* (weekly)
   > *Barrons* (weekly)
   > *M/G Financial Weekly* (weekly)
   > *Wall Street Transcript* (twice weekly)

   B. Journals and Periodicals (general investment topics)

   > *Business Week* (weekly)
   > *Financial World* (biweekly)
   > *Forbes* (biweekly)
   > *Finance* (monthly)
   > *Financial Executive* (monthly)
   > *Fortune* (biweekly)
   > *Institutional Investor* (monthly)
   > *Financial Analysts Journal* (bimonthly)
   > *OTC Review* (monthly)

2. Industry and Company (historical and statistical data)

   > *Statistical Abstract of the U.S.*
   > *Business Statistics*
   > Standard & Poors' *Statistical Service*
   >   *Basebook*
   > *Predicasts*
   > *U.S. Industrial Outlook*
   > *American Statistics Index*
   > U.S. Government Publications

3. Industry Data (general information)

    Dun & Bradstreet Key Business Ratios
    Robert Morris Associates' *Annual Studies*
    Value Line Investment Surveys
    Moody's Manuals

4. Company Data (general)

    Corporate Reports
    Security Prospectus
    SEC Reports (8-K, 9-K, and 10-K)
    Standard & Poors:
      Corporate Record
      Analysts Handbook
      Stock Reports
      Stock Guide
    Moody's Manuals
    Value Line Investment Service

5. Money Market and Bonds

    Money Manager (weekly)
    Weekly Bond Buyer (weekly)
    Bankers Trust Credit and Capital Markets
    Moody's *Bond Survey* (weekly)
    Value Line Options and Convertibles
    Moody's *Bond Record*
    Moody's *Municipal and Government Manual*
    Standard & Poors' *Bond Guide*
    Standard & Poors' *Convertible Bond Reports*

6. Miscellaneous Investment Advisors

    Value Line Options and Convertibles
    Vickers Guide to Investment Company Portfolios
    Weisenberger Investment Companies (annual)
    Investment Dealers Digest Mutual Fund Directory (semiannual)
    Mutual Fund Fact Book (Investment Company Institute)
    Commodity Yearbook
    Guide to World Community Markets

SPIN-OFF, SPLIT-OFF, SPLIT-UP

A spin-off is a distribution of subsidiary stock to the shareholders of the parent corporation giving them control of the subsidiary. The distribution is similar to an ordinary dividend distribution. A split-off is similar to a spin-off except that the shareholders in the parent corporation exchange some of their parent corporation stock for the subsidiary stock. A split-off is similar to a stock redemption. A split-up is essentially the distribution of the stock of two subsidiaries to shareholders of the parent in complete liquidation of the parent.

STAGFLATION

A simultaneous increase in the inflation rate and decrease in the level of aggregate output is called stagflation. The U.S. economy experienced stagflation as a result of the OPEC oil embargo that increased oil prices in 1973-1974. Aggregate supply decreased as firms adjusted to the higher cost of energy and, in many circumstances, looked for alternative sources of energy. The rate of inflation was increasing and output was decreasing.

STANDARD INDUSTRIAL CLASSIFICATION (SIC)

Industry groupings established by the Bureau of the Census within the Department of Commerce for classifying production activity are referred to as Standard Industrial Classifications (SIC). For example, within the manufacturing sector there are 20 major industrial groups, each coded by a two-digit classification number ranging from 20 through 39. These industry groups are referred to as two-digit SIC groups. These industries are listed in Exhibit S-5 on the following page. Within each two-digit SIC category there are a series of three-digit SIC industries corresponding to more finely defined product categories. For example, SIC 371 is motor vehicles and equipment within SIC 37. SIC categories go to the seven-digit level. SIC 3711321 is fire department vehicles.

STANDARDS

Standards provide several important economic functions:

1. *Information*: Verified data, terminology, test and measurement methods for evaluating and quantifying product attributes.

2. *Compatibility*: Properties that a product should have in order to be compatible with a complementary product or with other components within a system.

3. *Variety Reduction:* Limitations on the range or number of allowable levels of product characteristics, such as physical dimensions.

4. *Quality*: Specification of an acceptable level of product performance along one or more dimensions including reliability, durability, efficiency, safety and environmental impact.

Exhibit S-5
Two-Digit SIC Industries within the Manufacturing Sector

20: Food and kindred products
21: Tobacco manufactures
22: Textile mill products
23: Apparel and other textile products
24: Lumber and wood products
25: Furniture and fixtures
26: Paper and allied products
27: Printing and publishing
28: Chemicals and allied products
29: Petroleum and coal products
30: Rubber and misc. plastic products
31: Leather and leather products
32: Stone, clay, and glass products
33: Primary metal industries
34: Fabricated metal industries
35: Machinery, except electrical
36: Electric and electronic equipment
37: Transportation and related products
38: Instruments and related products
39: Miscellaneous manufacturing

STATEMENT OF CASH FLOWS

The Financial Accounting Standards Board (FASB) issued Statement of Financial Accounting Standards No. 95 which requires that a statement of cash flows be reported as a basic financial statement. The statement of cash flows replaces the statement of changes in financial position previously required by Accounting Principles Board Opinion No. 19. Statement No. 95 is effective for statements ending after July 15, 1988 with earlier application encouraged.

The Financial Accounting Standards Board outlined the importance of the statement of cash flows on funds flows, liquidity, and financial flexibility:

Funds Flows

Information about past cash flows or other funds flows may help users of financial statements improve their understanding of the activities of an enterprise, understanding the effects on funds flows of income-generating activities, and evaluate the investing and financing activities of an enterprise. In those and other ways the information may be used as a basis for making assessments of future cash flows associated with operating, investing, and financing activities.

Liquidity

Liquidity is an indication of the "nearness to cash" of the assets and liabilities of an enterprise. Nearness to cash can be regarded as the time that must elapse before assets and liabilities result in cash receipts and payments through normal operations. Information about liquidity may help to identify the relationship between income-generating activities and the related receipts and payments of cash. It also may help to identify the pay-back period on investments in operating assets. A short pay-back period may indicate a high level of financial flexibility.

Financial Flexibility

Financial flexibility is the capacity to adapt to favorable and unfavorable changes in operating conditions. For example, financial flexibility may enable an enterprise to undertake a new investment or to introduce a new product line. Equity investors may be particularly interested in this aspect of financial flexibility. When change has an adverse effect, financial flexibility may be critical to the survival of an enterprise. Declining funds flows from operations and reduced liquidity may signal an impending cash flow problem. The solvency of an enterprise may depend on its financial flexibility. Sources of financial flexibility include the ability to generate additional cash flows by financing, by liquidating assets, and by modifying operations. Information about past funds flows and the liquidity of assets and liabilities may be useful in assessing financial flexibility.

The statement of cash flows is a financial statement that reports cash flows relating to operating, financing, and investing activities of a company. Operating activities include all transactions and events that are not investing and financing activities. Such activities include revenues and expense transactions associated with the sale of products or the delivery of services, e.g., all activities that enter into the determination of net income. Investing activities include (a) lending money and collecting on those loans, and (b) acquiring the disposing of investments and productive long-lived assets. Financing activities involve liability and owner's equity items and include (a) obtaining cash from creditors and repaying the amounts borrowed, and (b) obtaining capital from owners and providing them with a return on their investment (dividends). (The statement of cash flows replaced the statement of changes in financial position, i.e., the funds statement.)

In the cash flows statement, cash flows include "cash and cash equivalents." Cash equivalents are short-term, highly liquid investments, such as treasury bills, commercial paper, and money market funds, purchased with cash that is the excess of immediate needs.

The statement of cash flows provides information about cash receipts and cash payments of an entity during a period. The statement helps investors and creditors assess the timing, amounts, and uncertainty of future cash flows. The statement of cash flows also provides information that can be used in (1) assessing the impact of operations on liquidity, and (2) assessing the relationship among cash flows from operating, investing, and financing activities. The statement helps users assess future cash flows, identify the relationship between net income and net cash flows, and provides information about the quality of income (e.g., the extent to which income has been turned into cash). The statement is also useful in understanding (1) the level of capital expenditures required to support ongoing and growing levels of activity, and (2) the major changes in the financing of a firm.

Cash flows from operating activities may be computed under either the direct method or the indirect method. When the direct method is used, the statement of cash flows reports cash inflows from operating activities as follows: (1) collections from customers, (2) interest and dividends collected, and (3) other operating receipts. A company reports its cash outflows from operating activities in four categories: (1) payments to suppliers and employees, (2) payments of interest, (3) other operating payments, and (4) payments of income taxes. When the indirect method of reporting operating activities is used in the statement, net income is adjusted for items included in the income statement that did not result in an inflow or outflow of cash from operating activities. The effect is to eliminate from net income any noncash transactions to determine the net cash flow from operating activities. The direct method of preparing a statement of cash flows is presented in the following statement:

ABC Company
Statement of Cash Flows
For the year Ended December 31, 19x5

Cash flows from operating activities:		
Cash received from customers	$76,000	
Cash disbursed for operating activities	21,000	
Cash provided by operating activities		55,000
Cash flows from investing activities:		
Purchase for plant assets	(8,000)	
Proceeds from sale of land	2,000	
Cash used by investing activities		(6,000)

(Continued)

Cash flows from financing activities

Proceeds of bond insurance	8,000	
Payment to retire bonds	(5,500)	
Proceeds from issuing capital stock	1,000	
Dividends paid	(1,500)	
Cash provided by financing activities		1,000
Net increase in cash		$50,000

The indirect method of reporting net cash flows from operating activities is illustrated as follows:

Net income	$100,000
Adjustments for differences between income flows and cash flows from operating activities:	
Depreciation expense	10,000
Increase in accounts receivable	(4,000)
Increase in inventory	(10,000)
Increase in accounts payable	12,000
Decrease in salaries payable	(3,000)
Amortization of bond premium	(1,000)
Net cash flow from operating activities	$104,000

Regardless of whether the direct or the indirect method is used, the amount reported as net cash flows provided (used) from operating activities will be identical. The direct method of reporting net cash flows from operating activities is preferred.

Cash flows associated with interest expense, interest revenue, and dividends earned are included in the computation of the net cash flows from operating activities. However, cash flows associated with dividends paid are included in financing activities.

Certain significant noncash transactions and other events that are investing or financing activities are omitted from the body of the statement of cash flows. Such items are included in either a separate schedule or a narrative description. Such items include the following:

1. The acquisition of assets by assuming liabilities by issuance of equity securities.

2. Exchanges of nonmonetary assets.

3. Financing of long-term debt.

4. Conversion of debt or preferred stock to common stock.

5. The issuance of equity securities to retire debt.

Stock dividends, stock splits, and appropriations of retained earnings are generally not reported.

Useful ratios using data from the statement of cash flows and income statement, and the balance sheet can be constructed:

1. *Quality of Earnings* (to support current level of operations and to generate future earnings)

    A. Net income to cash provided by operating income:
        Net income/Cash provided by operating activities

    B. Reinvestment activities:
        Capital investments/Depreciation + Proceeds from sale of assets

    C. Cash flow for adequacy:
        Cash provided by operating activities/Cash investments + Inventory additions + Dividends + Debt uses

2. *Financial Management* (reliance on outside financing for growth)

    A. Cash provided by sources:

        (1) Cash provided by operating activities/Total sources of cash

        (2) Cash provided by investing activities/Total sources of cash

        (3) Cash provided from financing activities/Total sources of cash

    B. Productivity ratio:
        Cash from operating activities/Capital investments

    C. Cash flow per share of outstanding common stock:
        Net increase in cash/Number of common shares outstanding

3. *Mandatory Cash Flows* (primarily interest and repayment of principal)

   A. Long-term debt payment ratio:
      Cash applied to long-term debt/Funds supplied by long-term debt

   B. Total fund sources required for long-term debt:
      Cash applied to long-term debt/Total cash

4. *Discretionary Cash Flows* (e.g., for dividends, to acquire other companies, to invest in short-term securities)

   A. Discretionary cash uses/Total sources of cash

   B. Individual discretionary use (e.g., dividends)/Total discretionary uses

   C. Dividend payout of cash from operating activities/Cash from operating activities

Reference:

"Statement of Cash Flows," FASB Statement No. 95 (Stanford, CN: FASB, 1987).

STATEMENTS OF FINANCIAL ACCOUNTING STANDARDS

Statements of Financial Accounting Standards are official pronouncements of the Financial Accounting Standards Board. The *Standards* are considered to be generally accepted accounting principles and are binding in accounting practice. The FASB employs due process procedures in the preparation and review of proposed standards before issuing them.

Rule 203 of the Rules of Conduct of the AICPA Code of Professional Ethics covers *Statements of Financial Accounting Standards:*

A member shall not express an opinion that financial statements are presented in conformity with generally accepted accounting principles if such statements contain any departure from an accounting principle promulgated by the body designated by Council . . . to establish such principles which has a material effect on the statements taken as a whole, unless the member can demonstrate that due to unusual circumstances the financial statements would otherwise have been misleading. In such cases, his report must describe the departure, the approximate effects thereof, if practicable, and the reasons why compliance with the principle would result in a misleading statement.

See also: ACCOUNTING PRINCIPLES
CONCEPTUAL FRAMEWORK OF ACCOUNTING
FINANCIAL ACCOUNTING STANDARDS BOARD
GENERALLY ACCEPTED ACCOUNTING PRINCIPLES
STATEMENT OF FINANCIAL ACCOUNTING CONCEPTS

Reference:

FASB, *Accounting Standards: Original Pronouncements* (McGraw-Hill, N.Y., 1985).

STATEMENT OF FINANCIAL POSITION

A statement of financial position (or balance sheet) is a report that shows the financial position of the enterprise at a particular moment of time, including the firm's economic resources (assets), economic obligations (liabilities), and the residual claims of owners (owners' equity). Assets are usually shown in the order of their liquidity (nearness to cash) and liabilities in the order of their maturity date.

The balance sheet is usually presented in one of the following formats:

1. Account form: Assets = Liabilities + Owners' Equity
2. Report form: Assets – Liabilities = Owners' Equity

The balance sheet discloses major classes and amounts of an entity's assets as well as major classes and amounts of its financing structure, including liabilities and equity. Major classifications used in the statement of financial position include the following:

1. Assets

    a. Current assets (cash, marketable securities, accounts receivable, inventory, prepaid expenses)

    b. Investments

    c. Property, plant, and equipment

    d. Intangible assets (patents, copyrights, goodwill)

    e. Deferred charges or other assets

2. Liabilities

    a. Current liabilities (accounts payable, notes payable, wages payable, accrued liabilities, unearned revenue)

    b. Long-term liabilities

3. Owners' Equity

    a. Capital stock

    b. Paid-in capital in excess of par or stated value

    c. Retained earnings

Working capital is the excess of current assets over current liabilities and can be computed from data shown on the balance sheet. This significant figure is useful in determining the ability of the firm to finance current operations and to meet obligations as they mature. The relationship between current assets and current liabilities is referred to as the current ratio and is a measure of the liquidity of the enterprise.

Balance sheets are usually presented in comparative form. Comparative statements include the current year's statement and statements of one or more of preceding accounting periods. Comparative statements are useful in evaluating and analyzing trends.

Assets and liabilities reported on the balance sheet are measured by different attributes (for example, historical cost, current (replacement) cost, current market value, net realizable value, and present value of future cash flows), depending upon the nature of the item and the relevance and reliability of the attribute measured. Historical cost is the exchange price of the asset when it was acquired. Current cost is the amount of cash or its equivalent required to obtain the same asset at the balance sheet date.

Current market value or exit value is the amount of cash that may be obtained at the balance sheet date from selling the asset in an orderly liquidation. Net realizable value is the amount of cash that can be obtained as a result of a future sale of an asset. Present value is the expected exit value discounted to the balance sheet date.

See also: ASSETS
CAPITAL MAINTENANCE THEORIES
CURRENT ASSET
CURRENT LIABILITY
FINANCIAL STATEMENTS
INTANGIBLE ASSETS
LIABILITIES
MEASUREMENT
PREPAID EXPENSE
PROPERTY, PLANT AND EQUIPMENT
RECOGNITION
SHAREHOLDERS' EQUITY

References:

SFAC No. 3, *Elements of Financial Statements of Business Enterprises* (FASB, 1981).

SFAC No. 5, *Recognition and Measurement in Financial Statements of Business Enterprises* (FASB, 1984).

STATEMENT OF RETAINED EARNINGS

The retained earnings statement reconciles the beginning and ending balances in the retained earnings account. This statement can be presented as a separate statement or in a combined statement of income and retained earnings. Generally accepted accounting principles require that a retained earnings statement be present whenever comparative balance sheets and an income statement are presented. A retained earnings statement reporting a prior-period adjustment would appear as follows:

Beginning retained earnings	$100,000
Deduct: Adjustment for failure to record	
depreciation prior year	10,000
Adjusted beginning retained earnings	90,000
Add: Net income for the period	110,000
	200,000
Deduct: Dividends	20,000
Retained earnings at end of year	$180,000

See also: INCOME STATEMENT
PRIOR-PERIOD ADJUSTMENTS

STOCK COMPENSATION PLANS

Most corporate compensation packages are either cash or stock. Currently bonuses are a function of both individual performance and corporate profits. Typical bonuses are a fixed percentage of corporate profit or of profits in excess of a specified return on stockholders' equity. Stock awards are assumed to create a positive relationship between the interests of top management and the shareholders. Disadvantages of stock awards include the possibility that top management will focus on short-term profits and/or an improper pattern of risk-behavior. Compensation plans for executives have been classified into three major categories:

1. *Market performance plans.* Market performance plans include compensation plans in which the value received by the employee depends solely on the market price, or movements in the market price, of the employer's stock. In the traditional plan the employee receives the right to purchase a specified number of a company's shares at a specified price over a specified period. In stock appreciation rights (SARs) plans, an employee is entitled to either cash or corporate stock in an amount equal to the excess of the market value of the company's stock over a predetermined price for a stated number of shares.

2. *Enterprise performance plans.* Enterprise performance plans are plans in which the value ultimately received by the employee depends solely on company performance. In performance unit plans, the employee is awarded performance units, each unit having a specified

dollar value based upon specified performance goals during the performance period (typically three to five years). Such plans are cash plans. Book value plans are similar to performance unit plans only they are related to changes in the book value of a company. Phantom stock plans are awards in units of numbers of shares of stock. After qualifying for the receipt of the vested units, the executive receives in cash the number of units multiplied by the current market price of the stock.

3. *Combination market—enterprise performance plans.* Such plans include those in which the value received by the employee depends on both company performance and the market price of the company's stock. Such a plan is similar to enterprise performance plans except that the award is in stock instead of cash. Junior stock plans and stock options with performance requirements fall under this category.

Various option pricing models have been proposed for management consideration. The minimum value option pricing method is expressed in a mathematical formula. The equation states that the value of a stock option cannot be negative and must be at least equal to the difference between the market value of the underlying stock and the present value (assuming a risk-free discount rate) of the sum of the exercise price and expected dividends during the exercise period. The minimum value of the stock option increases with:

an increase in the market value of the underlying stock
a decrease in the exercise price
a decrease in dividends paid by the company
an increase in the exercise period
an increase in the risk-free rate of return

The Black-Scholes option pricing model is more complex but similar to the minimum value option. The Black-Scholes option pricing model takes into consideration probability estimates relating to the future variation of the market price of the underlying stock. According to this model, the riskier the stock, the more valuable the option.

Formula based plans reduce some of the uncertainty and ambiguity about how performance will be evaluated. However, mechanistic formulas can lead to dysfunctional behavior. As a general rule, a company's incentive program should control for:

1. Increases or decreases in profits caused by accounting conventions instead of operating performance.

2. Increases in profits caused by the failure to adjust for price-level changes.

3. Increases in profits resulting from concentrating on short-term rather than long-term performance measures.

4. Actions that maximize divisional performance measures versus overall corporate welfare.

See also: MOTIVATION
              PERFORMANCE EVALUATION

STOCK DIVIDENDS

A stock dividend represents a distribution of additional shares of a corporation's own stock to its stockholders without consideration on a pro rata basis (that is, in proportion to the number of shares held). Stock dividends are usually motivated by a desire to give the shareholders some evidence of a part of their interests in accumulated corporate earnings without distributing cash or other property which the board of directors deems necessary or desirable to retain in the business.

A stock dividend does not change the enterprise's assets or shareholders' proportionate interests therein. Many shareholders look upon stock dividends as distributions of corporate earnings and usually in an amount equivalent to the fair value of the shares received, especially when the stock dividend is small (less than 20-25 percent of outstanding shares) because such dividends do not ordinarily reduce the market price of the shares. When the stock dividend is large, the market price of the shares typically declines but eventually tends to rise since a lower price can increase the demand for the shares.

When a small stock dividend is distributed, the corporation transfers from retained earnings to the category of permanent capitalization (capital stock and additional paid-in capital) an amount equal to the fair value of the additional shares issued. When a large stock dividend is distributed, the amount transferred is the amount established by legal requirements, which is usually legal capital.

See also: DIVIDENDS
LEGAL CAPITAL
RETAINED EARNINGS
STOCK SPLIT

STOCK OPTIONS

A stock option is the right to purchase shares of common stock in accordance with an agreement, upon payment of a specified amount. Stock option plans are compensation schemes under which executives are granted options to purchase common stock over an extended option period at a stated price. Nonstatutory stock options are not approved by the IRS Code and do not give special tax advantages to employees. Companies sometimes grant stock appreciation rights (SAR) that allow the employee to receive cash, stock, or a combination of cash and stock based on the difference between a specified amount per share of the stock and the quoted market price per share at some future date.

In compensatory stock option plans, the excess of the market price of the stock over the exercise price is considered the compensatory portion of the plan. This amount is computed on the date that the number of shares an individual employee is entitled to receive and the option or purchase price of the shares is known. This date is referred to as the measurement date. Compensation expense is recorded as the services giving rise to the stock option are rendered.

Where stock appreciation rights are concerned, total compensation expense to be allocated is estimated by the excess of the market value over the designated price. This amount is allocated to expense over the service period.

See also: OPTIONS
STOCK RIGHTS

STOCK RIGHTS

A stock right is the privilege attached to a share of common stock to purchase a specified number of shares of common stock or a fractional share. Stock rights indicate the price at which stock can be acquired (the exercise price), the number of shares that may be acquired for each right, and the expiration date. When a corporation issues stock rights to shareholders without compensation, one right is issued for each share. The number of rights required to purchase an additional share depends upon the agreement. Between the date on which the issuance of rights is announced and the date the rights are issued, the stock to which the rights relate is purchased and sold in the market rights on, which means that the value of the stock and the rights are united. After the rights are issued, the rights are traded separately from the stock and the stock is traded ex-rights.

Stock warrants (or stock-purchase warrants) are securities that give to the holder the ability to buy a specified number of shares of stock at a stated price for a specified period of time. Stock warrants do not pay current income. Warrants are often used to sell bonds or stock to make the securities more attractive when they are being issued. Warrants are purchased from the issuing firm or in the marketplace for cash. Stock rights are usually issued free to current stockholders who are entitled to purchase additional shares from a pending new issue of a stock in proportion to their present holdings (a preemptive right).

See also: STOCK OPTIONS

STOCK SPLIT

A stock split is a distribution of company's own capital stock to existing stockholders with the purpose of reducing the market price of the stock which would hopefully increase the demand for the shares. To accomplish the stock split, the par or stated value of the stock is adjusted. For example, a $10 par value stock that is split two for one will have a $5 par value after the split. Assume the following information about a stockholders' equity section of a corporate balance sheet. The stock is split 2:1. The effect of the stock split is illustrated on the following page.

Note that after the stock split, the components of stockholders' equity are the same as before the split. Only the par value of the shares and the number of shares outstanding have changed.

A reverse stock split is a stock split in which the number of shares outstanding is decreased.

	Before Stock Split	After Stock Split
Common stock, $10 par, 10,000 shares issued	$100,000	
Common stock, $5 par, 20,000 shares issued		$100,000
Additional paid-in capital	10,000	10,000
Retained earnings	90,000	90,000
Total	$200,000	$200,000

See also: STOCK DIVIDENDS

SUBSEQUENT EVENTS

Subsequent events refer to material events and transactions that occur after the balance sheet date but before the financial statements are issued. If the subsequent event, which provides additional evidence concerning conditions that existed on the balance sheet date, occurred after that date, the statements should not be adjusted. Disclosure should be made. For example, a lawsuit settlement after balance sheet date would require disclosure only.

See also: FINANCIAL STATEMENTS
FULL DISCLOSURE

SUBSTANCE OVER FORM

Financial accounting is concerned with both the economic substance and the legal form of transactions and events. When a conflict exists between the two, information concerning the economic substance of the transaction or event is considered more relevant, reliable, and representationally faithful than the legal form.

There are numerous accounting examples where substance takes precedence over the legal form of a transaction or event. For example, current accounting principles require that certain leases be reported as assets and liabilities even though the lessee does not have legal title to the property. Certain long-term notes receivable and payable are noninterest-bearing and legally have no claim to interest receipts or payments. In certain cases, accounting principles require that interest revenue and expense be recognized to reflect the time value of money. In computing earnings per share of common stock, convertible preferred stock and convertible bonds are sometimes considered common stock equivalents and used in the computation of earnings per share of common stock. In defining assets, the existence of future economic benefits is usually more important than legal ownership rights when considering whether an asset exists.

The concept of substance over form is not included as a qualitative characteristic of accounting information because it is a vague idea that is included in reliability and representational faithfulness.

The Internal Revenue Service often looks past the legal form of a transaction to its substance to determine its taxable status, especially in situations where the transaction has no valid business purpose other than saving taxes. Abusive tax shelters are a prime example of the application of substance over form by the IRS.

See also: CONSOLIDATED FINANCIAL STATEMENTS
DEFEASANCE
LEASES
PRODUCT FINANCING ARRANGEMENTS
QUALITATIVE CHARACTERISTICS OF ACCOUNTING
   INFORMATION
RELATED PARTY TRANSACTIONS
SALES WITH RIGHT OF RETURN
TAX SHELTERS

SUCCESSFUL-EFFORTS ACCOUNTING

Successful-efforts accounting for oil and gas operations capitalizes such costs as exploration, drilling, lease rentals associated with establishing the location of a natural resource only when the effort results in the discovery of a natural resource. Costs associated with unsuccessful wells are expensed. The full-cost method capitalizes the costs associated with all the wells, both successful and unsuccessful. Both methods of accounting for the cost of oil and gas properties are considered generally acceptable accounting methods and satisfy the needs of users of the financial statements. Large companies generally use successful-efforts accounting while smaller companies often use the full-cost method in order to reduce current expenses and increase income. Neither method reflects the economic substance of oil and gas exploration in that they do not include the current value of the oil and gas reserves in the statements.

See also: NATURAL RESOURCES

References:

AICPA, *Accounting and Reporting Practices in the Oil and Gas Industry* (AICPA).

Touche Ross & Co., *Oil & Gas Accounting: What Producers Must Know* (Touche Ross & Co., 1980).

SUPPLY CURVE

A supply curve or schedule is a graphical devise to illustrate that price and quantity supplied are positively related. The higher price is needed to provide the financial incentive for producers to make more of their product available, assuming all else remains constant. In the short run, a firm's supply curve is its marginal cost curve.

See also: MARGINAL COST

SUPPLY SIDE ECONOMICS

Supply-siders believe that excessive government purchases intended to stabilize the economy have, in fact, brought about growth only in the size of government and in deficit spending. Continuous deficits have crowded out private investment spending so that the growth rate of the nation's capital stock has been reduced. The growth of government has allocated resources to the public sector from the private sector, resulting in slower economic growth. Marginal tax rates have increased from the 1950s through the 1970s to pay for this growing public sector. Supply-siders believe in reversing these trends by shrinking the size of government and reducing the government's expenditures and regulatory influence. Supply-siders advocate supply management policies.

SURPLUS

The term "surplus" is generally disapproved for use in accounting. In law, surplus is defined as the excess of the net assets of a corporation over its stated capital; capital surplus refers to the surplus of the corporation other than earned surplus. In accounting, earned surplus has at times been used for retained earnings. This usage is not generally acceptable. Surplus suggests an excess that is not needed. In this sense, it is not particularly applicable to financial reporting.

In economics, the term surplus refers to a situation in which, at a given price, quantity supplied is greater than quantity demanded. To alleviate a surplus, price must fall.

See also: RETAINED EARNINGS
RESERVES

Tt

TAKEOVER

A takeover is a procedure whereby a company or individual attempts to acquire a target company. Takeovers were frequently attempted in the 1970s and 1980s in the United States. Takeovers can be either friendly or unfriendly. In a takeover, a formal tender offer to the stockholders of the target company is made stating that the acquirer desires to purchase their shares for a specified price during a specific period of time. The offer price is usually considerably above the current market price. The tender period is usually short, such as 60 or 90 days. The offer usually indicates the total number of shares the acquirers desire to acquire. By rejecting excessive shares, the acquirer hopes to be able to acquire such shares at a lower price following the takeover. Special terms associated with the takeover include:

Friendly takeover: a situation in which the management of the target company recommends to its stockholders that the tender offer be accepted. In a friendly takeover, the acquiring company usually purchases small amounts of the target company's shares in the open market until a significant percentage (such as 10 or 15 percent) is acquired. The acquirer makes an offer to management to acquire the remaining shares, of a major portion thereof, to company shareholders. Management may respond favorably, after which the acquirer makes a tender offer to the shareholders. If the management of the company recommends to its stockholders that the tender offer be rejected, the tender offer would represent a hostile tender offer.

Hostile tender offer: A situation in which the management of the target company recommends to its stockholders that the tender offer be rejected.

Shark repellent: Sections in a corporation's bylaws that are designed to discourage unfriendly takeovers. Such tactics include requiring a high percentage of the shareholders to approve a takeover.

Golden parachute: A strategy whereby the top management of the target company is to receive large rewards if the manager(s) positions are terminated as a result of a hostile takeover.

Greenmail: A situation involving the sale of shares acquired by the hostile acquirer back to the company, often   resulting at a handsome profit to the acquirer.

Poison pill: A situation in which the target company issues a very large amount of convertible preferred stock that can dilute the percentage of common stock to be acquired by the hostile acquirer or disposing of attractive assets to make the target company less attractive as a takeover prospect.

Pac-man: A strategy in which the target company tries to acquire the hostile takeoverer to foil the attempt.

White knight: A strategy of finding another company friendly to the target company to acquire it before it can be acquired by the hostile aggressor.

Scorched earth policy: A situation whereby the target company liquidates a significant portion of its assets to make the company undesirable to a suitor.

Leveraged buyouts: A takeover in which the acquirer arranges the transaction so that a significant amount of debt and a relatively small amount of equity capital is used to accomplish the buyout. In leveraged buyouts, assets acquired in the buyout are usually pledged as collateral for funds borrowed to purchase the target company.

TARIFF

A tariff is an excise tax imposed on imported goods. The purpose of a tariff is to increase the price of the imported products over that set by foreign manufacturers. Raising the price of imports gives domestic firms a price advantage in the marketplace and provides an incentive for domestic consumers to buy domestically-made products.

See also: PROTECTIONISM

TAX AVOIDANCE

Tax avoidance includes legal efforts by a taxpayer to arrange his/her tax-related transactions and affairs so as to reduce one's tax liabilities. Judge Learned Hand in S.R. Newman declared,

> Over and over again courts have said that there is nothing sinister in so arranging one's affairs as to keep taxes as low as possible. Everybody does so, rich or poor; and all do right, for nobody owes any public duty to pay more than the law demands: taxes are enforced extractions, not voluntary contributions. To demand more in the name of morals is mere cant.

The courts accept a corporation as being distinct from its shareholders. However, if it appears that a sham transaction occurs, the courts can rule that tax avoidance has taken place. For example, if there is no principal purpose for a tax-free acquisition, the courts can disallow deductions, credits or other allowances resulting therefrom. If there is a "principal purpose" other than stock avoidance, the taxpayer can have other purposes, such as tax savings.

TAX EVASION

Tax evasion involves illegal activities that are designed to reduce the tax liability. To be guilty of evading taxes, the individual must already have a tax liability.

See also: FRAUD
TAX AVOIDANCE

TAX INCIDENCE

Tax incidence refers to the individual(s) who actually bears the burden of the tax. Taxes on a retail store's activities can be passed forward to the buyer of the store's product, thereby shifting the incidence of the tax away from the store owner to the purchaser. Alternatively, the retailer could shift the incidence of the tax to his or her workers by lowering their salaries. If the retailer pays the tax from earned income, then there is not tax shifting and the incidence of the tax is the retailer, where it was originally intended.

TAX SHELTERS

A tax shelter is an investment at risk to acquire something of value, with the expectation that it will produce income and reduce or defer taxes and that its ultimate disposition will result in the realization of gain. Tax-sheltered investments are often public offerings that have been registered with the Securities and Exchange Commission for interstate sale, or with a state agency. Private offerings are not registered. Most tax shelters are structured as limited partnerships in which the investors are the limited partners. Subchapter S corporations are also used to structure a tax shelter. The tax losses generated by most tax-sheltered investments are attributable to deductions for depreciation and interest on borrowed funds that provide leverage for the investment. Investment tax credits and rehabilitation credits frequently add to the attractiveness of tax shelters.

Tax shelters have frequently been abused. An abusive tax shelter is a transaction without any economic purpose other than the generation of tax benefits. Such shelters frequently overstate the valuation of assets. The Internal Revenue Service disapproves of abusive tax shelters.

See also: PARTNERSHIP

Reference:

Arthur Andersen & Co., *Tax Shelters—The Basics* (Arthur Andersen & Co., 1982).

TAXES

Governments (federal, state and local) finance their expenditures through taxation. About 80 percent of the federal government's expenditures are financed from tax revenues.

Taxes are levied on the basis of two broad principles: the benefit principle and the ability-to-pay principle. The benefit principle of taxation suggests that those consumers who directly receive the benefits from public goods and services should themselves finance these expenditures. User taxes, for example gasoline taxes earmarked to finance highway construction and repair, are levied according to the benefit principle. This principle underlies the rationale for every citizen being taxed to pay for public goods, such as national defense.

The ability-to-pay principle of taxation is based on the equity concept that those who earn more can afford to pay more taxes. This principle underlies the U.S. individual income tax program. The more income a person earns, the larger the percentage of that income that is taxed.

See also: EXCISE TAX
PAYROLL TAXES
PROGRESSIVE TAX
PROPORTIONAL TAX
REGRESSIVE TAX

TECHNOLOGICAL CHANGE

Technological change refers to technology changing over time. The term technology has been used in a variety of ways. In a narrow sense, technology refers to specific physical tools, but in a broader sense it describes whole social processes.

One useful approach to this definitional issue is to conceptualize technology as the physical representation of knowledge. Any useful technological device is, in part, proof of the knowledge-based or informational assumptions leading to its creation. This informational view of technology implies that technology per se is an output from a consciously undertaken process. Such an idea highlights the role of research in the generation of technologies. Thus, technologies can be distinguished, although imperfectly, by the amount of embedded information. Underlying research and development expenditures is one such measure.

TENANCY

A tenancy in common is a form of co-ownership in which each tenant (owner) holds an undivided interest in property. The ownership interest of a tenant in common does not terminate upon the owner's prior death.

A joint tenancy is one which provides for the undivided ownership of property by two or more persons with the right of survivorship. Right of survivorship gives the surviving owner full ownership of the property.

A tenancy by the entirety is essentially a joint tenancy between husband and wife. As in a joint tenancy, upon the death of one tenant by entireties the entire title automatically and immediately vests in the survivor.

TRANSFER PAYMENTS

A transfer payment refers to an amount of money that an individual receives from the federal government as a grant. Literally, this money is transferred from the government to individuals.

TRANSFER PRICING

Divisions of an enterprise frequently buy and sell to one another. A price must be established for these transfers. This price is referred to as the transfer price. Various alternatives to establishing a transfer price include the following:

1. The transfer price should be set equal to the manufacturing cost of the selling division.

2. The transfer price should be the amount the selling division could sell the product to an outside firm.

3. The transfer price should be the amount the buying division could purchase the product for from an outside firm.

4. The transfer price should be a negotiated amount agreed upon by the buying and selling divisions.

5. The transfer price should be the costs incurred to the point of transfer plus the opportunity costs for the firm as a whole. The opportunity cost would be the next best alternative for the firm. For example, if the selling division was operating at less than full capacity, the opportunity cost would be zero. If the selling division was operating at full capacity, the opportunity cost would be the lost contribution margin (selling price minus variable costs) resulting from foregoing outside sales to sell to the buying division.

The choice of method depends upon a number of factors, such as the autonomy allowed to divisions, the degree of market competition, the extent to which the goals of the division are expected to correspond to the goals of the firm, short-run supply and demand relationships, and how divisions are evaluated by the firm.

See also: COST ACCOUNTING

TREASURY BILLS

Treasury bills (T-bills) are debt obligations of the U.S. Government that mature in one year or less. The U.S. Treasury regularly sells bills with maturities of three months, six months, and one year. All bills are sold at discount so that the return to the investor is the difference between the purchase price of the bill and its face or par value.

The volume of bills outstanding has grown very substantially in recent years because of the large federal budget deficits. By the second half of 1986, the outstanding volume totaled $411 billion, making T-bills the most popular money market instrument.

Treasury bills are held by a wide variety of investors including individuals, businesses, commercial banks, money market mutual funds, the Federal Reserve System, and foreigners. The popularity of T-bills stems from their unique characteristics. First, T-bills are considered to be essentially free from default risk. Second, they are highly liquid because there is a very large and efficient secondary market that enables investors to easily and quickly convert bills to cash. Third, the income earned on T-bills is exempt from state and local income taxes. And finally, bills are sold in minimum denominations as small as $10,000 and in multiples of $5,000, making them appropriate for the needs of both large and small investors.

The U.S. government first offered T-bills for sale in 1929. At present, the Treasury conducts public auctions of three- and six-month bills every week and one-year bills every month. Occasionally, the Treasury also sells "cash management" bills with maturities that have ranged from 3 to 168 days. These special issues are designed to bridge low points in the Treasury's cash inflows.

In order to reduce the cost of issue of the large volume of bills which the Treasury sells, T-bills are only issued in book-entry form. Purchasers do not receive actual physical certificates. Ownership is recorded in a book-entry account established at the Treasury, and investors receive only a receipt as evidence of purchase. The book-entry system for Treasury securities is a "tiered" custodial system whereby the ownership of T-bills is represented by entries on the books of a series of custodians. This system extends from the Treasury itself through the Federal Reserve Banks and depository institutions to the ultimate owner.

The weekly auctions of three- and six-month bills are held each Monday. The amount of bills that the Treasury intends to sell at each weekly auction is announced on Tuesday. Bids must be presented at the Federal Reserve Banks or their branches by 1:00 p.m. New York time of the day of the auction. Payment and delivery of bills is on Thursday following the Monday auction.

Potential investors may enter bids in two categories: competitive and noncompetitive. Under a competitive bid, the bidder states the amount of bills he is willing to purchase and the price he is willing to pay. Competitive bids are usually made only by large investors. Smaller investors may enter noncompetitive bids. A noncompetitive bidder states the quantity of bills he is willing to buy and agrees to pay a price equal to the weighted average price of bills sold to investors in the competitive-bid category. Noncompetitive bids are limited to a maximum of $1 million of each new offering.

The Treasury fills all noncompetitive bids first. In recent years, the volume of noncompetitive bids has averaged between 10 and 25 percent of the issues sold. The remainder of the issue after the noncompetitive bids have been filled is allocated to competitive bidders according to the price of their bid, from the top bidder down.

Investors wishing to buy bills other than at regular auction and those wishing to sell bills prior to maturity may do so easily in the secondary market. The secondary market in Treasury bills is the largest and most efficient of any money market instrument. One measure of its efficiency is the narrow spread between the bid and ask prices on bills. This spread is normally only between 2 and 4 basis points, that is only $200 to $400 per $1 million traded.

The secondary market in bills is maintained principally by a group of security dealers known as primary dealers. In 1986, there were 37 primary dealers, of which 14 were commercial banks. In addition, there is a large and growing number of secondary dealers.

Trading in bills takes place "over the counter," rather than on a formal exchange. Dealers are in almost constant contact over the telephone. Primary dealers are in contact also with the Federal Reserve, and the Fed conducts its open-market operations in government securities only through primary dealers. In 1987, the average daily volume of T-bills traded by primary dealers amounted to more than $40 billion.

The yields on T-bills are usually quoted on a discount basis using a 360-day year. For example, the yield on a 91-day (three-month) bill selling for $97.345 per $100 of face amount normally is calculated as follows:

$$(\$100 - \$97.345)/\$100 \times (360/91) = 10.5\% \qquad \textbf{(1)}$$

To convert this to a bond-equivalent yield, the discount should be divided by the purchase price and a 365-day year should be used as follows:

$$(\$100 - \$97.345)/\$97.345 \times (365/91) = 10.9\% \qquad \textbf{(2)}$$

In this example the bond-equivalent yield is substantially higher than the discount yield.

Another factor to remember in comparing yields on T-bills with those on other securities is that interest on T-bills is exempt from state and local income taxes. Accordingly, the T-bill rate should be adjusted upward to put it on an equivalent basis with an instrument that is fully taxable. For example, a T-bill having a bond-equivalent yield of 10.9 percent and owned by an investor who is in a 7-percent marginal state income bracket is equivalent to a fully taxable security that yields 11.2 percent (that is, 10.9% / (1 - .07) = 11.2%).

T-bills have lower rates than other money market instruments such as certificates of deposit (CDs) and commercial paper because investments in T-bills generally are considered to be free from default risk. The spread between the T-bill rate and that on other instruments is not constant but varies over time and with economic conditions. Over the past several decades, the spread been the CD rate and that on T-bills has ranged from a high of more than 200 basis points to less than 30. Commonly, the spread tends to widen in bad economic time as investors tend to seek the security of default-free T-bills and to narrow in good times as the market becomes less concerned about default risk.

See also: MONEY MARKET
    REPURCHASE AGREEMENT

Reference:

Cook, Timothy Q., "Treasury Bills," in Timothy Q. Cook and Timothy D. Rowe, eds., *Instruments of the Money Market* (Richmond, VA, Federal Reserve Bank of Richmond, 1986).

TREASURY STOCK

Treasury stock is a corporation's own capital stock that has been fully paid for by stockholders, legally issued, reacquired by the corporation, and held by the corporation for future reissuance. The reacquisition of the shares results in a reduction of shareholders' equity. Treasury stock is not an asset because the corporation cannot own itself. Neither can a corporation recognize a gain or a loss when reacquiring or reissuing its own stock. Treasury stock is treated as a reduction of stockholders' equity. Treasury stock does not possess voting right or the preemptive right, nor does it share in dividend distributions or in assets at liquidation.

A corporation might reacquire its own shares for a number of reasons: to have shares to use for stock options, bonus, and stock purchase plans; to use in the conversion of convertible preferred stock or bonds; or to maintain the market price of its stock.

Treasury stock can be reported in the stockholders' equity section of the balance sheet as contra to shareholders' equity as follows:

Contributed capital:	
Common stock	XXX
Additional paid-in capital	XXX
Total contributed capital	XXX
Retained earnings	XXX
Less: Treasury stock	
(10,000 shares at cost)	(15,000)
Total stockholders' equity	$XXXXXX

See also: CAPITAL STOCK
                SHAREHOLDERS' EQUITY

TRIAL BALANCE

A trial balance is a list of ledger accounts and amounts. A trial balance provides evidence of the equality of total debits and credits in the ledger. The equality of debits and credits on a trial balance does not prove that the correct accounts were debited and credited. Trial balances can be taken at various times during the accounting cycle and therefore provide unadjusted, adjusted, and postclosing trial balances. A condensed trial balance would appear as follows:

	Debits	**Credits**
Assets	XXX	
Liabilities		XXX
Owners' Equity		XXX
Revenues		XXX
Expenses	XXX	
Total	XXX	XXX

Note that assets and expense accounts usually have debit balances; revenue, liability, and owners' equity accounts usually have credit balances. This is a result of the basic rules for double-entry accounting.

See also: ACCOUNTING SYSTEM
DOUBLE-ENTRY SYSTEM
LEDGER

TROUBLED DEBT RESTRUCTURING

A troubled debt restructuring is a debt restructuring if the creditor, for reasons related to the debtor's financial difficulties, grants a concession to the debtor that it would not otherwise consider at a point earlier than the scheduled maturity date. The two principal types of debt restructuring include a transfer of assets or equity interest from a debtor to a creditor in full settlement of a debt and a modification of terms. Modification of terms includes such arrangements as interest-rate reductions or maturity-date extensions. Debtors experience gains and creditors recognize losses on troubled debt restructurings.

The accounting procedures for troubled debt restructurings can be summarized as shown below for the debtor and creditor:

Accounting for Form of Restructure	Debtor and Creditor
1. Settlement of debt: a. Transfer of assets.	a. Debtor recognized gain; creditor recognizes loss on restructure. Debtor recognizes gain or loss on asset transfer.
b. Granting an equity interest	b. Debtor recognizes gain creditor recognized loss on restructure.
2. Modified terms: debt continues: a. Carrying amount of debt is less than total future cash	a. No gain or loss is recognized on restructure; however, a new effective interest rate must be computed.

b. Carrying amount of debt is greater than total future.

b. Gain or loss is recognized on restructure; debt reduced to the amount of future cash flows. No interest expense or income is recognized in subsequent periods when only principal is repaid over the remaining life of the loan.

See also: BANKRUPTCY
LIQUIDATION
QUASI-REORGANIZATION
REORGANIZATION
SOLVENCY AND INSOLVENCY

Reference:

SFAS No. 15, *Accounting by Debtors and Creditors for Troubled Debt Restructuring* (FASB, 1977).

TRUST

A trust is a fiduciary relationship under which property is held by one person (a trustee) for the benefit of another (the beneficiary). The income beneficiary is called a cestui que trust: he or she is also a life tenant if he or she is to receive income for life. The eventual recipient of the principal is a remainderman. The trust agreement provides for the distribution of trust principal and the income earned thereon. A trust is usually created by the owner of property (the trustor or grantor) who transfers property to the trustee. A trust established while the grantor is alive is referred to as an inter vivos or living trust. A trust established by will is a testamentary trust. The administration of trusts usually proceeds without any involvement of the courts. Trust administration involves primarily the prudent management of funds to provide continuing benefits to an income beneficiary and then to a remainderman. Estate administration is primarily a liquidating process.

Uu-Zz

UNCERTAINTY

Uncertainty is a situation in which a decision maker does not have information about the outcomes of an action, and, unlike with risk, no estimates can be made about the probabilities associated with alternative outcomes. Decision making is guided by the consistent use of selected criteria, such as the maximin and maximax criteria.

See also: MAXIMIN CRITERION
MAXIMAX CRITERION

U.S. RULE AND MERCHANTS' RULE

According to the U.S. Rule, interest is computed on the unpaid balance of a debt. The payment is first applied to interest. The excess payment reduces the balance of the debt.

The merchants' rule is a method for allowing interest credit on partial payments made on an installment basis. One variation of the merchants' rule requires that both debt and all partial payments are considered to earn interest up to the final date. The final amount due is their difference.

See also: INTEREST

609

VALUE

The term value is used in accounting accompanied by an adjective: book value, par value, no-par value, stated value, appraisal value, fair market value, disposal value, salvage value, scrap value, exit value, entry value, discovery value, replacement value, maturity value, carrying value, and others.

VALUE ADDED STATEMENT

Value added refers to a portion of the selling price of a commodity or service attributable to a specific stage of production. A value added statement is used by many British companies to report on the wealth-creation process. Value added represents the income of shareholders, suppliers of debt capital, employees, and governments. Value added can also be conceptualized as sales revenue minus the cost of materials and services which were brought in from outside suppliers. The value added statement can be presented in the following format:

Sources:			
Sales			$500,000
Less:	Brought-in materials, services	$100,000	
	Depreciation	50,000	150,000
Total value added			$350,000
Applied as follows:			
To wages			$200,000
To interest (banks and other lenders)			25,000
To taxes			75,000
To dividends			30,000
To retained earnings			20,000
Total value added			$350,000

VALUE-ADDED TAX (VAT)

A value-added tax (VAT) is a tax levied on value added at each stage of production rather than only on the final selling price. VATs are common in Europe. The advantage of a VAT is that it is difficult for any producer to evade the tax, but a disadvantage is than final consumers are unaware of the total VAT at the time of purchase because little value is added by the retailer.

VARIABLE COST

Although some factors of production remain fixed in the short run, other inputs vary with the level of production. Variable cost is associated with these factors. Total variable cost (TVC) is the total cost associated with the variable factors of production. TVC increases with output. Average variable cost (AVC) is total cost per unit of output and it equals TVC divided by output. AVC is U-shaped: first AVC decreases and then increases. The economic reason for this shape comes from the law of diminishing returns.

See also: FIXED COST
                  LAW OF DIMINISHING RETURNS
                  TOTAL COST

VARIANCE

A variance is the difference between actual and standard, or between budgeted and actual expenditures or expenses. Variance analysis is based on the concept of management by exception. A variance system provides management with information only when conditions, performance, or activity varies from what they should be. Variance systems are designed and used primarily for control and evaluation purposes. An effective variance system would focus on matters which require management's attention. Variance analysis is also widely used to evaluate performance.

Variance systems typically require:

1. accurate performance standards or bench marks,

2. variables that are subject to control,

3. accurate measurement procedures for inputs and outputs, and

4. responsibilities assignable, preferably through responsibility centers.

Actual cost can differ from standard or budgeted cost because (1) the actual price or rate differs from the standard or budgeted and (2) actual usage or efficiency differs from the standard or budgeted. A price or rate variance indicates that more or less was paid for the cost factor than the standard or budgeted required. A usage or efficiency variance indicates that more or less of the cost factor was used than was anticipated by the standard or budgeted.

See also: CONTROL FUNCTION
DISTRIBUTION COST CONTROL
GOALS AND OBJECTIVES
GROSS MARGIN ANALYSIS
MANAGEMENT
ORGANIZATIONAL BEHAVIOR
PERFORMANCE EVALUATION

VELOCITY OF MONEY

The velocity of money is the rate at which the money stock turns over each year. Formally, the velocity of money is defined as

$$V = GNP/M = (p1q1 + p2q2 + \ldots)/M \tag{1}$$

where

V = velocity of money
GNP = gross national product
M = money stock
$p1q1$ = the price of the ith transaction times the quantity
              of the ith transaction

Note that the sum of all final transactions during any one year is equal to gross national product (GNP).

Equation (1) can be rearranged to yield the quantity equation of exchange as follows:

$$M \times V = P \times Q \tag{2}$$

where

> P = average price level of all final transactions
> Q = aggregate quantity of all final transactions, or real GNP

Equation (2) states that the money stock (M) multiplied times the velocity of money (V) is equal to the average price level (P) times aggregate quantity (Q). Price (P) times quantity (Q) is equal to nominal GNP.

Equation (2) can be rearranged to show the relationship between the velocity of money and the demand for money:

$$M = (1/V) \times P \times Q \tag{3}$$

When all markets are in equlibrium, the stock of money (M) equals the demand for money (MD) that people wish to hold, so that equation (3) becomes

$$MD = k \times P \times Q \tag{4}$$

where k equals the reciprocal of velocity (1/V).

The quantity theory of money as advanced by the famous American economist Irving Fisher in his classic book *The Purchasing Power of Money* (1911) and more recently by Milton Friedman asserts that k is a stable function at least over the long run because the velocity of money is stable.

Because velocity is thought to be stable, Fisher, Friedman and other "monetarist" economists traditionally propound the "quantity theory of money," which states that nominal income (P × Q) is determined solely by movements in the quantity of money. Using equation (2), the quantity theory of money predicts that if the money stock were to double, nominal income also would double because velocity would remain stable.

Monetarists stress that over the long run with the economy at or near full employment, aggregate real output in the economy (Q) is not affected by changes in the stock of money. However, changes in the money stock do affect the level of prices. Thus, equation (2) tells us that there is a direct relationship between the stock of money and the price level. And according to the monetarists, changes in the price level result solely from changes in the quantity of money.

See also: MONETARISM

References

Fisher, Irving, *The Purchasing Power of Money* (New York, NY: Macmillan, 1911).

Friedman, Milton, "The Quantity Theory of Money: A Restatement," in Milton Friedman, ed., *Studies in the Quantity Theory* (Chicago, IL: University of Chicago Press, 1956).

VERTICAL INTEGRATION

A firm is vertically integrated if it had some controls over inputs into its production process and/or some control over markets to which its product is sold. A firm is said to be backward integrated if it owns, for example, a plant that produced an input used in making its final product. A firm is said to be forward integrated if it controls, say, the distribution of its product to final consumers.

Vertical relationships can be achieved through outright purchases or through vertical mergers.

WARRANTIES

A warranty or guaranty is a promise by the seller relating to some aspect of the sale, such as the quality or quantity of the goods or title of the goods. Warranties are either express (made part of the contract by seller's oral, written, or printed words) or implied (made part of the contract by operation of law without any action by the parties).

Express warranties can be an affirmation of fact or promise, description, or sample or model. "Puffing" or opinion are not warranties. An express warranty can be excluded or disclaimed by words or conduct if consistent with a written contract. Express warranties relating to the quality of goods can be made by promise or by description. Implied warranties include warranties of merchantability and fitness for a particular purpose. Such warranties are implied by law. A fitness-for-particular-purpose warranty can only be excluded or disclaimed in writing. A seller's title warranty relates to the assumption that the seller owns the goods and the goods are not subject to any security interests or liens held by other persons. A warranty of title can be excluded or modified only by specific language. A seller's infringement warranty is an implied warranty and affirms that the goods will not be subject to a patent or trademark infringement suit by a third party. A buyer's infringement warranty affirms that if the buyer supplies the specifications, the buyer warrants that the seller will not be subject to a patent or trademark infringement suit by a third party due to the seller's manufacturing.

The Magnuson-Moss Warranty Federal Trade Commission Improvement Act was passed in 1975 and applies to consumer goods sold to consumers. The Act requires specified disclosures in any written warranty given for consumer goods that cost more than $15. The Act does not require that a written warranty be issued. The Act provides remedies for consumers who have been harmed.

Warranties for services result only if there is a sale of goods involved. There are no sales warranties for contracts involving services.

See also: CONTINGENCIES
          LIABILITIES

WORKING CAPITAL

Working capital is the excess of current assets over current liabilities. The amount of working capital is computed by subtracting current liabilities from current assets. Current assets include those resources that are in the form of cash and those that are reasonably expected to be sold, consumed, or converted into cash during the normal operating cycle of the business, or within one year if the operating cycle is shorter than one year. The normal operating cycle of a business is the average time it takes to convert cash into inventory, sell the inventory, and collect the receivables. Current liabilities are obligations that are to be paid, liquidated, or settled with current assets.

Working capital is useful in determining the ability of the firm to finance current operations and to meet obligations as they mature. Adequate working capital is necessary for a business if it is to operate efficiently and effectively.

Working capital management is often the most critical factor for business firms. Liquidity is crucial to survival and success. Short-term credit must be obtained usually through trade credit, but this can be costly if discounts are not taken. The areas of finance that are of utmost importance to small firms include the following:

1. Reliance on internal financing, especially through profits retained in the business, or funds supplied by owners

2. Reliance on financial controls, especially financial ratios and trend and variance analysis

3. Reliance on working capital management so that limited resources are efficiently and effectively employed

See also: CASH MANAGEMENT
FINANCIAL STATEMENT ANALYSIS
FORECASTING FINANCIAL REQUIREMENTS
LIQUIDITY
RATIOS

Reference:

Woelfel, Charles J., and Charles D. Mecimore, *The Operating Executive's Guide to Profit Planning Tools and Techniques* (Probus Publishing Co., Chicago, Ill., 1986).

WRAPAROUND MORTGAGE

A wraparound mortgage or wraparound deed of trust encompasses existing mortages and is subordinate to them. The existing mortgages stay on the property, and the wraparound mortgage is made for an amount that includes the sum of the existing mortgages plus some portion of the owner's equity. This kind of arrangement is used commonly as a method of seller financing.

Suppose a homeowner wants to sell his home valued at $120,000. He has an assumable mortgage of $20,000 at a fixed rate of 7 percent. He finds a buyer with $60,000 in cash who needs to borrow an additional $40,000 to buy the property.

If the buyer must refinance the entire $60,000 with a new first mortgage, he will pay the going market rate of 12 percent. However, if the seller is willing to make a *wraparound mortgage* for $60,000 at 10 percent, they may both gain. The buyer gets the lower rate of 10 percent. The seller earns 10 percent on $60,000, but has to tie up only $40,000 of additional capital. His return on his $40,000 is actually 11.5 percent. That is, he gets 10 percent on $60,000, or $6,000. He must pay 7 percent on the $20,000 first mortgage, or $1,400. He is left with a gain of $4,600—a return on his marginal investment of 11.5 percent ($40,000)

Often a seller will consider a wraparound mortgage if it is the only way to sell his property, because buyers can't afford the cost of refinancing at high market rates of interest. In the above example, a wraparound mortgage may be the factor that permits the property to be sold. In such a case, the seller at least gets some of his equity out of the property in cash and takes a wraparound mortgage that covers both his remaining equity and the amount of the first mortgage.

Wraparound mortgages will not work if the first mortgage is not assumable, because of a due-on-sale clause. Sometimes wraparounds also may be made by a third-party lender who might put up the $40,000 and take a wraparound mortgage for $60,000. In this case, the seller would continue to make the payments on the outstanding first mortgage.

See also: MORTGAGE

X-INEFFICIENCY

An important assumption in economic theory is that firms allocate resources and produce efficiently. Harvey Leibenstein has developed a theory of X-inefficiency. He posits that in economic circles inefficiency is the norm arising from organizational entropy, human inertia, incomplete contracts between economic agents, and agency problems. In such a world there is persistent slack. There are many skeptics of this theory.

YIELD CURVE

The yield curve is a relationship that shows the rate of return currently available to investors in the market on debt obligations of varying maturities. Information to plot the yield curve on government securities is published every day in the *Wall Street Journal*. The *Journal* column shows the yield and the maturity date on outstanding debt obligations of the U.S. Treasury.

The shape of the yield curve does not remain constant over time but changes with changes in the market. The usual shape of the curve is upward sloping, but in poor economic times (for example, during much of 1982) the curve may slope downward, indicating that shorter-term obligations pay a higher yield than those of longer term. Occasionally, the yield curve may be flat or even humped.

The yield curve is a useful concept for fixed-income investors because it provides a picture of the trade-off offered in the market between yield and maturity. By scanning the shape of the yield curve, investors can get a clear picture of the yield-maturity trade-off available in the market. In normal times when the curve is upward-sloping, investors must buy securities with longer maturities in order to get higher yields. And because longer-term obligations are generally thought to subject investors to greater risk, buying longer-term securities thus involves an implicit trade-off of risk and return. When the curve is downward sloping, however, investors can get higher yields without the additional risks of longer maturities.

YIELD TO CALL

The yield to call is the rate of return earned on a bond if it is redeemed before it matures. Like the yield to maturity, the yield to call on a bond or other security is the rate of discount that will make the present value of the cash inflows (both interest and principal) from the security exactly equal to the market price of the security. This relationship is express as follows:

$$MP = C/(1 + i) + C/(1 + i)^2 + \ldots + C/(1 + i)^m + A/(1 + i)^m$$

where

MP = market price of the bond or security
C = annual coupon payment
A = par or maturity value of the security plus any call premium
m = term (years) to call
i = yield to call (discount rate)

The yield to call may be approximated as follows:

$$i = [C + (A - MP)/m] / [(A + MP)/2]$$

See also: YIELD TO MATURITY

YIELD TO MATURITY

The yield to maturity on a bond or other security is the rate of discount that will make the present value of the expected cash inflows (both interest and principal) from the security exactly equal to the market price of the security. This relationship is expressed as follows:

$$MP = C/(1 + i) + C/(1 + i)^2 + . . + C/(1 + i)^m + A/(1 + i)^m$$

where

MP = market price of the bond or security
C = annual coupon payment
A = par or maturity value of the security
m = term to maturity
i = yield to maturity (discount rate)

The yield to maturity may be approximated as follows:

$$i = [C + (A - MP)/m] / [(A + MP)/2]$$

The yield to maturity is the rate of return that the buyer of a security can expect if the security is held to full term, assuming that all interest payments are made on time and in full.

The yield to maturity on a bond that sells at par consists entirely of the interest yield (coupon payments). But if the security sells above or below its par value, the yield to maturity consists of the interest yield plus a positive or negative capital gain.

The yield to maturity changes whenever the market price of the security changes, which may occur daily. An investor who buys a security and holds it until it matures will receive the yield to maturity that exists on the purchase date, but the security's quoted yield to maturity may change frequently.

See also: BOND

ZERO SUM GAME

A zero sum game in game theory is one in which the gains to one player exactly equal the losses to another player. One benefits directly at another's expense.

See also: GAME THEORY